John Smith's Chesapeake Voyages, 1607–1609

John Smith's Chesapeake Voyages 1607–1609

Helen C. Rountree, Wayne E. Clark,
and Kent Mountford

Contributing Authors: Michael B. Barber, Grace Brush, Robert
Carter, Edward W. Haile, Alice Jane Lippson, Robert L. Lippson,
E. Randolph Turner III, John Wolf

*Published in Association with the Chesapeake Bay Gateways
Network and the U.S. National Park Service, Virginia Department
of Historic Resources, and Maryland Historical Trust*

University of Virginia Press
Charlottesville and London

Publication of this volume was made possible with the generous
support of the Office of the President of the University of Virginia.
University of Virginia Press

First published 2007

9 8 7 6 5 4 3 2 1

LIBRARY OF CONGRESS CATALOGING-IN-PUBLICATION DATA
Rountree, Helen C., 1944–
    John Smith's Chesapeake voyages, 1607–1609 / Helen C. Rountree, Wayne E. Clark, and
Kent Mountford ; contributing authors, Michael B. Barber ... [et al.].
        p.   cm.
    "Published in association with the Chesapeake Bay Gateways Network and the U.S.
National Park Service, Virginia Department of Historic Resources, and Maryland
Historical Trust."
    Includes bibliographical references and index.
    ISBN-13: 978-0-8139-2644-5 (cloth : alk. paper)
    1. Smith, John, 1580–1631—Travel—Chesapeake Bay Region (Md. and Va.)
2. Chesapeake Bay Region (Md. and Va.)—Description and travel. 3. Chesapeake Bay
Region (Md. and Va.)—History—17th century. 4. Indians of North America—Chesapeake
Bay Region (Md. and Va.)—History—17th century. 5. Explorers—Great Britain—
Biography. 6. Explorers—America—Biography. 7. America—Discovery and exploration—
English. I. Clark, Wayne E. II. Mountford, Kent, 1938– III. Barber, Michael B.
IV. Chesapeake Bay Gateways Network. V. United States. National Park Service.
VI. Virginia. Dept. of Historic Resources. VII. Maryland Historical Trust. VIII. Title.
F187.C5R675 2007
917.55'18—dc22   2006037564

Frontispiece: Engraving of John Smith from *Generall History of
Virginia, New-England and the Summer Isles,* 1624. (Courtesy of
the Library of Virginia)

Contents

Preface

John Smith. To modern ears the name sounds too ordinary to stand at the center of a story as extraordinary as the arrival of Europeans on the Chesapeake Bay. But as every young schoolchild in the nation learns, Smith's arrival in 1607 at the mouth of the bay near Cape Henry was anything but a commonplace event.

It marked a historical pivot point of momentous proportions, setting the Chesapeake Bay region on a course that would forever transform its culture, its commerce, and its environment. Smith's arrival also set the stage for revolutionary political, social, and economic developments destined to shape the broader course of Western civilization. Of course, Smith's story also makes for a grand personal drama; it was thanks to his talents as a writer and promoter that we have such a vivid, fascinating picture of what it was like to travel the bay and its rivers four centuries ago.

This book is an effort to recount the full story of the Chesapeake Bay in John Smith's time. Developed for the Chesapeake Bay Gateways Network, it is a joint project of the National Park Service, the Maryland Historical Trust, and the Virginia Department of Historic Resources. Its goal has been to bring together the best and most current of historical, scientific, archaeological, and ecological knowledge on the eve of the four hundredth anniversary of the series of voyages Smith took through the Chesapeake region between 1607 and 1609. In the process, it addresses some enduring questions about Smith's enterprise and its impacts.

For example, exactly where did Smith travel and what did he encounter as he explored along the thousands of miles of tidal shoreline embraced by the Chesapeake and its tributaries?

Who were the indigenous peoples of the region? How did they interact with the broader bay environment? How did they react to the exotic newcomers who appeared so suddenly in their midst?

How did the British settlers manage to survive in their new, strange environment? How did they regard a place so exotic that it appeared to them as a whole "New World"?

What was it about the arrival of European settlers that presaged such monumental change for the Chesapeake region? How did the actions those settlers took and the choices they made shape the bay we know today?

What was the natural state of the Chesapeake Bay in the seventeenth century? How has the environment changed, and can that knowledge inform our ongoing efforts to restore the bay today?

The Chesapeake Bay region is one of the world's great natural treasures, and it has been the backdrop for an array of thrilling historical stories, the Smith expeditions being but one of them. This volume has been created in the hope that its readers will discover an even fuller, richer tale—a painstakingly researched description of people, places, events, and natural conditions representing the whole Chesapeake Bay in Smith's times. This comprehensive historical portrait will naturally shine a light on the state of the bay today—and on the work that needs doing if we are going to conserve and preserve for future generations the natural treasure that Smith explored four centuries ago.

Acknowledgments

This volume was made possible by many hands pulling at the oars. Its concept originated with the National Park Service Chesapeake Gateways Working Group. Special thanks go to Jonathan Doherty, former director of the Chesapeake Bay Gateways Program, for turning the concept into a funded agreement and for his strong dedication to the project. His successor, John Maounis, also assisted us. Elizabeth Hughes of the Maryland Historical Trust and Robert Carter of the Virginia Department of Historic Resources, who serve on the Gateways Working Group, nurtured the project since its inception, with Carter also serving as a co-manager, researcher, and author of the final chapter. Wayne E. Clark served as contract administrator and contributed as a research scholar for chapters dealing with Maryland and the major bay voyages. Helen Rountree and Kent Mountford led the cultural and natural resource production teams, with Rountree serving as principal editor and writer. The cultural resources team benefited greatly from the excellent insights and contributions of Randolph Turner III, Michael Barber, and Edward W. Haile. The natural resources team included leaders in the environmental sciences. Grace Brush provided wonderful expertise on forest ecology and composition. Contributions by Alice Jane Lippson and Robert L. Lippson were many and insightful. John Wolf's GIS expertise and map production made him an invaluable addition to the team.

Editorial and other graphic production assistance were ably provided by Beverly McMillan, Irene and Nick Kirilloff, Jon Dean of Jefferson Patterson Park and Museum, and Katherine Mansfield of the Virginia Institute of Marine Science. Sharon Raftery of Jefferson Patterson Park and Museum supplied electronic files of several images and Jennifer Chadwick-Moore of the Maryland Historical Trust assisted in site data search for Maryland using the GIS program. Kathy Opferman of the Maryland Historical Trust provided administrative assistance throughout the project. Contract and budget support was provided by Betsey Corby and Elizabeth Ragan of Salisbury University and Betty Hobgood of the Maryland Historical Trust. Our special thanks to the many organizations and individuals who granted permission for use of photographs and other graphics included here.

The Technical Advisory Team supplied timely and meaningful review comments, dialogue, alternative ways of seeing the past, and support for the goals of this project. The team included Stephen Potter of the National Park Service, Antony Opperman of the Virginia Department of Transportation, Thomas Davidson of the Jamestown-Yorktown Foundation, Melanie Perrault of Salisbury University, Julia King of Jefferson Patterson Park and Museum, and Lois Carr of the Maryland Historical Trust.

Native American representation and perspective were provided by Mervin A. Savoy, of the Maryland Commission on Indian Affairs, and Deanna Beacham, program specialist for the Virginia Council on Indians, who also coordinated comments from Virginia tribal leaders, VCI members, and other members of the Virginia Indian community. Specifically, helpful comments were received from Karenne Wood, VCI chair; Chief Anne Richardson of the Rappahannock Indian Tribe; Mitchell Bush, VCI member; Reeva Tilley, Rappahannock; Buck Woodward, VCI member; Ed Reagan, historian for the Rappahannock tribe; and Blair Rudes of the University of North Carolina–Charlotte.

Natural resource reviewers included Jeffrey P. Halka of the Maryland Geological Survey, James Cummins of the Interstate Commission on the Potomac River Basin, John R. Davy Jr., and Thomas L. Smith of the Virginia Department of Conservation and Recreation. Many other scholars willingly gave of their expertise and knowledge, including W. Lauck Ward, who provided dates for cliffs around the bay. The meetings of the Technical Advisory Team were open to Gateways staff and other interested persons, many of whom took the time to attend and to share their insights, desires, and suggestions. This book is better for their comments and involvement.

There are many paths to understanding the Chesapeake Bay's diverse heritage. We have examined numerous interpretations of the evidence left to us in the ground, on paper, in the sediments of the bay bottom, in living biological systems, and in the traditions of the rich cultural tapestry of descendent communities. We offer this analysis of the Chesapeake world of 1607–9 as one well-researched twenty-first-century interpretation of this evidential record. May it help enrich our changing views of the Chesapeake and its many cultures over time.

John Smith's Chesapeake Voyages, 1607–1609

1

The Chesapeake Environment in the Early Seventeenth Century

Kent Mountford, Robert L. Lippson, and Alice Jane Lippson

Prologue

The Chesapeake Bay is a product of geology.[1] Its underpinnings were first shaped 35 million years ago by the impact of a huge object from outer space colliding with the earth roughly where Cape Charles stands today. That spot was then underwater, on the continental shelf; the Eastern Shore and the Chesapeake Bay west of it developed much later (see box on p. 198). Over subsequent eons, over a thousand feet (305 meters) of sediment accumulated in the crater, which is now hidden but still has effects upon the modern Hampton Roads area.[2] Then, long before humans appeared, a series of glaciers advanced and retreated across the North American landscape over hundreds of thousands of years. During the Ice Ages, substantial amounts of the earth's water were locked up in the ice sheets, and as a result, the sea withdrew far eastward from the shorelines of warmer periods. During the interglacial periods, when ice-melt again raised sea level, embayments (semi-enclosed bodies of water) formed where fresh river waters and salty seawater blended. These were estuaries, and a sequence of them was created and drained during other glacial epochs long before the present Chesapeake Bay came into being.

Prehistory

When the last great ice sheet occupied what would become the upper Chesapeake drainage, in modern Pennsylvania and New York, some 18,000 years ago,[3] the seacoast was over one hundred miles (160 kilometers) east of where it is today and the bay was a forested river valley. Today's Chesapeake follows the course of the old proto–Susquehanna River draining down from the glaciated north. Humans may have lived south of the ice front, in the dry, cold climate typically found downwind from glaciers, during some or all of that time. Permafrost has been documented as far south as Cape May, New Jersey, at the same latitude as Washington, D.C.; it may have extended even farther south.[4] As the last glaciers melted and receded northward, sea level rose and flooded the adjacent land. The modern Chesapeake began to form. River gorges, notably the proto-Susquehanna carrying snowmelt and rain from the increasingly moist climate, scoured deep into the landscape, eventually creating the bay's navigable channels.

Humans were certainly present by fifteen thousand years ago.[5] As the sea advanced and estuaries formed literally at the people's hearthsides, they relied more on the species in the surrounding waters. It is a pity that the sites they left behind have been swallowed up by shoreline erosion. Archaeologists are just beginning to learn how to study this submerged history, once thought lost. By about three thousand years ago, the bay had assumed a shape that modern people would recognize. The shorelines would still recede—they are doing so today—but the basic environmental template was there.

Climate

The Chesapeake basin is large enough that seasonal differences of three or more weeks can be present from north to south. As a rule of thumb, "spring" moves northward from the Carolinas to New York State at about fifteen miles (24.1 kilometers) per day. This roughly twenty-three-day difference means that snowpack can still be melting at the upper end of the basin while early shrubs and forest floor vegetation are leafing out in Virginia Beach. The English initially settled near the bay's southern extreme, and they were unprepared for the ferocious thunder squalls and intense summer heat (which they didn't like) or for the extended "Indian" summer that often lasted far into autumn (which they did like). Similar climatic differences exist east-to-west, from the seacoast to as far as 225 miles (362 kilometers) inland to the summit of the Appalachians, where a thirty-degree temperature difference can occasionally be experienced. The massive ocean and Chesapeake Bay temper coastal weather: it gets warm more slowly in spring because the waters are still cold, and it gets cold more slowly in autumn because the waters are still warm. Given the alternation of cold fronts from the northwest and warmer winds from the southwest, it is not uncommon for the Chesapeake region to experience "warm snaps" of shirtsleeve weather during the winter. John Smith wrote: "In the year 1607 was an extraordinary frost in most of Europe, and this frost was found as extreme in Virginia. But the next year for 8 or 10 days of ill weather, [an]other 14 days would be as summer."[6]

The region's climate reflected major world patterns. After a "medieval warm period" characterized by somewhat dryer and warmer conditions than the present, with resultant wildfires, the weather reversed itself and turned somewhat colder than modern conditions in the Northern Hemisphere. This "Little Ice Age" extended from the 1400s through the 1700s with repercussions on both sides of the Atlantic.[7]

Ironically for both Native Americans and English, the mid-Atlantic region was less hospitable than usual when Europeans came calling. Tree-ring analysis suggests that multiyear droughts were in progress during the first three colonizing efforts: 1570 (Spanish on York River), 1585–87 (English on the Outer Banks), and 1606–12 (English at Jamestown).[8] When these ill-supplied colonies started trying to secure food from the native people already suffering from the drought, the result was disaster.

The Europeans who left the first written records about the bay were interlopers, without much insight about either the native peoples or the extraordinary environment that had evolved here. In many ways, the 15 to 16 million people occupying the bay's drainage today are similarly lacking in insight, and their footprints are much heavier and more damaging. Perhaps a better understanding of what the bay used to be like will ameliorate that situation.

A World of Intertwined Lands and Waters

Although it was visited by previous explorers (see chapter 3), the Chesapeake Bay was first described through the writings of John Smith in 1607-8. While the bay was in some ways a markedly different environment from today's version, it was close to its present size: about 180 miles (290 kilometers) long, a relatively narrow 35 miles (56.3 kilometers) at its widest, oriented north-south roughly parallel with the Atlantic coast, and with all its estuarine (as opposed to riverine) shoreline lying inside what is now Virginia and Maryland. This vast, shallow estuary is highly branched, and that shoreline is deeply and irregularly incised by hundreds of embayments and tributaries of various sizes, many of them navigable for many miles by seventeenth-century ships and boats. Nineteen principal rivers and four hundred lesser creeks and streams have a combined tidal shoreline, by one estimate, of eleven thousand miles (17,703 kilometers), an amazing labyrinth for a bay less than two hundred miles (322 kilometers) long.

Sources of the Water

Rivers of the bay's western shore are generally larger than those on the Eastern Shore, with much larger drainages extending at least into the Piedmont. The James, Potomac, and Susquehanna arise far up in the mountains, making them the principal sources—80 percent—of the freshwater entering the bay other than by rainfall. Eastern Shore rivers, by contrast, cut across most of the low, flat countryside of the Delmarva Peninsula and flow through large expanses of wetlands.[9] These tributaries drain an immense watershed spanning sixty-four thousand square miles (165,759 square kilometers). The Chesapeake is unique, compared to other estuarine systems on earth, in having an immensely large drainage basin relative to its water area.[10] That proportion meant that very large areas of mostly forested landscape (which release only small amounts of nutrients) sustained the bay's living resources. Before European farmers disrupted the system, the bay's ecological processes and Native American actions had achieved a fine-tuning among the needs of many species, supplying enough nutrients to sustain an estuary with vast quantities of fish, shellfish, and aquatic vegetation. That fine-tuning meant in turn that the bay and its ecosystem were extremely sensitive to the large-scale landscape disruption caused by later generations of Europeans in the eighteenth and nineteenth centuries.

What the Waters Were Like

In the 1600s, all the Chesapeake's tributaries drained watersheds that were largely in forest, rather than an open agricultural landscape or the impervious (paved and roofed) surfaces that our urban areas create today. Much of the rainfall was therefore stored as groundwater, and there was less runoff into streams. Cores extracted from the bay floor show that even large storms resulted in only modest deposits of sediment, which contrasts with the massive loads of sediment, nitrogen, and phosphorus the rivers carry today. Because they drain more open, unforested watersheds, modern streams are also "flashy": their runoff volume increases quickly after rainstorms and thus scours sediment from bottoms and banks, carrying it downstream in immensely greater quantities than in the past.

Broad areas of natural forest topsoils stored more water, and immense amounts of moisture were pumped into the atmosphere by the largely undisturbed plant communities. In dry periods, the water stored in soil and roots was released naturally and more slowly, so that river flows probably decreased less during droughts than is the case today, resulting in less stress on plants and animals in all bay tributaries and their watersheds.[11]

Because of less sediment and contaminants borne in runoff four centuries ago, the waters in the bay would have been much clearer than they are nowadays. More light would have reached the bottom, allowing for larger animal communities that depended on resources attached to or burrowing in the bottom, rather than on microscopic plankton food sources floating freely about.

Another effect of less runoff may have been that salt water penetrated farther up the main stem and tributaries of the Chesapeake Bay in the early seventeenth century than it does now,[12] in spite of sea level being lower by a possible 1.36 meters (4.5 ft).[13] The effects on food resources for humans were both good and ill: saltwater shellfish such as oysters and hard and soft clams occurred somewhat farther upstream than they do today,[14] but the brackish and tidal freshwater nurseries for fish would have been compressed into a smaller area, though their habitats extend into the Piedmont and beyond.

Water Depth

The Chesapeake Bay is extremely shallow compared with the Atlantic Ocean, with an average depth in the main stem of only about thirty feet (9.1 meters). Including the tidewater tributaries, that average decreases to about twenty feet (6.1 meters). Broad shoals and extensive flat-bottom areas are common in the bay, so that Native Americans who lacked deepwater fishing gear still had access to huge sections of the bay for fishing and shellfishing. Along the course of the Ice Age Susquehanna, there still remain deep holes and channels that have yet to fill up with sediment. The upper bay just west of Kent Island off Bloody Point reaches a depth of 174 feet (53 meters), and the water near the mouth of the Patuxent River is 120 feet (36.6 meters) deep. There is a trough over eighty feet (24.4 meters) deep along the lower Eastern Shore of Virginia near the bay's mouth, where the

Ice Age Susquehanna turned eastward toward what is now the continental shelf.

Tides in the bay have always risen and fallen twice a day, with tidal heights varying along the length of the bay from about four feet (1.2 meters) at its mouth to about a foot (30 centimeters) in the vicinity of Annapolis, increasing again to two feet (60 centimeters) northward to the head of the bay (which is the head of tide). A similar increasing tidal range upstream is present in the bay's major rivers. Using the Potomac as an example, average tidal rise is about one foot (30 centimeters) near its junction with the main stem of the Chesapeake, but it increases to about three feet (90 centimeters) at the head-of-tide, which as with the James is also at the fall line. These tidal ranges were small compared to those the English were familiar with on the coast of Britain, where the amplitude can exceed twenty feet (6.1 meters).

This daily rise and fall creates immense areas of shallow peripheral and shoreline habitat, with water flow bringing a continually changing supply of plankton and land-based debris that is useful to many species as food. Estuarine organisms have adapted over many thousands of years to thrive in varying saltiness, from seawater to nearly freshwater, and changing seasonal water temperatures ranging from freezing to above 90 degrees. The result in the precolonial Chesapeake was a richly varied shallow-water community, with certain species developing phenomenal abundances of organisms that were relatively easily harvested by the native people of the region.

Salinity is one of the most important factors (the other being temperature) regulating the distribution of plants and animals in estuaries such as Chesapeake Bay. Unlike the ocean, where salt content varies little over vast regions, the bay encompasses waters that range from nearly the saltiness of the Atlantic outside its mouth (30–32 parts per thousand) to fresh near the river fall lines (zero parts per thousand), with additional seasonal changes along the rivers (fresher in spring, saltier in fall).[15]

Where the waters are fresh, the adjacent wetlands can be especially rich in broad-leaved plant species with parts edible by people. Downstream in the rivers and fringing many areas of the main stem, especially on the Eastern Shore, are marshes with plants that tolerate more salt in the water, many of them being reeds useful for mat making by Indians (chapter 2) or thatching by Englishmen who would also fasten upon these wetland meadows as natural pastures for livestock.[16]

Wetland resources sustained immense populations of waterfowl, many

of which were migrants from other parts of the continent. We discuss
later on.

Life in the Waters

In shallows beyond the marshes, the seventeenth-century Chesapeake is believed to have had vast underwater meadows, running to hundreds of thousands of acres, of submerged rooted and flowering plants, today classed as
submerged aquatic vegetation, or SAV. There were at least a dozen species
living in freshwater streams, including wild celery, common waterweed,
horned pondweed, and redhead grass. Downstream into tidal fresh and
brackish waters, the number of species would have gradually decreased
with only widgeon grass and eelgrass in the saltier waters of the bay. These
SAV beds were protected havens for juvenile fish and blue crabs as well
as habitat for many invertebrates and small fish species. All the SAV beds
served as winter food supply for legions of visiting waterfowl. The eventual
decline and disappearance of once-rich SAV beds has been one of the key
signals of a declining ecosystem, modern acreages hovering in recent years
around only seventy-four thousand (52.6 thousand hectares).

Along the edges of the waterways and in the marshes, there would have
been lush stands of emergent vegetation. Numerous species would be found
in freshwaters and tidal fresh and brackish waters; these included tuckahoe
(commonly called arrow arum today), pickerelweed, wild rice, and cow
lily. Where salinity is greater, marshes would be dominated by saltmarsh
cordgrass with large broad meadows of salt marsh along the low profiles
of the Eastern Shore and smaller stands, some merely "pocket marshes,"
elsewhere throughout the bay and along almost every tributary stream or
creek. Black needlerush, three-square sedges, and other species would provide valuable seed food for waterfowl and shorebirds.

The bay has always played host to migrating and visiting fish, as well as
being home to many permanent residents. All but one of the migrants are
anadromous fishes that live in salty waters and migrate to freshwater areas
to spawn. This category includes shad, herring, alewives, striped bass, and
sturgeon. Another bay migrant, the American eel, is catadromous: adults
live in the bay and up its freshwater tributaries but head out into the Atlantic to spawn. Shellfish and many other invertebrate species are full-time
residents of the bay's waters, while several species of mammals—ranging
from migratory bottlenose dolphins to resident river otters—also utilize

Examples of wetland plants that were used heavily by native peoples around the bay. Tuckahoe, or arrow arum (*Peltandra virginica*), left, and pickerelweed (*Pontederia cordata*), right. (A. J. Lippson)

the bay and its tributaries. Reptiles are represented by migratory animals such as the loggerhead sea turtle and resident diamondback terrapins.

Anadromous Fishes

All rivers in the pre-European Chesapeake probably had spring fish runs, for even some very small tributaries experience them today. Spawning anadromous fishes were an essential resource for Native Americans all along the Atlantic coast. The young hatch in tidal fresh and brackish spawning areas of the upper bay and its tributaries, grow to juveniles as they move down into shallow saline waters, and use most of the bay as a gigantic summer nursery. Some young fish leave the bay by autumn, with others remaining until their second year. They then range the Atlantic coast from Labrador to northern Florida, eventually returning to their natal rivers[17]—unless caught or prevented by new human-erected obstacles. Since precolonial times, when each spring saw literally billions of spawning adult fish passing through, the old migratory routes have been blocked by about 2,500 such obstructions, so that by now only remnant populations remain in most rivers. In the Mattaponi and Pamunkey rivers, Native Americans descended from the old Powhatan "empire" still manage a sustainable shad fishery, supplemented by their own tribal hatcheries.

Adult anadromous fishes can make more than one annual spawning run, and there were once small autumn runs as well. When these populations were immense, they contributed significant quantities of energy and

John Smith's Chesapeake Voyages, 1607–1609

organic material—eggs and milt, as well as waste material from the juvenile fish and adults caught in narrow upstream waters by predators (fish, mammals, and birds)—fertilizing those waterways at a time when nutrients in the surrounding forests were being conserved.[18] The several species of herring and shad will be described in chapter 7.

In the seventeenth century, only three major freshwater predatory (piscivorous) fishes were present to feed on the anadromous species' eggs and juveniles in the spawning areas: the longnose gar, the bowfin, and the chain pickerel.[19] In addition, striped bass feed on other fishes during their spawning sojourns up bay tributaries. A number of predators have been introduced into the bay since then (see chapter 14).

Atlantic menhaden are herring that are closely related to shad and river herring; they have many common names: bunkers, mossbunkers, skipjacks, pogies, fatbacks, and alewives. They are not anadromous but spawn in the coastal ocean, after which the tiny young swim and are swept by wind and tide into the Chesapeake and other estuaries. They aggregate in the main stem of the bay as well as the tributaries, filter-feeding on microscopic plankton. Schooling menhaden swim closely packed, going in tight circles so close to the surface that they often ruffle it with their mouthparts. It is likely that, in the first third of July 1608, this was the species John Smith and his compatriots tried to catch with a frying pan while exploring the Potomac River in 1608.[20] An illustration on the original title page of Smith's *Generall Historie* also suggests this association.[21]

There were also several kinds of bass in the bay, the premier Chesapeake food and sport fish being the striped bass, a species that ranges from the Canadian Maritimes all the way to northern Florida.[22] Other names for it are striper, rockfish, and rock. The first explorer to illustrate this fish was John White in 1585; the first culinary description of it may be that of Jasper Danckaerts in 1679, who was given the fish by Nyack Indians in New York: "two fine bass . . . We ate of them also in the evening, . . . and had not tasted any better in the country. They were fat and hard, with a little of the flavor of the salmon."[23] Sea-run striped bass grow to a weight of one hundred pounds (around 40 kilograms) or more, and though they spawn in other rivers along the coast, the Chesapeake Bay has historically been their major spawning ground. They come in from the sea in early spring and begin gathering in fresh and brackish waters in April and May. The males and the larger females (called cow rocks) prefer to spawn in rivers with a salinity of about three parts per thousand, or about one-tenth the salinity of the Atlantic Ocean.[24] Even in the twentieth century, the tales of the upper Nanticoke River roiling with fish and viscid with the release of eggs and milt hint at what this species' abundance might have been centuries ago.[25]

The white perch is a smaller species, closely related to the striped bass. White perch are essentially an estuarine species, staying within the bay during their entire life cycle, but returning to the tidal fresh and brackish waters in the same river where they were spawned. They are often referred to as semianadromous fish. Some of the major perch spawning grounds historically are the Potomac River above Morgantown, Maryland; the Nanticoke River near Vienna, Maryland; and on the Susquehanna Flats in the upper bay. Today white perch also traverse the Chesapeake and Delaware Canal, which has directly joined the two bays since 1927, and they also spawn in the York, James, and other rivers along the Eastern and Western shores.[26]

The sturgeon group has been in existence at least 200 million years, and the Atlantic sturgeon reflects this ancient heritage. The body is armored with five rows of hard, bony plates or shields, rather than small scales like other fishes; these plates are sharp-edged in younger sturgeon but become blunt with age. The adult plates, or "scutes," have been recovered by archaeologists inside the English fort at Jamestown,[27] where John Smith and others reported them to be a life-saving food resource, taken sometimes in large numbers by net. One fish could feed a lot of people: sturgeons have been recorded with lengths over twelve feet (3⅔ meters) and weighing over eight hundred pounds (315 kilograms). Their roe, the highly valued caviar, was something the colonists failed to export, lacking proper preservation techniques. The species is anadromous, spawning in fresh or slightly brackish waters where the water is swift and the bottom stony and rough. However, sturgeon need muddy bottoms for feeding, detecting mollusks, worms, and insect larvae with four sensory barbels that project in front, then sucking the food into their soft, protractive, toothless mouths. Young Atlantic sturgeon, which now spawn in certain parts of the James and York rivers, may remain in the bay for five years, attaining a length of three feet (90 centimeters) before venturing into the ocean. A second species, the shortnose sturgeon, looks similar but grows to a lesser length. This fish had been documented to spawn only in the Potomac River but is apparently not to be found anywhere in the bay today. Atlantic sturgeon are present but uncommon now in the Chesapeake, whereas the early colonists reported catching many that were several feet (perhaps as much as two meters) long.

Catadromous Fishes

The American eel is the only catadromous fish in the Chesapeake Bay. Like its European cousins, it lives in rivers and spawns in the Sargasso Sea, which is an unusually salty part of the Atlantic east of the Bahamas and north of the West Indies. The adults then die, while the eggs develop into larvae and then into translucent "elvers." The elvers follow major ocean currents for thousands of miles west and north and enter estuaries and rivers all along the North American coast. Making their way upstream, the males tend to stay in nearly fresh waters, while females continue upstream, around or over waterfalls, where they spend from five to twenty years before returning along with the males to the Sargasso Sea to spawn and die, as their parents did.

Visitors

Other species are essentially ocean fish that enter the bay to feed, especially in summer. The Jamestown colonists would recognize all of them, but their abundances are changed nowadays. Predatory bluefish and Spanish mackerel often invade the bay by the millions. Bottom-feeding kingfish, black drum, and red drum feed on mollusks and worms. Atlantic spadefish, cobia, Florida pompano, and hakes all come to the bay to feed. Various sharks are seen annually, most often the sandbar shark, which uses the lower bay as its principal nursery ground. The sharks' close relatives, rays and skates, are often abundant. One species, the cownose ray, which is locally known as the double-head, swarms into the bay in the spring, sometimes forming huge schools. They feed mainly on clams and crabs and are often seen in the shallows, flapping their wings like great underwater birds and blowing the silt off razor clams and soft-shell clams before crushing them with their platelike teeth.[28] In the 1960s and 1970s, schools containing millions of cownose rays significantly damaged the bay's underwater grass beds by feeding and coincidentally uprooting the plants. John Smith and his companions surprised such a school at what became Stingray Point at the mouth of the Rappahannock River. Both the cownose ray and the southern stingray have poisonous spines at the base of their whiplike tails, and Smith took a hit in the wrist from one that nearly killed him.[29] A related but different species, the skate, produces the leathery egg capsules ("mermaid's purses") found on beaches of the lower bay.

Marine mammals were another component of the bay system in 1607. Atlantic bottlenose dolphins, which feed voraciously on bay fishes, roamed the waters from the capes to the upper bay near Annapolis and St. Michaels, where occasional ones are seen today. Up until 1884, notably before the widespread use of propeller-driven vessels, dolphins were described as common in the lower part of the Potomac, but they were rarely seen there by the 1920s. "Grampus," or pilot whales, were reported in the early seventeenth century,[30] and at one time there were the first glimmerings of a whale fishery near the bay's mouth.

Loggerhead turtles still use the bay by the hundreds, entering during the summer, when they feed on crustaceans and finfish. Loggerheads are large animals, and the hungry Jamestown colonists left the shell of one they'd eaten among the garbage inside the fort.

Permanent Residents

There are many freshwater fishes living in the tidal waters of the inner coastal plain that move lower into brackish waters at times. Yellow perch and white catfish, as well as three species of bullheads, are found throughout the bay system in fresh and brackish waters. Several other species of fish that are effective predators on smaller fishes in fresh and slightly brackish waters, are non-native, being imported and released into the bay or tributaries in the nineteenth century. The best known of these are the channel catfish, the largemouth bass, and the smallmouth bass.

There are many estuarine fish that live their whole life within the bay and would have been abundant in the seventeenth century. Darting schools of bay anchovies and silversides would be prey for striped bass, bluefish, and other large predator fish. The oyster communities would be home to gobies, blennies, and toadfish; small killifishes would congregate in the shallows, and hogchokers and winter flounder would hover at the muddy bottoms.

Blue crabs were a favored food to the Native Americans, as they are for us. They would have been abundant throughout the bay and easily accessible in the shallow waters as hard or soft crabs. Blue crabs are swimming crabs, for their hindmost legs have flattened paddles rather than being the pointed walking legs typical of most other crabs. They have developed a large muscle for these paddles to propel themselves rapidly through the water, and this is the source of lump, or backfin, crabmeat, so desirable in Chesapeake crab cakes. Blue crabs are relatively short-lived, surviving three or sometimes four years. They prefer underwater grass beds, especially when young; about thirty times as many crabs are found in grass beds as on bare bay bottom, so decreases in underwater grasses mean less favorable conditions for crabs. Their remains have been found in large quantities at some archaeological sites.[31]

John Smith's Chesapeake Voyages, 1607–1609

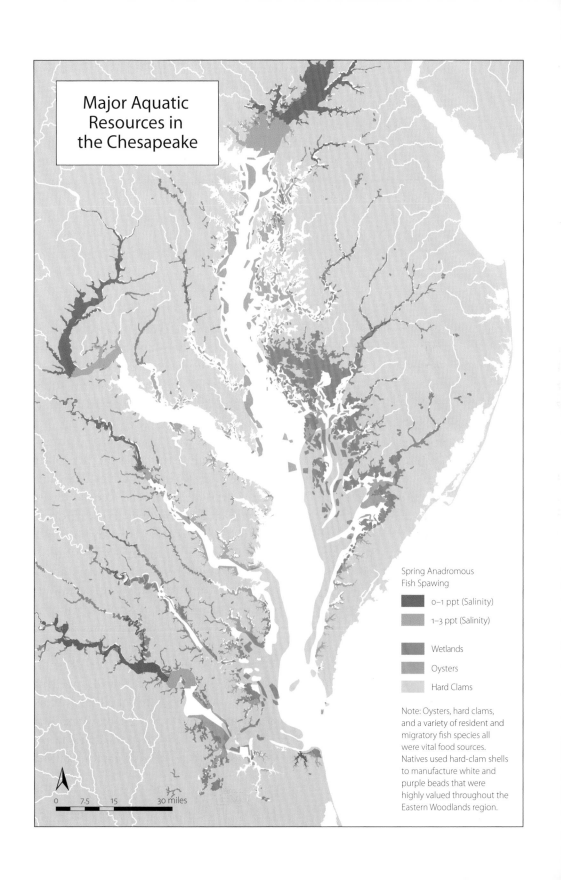

Major Aquatic
Resources in
the Chesapeake

Spring Anadromous
Fish Spawing

0–1 ppt (Salinity)

1–3 ppt (Salinity)

Wetlands

Oysters

Hard Clams

Note: Oysters, hard clams,
and a variety of resident and
migratory fish species all
were vital food sources.
Natives used hard-clam shells
to manufacture white and
purple beads that were
highly valued throughout the
Eastern Woodlands region.

0   7.5   15   30 miles

Significantly, no records have been found of the bay's infamous "stinging nettle" jellyfish until the mid-eighteenth century.[32] The Portuguese man-of-war "sea nettle" was encountered offshore, probably in the Gulf Stream, but it was not the same as today's pest. Records from the Civil War era and late nineteenth century indicate that jellyfish have increased since European contact.[33]

Oysters occur all through the saltier portions of the bay and its tributaries, while various species of clams and mussels grow in all waters.[34] Those at shallower depths were easily harvested at low tide by Native Americans, who are also known to have dived for them.[35] Others formed reef systems, some shallow enough to be noticed by early cartographers like Robert Tyndall in the James and York rivers. These reefs, or "rocks," as they came to be called, were often emergent at low tide in the lower bay. Farther up the bay, the reefs were subtidal but still abundant. Too much exposure to the air, with its seasonal heat and freezing that killed the topmost oysters, was the only limit to the slow, inexorable growth of these natural structures, which had steadily advanced in height and mass as sea level rose in the Chesapeake after the last Ice Age.[36] Often located near points of land onshore, the outer layers of oysters inhabiting the reefs as a living veneer fed on microscopic plankton in passing waters, in the process filtering large fractions of the bay's daily tidal prism.[37] Thus they were a great natural engine for cleaning and clarifying the waters at a phenomenal rate. The resulting debris, including waste products, were excreted and fell to the bottom around the reefs, there to be fed upon by other scavenger species, and their potentially polluting nutrients were mineralized by bacterial processes. The millions of amassed oysters created a living, hard bottom that enabled dozens of invertebrate species to dwell within the recesses among their shells. Worms moved over the surfaces or built tubes attached to them, sponges grew atop them or bored into them. Delicate plantlike anemones and hydroids and tougher barnacles all attached themselves, while fishes of all sorts deposited their eggs as well. This teeming community, swarming with life, produced literally billions of larvae that in turn were fed upon by passing predators.

Whelks, or "conchs," are carnivorous saltwater snails. Because of their size, their shells were a prized trade item accessible to Native Americans near the coast, especially the Nanticokes, so they will be discussed in chapter 9. Of the clams and mussels that live in various water salinities, two are well known to the public. Hard clams live in mud bottoms up to twenty feet (6.1 meters) deep, require relatively high salinities, and get their name from the density of their shells. They have a number of names these days, based

John Smith's Chesapeake Voyages, 1607–1609

mainly on their size: quahogs (a Native American name), littlenecks, and chowder clams; cherrystones were named after their original harvest site on the Virginia Eastern Shore. Soft clams are variously called manninose (the Indian name), piss clam, longneck clam, steamer, and belly clam. They have thin, fragile shells that do not completely close at the ends, making for another name, gaper. They live subtidally in fine sand or sandy mud, meaning that Native Americans would have had to dive or dig in the bottom at very low tides to harvest them. Shells on some middens show clear evidence of being cooked, discarded, and then broken by footsteps around the campfire.[38]

The Chesapeake Landscape in 1607

The English adventurers first encountered the southern end of the bay, where the land is low and the fringe marshes ubiquitous. As they moved northward up the bay, and chiefly westward into the tributaries, they discovered that the land became higher, in many places with exposed cliffs actively eroded into the waters they traversed by the action of sea level rise, waves, and tide.[39] Likewise, as the rivers narrowed upstream, the uplands between them became more extensive and the climatic extremes more continental. Finally, along all the rivers that were long enough, a "fall line" would be reached, where the coastal plain sediments lensed out and outcroppings of bedrock prevented further exploration except on foot. Those points would later be the sites first of trading ports and still later of cities like Richmond, Fredericksburg, Washington, and Baltimore.

Prehistory
The coastal plain is in fact a partially flooded landscape. As sea level rose after the last Ice Age, valleys previously cut by meandering streams were inundated with a combination of fresh river water and seawater. Some of the last Ice Age's meanders are still visible along the James, and the modern Pamunkey and Chickahominy are still distinctly sinuous. The depositional effects of meanders from earlier epochs can be traced in the margins of the floodplains of rivers from the Rappahannock southward; on those floodplains are some of the best, naturally fertile corn-growing soils in the region.[40] As sea level rose, low peninsulas became islands—as New Point Comfort has recently done—and then the islands slowly disappeared, their vegetation changing from mixed hardwood forest[41] to pine woods to water-

tolerant grasses such as saltmarsh cordgrasses and black needlerush, before vanishing altogether.

The Delmarva Peninsula, colloquially called the Eastern Shore, widens as one moves north, with a complex landscape interdigitated by several long, often deep rivers that transect low hills of buried sand dunes from geologically ancient, pre-Chesapeake sea beaches. The landscape is dotted with circular ponds that are now called "Delmarva Bays." Geologists have recently proposed that these are relics from the last glaciation, when this region was a near-desert swept by fierce winds roaring down from the distant ice.[42] Parts of the permafrost melted, and these sites dried and were scoured of their fine, windblown soils, or "loess." Today the resulting depressions capture rainfall. The higher ground has sandy loam soils that Native Americans and Europeans both used for farming.

Where the Chesapeake or its tributaries have cut into higher ground, bank and cliff collapses have revealed a cross section of the landscape's ancient past: myriad fossils ranging in age from 1 to 14 million years. The closer to the fall line, the older the sediments exposed in cliffs. Native Americans of the region are known to have used fossil shark teeth to decorate clothing and to incise decorations in some of their tobacco pipes. At least one tiny fossil snail species was used to ornament a chief's garment, the famous "Powhatan's Mantle" described in chapter 7.

Forests

Nearly all of the Chesapeake drainage was clothed in a deep, sometimes ancient forest whose annual deposit of leaves had created a humus layer a full foot (30 centimeters) thick. In what is now Lancaster County, Pennsylvania, the original topsoil layer was sixteen inches (40.6 centimeters) thick, about half of which has been eroded away thanks to clear-cutting of fields and intensive farming.[43] The forest creating such a layer of humus was deciduous, with oaks, hickories, chestnut, and other species that could grow to immense size. The English, delighted that they had come upon this extractable resource to send home to their nearly denuded island, waxed lyrical about it at times.[44] John Smith wrote that "many of their oaks are so tall and straight, that they will bear two feet and a half square of good timber for 20 yards long . . . wood we call cypress . . . and of those trees there are some of three fathoms [18 feet or 5.5 meters] about at the foot, very straight, and 50, 60, or 80 [feet] without a branch."[45] He added that "a man may gallop a horse amongst these woods any way, but where the creeks or rivers shall hinder."[46] Father Andrew White wrote even more ecstatically about the north bank of the Potomac in 1634: "a coach and four horses may travel [through them] without molestation."[47] Both writers were depicting parklike forests, with little undergrowth, on the narrow eastern ends of river necks: the Virginia Peninsula and the St. Mary's River area. There the deer had browsed extensively and the native people had gathered firewood. Basinwide, where land areas were less constricted, the reality was far more complex, since all forests are living, changing systems. The difference today is that mature trees are scarcer thanks to logging, and the forests cover much less ground thanks to farming and suburbanization. In the resulting open lands, at least half of the herbaceous species were brought over—intentionally or not—from Europe.

Whether parklike forests and open spaces characterized the forests throughout the region is subject to some speculation. The forests that Smith and White were writing about were plainly mature, with large trees, a closed canopy, and little undergrowth. However, the species composition of forests did vary, depending on the topography of the land, the chemical composition of the soils, and the amount of moisture therein. Trees, like other plants, are adapted to specific conditions. For instance, "oaks" will grow nearly everywhere sooner or later, but there is actually a myriad of species of oaks, some tougher and some more finicky than others, such as water oak, which grows in open water, and chestnut oak, which occupies the driest sites. The Chesapeake region contains areas ranging from dry coastal sands and interior serpentine barrens to moister uplands and lowlands between the rivers and from there to swampy heads of waterways and inland depressions like the Great Dismal Swamp, where the land is always soggy. The soils varied in composition, too: coastal-plain soils were deposited by either wind or ancient seas, while Piedmont soils come from rock that decomposed (or weathered) in place. The tree cover on all these soils varies from place to place, sometimes minutely, sometimes dramatically.

In addition, weather patterns have not changed substantially over the past few centuries. Therefore, disturbances such as we experience today also affected the region's forests: hurricanes, wind storms, droughts, fires, floods, not to mention the shifting gardens of the Indians and the fires they set for their surround-hunting of deer in autumn. So all Chesapeake forests were (and are) a mosaic of different stages of growth. Where enough light penetrated into recent clearings, low-growing herbaceous plants flourished until overshadowed by colonizing trees and shrubs. Sometimes the trees did not gain a toehold, and a natural meadow would result; such meadows may have made up as much as 15–17 percent of the land area of eastern

North America.[48] But usually young pines and others became established, only to be crowded out later by the big hardwoods: oaks, red maples, hickories, and the like. In the case of Indian gardens, which were freer of wild vegetation than most natural clearings, abandonment set up a series of successive changes, each of which produced wild foods for people.[49] More comprehensively cleared Indian village areas would take a longer time to return to mature forest; recent studies along the New River suggest that the necessary span is approximately 140 to 160 years.[50]

Hence the early colonial descriptions of the Chesapeake's landscape could have varied considerably, depending on the viewer's route. A traveler could see the forests that Smith and White described, or a forest with an impenetrable understory of American holly or mountain laurel (which also grows on the coastal plain), or a low-lying area where trees were hung with vines of wild grapes, Virginia creeper, trumpet vine, greenbriers, and poison ivy, or pine forests on sandy soils maintained by natural or man-made fires. Or the traveler might encounter grassy barrens typifying the serpentine domes that are scattered throughout southeastern Pennsylvania and adjacent Maryland, or saltwater marshes with stands of loblolly pines, or freshwater marshes and swamps containing bald cypress, Atlantic white cedar, and black gum. It is plain that John Smith and later writers were selective in what they said about forests; they were advertising to prospective colonists what Englishmen were more interested in at the time.[51]

During the last Ice Age, the Chesapeake region—and the exposed continental shelf to the east of it—was forested mainly by fir and spruce, with some pines, birches, ashes, hornbeam, and alders present, as well as grasses and sedges.[52] The fir and spruce today are found mainly at high altitudes in the Appalachians, where tundra existed back then.[53] The Ice Age did not end gradually and smoothly, but in a series of back-and-forth warmer and colder periods, but the result was a somewhat warmer climate in which eastern hemlock was the dominant tree, with pine prominent and black gum, ashes, and birches present. Remnant stands of hemlock still exist in the western Piedmont, and a few small coves occur on the coastal plain. Oaks and hickories made their appearance as the climate warmed further, and recurring fires created meadows in which blueberries and arrowwood (also called wild raisins) flourished. By four thousand years ago, the forest composition was much as it is today:[54] deciduous species except along the coast, where pines are prominent and, in very low, saltwater-flooded areas, dominant. During wetter periods in the last few millennia, black gum, sweet gum, and river birch predominated, with cinnamon fern beneath

A 520-year-old bald cypress tree, located in Maryland's Battle Creek Cypress Swamp Reserve. When it was photographed in 2006, this specimen's circumference measured nearly eighteen feet. John Smith also reported seeing bald cypresses "three fathoms [eighteen feet] about the base." Natives used bald cypress for their log canoes, some of which could accommodate as many as forty individuals. (Photograph by Dwight Williams)

them. In dryer periods, the trees would be mainly oaks, hickories, and chestnuts, with American holly appearing frequently in the understory.

The foregoing is a very coarse-grained view of forests in the Chesapeake in recent centuries. There is tremendous variation among combinations of hundreds of species of trees, shrubs, and many more species of herbaceous plants making up plant communities that, like the lands they inhabit, tend to grade into one another. Several broad associations of trees and other plants can be delineated for the region.[55]

Bald cypress, the premier canoe-making tree for the Indians, grows in peaty muck that is at least permeated by freshwater and, more usually, standing or gently flowing freshwater, above which some of its roots protrude as vertically growing "knees." It is a southerly species that occurs along the middle reaches of the James and Pamunkey, the head of the Piankatank, in Battle Creek, a tributary of the Patuxent, and along the middle and upper reaches of the Pocomoke. Often growing near or among these trees are black gum (which also produces "knees"), sweetgum, green ash, and red maple, with an understory of poison ivy, American holly, Virginia creeper, coastal pepper bush, and southern arrowwood.

The American chestnut was a strong component in pre-Contact and later forests, ranging from 20 to 30 percent in upland habitats. An excellent and rot-resistent timber species, it appears in many colonial structures; its nuts, falling in September and October, were sought by the native people and colonists alike. A European blight all but wiped it out in the 1930s,[56] delivering a blow to humans and animals alike. The forest's composition was not much affected, however, since chestnuts did not grow in "pure" stands. Their place in the landscape was taken by whatever was growing close to them: oaks, tulip poplars, hickories, and other species found widely in mesic soils (well-drained, with a high water-holding capacity) on the peninsulas of Virginia and the gently rolling country of Maryland.

The chestnut oak–post oak–blackjack oak association grows on soils that are very dry, being either fragipan (having a hard layer close to the surface), gravelly (which drains rapidly), or serpentine (which does not form soil). Found in scattered places around the coastal plain, this stunted-looking forest includes the three above-named oaks, Virginia pine, and occasional pitch pines, with an understory of red cedar, serviceberries, blueberries, sassafras, mountain laurel, and chinquapin.

There are two floodplain associations in Virginia and Maryland, one being the sycamore–green ash–box elder–silver maple one that is common in the Piedmont and mountains. The one that we can be sure John Smith saw is the sycamore–river birch association of the coastal plain and (for the Potomac River) the Piedmont. The dominant trees are sycamores and river birches, with slippery elms, tulip poplar, red maple, and black gum added to the upper story, and green ash, spicebush, southern arrowwood, poison ivy, Virginia creeper, and greenbriers in the understory.

There are several kinds of loblolly pine and oak associations in the coastal plain. Along tidal marshes are pure stands of loblolly pine, a southern species adapted to occasional floodwaters of different salinities, with wax myrtle, poison ivy, Virginia creeper, and—in southern Virginia—green bay in the understory. The basket oak–loblolly pine association grows mainly on sandy loams, silts, and floodplains. In addition to its pines and basket oaks, there are sweet gum, black gum, and white oak, with an understory of American holly, coastal pepperbush, common highbush blueberry, and greenbrier. The basket oak–loblolly pine association is an extension of the previous one, except that it extends beyond the northern limit of loblolly pines in Maryland, occurring on sandy loams and silts and including tulip poplar and shadbush. Willow oak–pine forests are extensive to the west of the Chesapeake Bay and are intermixed with the chestnut oak–post oak–blackjack oak forests, preferring sandy loams and silts. This association resembles the basket oak–loblolly pine one except that basket oaks are absent instead of the pines.

English Interest in Forests

By 1607, most forests in England had been cut for domestic and industrial use. The Jamestown colony was expected to export wood products (timber, charcoal, and ash), and the trees in which John Smith and his compatriots took the greatest interest were the larger ones. The "walnuts"—black walnut, butternut, and hickory—as well as oaks, poplars, pines, and beech, appear in the early accounts.[57] The oaks were described as being so big that a timber thirty inches (over 76 centimeters) square and sixty feet (18.3 meters) long could be cut from a single log. The English especially wanted timber for sailing ship masts, such trees rarely being available even on the Continent. The vessel *Starre* was modified to accept such a cargo through "scuppers" (portholes) in the stern of the hull, but only half of the timbers prepared would fit without being shortened first.[58] Elm and ash were burned to make soap-ashes.

The colonists also paid close attention to which trees produced fruit people could eat: mulberries, crabapples, persimmons, and wild plums. They only mentioned the fruit-bearing shrubs in general—blueberries, blackberries, raspberries, elderberries, huckleberries, wild raisins, and wild grapes. They gave more notice to passion fruit (called *maracock* by the Powhatans and later Anglicized to "maypop") because it grew around the edges of Indian fields. Among the nonwoody plants, the English colonists noted that there were plenty of "salad" plants, but they only mentioned two plants by name because the native people processed them into bread flour: little barley (called *mattoume* by the Powhatans), which grew in the wetter abandoned fields, and tuckahoe (arrow arum; the berries were given a separate name, *ocoughtamnis,* later Anglicized to "cuttenemons").

Birdlife

Aside from songbirds, many of which (such as the cardinal) were strange to Europeans, John Smith and other early writers mentioned quails, eagles, wild turkeys, and several kinds of hawks. There was also the stupendously abundant passenger pigeon, which darkened the skies during the winter with flocks estimated at up to 2 billion birds.[59] Audubon separately estimated that at times 300 million flew over him in an hour, in a flock that took three days to pass.[60] Clouds of the birds bowed the limbs of roosting trees and provided thousands of easily obtained squabs as food. The species was brutally market-hunted by nineteenth-century Americans until the population crashed to extinction. The Carolina parakeet was also common in colorful flocks. Considered a pest on grain and fruit crops, it was also driven extinct by hunting and habitat destruction.[61]

Waterfowl, particularly from autumn through spring, provided native people and colonists alike with remarkable seasonal bounty. The species distribution of waterfowl in the bay and its tributaries changes with salinity. Wood ducks, green-winged teal, and ring-necked ducks are seldom seen in the saltier waters favored by pintails, old squaws (now called long-tailed ducks), common loons, and scaups. Availability of SAV further affects some migratory birds, for the stalks, tubers, and roots present at the end of the growing season are food for these birds. In the early seventeenth century, all these waterfowl were so abundant that the English were stunned at their seasonally great numbers.[62]

Land Animals

John Smith recorded a comprehensive list of the larger land animals in Virginia: deer, raccoons, several squirrels (including flying squirrels), muskrats, rabbits, opossums, bears, wolves, bobcats, foxes, martens, skunks, weasels, minks, otters, and last but not least (for the Powhatans considered their tails a delicacy, and Europeans soon would, too),[63] beavers. There was also a variety of turtles and snakes. The raccoons and opossums were new to Europeans, who adopted Powhatan names for them that we still use. Of this list, deer, wild turkeys, and box turtles are the animals whose remains are most frequently found in Native American sites, except for those that are obviously primarily fishing camps. At freshwater fishing sites, sturgeon, gar, and catfish turn up the most often (though fish with finer bones, more subject to decomposition, were probably also eaten).

Bison are conspicuous by their absence from the archeological records of Virginia and Maryland. No *Bison bison* bones have yet been recovered in any aboriginal context, nor have they been identified from colonial sites. However, in the seventeenth and eighteenth centuries there were still sightings of buffalo within Virginia and Maryland and perhaps in Pennsylvania as well. In 1613, describing an experience that likely occurred within fifteen miles (24.1 kilometers) of Washington, D.C., Samuel Argall wrote: "I found great store of cattle as big as Kine [cows], of which the Indians that were my guides killed a couple, which we found to be very good and wholesome meate, and are very easie to be killed, in regard they are heavy slow, and not so wild as other beasts of the wildernesse."[64] In the early 1630s, Henry Fleet wrote about the upper tidal Potomac near the Anacostia River: "And as for deer, buffaloes, bears, turkeys the woods do swarm with them."[65] Spaniards visiting the Rappahannock fall line spoke of a "wild cow." As early as the sixteenth century, a watercolor by John White at Roanoke Island (now North Carolina) depicted a Native American male dressed in loincloth attire but with a long tail hanging down in back that could have been that of a buffalo or, more likely, a puma.[66] There are also several place-names in the western part of Virginia including "bull" or "cow" or "calf" as possible references to bison—or to elk, which were also residents in those days. A Native American comb carved from elk antler was found at a site currently occupied by the Whitehurst Freeway in Washington D.C.[67]

All of the attested animals in John Smith's list were forest dwellers, since forest was the commonly available habitat; as already noted, meadows for grass-eaters like bison were not plentiful.[68] Carnivores included the cats, wolves, otters, weasels, martens, and minks. Omnivores included the bears, raccoons, and opossums. Other animals, such as deer, were herbivores. And most of those in turn were forest-adapted, eating bark, leaves, seeds, and nuts rather than grass. The nut-eaters (including the omnivores) became major prey for human hunters in autumn—hunters who were stalking the competition, for humans are nut-eaters, too.

Beavers were abundant in the Late Woodland period and served a significant ecological role, building low dams along countless small streams, which locally modified forests by drowning trees and creating ephemeral wetlands that conserved sediment and nutrients leaking from neighboring woodlands. Though Native Americans all around the Chesapeake used beaver pelts and meat, the intense hunting spurred by European commerce took place (in the 1630s through 1670s) from the Potomac and Maryland Eastern Shore rivers northward. There the winters were cold enough that the animals grew thicker and more desirable pelts. Some believe that a million beavers were eventually killed in this trade,[69] which virtually extirpated the species in the Chesapeake by 1700.[70] Beavers were reintroduced to the East in the twentieth century and have succeeded well enough to be a problem for modern residents in some areas.

Most of the animals on the list were medium-sized or small by Old

World standards. Even the wolves were not large: "they are no bigger than our English foxes."[71] Since the end of the last Ice age, when the North American relatives of horses, camels, rhinos, and elephants became extinct, the continent had been nearly devoid of large herbivores other than buffalo, moose, elk, bighorn sheep, caribou, and musk ox. Several of those did not live anywhere in the Eastern Woodlands, and none of them lived in the Chesapeake region. Thus there were no large animals for the native people to domesticate for eating, drawing heavy loads, or any other purpose; they had only small, near-feral beagle-sized dogs, which they used for hunting wild turkeys.[72] That lack of domesticated animals dictated that any meat in the people's diet had to come from hunting and fishing; it also meant that their farming would be carried out on a relatively small scale. The result was an Indian world far different from that of the Europeans.

2

The World of
Algonquian-Speaking Peoples

Helen C. Rountree

THE PEOPLE NATIVE to the Chesapeake region used most of its natural resources, as far as their technology and cultural values would allow, yet they had a much smaller impact on the land than modern people do. That was not due so much to being perfect conservationists—they weren't[1]—as to the fact that there were many fewer people using the land in 1607–9 and they were doing it without heavy machinery or chemicals.

Native Ways of Life

Variations in environment made for some slight subsistence differences among the people, depending upon the elevation of the land and the salinity of the waters, as well as the access different groups had to long-distance trade. Just as the Chesapeake Bay and the lands surrounding it were not uniform, the Native American groups living on those lands and using the bay were not carbon copies of one another.

Algonquian Indians fishing in Albemarle Sound, as rendered in the late sixteenth century by Theodor de Bry, based on an illustration by John White. A talented artist, White accompanied the colonists who tried (and failed) to establish a settlement on the island of Roanoke (North Carolina) in 1585–86. (From the collections of The Mariners' Museum, Newport News, Va.)

Language

The native people of the Virginia and Maryland coastal plain spoke languages that belonged to the Algonquian language family, a large group (named for the Algonquin tribe of what is now Quebec) that extended along the coast from Canada's Maritime Provinces (e.g., Montagnais) to North Carolina (e.g., Pamlico), as well as westward through the Great Lakes (e.g., Ojibwa) and out onto the Great Plains (e.g., Cheyenne and Arapaho). People living near each other spoke similar dialects; but the farther apart people lived, the more difficulty they had understanding one another. The speech of the Algonquian speakers of North Carolina (Roanokes and others), the Maryland Eastern Shore (Nanticokes and others), and Virginia (collectively called Powhatans) may have differed enough that we can recognize at least three separate languages.[2] The region's linguistic diversity had already been noticed by the Spanish in the 1570s.[3]

John Smith may have carried to Virginia a Roanoke word list collected in the 1580s.[4] He may or may not have learned a fair amount of the Powhatan language during his captivity, but he said he served as his own interpreter thereafter,[5] including the two expeditions he made around the Chesapeake. When he arrived at the head of the bay, he found that he could not communicate with the Tockwoghs (whose language may have been closer to that of the nearby Delawares/Lenapes than to that of the Pamunkey River people who had held him captive). To talk to them he needed an interpreter. To talk to their neighbors, the Susquehannocks—who belonged to an entirely different language family (Iroquoian, which included the Five Nations)—that interpreter in turn needed an interpreter.[6] A similarly skilled person was needed for Smith's "interviewing" of the Mannahoac man during the second expedition; that may have involved a language from a third major language family (which included the Siouan-speaking Catawbas and Lakotas).[7] Fortunately, in the multilingual Late Woodland Indian world,[8] such facilitators were usually available.

Most Algonquian place-names in the region cannot be translated today, even though a few of them (e.g., Pamunkey, Piscataway) appear repeatedly up and down the Atlantic coast. The meaning of the name of the great bay itself is uncertain. Philip Barbour wrote that it meant "country or people on the great river,"[9] which accords with the English of the Roanoke colony originally hearing the name in connection with the Chesapeake Indians, not with the bay at all. The Spanish called the great estuary Bahia de Santa Maria (St. Mary's Bay), and their sometime guide Paquinquineo (Don Luis) called the region he knew Ajacán.[10] But nobody recorded the native names (probably plural) for the bay.

Physical Appearance

All of the people of the region, except for two persons observed to exhibit European ancestry,[11] were American Indian in their physical type.[12] They had sallow-white skin that tanned readily; and it was made redder by the dyeing properties of the puccoon-root paint that people applied to their faces, necks, and shoulders on special occasions (i.e., whenever Europeans showed up during peacetime). Those same areas might be tattooed, in the case of the women. Hair was coarse, straight, jet black, in old age thinning somewhat and turning gray or white. Eyes ranged from brown to black. Women usually wore their hair long and loose, while Powhatan men and many men in the Maryland groups shaved half their heads, left a stiff roach along the center, and knotted up the long hair on the left side. Men's beards and other body hair were sparse. Younger men grated away their whiskers with mussel-shell tweezers, while old men like Powhatan let the beard grow. Old age also brought tooth loss.[13]

The native people of the Chesapeake region appeared relatively unclothed to European observers like John Smith. Tailored clothing did not exist, except for the protective leggings and moccasins that both sexes wore in the forest. Other clothing was not sewn, unless it was embroidered with shell beads; that embroidery, plus tattooing and painting and differing hairstyles, usually said more about a person's tribal identity than did clothing per se. Clothes were made of animal skins and were draped: women's aprons and men's breechclouts from waistbands, and mantles around shoulders in cold weather (the forerunner of "Indian blankets").[14] That kind of winter clothing was not practical for very active work, such as a hunter chasing a wounded deer or men and women paddling dugout canoes. Therefore people made a virtue of necessity by valuing endurance and acclimatizing themselves every year.[15]

The kinds of work people did also affected their physical appearance, just as it does now. Men's primary work involved hunting and war; warfare was guerrilla war, which meant hunting people. A great deal of running was required, so that early eyewitness accounts mention men's leanness and speed as runners.[16] In other words, they were accomplished cross-country runners and looked it. Women, on the other hand, did heavy physical work like collecting firewood in the forest, weeding gardens, digging deep-growing tuckahoe (arrow arum) roots in the marshes, and pounding corn into cornmeal at the end of a workday, so that they were usually heavily muscled.[17] Children grew up doing what their same-sex parent did, and they would have been wiry or heavily muscled accordingly (the Disney cartoon's Barbie-doll Pocahontas is a modern-day myth).

John Smith and others wrote that the Algonquian speakers were "tall," especially those chosen as bodyguards for paramount chiefs like Powhatan.[18] Some engravings of the time, such as the one of John Smith facing off with Opechancanough, show an extreme disproportion between tall tribesmen and short Europeans. The reality was less spectacular. Although Smith recorded that some people tended to be short, like the Eastern Shore Wiccocomicos (later called Pocomokes), and others were very tall, like the Susquehannocks,[19] the archaeological evidence for the whole region indicates an average adult male height of 5 ft. 7–7.5 in. (170.4–171.4 cm) and an average adult female height of 5 ft. 2–3 in. (159–161 cm), with coastal plan inhabitants being slightly shorter

A 1645 etching of a twenty-three-year-old Virginia Indian man, by Wenceslaus Hollar. Nothing about the man himself was recorded, but there was a war going on in the Virginia colony in 1645. Presumably he came from one of the tribes friendly to the English, such as those on the Eastern Shore, Rappahannock River, or Potomac River. (Library of Congress)

than those of the Piedmont. Even the Susquehannock men averaged about the same.[20] On the other hand, averages for the London English of that time were 5 ft. 6 in. (169 cm) for men and 5 ft. 1 in. (155 cm) for women.[21]

Food Getting

Seasonal variations in diet affected how the coastal plain people looked. John Smith wrote: "It is strange to see how their bodies alter with their diet, even as the deer and wild beasts they seem fat and lean, strong and weak."[22] The leanest season was spring, when the previous year's stores were gone and this year's crops and wild fruits were not yet ripe; the fattest was early winter, after harvesting crops, nuts, and acorns. Available foods year-round were relatively low in fat and sugar and high in fiber; what varied seasonally was energy-rich starch.[23] Much of the native diet came from wild sources (described in more detail shortly) and was procured by both men and women.[24] In the near-absence of domesticated animals (there were only dogs), meat had to be hunted or fished for by the men. Women handled plants, assisted by children. Corn, beans, and squash were the domesticated plants they cultivated; there is no record of who raised the tobacco, but it may have been men. None of these four plants are native to the region, and they suffer in the dry summers that occur approximately every third year. Even in a good year, a plague of insects or a raid by enemies could wipe out the crop. So it made excellent sense for the women to keep up the ancient knowledge (dating back several millennia) of the region's 1,100-plus native wild species that have edible parts at various seasons.[25]

Some plants produce food edible by humans at all seasons—for example, tuckahoe roots for starch and greenbrier leaves for greens. But in early spring (in Powhatan, *cattapeuk*),[26] it took a lot of energy to get those roots, and the leaves were sparse, tough, and bitter. At least the fish runs brought nice, oily shad and herring to the rivers. After that, in the planting season (*cohattayough*), the mulberries and other wild plants ripened while the corn grew. If there was enough rain distributed over the whole summer, there would be a good harvest in August through October (in Powhatan, *nepinough*). In *taquitock,* the autumn nuts and acorns were gathered and added to stores of corn, and communal hunts were held to bring in large quantities of venison and deer hides. That was the people's major time for both war and ritual. Then *popanow,* winter, was the "fat" time when people were less active and lived on the foods they had put away. When the stored foods ran out, it was early spring again, and people went foraging and became lean once more.[27]

Like Algonquian speakers to the north, each year the people of the Virginia and Maryland coastal plain staged two major dispersals out of their towns: one in spring and one in autumn, both seasons when people lived on wild foods. The result was a much more varied diet than the relatively starchy one consumed by the English (and the starchy, fatty, and sugary one many modern Americans have). That probably accounts for the Native Americans being slightly taller, on the average, than the English. It also meant that the native people's towns, which lacked latrines, could get a semiannual airing out, a sanitation measure unavailable to all but the rich-

John Smith's Chesapeake Voyages, 1607–1609

A STREAM VALLEY IN CROSS SECTION

showing the locations of the various plant and animal resources the native people utilized. (Helen C. Rountree)

Uplands with
Deciduous Forest
(Foraging)

Lower Terrace:
Houses & Fields
(Living, Farming, Foraging)

Yr. 1: girdle trees
Yr. 2: clear, cultivate
  (very good yield)
Yr. 3: cultivate
  (good yield)
Yr. 4: cultivate
  (fair yield)

All Year:
Firewood
Cedar bark
  for fabric
Deer
Bear
Wild turkeys
Raccoons
Opossums
Box turtles
Passenger pigeons

Fall:
Acorns
Walnuts
Hickory nuts
Beech nuts
Chestnuts
Chinquapins

Seasonal:
Medicinal herbs
Bloodroot
Oak/Elm bark for
  Shingles
Saplings for structures

Yrs. 1-2 fallow:
Little barley
Maypops
Cordage plants
Blackberries
Raspberries

Yrs. 3-7 fallow:
Cordage plants
Blackberries
Raspberries
Black cherry
Wild grapes
Groundnut
Hog peanut
Wild potato vine
Cleavers
Wild rose
Var. briars
Persimmon
Sassafras
Chinquapin
Small pines
Small oaks

Yr. 7+ fallow:
Last 7 items, in the form of
  saplings squeezing out
  briars and roses

Marsh
(Salt or Fresh)
(Foraging)

Reeds for mats
Arrow arum tubers
  (Tuckahoe)
Wild rice
Muskrats
Raccoons
Snapping turtles
Sora rail birds

Waterway
(Salt or Fresh)
(Transport, Foraging)

Fish
Crabs
Crayfish
Mussels
Oysters
Clams
Arrow arum berries
  (cuttanemons;
  floating in fall)
Migratory ducks
Migratory geese
Beavers
Otters

est Europeans of the time. Later on, dispersals meant that European diseases like tuberculosis were less likely to cause the horrendous mortality that occurred among the urban Aztecs and Incas. The first real epidemic recorded in Virginia did not occur until 1617, and it was bloody flux (hemorrhagic dysentery) rather than an eruptive disease like smallpox.[28] Worse threats to health came from drought and famine, human enemies, and storms while canoeing, though there were some native infectious diseases.[29]

Lean times could mean malnutrition, which is a damper on the size not only of human beings but also of human populations. Combined gardening and foraging was another damper, for the carrying capacity of the Chesapeake region for humans was considerably less under that regime than it would become with European intensive plant and animal husbandry, especially more recently with mechanized farming. A further lowering of the birth rate stemmed from the marital chastity required during women's menstrual periods and men's ritual activities. John Smith and others noticed that there were fewer people on the land than they were used to seeing, and the majority were women and children (thanks to unremitting warfare as described below). Smith estimated that there were only about five thousand people within sixty miles (96.5 kilometers) of Jamestown, while Henry Fleet postulated a similar number for the Potomac River valley below the fall line.[30] We will consider the population of specific districts in later chapters of this volume, using Randolph Turner's 1982 estimates, which are based on Smith's and Strachey's "warrior-counts" for each district.[31]

Farming and Living in Towns

The Indian people of the Chesapeake region spent the year in a variety of settlements, ranging from settled villages to small seasonal hunting camps. The latter were located at good fishing spots along the waterways and in the forests of the uplands. The villages, however, were always to be found along the waterways, specifically where several conditions existed: a landing place that had minimal fringe-marsh to cross for canoe launching and, if the town was on a bluff, a natural ramp or dry ravine leading from water's edge to town's edge (people-power hauled everything up to the town); large nearby stands of reeds (for mats) and/or emergent plants (for food) to be gathered; and good-quality farmland that was level or nearly so.[32] Most Indian towns—in both the coastal plain and the Piedmont[33]—were therefore built on lowish alluvial terraces along the rivers (exactly where developers want to build houses today).

The main water supply for each town was the stream in front of it, which was primarily used for bathing. Where that water was brackish, the people obtained drinking water from the many small springs (most of them rather like seeps) that flowed in this forested region. Unlike modern Americans, some Algonquian speakers did not expect to bathe in drinking-quality water.

The native people of the Chesapeake region—and of the Eastern Woodlands in general—practiced shifting cultivation, a method that is still common in tropical latitudes. Soil becomes played-out in a few years if it is not fertilized (pest infestation can have the same effect), but fertilizing with fish or anything else would have meant more work for people who were already busy foraging for much of their food.[34] Someone would have had to catch and transport those extra fish, to grow crops that might fail anyway. It made better sense to clear a few new fields each year, especially given that the trees killed in the process could become firewood. Most towns in the region consisted of houses scattered among gardens, and the various components of these "towns" moved continually. When the new fields became far enough away, the women and children who cultivated them would abandon the old family houses—sapling-and-mat affairs that lasted only a few years anyway—and build new houses nearby. Native towns thus would move, amoebalike, up and down the banks of the waterways. Even the densely built palisaded towns (described shortly) would be moved at intervals of perhaps twenty years.[35] All that movement means that John Smith's map, originally sketched as early as 1608, is a snapshot in time: it shows where settlements were in that year. It does not show where they were a decade before or after, or what their earlier or later names (apparently tied to specific localities) would have been.[36]

No Algonquian-speakers' town of 1607–9 would have seemed sizeable to us. The largest had only had a couple of hundred people, and the great majority of people living away from the frontiers dwelled, as Gabriel Archer put it, "by families of kindred and alliance, some 40 or 50 in a . . . small village; which towns are not past a mile or half a mile [1–1.5 kilometers] asunder in most places."[37] That is why there are so many towns on John Smith's map, despite the rather sparse population. This scattering of the people was an additional reason, besides the twice-yearly dispersals, why epidemics did not cut such a swath in the Chesapeake region as they did in Mexico and Peru. Cities are vulnerable; hamlets are less so.[38] For the names of most of those native settlements we are indebted to John Smith (who was also the author of the 1608 "Zuñiga" sketch-map).[39] It is a pity that he did not

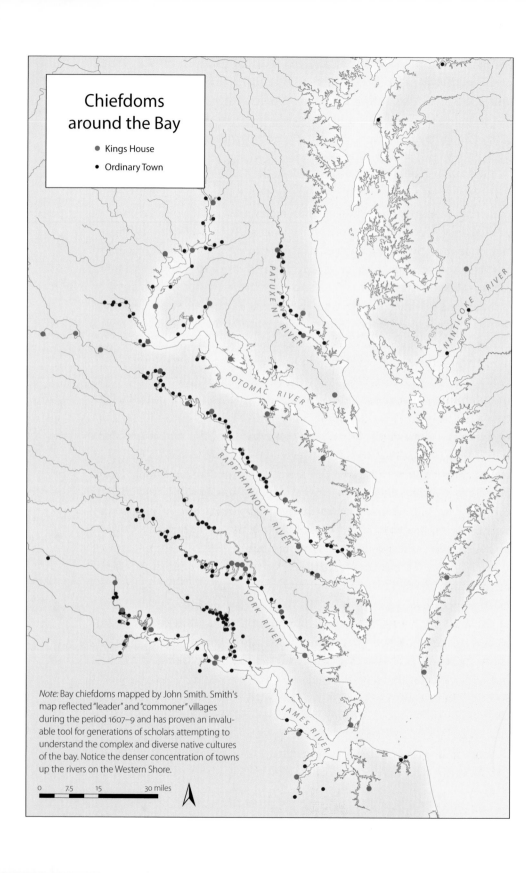

Chiefdoms around the Bay

- ● Kings House
- • Ordinary Town

PATUXENT RIVER

NANTICOKE RIVER

POTOMAC RIVER

RAPPAHANNOCK RIVER

YORK RIVER

JAMES RIVER

Note: Bay chiefdoms mapped by John Smith. Smith's map reflected "leader" and "commoner" villages during the period 1607–9 and has proven an invaluable tool for generations of scholars attempting to understand the complex and diverse native cultures of the bay. Notice the denser concentration of towns up the rivers on the Western Shore.

0   7.5   15   30 miles

inquire (perhaps because it would have been very time-consuming in the absence of a truly skilled interpreter) which settlements belonged to which chief.

Chiefs

Most Algonquian-speaking people of the Chesapeake lived in chiefdoms, presided over either by local chiefs or by paramount chiefs who ruled multiple local chiefs. There were four of the latter organizations: the Powhatans (covering all the rivers of eastern Virginia except the Chickahominy), the Piscataways (the north bank of the Potomac from at least Port Tobacco to the Anacostia River), the Nanticokes (the Nanticoke River and several rivers to the south), and the Asseateagues (Atlantic bays, Pocomoke River, and smaller rivers to the north).[40]

The Nanticokes were one of the first people to develop such "emperors," as John Smith's compatriots called them.[41] In the early 1660s, Piscataway oral tradition stated that they had gotten the idea from that Eastern Shore group thirteen "generations" (probably thirteen chiefs' reigns) before,[42] which would take it back at least to the early sixteenth century and possibly back into the 1400s, with the Nanticoke version being even older. Powhatan's paramount chieftaincy, on the other hand, seems to have dated only to the early to mid-1500s: he inherited six districts and added the twenty-odd others that he dominated in 1607.[43] There is also linguistic evidence that he did it independently of the Maryland "emperors": the word for paramount chief in Virginia was *mamanatowick*,[44] while in Maryland it was *tayac* (Piscataway)[45] or *tallak* (Nanticoke; feminine version *tallakesk*).[46] If Powhatan had simply copied the Piscataways, the word for his exalted position would logically have been a cognate (i.e., a recognizably similar word with similar meaning) of *tayac*. (Both *-sk* and *-squa* were feminine endings in coastal Algonquian languages, giving rise to the now-derogatory word "squaw" for an Indian woman.)

Paramount chiefs, or "emperors," among the Powhatans and Piscataways, at least, inherited their positions matrilineally—that is, through the mother's line. This meant that a chief's heirs were not his or her children, but the chief's brothers, with sisters and sisters' children respectively next in line.[47] The result was that although two of Powhatan's sons are known to have been chiefs—because he appointed them as such—his daughter Pocahontas was not a "princess" in the European sense. This heirs-of-females practice may have been borrowed from the mound-building chiefdoms of the Southeast (there is no recorded oral tradition on that point), but it also

John Smith's map of Virginia, first published in 1612 and used by colonists as the primary map of the bay region until the 1670s. In Smith's time, English mapmakers did not follow the convention of putting north at the top of the map. Thus the Chesapeake is laid out as the English would approach it by sea. (Library of Virginia)

Native Words for Politico-Military Positions

Maryland
    Piscataway
        Weroance—district or hamlet chief
        Wiso—councilor
        Jan Jan Wizous—true king
        Cockaroose—war captain
        [not recorded]—speaker
    Nanticoke
        Matt-ah-ki-ween—warrior

Virginia
    Powhatan
        Weroance—district or hamlet chief
        Weroansqua—district or hamlet female chief
        Cronocoe—councilor
            (Chickahominy dialect): Cawcawassough—elder (Original text
            says "cawcawassoughs . . . elders"; the Algonquian plural here
            would have been -as, rather than the English -s.)

Sources: Anonymous 1910 [1635]; Browne et al. 1883-1972; Haile 1998; J. Smith 1986 [1608]; Speck 1927; Strachey 1953 [1612]; A. White 1910 [1634].

had practical value, for it eliminated potentially lethal competition among the sons of male chiefs. There were dozens of such sons, some possibly born on the same day, because male chiefs had many wives.[48] The practice also avoided a scourge of sixteenth-century royal governments in the British Isles: a child succeeding to the throne and then being manipulated by a regent, courtiers, or others. In the Algonquian speakers' world, the next generation came to power only when they had reached adulthood and after the previous generation had died. Even female chiefs, who would have learned about warfare mainly secondhand, had ample time while their brothers ruled to absorb what they would need to know to protect their people when they inherited the chieftainship.

Chiefs, called *weroances* by the Algonquian speakers, governed with the assistance of priests and councilors, who were either lesser chiefs or else proven war captains. These positions were probably far older in the Algon-

POWHATAN CHIEFLY SUCCESSION

Example of how matrilineal succession determined who could become a Powhatan chief.
Red *type indicates potential rulers.*

Powhatan's Mother

Powhatan	Opitchapam	Opechancanough	Kekataugh	2 sisters (unnamed)
Pocahontas (many others)	(many children)	(many children)	?	Eldest's sons, then her daughters

quian speakers' culture than paramount chiefs, since they represented local power structures and often had cognate terms denoting them (see the box on native words for politico-military positions).

Chiefs' duties were primarily in military, diplomatic, and religious matters, in all of which they acted as official representatives of their people. Regrettably, whenever a European came to call, the occasion became a special one. That probably accounts for John Smith and others saying that Powhatan and his confreres had life-and-death power over their people, at the same time that Powhatan went on record as saying he could not control all his people.[49] On a day-to-day basis, chiefs seem to have had limited power over their "subjects," both because the people were not yet accustomed to being much interfered with and because there were no standing armies to enforce chiefs' will. Two episodes from the life of Powhatan's brother Opechancanough illustrate the limitations upon native VIPs. Opechancanough's favorite wife was seduced away by another chief, and though Powhatan demoted the chief, the wife could not be retrieved. And when John Smith was newly captured in late 1607, and the father of a man he had killed while being taken prisoner tried to take revenge upon him, Smith's captor, Opechancanough, had no power to order the bereaved father to desist. Instead he had to remove Smith to another district (from the headwaters of the Chickahominy River to the upper Pamunkey River).[50]

Order was kept in the towns by other means. Good manners, meaning self-restraint, went a long way. An observer of the Piscataways and others remarked on how polite and deliberately inoffensive people were to one another, especially in council meetings, where interrupting speakers was unheard of.[51] People lived among and worked on behalf of their relatives all their lives,[52] which made for very strong interpersonal ties. Infractions of customary law were enforced by the many local deities (John Smith's

Intertribal Hostilities in the Early Seventeenth Century

A = Algonquian speakers
I = Iroquoian speakers
S = Siouan speakers

Powhatans [A] against:
    Monacans [S]
    Mannahoacs [S]
    Massawomecks [I]
    Chowanocks [A] (by 1620s)

Patawomecks [A] against:
    Massawomecks [I]
    Piscataways [A] (1623)
    Nacotchtanks (Anacostians) [A] (1622)

Piscataways [A] against:
    Massawomecks [I]
    Nacotchtanks/Anacostians [A]
    Susquehannocks [I] (by 1642)
    Patawomecks [A] (1623)

Patuxents [A] against:
    Massawomecks [I]
    Accomacs [A] (by 1621)

Tockwoghs [A] against:
    Massawomecks [I]

Susquehannocks [I] against:
    Massawomecks [I]
    Yoacomocos [A] (by 1634)
    Wicomisses [A] (by 1634)
    Piscataways [A] (by 1642)

Sources: Anonymous 1910 [1635]; Bland et al. 1911 [1651]; Fleet 1876 [1631–32]; Haile 1998; Jesuit Letters 1910 [1631–32, 1642]; Kingsbury 1906–35; Pory, in Smith 1986c [1624]; J. Smith 1986a [1608]; J. Smith 1986b [1612]; J. Smith 1986c [1624]; Strachey 1953 [1612]; A. White 1910 [1634].

okees), who could either be vengeful by themselves or else could identify malefactors to the shaman-priests,[53] who told the chiefs.[54] Yet another useful mechanism, employed by some modern governments, was to direct people's frustrations and hostilities outward onto foreign enemies.

John Smith's Chesapeake Voyages, 1607–1609

War

Warfare went on all the time throughout the Eastern Woodlands before Europeans arrived to complicate matters further.[55] The Powhatans and Monacans are known to have raided each other annually at least from the 1570s through the early years of the Jamestown colony, after which both sides concluded that the English were a mutual enemy.[56] The situation was fluid, though. Alliances were made and cemented by trading and visiting thereafter; enmities flared up and then were sometimes patched up by diplomatic means. Wars were vicious while they continued, however. Boys were raised to be professional hunters of people as well as of animals, and to be ready to die stoically under the torture that was often meted out to male captives.[57] Long-distance raids were carried out, and the prisoners taken included women and children who were adopted into their captors' tribes. Thus there was a constant small-scale moving-around, which, in addition to the long-distance trade evidenced in the archaeological record, meant that people in any one area would know individuals from elsewhere and also would probably speak some of their languages.

Warfare usually but not always occurred along linguistic cleavages, as the following list will show. Unless otherwise noted, the accompanying box shows the intertribal antagonisms at the time of John Smith's explorations.

An arms race was already on when John Smith came calling in 1607–8. The Massawomecks were especially feared because, living in the Appalachians to the northwest, they had two advantages: iron hatchets from the French and birch-bark canoes that could easily outrun the Algonquian speakers' heavy log dugouts.[58] That arms race accounts for the avidity with which the people Smith met in his travels sought to buy English hatchets and knives; the Virginia Powhatans were well-supplied with them by 1612.[59] (Other popular trade items were metal shovels and hoes, which the women used in gardening.[60])

Fortified Towns

A byproduct of the fear of enemy raiders were the densely clustered, palisaded towns built by people who were struck too often. Most Algonquian speakers' towns were dispersed, "rural" settlements, but in certain places the people built their houses close together—at least at the chiefs' towns—and erected a pole-and-bark palisade around the perimeter. The famous de Bry engraving showing only a circle of upright poles around the town depicts an incomplete palisade, so that viewers can see the houses.[61] A finished palisade would have no open spaces for enemy snipers to shoot through. The overlapping entranceway, however, is accurate. Such fortified settlements are known both historically and archaeologically. John Smith mentioned Tockwogh and Powhatan town.[62] Excavations have added to the list, including the Great Neck site (located in modern-day Virginia Beach and probably "Chesipiuk" of 1585); the Accokeek Creek site (which would have been in the vicinity of Moyaons on the Smith map, the Piscataway capital); and Patawomeck (two adjacent sites, one of John Smith's time and one slightly earlier). Archaeological survey has suggested others, such as the Buck site within Chickahominy territory; Chicone ("Kuskarawaok" on Smith's map), where the later Nanticoke "emperors" lived; and the Cumberland site on the lower Patuxent River (in the area of "Opanient" on Smith's map).[63]

Trading

Trade as well as war went on among the peoples of the Chesapeake region. That trade was mainly in luxury goods such as copper[64] (available by long-distance connections with the Great Lakes, regardless of the Monacans), shell jewelry (marine shells from the Atlantic littoral or the saltier portions of the Chesapeake Bay), freshwater pearls (available in freshwater streams), and the red-dyeing root puccoon (available by trade from the Meherrins or by long-distance connections through middlemen in the Carolina Piedmont to the sand hills of South Carolina).[65] Most luxury goods wound up in the hands of chiefs, who wore them on special occasions to impress visitors with their wealth and power.

There may also have been a more ordinary trade between upriver and downriver districts within the southern part of the coastal plain. People like the Kecoughtans and Accomacs lived in a saltwater area lacking the starchy root tuckahoe (arrow arum, a freshwater marsh plant). They also inhabited the narrow ends of peninsulas, where the deer had been overhunted. They therefore raised more corn and caught more fish and shellfish; shelled corn and dried seafood[66] could be traded for dried venison, deerskins and perhaps other furs, and cakes of rendered deer suet (eaten on cornbread).[67] Even when trading with foreigners for tools, for the common folk the aim was improving food procurement, for "their victual is their chief riches."[68]

The people's food, like their clothing, tools, and houses, nearly always came from sources immediately around them. Farmers though they were, complex politically though they were, they still lived for the most part directly off the land.

The Indian village of Pomeiooc on Albemarle Sound as rendered by Theodor de Bry, based on a painting by John White. The palisade is unfinished, to show the houses better. A completed palisade would be covered on the outside with bark, so that enemy sharpshooters could not see the people inside to shoot at them. (From the collections of The Mariners' Museum, Newport News, Va.)

The Land as Shopping Center

The Algonquian speakers of the Chesapeake region knew their land intimately, for that kind of knowledge—plugged into memories like a computer—was required for survival, even in a rich environment. John Smith was dead wrong when he wrote of people living "from hand to mouth," for it took planning to put the knowledge into effect. That was doubly true of people who lacked metal tools, draft animals, and the wheeled vehicles that draft animals make feasible. Let us examine some basic situations, which modern Americans solve by going shopping, to see how the native people handled them.

Transport

Everyone needs transportation, both for long-distance travel and to bring home heavy burdens. The solution—for everyone in the Chesapeake until the 1930s[69]—was water-based travel by boat. Waterways, in the Indian world, were the centers of tribal territories, not boundaries between them. "Boats" before 1607 meant log canoes, which were just as expensive, in a native family's time-budget, as cars are monetarily for us. Canoes had to carry considerable loads of people and goods: up to forty people and, if an overnight trip was planned, cooking gear and the makings of a temporary house. Therefore those craft had to be large—a 45-footer (13.7 meters long) was measured in 1607. Most canoes could carry "10 or 20 [persons] with some luggage," and heavy as they were, they could be paddled faster than the English could row their own small craft.[70] So even a workaday canoe had to be built from what we would consider a very large tree indeed.

A likely tree growing along (cypress) or reasonably near (other species) a waterway had to be located and then laboriously chopped down and delimbed with a stone axe (not as sharp as an iron one), probably by several men from the same extended family. They then dragged the log out into the waterway and towed it home (using the old canoe they were replacing). After dragging it up the landing and into the yard, they and probably the rest of the family would proceed to hollow the log out, not with hatchets but by burning patches, scraping the charcoal out with shells, burning more patches, and so on—a slow, laborious process.[71] The larger the canoe, the longer it took. The finished canoe was then used by family members for visiting, courting, politicking, fishing, lugging reeds and tuckahoe from marshes, war making, and other tasks. The tributaries of the Chesapeake were as busy with watercraft in pre-Contact times as they have been in post-Contact ones.

Even going back and forth from town to obtain garden produce and firewood meant that women and children needed carrying equipment. One essential item—found in all human cultures—was a baby carrier, which for the Powhatans meant a flat wooden cradleboard and twine for strapping the infant onto the board and the board onto mother's back.[72] (The baby's diaper, like the other "linens" used by the native people, was made either of Spanish moss, which then grew farther north and west than it does today,[73] or of the soft fibers from red cedar bark.) Twine was also needed for tying bundles of firewood, and it was woven into carrying nets and bags for the groceries. The women made their own twine—miles of it—from scratch.[74] Some of the best plants for this purpose, such as Indian hemp, grow in first-year abandoned fields, the best time to harvest the stalks being when nature has dried them out—midwinter through early spring.[75] The fibers in the stalks can then be easily removed, without the plants' sticky sap interfering, and cleaned and separated, ready for hand-twining, which went on all year.

House Building

At least a mile of twine, as well as other materials, had to be ready in advance when a house was to be built—probably by the same women who made the twine.[76] The houses of Algonquian speakers up and down the Atlantic coast were lashed-together bent-wood frameworks with mat or bark coverings added. That sounds simple, but even with many of the materials purchased, a large house (30 ft. by 15 ft.) built recently at Jamestown Settlement took well over five hundred man-hours to erect.[77] Making over a mile of twine would have been only one part of the preparation four centuries ago.

Bark can be removed from trees (most easily in April and May) and used soon thereafter. But mats require advance planning. Harvesting the dead, dry reeds in midwinter through early spring is easiest, when new growth does not interfere; although less subject to natural rot, green reeds are more difficult to cut and must be dried back in town. Any hollow-stemmed reed will do, and there are usable species in marshes of all salinities.[78] Marshes are muddy, however, and even in the cold weather the activity of harvesting is hard, backbreaking work, especially if one does not have a machete (English swords would have served the purpose after 1607). Bundled reeds are also surprisingly heavy, so canoes would have been the only efficient means of transporting them in bulk from the marsh back to town. The

Replica of an Indian house at Jamestown, Virginia, showing woven mats used as coverings. Archaeology has shown that Virginia Algonquian houses had circular or oval floor plans, unlike what John White painted. Houses with rounded ends can withstand higher winds. (Helen C. Rountree)

reeds would then have to be woven or sewn into mats, one mat at a time, a job that probably went on all year.

The last materials to be collected for the house were the saplings for the framework. Most of these needed to be at least eighteen feet (5.5 meters) long to provide the headroom shown in sixteenth- and seventeenth-century engravings, and there had to be at least fifty of them to build a small house: uprights to bend together, horizontal battens to brace the structure, and internal posts as additional bracing and built-in beds along the walls. All of these saplings needed to be peeled to discourage wood-eating insects and then used in the building process before they dried out (unlike reeds and cordage plants, which were used dry). House raising was probably a group effort by an extended family, for parts of that task literally require many hands at once.

In addition to the oblong houses of the agricultural villages, the Algonquians also constructed bent-pole circular houses for individual families who went to the interior winter hunting quarters. Each day the hunters (and perhaps the women) agreed where the camp would be that evening, and then while the men and boys hunted, the women and girls went to set up temporary houses, cutting saplings and bending and lashing them into low frameworks (such houses being mainly for sleeping) and then covering these structures with mats they brought with them. In about two hours, the camp was ready.[79]

Where the Food Came From

Everyone has to eat, so every family needs food coming into the house. People also need to be decently clothed, which in the Algonquian speakers' world, with its deerskin garments, went hand-in-hand with food-getting. The tribal territory generally included enough species of wild plants and animals so that each family could be self-sufficient, unless a severe drought struck.

Indian women cultivated several fields each year, staggering the planting across a three-month period. Most fields were a year or two old while others were newly cleared by the men. The women had learned, from centuries of trial and error, where the best soils were for producing corn (a non-native plant) in eastern North America's less-than-perfect climate. Such soils were ideally naturally fertile, though in reality they were confined to the alluvium of the floodplains of the James, York, and Rappahannock rivers.[80] Otherwise, the favored soils were level or nearly so, fine-grained but easy to till, well-drained but not too dry, and possessing a low winter water table, a characteristic that allowed them to warm up quickly in the spring.[81]

Abandoned fields, in various stages of regrowth, provided a great variety of wild foods. On newly fallow plots grew not only cordage plants but also many edible greens like wild plantains and wild lettuce (all of which most people consider weeds today). Some meadows grew grain-producing little barley, which the Powhatans called *mattoume* and ground into flour for bread.[82] After several years, the old fields would begin to sprout the low, thorny bushes that produce raspberries, blackberries, and the like.[83] These fruits would attract berry-loving animals such as raccoons and opossums, which could be hunted. Thus "abandoned" fields were not really abandoned by people once they ceased to be cultivated.

Men provided the deer carcasses—and carcasses of wild turkeys and other fowl and animals—that yielded meat for the stewpot, hides for clothing, and bones for tool-making. Men had to produce those carcasses year-round, although there was less pressure to hunt in the very cold months thanks to the large-scale hunting that went on in autumn. A man whose family wanted another carcass did not have the luxury of wandering out into the forest, hoping to meet a deer. He had to know what deer prefer to eat at each season and where those plants grew within his tribal territory. In autumn and winter, that meant the uplands' deciduous forest, where nuts and acorns were plentiful. The forest also attracted other nut-lovers such as wild turkeys, raccoons, opossums, bears, and the like, all of them edible and sporting other useful things like bones, hides, feathers, and antlers.

Not Primitive at All: Indian Houses

The term "sapling-and-mat" houses makes many people think immediately of flimsiness and impermanence. The Algonquian speakers' houses were impermanent; they moved every few years anyway, and instead of selling or renting their "old" houses as modern mobile families do, they let theirs fall down—no one was going to occupy the sites for a while—and simply biodegrade.

The houses were not truly flimsy, though, as long as the pole framework's lashings were kept tight. Smaller houses were conical; longer houses had rounded ends that provided bracing. Such frameworks can withstand hurricane winds; although the mat or bark coverings would need repair or replacement afterward, the house would not be completely roofless. Such frameworks, especially the conical ones, can also withstand heavy snowfalls, which is why conical houses were standard among the northern Algonquian speakers from New England and the Canadian Maritime Provinces westward to the Great Lakes.

In winter, men went fowling. Geese and dabbling ducks such as mallards require shallow water, so men knew the relative depths of all the waterways in their tribal territories. Men also built fish weirs, traps that caught fish for much of the year. In the Piedmont and farther inland, a weir was a V-shaped rock wall with a reed-constructed conical trap inserted at the point, which was downstream. This type of trap could be constructed almost anywhere unless a river was too wide and deep. But in the very wide estuary of the Chesapeake Bay and its tributaries, weirs were arrow-shaped pole-and-reed-fence affairs (described in chapter 8) extending outward at least a hundred feet (over 30 meters) from a shore. Native technology limited the desirable diameter and length of the cut poles, and thus the depth of water in which the weir could be built (six feet [1.8 meters] at low tide),[84] so that knowledge of local depths was a necessity.

Knowledge of the characteristics of the bottoms of the waterways was also important, especially among the people living near the bay who did not have access to freshwater-loving tuckahoe. Raising more corn solved the problem only in good crop years; in bad ones, they made up the difference by going oystering and clamming more often. Freshwater streams produced clams and mussels of other species. All could be gathered by wading or, if necessary, diving.[85]

Women and children were constantly going out of town (away from houses and gardens) to obtain plants for food, clay for pottery, and wood for building or fuel; they, too, used canoes for some tasks, since their work could take them all over their tribal territories. Both sexes had to know the land like the backs of their hands.

One place people—men, women, and children—had little reason to go for plant foods was the beach. The same was true of the dunes and sandy lands behind them, which offered little to eat and had soil poor for gardening. Anglo-Virginians would later call such lands (e.g., First Landing State Park) "deserts." However, the beaches of the lower bay, the Atlantic shore, and the back barrier bays were excellent places to gather clams and whelks, whose meat was edible and whose shells were highly valued for jewelry making and trading throughout the Chesapeake region. Beaches also had outwashes of cobbles in places, which in the nearly stone-free coastal plain provided lithic deposits crucial for stone tool manufacture. Along the bay's western shore, Miocene-era fossil shark teeth were found and used for decorative purposes. The cliffs along the rivers, like the high Calvert Cliffs, may have also served as hunting camp locations and as watch stations for monitoring the canoes of friends and foes.[86] On the other hand, the English and their descendants did not value beaches highly until the 1880s, when railroads brought in food and people, creating resorts. Today, overcollecting of shells, fossils, and stone tools by beachcombers has greatly diminished resources that were still available in the first half of the twentieth century.

Swamps were good places to go, although intruding Europeans did not understand why. There are fish and turtles to catch in the waters; shallows open to the sun produce some of the same useful plants as freshwater marshes, and in shady places a few emergents such as tuckahoe will grow to some extent. Swamps have edges and also higher grounds (hammocks) within them where food-producing trees may grow: oaks for acorns and persimmon trees for fruit. Such resources draw mammals such as deer and birds such as wild turkeys, so that hunting, while not as productive as in the upland forests, can bring in enough meat to feed a family. The wet edges of swamps are a good place to find groundnuts and other edibles.

Deciduous forest—found over much of the Chesapeake region right down to the waterside (extensive pine barrens are in New Jersey but are otherwise a more southerly phenomenon)—is rich in huntable animals thanks to its plethora of nut-producing trees yielding acorns, walnuts,

One Person, Several Names

Most modern people have several names—those on the birth certificate, a childhood name within the family, a nickname in the schoolroom, perhaps another (and less palatable) nickname on the playground, a more grownup name in adolescence, and (for many people) a switch to a middle name or a legal name-change altogether in adulthood.

The Powhatans and probably the other peoples in the Chesapeake region also had multiple names, but they came by them in somewhat different ways. No one had a surname, partly because the population was small enough that surnames were not needed to avoid confusion and partly because Indian names carried recognizable meaning, in contrast to modern given names, of whose meanings and origins we are often unaware.

Every child started out life with two names. One was a secret, profoundly personal name that parents bestowed; one daughter of Powhatan received the name "Matoaka," the meaning of which is unknown. The other name was the one used in daily life while the child was small; Matoaka's public name was "Amonute," also untranslatable today. As they grew older, boys and girls earned other names. Those of boys reflected how well they were doing at becoming hunters of animals and people; they may have had nicknames as well (the record is silent on the matter). Girls could definitely earn nicknames: this same daughter of Powhatan teased her powerful father, who jokingly dubbed her "Pocahontas," meaning a combination of undisciplined, lewd, and cruel (to her poor, harassed father).

In adulthood, males went on to earn numerous other names to reflect their exploits, and the names would be formally bestowed by a chief grateful for their services. The chiefs themselves are known to have taken new names. When Powhatan died in 1618, Opitchapam, the brother who succeeded him, took the "throne" name Otiotan (or Itoyatin; meaning unknown). "Powhatan" was an early throne name for Pocahontas's father, used by the leaders of neighboring peoples like the Monacans. His public personal name in 1607–9 was Wahunsenacawh (meaning unknown); we do not know how long he had carried this appellation, and his secret personal name was never recorded.

hickory nuts, beechnuts, hazelnuts, chinquapins, and (formerly) chestnuts. This is the prime ecological zone in which to find nut-lovers such as deer and wild turkeys, the staple land animals in the native people's diet. Since the native people also laid in large supplies of nuts and acorns in the fall, whole families left the towns to find food, the women and children to harvest nuts and the men to hunt the competition. At other seasons there were hog-peanuts and various greens to gather for the stewpot.

The real "breadbaskets" in the region, in terms of producing starchy seeds and tubers used in bread making, were the freshwater marshes, especially the large ones in the wide floodplains crossed by meandering rivers. The most prominent plant in John Smith's writings was tuckahoe (arrow arum), which we have met already and which grows abundantly in many such meanders; with it often grow pickerelweed and wild rice, which produce edible seeds. In other wide marshes there is spatterdock (cow lily), which has thick, pipelike edible roots. Spatterdock and tuckahoe both produce edible seeds as well; those of the latter were so plenteous and commonly used that Smith recorded a separate name for them, *ocoughtanmnis* (later corrupted to "cuttanemons"). The locations of "breadbaskets"—which in this volume we define as marshes at least ten acres (4 hectares) in extent that contain at least 30 percent wild rice or 50 percent tuckahoe or spatterdock—would have been basic knowledge for women who had to feed the "six to twenty [people] in a house[hold]" that John Smith wrote about.[87]

Spiritual Life

Going out to collect—with a limited toolkit—so many of the things needed for survival was extremely physical work. Even paddling a heavy dugout canoe—a multiperson job—was strenuous. The native people began to develop arthritis in their thirties,[88] which was near the limit of life expectancy (especially for women).[89] Going out and about was also dangerous work, to be undertaken in groups and with proper ritual precautions. They were prescientific people, like the English they met, so they were somewhat more exposed to dangers from weather and large predatory animals (such as bears and wolves). Not surprisingly, "all things that were able to do them hurt beyond their prevention, they adore[d] with their kind of divine worship."[90] That was only part of the story, though: the Chesapeake region's Algonquian speakers led an intensely spiritual life. The Powhatans are known to have said prayers and made offerings each morning after they bathed in the rivers,[91] and they gave thanks before meals.[92] There were also ceremonies involving whole towns when there was "some great distress of want, fear of enemies, time of triumphs, and gathering together their fruits [crops]."[93]

The people of the Chesapeake region probably shared in the widespread Native American view of human beings being assigned a role by their Creator that required living with, rather than dominating, the world around them. For such people, populating that world with a variety of moderately powerful deities, rather than one omnipotent but (for many modern people) distant deity, brought their surroundings—waters, land, plants, and animals—to life to a degree that cannot be overestimated. In their cooperative attitude, as well as their in-depth knowledge, they did indeed live much closer to the land than we do today.

3

Englishmen in the Chesapeake

Helen C. Rountree

THE WORD "ENGLISHMEN" is accurate here, for until mid-1608, when two women joined them, the intruding English colonists (and the Spanish ones who preceded them) were male. Hence, apart from the language barrier, there was a sexual barrier that hindered the "visitors" in understanding how the native people's society worked—assuming they wanted to know. Most did not. John Smith, possessing notable intellectual curiosity, was an exception.

An Early Colonization Effort

Europeans came to the Chesapeake for definite reasons, most of which had nothing to do with the region's human inhabitants. The two most pressing goals were to find treasures of gold and silver and, failing that, to discover a water passage across North America that would enable them to reach China—where great trade profits awaited—without having to sail around Africa and across the Indian Ocean. In the Jacobean period, the English had high hopes that one or both of these aims could be fulfilled, enabling them to compete successfully with the colonizing Spanish. Notwithstand-

Europeans in the Chesapeake before 1607

1524	Giovanni di Verazzano may have visited.
1559	Joining of Spanish by Indian leader Paquinquineo (Don Luis de Velasco) from Bahia de Santa Maria, the sixteenth-century Spanish name for the Chesapeake Bay.
1570–72	Spanish Jesuit mission destroyed; Spanish military retaliation.
1585–86	English from Roanoke colony stayed several months with Chesapeake tribe.
1588	Spanish military reconnaissance (sent from Havana) in Potomac River.
1603	English party, probably landing on Eastern Shore.
ca. 1603	Unidentified European ship visited Werowocomoco and Rappahannock.

Sources: Canner 1904–6 [1603]; Haile 1998; Lewis and Loomie 1953; Quinn 1955; Scisco 1945 and 1946; J. Smith 1986a [1608]; Wingfield 1969 [1608]; Wroth 1970.

Note: Though Paquinquineo was from the Paspahegh chiefdom, he encountered the Spanish somewhere on the North Carolina Outer Banks and went with them willingly.

ing James I's peace accord with Spain in 1606, competition with the Spanish was a driving force behind many of the decisions that London would inflict upon John Smith and his Jamestown compatriots, regardless of the actual conditions in Virginia. Spain still claimed the Chesapeake region as part of its North American territory, called "La Florida." In the early seventeenth century, there was always the possibility that a marauding military force from the large Spanish base in Havana would come north to make good that claim and rout any interlopers. Even after the native people mounted a major assault on the English in 1622, the residents of Jamestown remained at least as afraid of the Spanish as they were of the Powhatans.[1]

Jamestown was the first of several English colonizing attempts on the east coast of North America that actually "stuck." Earlier efforts on Roanoke Island, North Carolina (1585–87),[2] and in what is now eastern Canada had failed for a variety of reasons. The Jamestown colonists did not know, as we do, that their project would ultimately succeed. In fact, after John Smith left Virginia in the autumn of 1609 and a famine wiped out most of those who stayed behind, the colony teetered on the edge of extinction just as its predecessors had done. In his later writings, Smith would lecture long and loud on what it took to populate and sustain a working colony in North America. But he himself learned those lessons the hard way during his sojourn in Powhatan's country from April 1607 to October 1609.

The Jamestown colony, like the prior English efforts, was very much an economic enterprise. It had a relatively small religious component, unlike the major religious impulse of the Pilgrim venture of 1620, and that component was limited to converting to Christianity a native people who, they soon discovered, were deeply attached to their own ancient religion. The failure to win converts would make the Virginia colony almost exclusively profit-driven.

A Diverse People

English society in the early seventeenth century was in a state of flux. Rising socially by acquiring land or adding to one's holdings was a desirable goal for many people below the highest stratum of society.[3] People hoped to rise at least a couple of rungs within a pyramidal, multilevel social structure, in which landless laborers were on the bottom, tradesmen and yeoman farmers were in the lower middle, gentlefolk (owning enough land to pay at least 40 shillings annually in taxes) occupied the upper middle, titled aristocracy were farther up, and the royal family was at the apex. Money was the key to moving up through the lower three levels; both money and patronage were required to advance beyond them. Money, land, and titles were often inherited, unlike the case of most Algonquian-speaking people, whose wealth was mostly foodstuffs and among whom prestige was individually earned. Also unlike the Indians' matrilineal system of chieftainship, inheritance for all but the royal family and the oldest titles was strictly patrilineal. Men-on-the-make therefore aimed at both advancing themselves and having male progeny to benefit from their efforts.[4] One avenue for advancing one's family was the custom of "fostering out"—placing one's children after age eight or so in other, higher-status families where they could make advantageous connections (the forerunner of sending children to prestigious boarding schools). The practice was already common in 1500 in families from the yeoman level up through the aristocracy (which was itself ranked, of course). When the English colonists offered to rear Indian children to "improve" them, the parents—who trained their own children—were horrified.[5]

Before 1624, King James of England invested little money in the Virginia enterprise. Instead, he put the Virginia project into the hands of investors, organized into the Virginia Company of London.[6] Those investors, hoping for great profits from the venture, came mainly from the gentry and lower nobility, although an exception was colonist George Percy's brother, the Earl of Northumberland. The men at Jamestown during John Smith's time (April 1607 to October 1609) were a diverse lot, but it was not always a diversity that fostered the common welfare. Some of them knew trades back home, but there were not enough of such people to do the pioneering work of building and maintaining houses, farming, and cutting timber for export. There were too many gentlemen, and here the pervasive English class system had a truly destructive effect. John Smith was arguably the most able leader in Jamestown, but as the son of a yeoman he did not command the respect of many gentlemen (Gabriel Archer, a gentleman, and George Percy, an aristocrat, were especially inimical to him). Smith rose to be president of the colony despite his class background, not because of it. Moreover, there was a strongly ingrained feeling in everyone that a gentleman should not do manual work, for such work was socially beneath him. That attitude may have served the English well in towns and cities back home, but it did little good in a place where houses had to be built, trees felled, food raised, and new ways of living discovered in a challenging environment.

Even though numerous gentlemen and even an earl's brother took up residence at Jamestown, the living quarters were crude by the standards of later centuries. The English borrowed few building techniques from the Powhatans, and then only later.[7] Instead they erected an English-style stockade around a collection of houses that initially resembled the hovels of the poor back home. Before long, as the colony became better organized, they would build the post-in-ground, wattle-and-daub, half-timbered houses that tourists can see at Jamestown Settlement's English Fort. Higher-status persons had larger quarters with more furnishings in them, including a Bible and paper and quill pens (literacy was not widespread at the time in England). The second-largest building in town was the church. Unlike the temples of the Algonquian speakers, which were large but outside the towns and off-limits to common folk, the English church was in town center, open to all.

The English were religiously and socially diverse, but they were not yet divided to the degree that would lead their country to civil war by the mid-seventeenth century. The Puritans were emerging as a faction in the Church

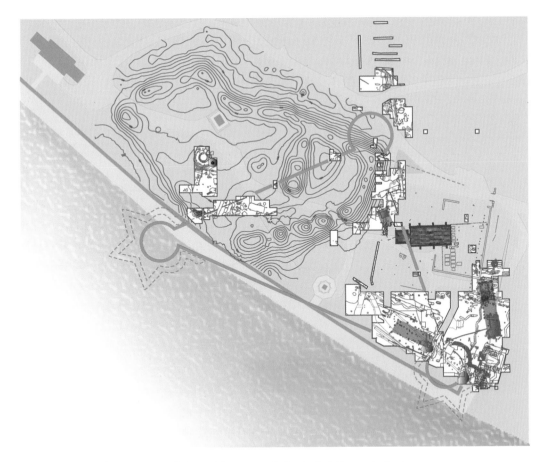

Model of the site of James Fort on the James River, 2003. Archeological discoveries have confirmed the method used to construct the palisade and defense works, as well as the fort's precise location and layout. (Courtesy of APVA Preservation Virginia)

of England; John Rolfe (Pocahontas's husband) shows in his writings that he was one such. There is little indication of where John Smith stood on the matter. But he followed the rules, as everyone at Jamestown had to, which decreed daily prayer and compulsory church attendance on Sunday. Englishmen were supposed to hold a daily prayer service even when they were out exploring, as Smith and his companions did in the presence of several bemused Susquehannocks. The English, like the Algonquian speakers whom they encountered, were prescientific people who looked to superhuman forces to explain the world around them. Both groups appealed to those forces to bring them what was beyond their paltry human power to grasp. The pity is that the English—and perhaps the Indians, though they left no records—were consistently blind to how their actions affected others. For the English, it was always God "moving the hearts of the savages," not Englishmen trespassing against Indians or angry Indians holding Englishmen accountable for broken promises.[8]

Hindrances to Exploration

Serious exploration of the Chesapeake region did not begin until mid-1608, over a year after Jamestown was founded. A major factor in this delay was the colony's fractious politics in its early years. The first charter, in effect from late 1606 to mid-1610, provided for a seven-member council that elected a president to run the show. Factionalism and strife among council members, exacerbated by frequent changes in personnel and policy, ultimately led the Virginia Company in its second charter (written 1609, in effect from mid-1610) to turn matters over to appointed governors. The first such governor, the aristocrat Baron de la Warr, took things in hand with a vengeance. Before de la Warr's arrival, however, one council would issue a directive, only to find it countermanded by a new majority on council. The "bosses" who could settle such disputes, analogous to the chiefs among the Native American tribes in the region, were thousands of miles away in London. Outside of council, disagreements among the early settlers were also rife. For instance, in the hungry late spring of 1608, part of the colony was sent to Old Point Comfort to live on oysters and fish, but "in 6 weeks they would not agree once to cast out their net."[9]

We know today that the bickering may have been due in part to salt poisoning, which makes people cranky as well as debilitated.[10] No one—not even John Smith, apparently—thought to dig a well inside the fort until the spring of 1609![11] Before then, they drank ale or beer from home—where most adults were drinking at least a gallon of it per day.[12] When the beer ran out, they relied on the James River for water, which then as today becomes somewhat brackish after fresh waters from the spring thaw in the Appalachians have passed through. Apart from this physical cause, disagreements among the colonists sprang from the very nature of the colonizing experiment. The people engaged in this experiment disagreed continually about what tasks to assign, which projects to undertake, and how to get the jobs done.[13] Uncertainty over what it would take to make the experiment work was compounded by a terrible insecurity, felt by everyone in Jamestown Fort, about trying to gain a toehold in an unknown country while being outnumbered by the country's native landowners (although that ownership was not acknowledged).

Hunger made the English cranky, too, as the native people soon found out. Without yet offering them the incentive of land ownership, the Virginia Company expected its employees to do what we today call "multitasking." Besides raising their own food—during a series of dry years, no less—the colonists were expected to export commodities such as timber and soap-ashes (chapter 1) to England for the company's profit and still find time to explore a sizable portion of North America. Mariners like Christopher Newport, who were charged with bringing the colonists food and tools from England, were tapped to assist in diplomatic and exploring maneuvers in the Chesapeake, which kept Newport in Virginia for extended stays. No wonder food shortages developed! Depending on the native people proved a dicey proposition, and despite repeated pleas from the colonists, the profit-conscious Virginia Company was slow to fill in the gap. Like the Roanoke colonization effort of the 1580s, the Jamestown enterprise was horribly ill-supplied from home during its first few years, so badly supported at times that one wonders if the London investors simply considered such colonists to be "disposable."

The first English at Jamestown were left, on June 22, 1607, with enough food (supposedly) for about fourteen weeks,[14] after which the colonists were expected to buy food from the Powhatans, which they managed to do. The First Supply was expected in November 1607 but did not come: one ship captained by Christopher Newport arrived on January 2, 1608—much of this cargo burned five days later—but the second ship, captained by Francis Nelson, was blown off course and did not arrive until April.[15] Newport did not return for more food and tools until after that, which meant that he and his mariners, besides the colonists, had to live off the Indians for over three months. Newport brought the Second Supply—and a cadre of new colonists to eat the food—to Virginia in late September of 1608.[16] By then the Algonquian speakers in the James and York river valleys were so alienated by Smith's expeditions up the bay that they were not giving up corn unless forced. Before he headed home, Newport worsened things by making an expedition into the Monacan country against Powhatan's wishes. That same winter, with supplies low and no corn crop because of other duties during the summer and fall, John Smith and his men forcibly took the winter stores of the York, Pamunkey, and Mattaponi river people, thereby breaking the already fragile alliance with Powhatan.

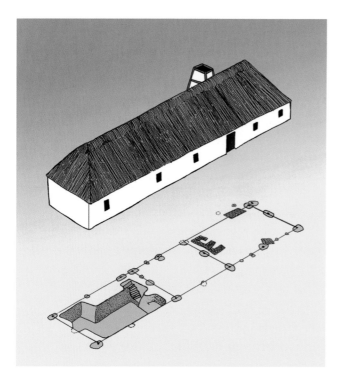

The Jamestown store and workshop. Conjectured reconstruction of the building, with the associated archaeological plan. The excavation of the building's site reveals wall postholes and three rooms. Such rows of apparently unrelated rooms—storage cellar, commoners' barracks, and VIP bed-sitting room (*left to right*)—were common in English towns at that time. (Courtesy of APVA Preservation Virginia)

By late spring, the colony was hungry again and hoping for food from home, but the Third Supply did not even depart from London until June 1, 1609, due to delays in assembling the funds to secure any supplies at all. Then the nine ships (bringing five hundred more mouths to feed) were dispersed by a hurricane. A few vessels managed to reach the colony in August of that year, finding that the Jamestowners had tried to spread into satellite settlements but had been driven back by the native inhabitants. The winter of 1609–10 was the famous "Starving Time." The new governor's portion of the fleet did not reach Virginia until June 1610, when the advance party found the decimated, emaciated colonists clamoring to be evacuated from what to them had become a pesthole.[17] Colonists in Virginia would not manage to feed themselves until the 1630s.

In addition to the hardship of poor supplies, constant hunger, and brackish water, the English found Virginia to be an "unhealthy" place for Europeans. "New" diseases worked both ways: it wasn't only Native Americans who succumbed. The English kept the records, and therefore we hear more about their losses. There were so many native "bugs" to which they had no immunity that most newcomers from England fell sick in the first year—a year that rapidly came to be known as a time of "seasoning." Dysentery, paratyphoid, and probably other ills weakened the newcomers. During John Smith's second Chesapeake Bay expedition, more than half his men, most of them new arrivals, would fall sick, and one would die (see chapter 5). Early colonial cemeteries present a stark picture of what the colonists' lives were like. The one at Jordan's Point in Prince George County, Virginia, where there are Native American burials nearby for comparison, shows that the Indians were far healthier: in their skeletons "pathology frequencies were low."[18] The English, meanwhile, died young: 43.2 percent of them in their teens, 32.4 percent of them in their twenties, 19 percent in their thirties, with only one person surviving to age forty. (Of course, the data from Jordan's Point reflect who died at the site; we can't measure the health of those who survived and did not end up in the cemetery.)

The people buried in the cemetery had not been healthy back in England, either. Eighty percent of those living long enough to have permanent teeth (thirty-five individuals) had teeth showing enamel hypoplasia, a thinning of enamel that occurs while teeth are forming during early childhood. Such thinning probably reflects extended periods of malnutrition, either because of dire poverty or because of the child's being too sick to eat or drink (in those days before intravenous feeding). Poor hygiene must also have played a role in the high mortality rate. Most of the Jordan's Point English who survived past their mid-twenties had lost several teeth to cavities that had turned into abscesses, and at the time of death they suffered from other abscesses that were destroying other teeth. One woman aged twenty-five to thirty-five had lost ten of her thirty-two teeth, and the others would have gone before too long; she was already a prime candidate for malnutrition from not being able to chew well.[19] Aside from being in constant pain, once she was seriously malnourished she was a sitting duck for any pathogen that came along.

It did not help that the Jacobean English did not believe in bathing or washing their clothing very often. They came from a cold climate where wood for heating water had become scarce and baths were uncomfortable; also, many people believed they caused disease. English clothing of that era was heavy, being mainly of wool and linen, and it covered nearly all of the body even in the summertime. When men added chain mail for defense against enemies, the result would have been stifling; wearing armor in a Virginia summer would have meant roasting alive. The lack of bathing or clothes washing attracted fleas and lice to English bodies—the Indians had them, too, but took daily baths to keep them —not to mention a myriad of germs—at bay.

Englishmen in the Chesapeake

The death rate of the English colonists for the first twenty years of the colony was appalling. Of the original 104 colonists who arrived with John Smith in April 1607, only thirty-eight were alive to greet the First Supply in January 1608. Nothing daunted, the Virginia Company continued to ship new colonists even though they died in droves due to hunger and illness. Of the 220 colonists alive in December of 1609, at the start of the "Starving Times," only sixty remained in the next spring. By 1616, death and immigration back to England had reduced the Virginia colony to only 350 people. Those returning to England revealed that the Chesapeake was not the "Earth's Only Paradise" as billed by its business promoters, but a death trap,[20] offering little incentive or reward for the commoners whose labors were expected to support the transported gentry and stakeholders back in England.

English Watercraft

All the small craft used by John Smith and others in food getting and exploration could be sailed, which conserved the energy and lowered the nutritional needs of the occupants. However, the various riggings of the time did not permit sailing quite as close into the wind as is possible with today's sailboats (which is 45° off the direction the wind is coming from). Thus the English boats were somewhat more dependent than modern sailboats on "fair" winds to travel where they wanted to go under sail instead of by rowing. Large square-rigged ships were far less flexible than the smaller craft, needing winds from the quadrant behind them to make any time at all. That explains why it took the first three English ships—which of course were far too large to be rowed—four days in May 1607 to travel only fifty miles (80 kilometers) from Old Point Comfort up the James to the mouth of the Chickahominy River. Lack of wind is probably not the culprit; "unfavorable" wind direction is more likely. In May in that part of Virginia, the winds are changing from the northwest-to-west of the cooler months to the southwest of the warm months. And the ships were heading west to Newport News, then turning northwest (for a long reach) and north around what is now Fort Eustis, then west and southwest around Hog Island, and finally heading northwest and then west to the Chickahominy's mouth. It required a great deal of tacking to journey up the James in a square-rigged ship.[21] And aside from the awesome size and height of those ships, that

Susan Constant replica under sail. Given the often hectic travel schedule of this replica, the vessel is discreetly equipped with powerful diesel engines and modern radar and sonar, in order to reach its destinations safely and on time. (Courtesy of the Jamestown-Yorktown Foundation)

crosswise back-and-forthing must have perplexed the native people, who were accustomed to paddling dugout canoes wherever they wanted to go.

It only made sense for exploring or food-buying trips to be made in more maneuverable boats that also had a shallower draft, even though those boats were more vulnerable to strong winds and heavy seas. What these craft were like, however, is somewhat obscure. In the early 1600s, people who built boats and ships were workmen uninterested in keeping records.[22] Scholars are uncertain even about the "big" deep-draft ships (the replicas of which at Jamestown Settlement seem so cramped to us) that brought John Smith and his compatriots across the Atlantic. Recently scholars have revised their estimates of the sizes of those vessels; their "tunnes burthen," or barrel-holding capacity—the only recorded indication of their size—is now being interpreted to mean larger ships, which is being reflected in the new replicas at Jamestown Settlement.[23] So it is not surprising that what the "ships" and "pinnaces" and the "shallops" or "barges" (the early seventeenth-century English applied a variety of terms to similar vessels) were like is still a matter of controversy.[24]

A pinnace was at least forty to fifty feet (about 12–15 meters) long, which allowed room for a cabin and at least two masts with square-rigged sails. Modern tourists can see a pinnace at Jamestown Settlement: the smallest of the ships, the *Discovery,* is such a craft. But thanks to the English not caring much about precision in labeling back then, ships larger even than the replica of the *Susan Constant* (the largest of the three ships) could be also called pinnaces at times. The hull always had a keel, which made the boat draw anywhere from five to twelve feet (1½–3⅔ meters) when unladen. Pinnaces were used for voyages to visit Indian tribes like the Patawomecks, from whom the English expected to buy a quantity of corn. It was also an unnamed pinnace (so we cannot guess its size) in which Captain Christopher Newport remained—probably out of sight in the cabin—on the first day of the first formal diplomatic-cum-trading mission to Powhatan's capital in February 1608, in order let John Smith run interference for him before he staged a dignified entrance the next day.

The large rowboats that went back and forth between shore and pinnace, and the type of vessel John Smith chose for his travels around Chesapeake Bay, were called shallops or barges. This was "a narrow-beam, undecked vessel that sacrificed cargo space and sail-carrying ability for the sake of being more handy as a rowed vessel with a shallow draft for putting ashore anywhere along the riverbank."[25] Its length was probably at least thirty feet (9.1 meters), which accommodated the fifteen men who went on Smith's first Chesapeake Bay expedition plus their food supplies, and it had a mast that supported either a lug sail or a sprit-rig sail. Both sails were quadrilateral and suspended from a moveable wooden spar attached to the mast, as opposed to modern triangular sails suspended from the top on a halyard and spread out at bottom by a wooden boom. Scholars differ on whether barges had flat bottoms, and therefore drew less water, or rounded ones with keels. On Smith's map of 1612, in the area of the Susquehanna Flats at the head of the bay, a barge is shown with a single sail and what appear to be rounded sides. Either hull, drawing about eighteen inches (nearly 46 centimeters) of water when empty,[26] could be defeated by the shallows of the bay and its tributaries; John Smith ran aground numerous times, often when he was trying either to stage a dramatic departure or to make a hasty getaway. At least one barge was taken to Virginia in 1607, and it was carried disassembled aboard one of the three ships and put together upon arrival.[27] Because the boatbuilders left no assembly instructions, pending

John Smith's Chesapeake Voyages, 1607–1609

future experiments scholars remain uncertain of how the sections were constructed (top and bottom? bow, midships sections, stern?)[28] and how they were joined (bolts and caulking?).[29]

Seeing What They Were Looking For

The English who went out on expeditions around the Chesapeake in 1607–9 drew on a certain amount of prior estuarine exploration[30] and saw a natural world that was only gently touched by the Native Americans and only slightly affected by previous visiting Europeans. It is a pity that they were so intent upon their own business, for not only did they alienate many of the native people in the process (they were nosey, especially on those two major exploring trips in the summer of 1608), but they also ignored many details that modern people might like to know about.

For example, the English explorers frequently took notice of how much corn the local people were raising, for they themselves were periodically in a near-famine state. On the other hand, they did not pay much attention to other crops, and no one bothered to write down who cultivated the tobacco that had such ceremonial significance in the Amerindian world. The native people used a great many other plants in their territories, and due to their relatively small populations they did not use them excessively. For the English it was different. Not only did they have a far more exploitative attitude toward natural resources, based upon their understanding of Genesis 1:26, 28 (God giving Adam dominion over the earth),[31] but they also had a much larger population at home to consider. So except for tuckahoe (arrow arum), which supported Indian families but which the English had no intention of digging, the colonists' accounts describe only three categories of plants: berry bushes and fruit-producing trees with easily gatherable food, plants thought to produce exotic medicines (such as sassafras), and—above all—big trees. After seven-and-a-half millennia of raising plants and animals and a millennium of *intensive* farming, England had long since been turned almost entirely into a land of agricultural fields and pastures, so there was a serious shortage not only of firewood but also of large timber trees for ship building and masts. More timber, more ships, more riches! The English practiced the extraction from foreign soil of resources they had exhausted at home.

As to Indian populations, John Smith made estimates of how many warriors inhabited each district he visited mainly because he and his compan-

The Discoverie Barge

We don't know what the barge that Smith and his adventurers used actually looked like. It was simply incidental to their tale, and none of the crew especially praised its performance. We hear mostly about limitations: that it was small for the number of men aboard on Voyage One and the arms and provisions they carried, but that on Voyage Two, with a smaller crew, they took on five Susquehannock chieftains and two interpreters bound across the bay in rough weather for the Sassafras River. The craft was variously described as being of two "tun" or three, not a measure of its weight but rather of its capacity for large casks in which cargo might be shipped.

The barge was "overraked" by the short seas of five feet (1.5 meters) or so in a Tangier Sound thunder squall. Its foremast apparently broke and, being unstayed, went overboard. They had to cut a replacement for it. "Foremast" implies, but does not guarantee, that the barge had two masts. This makes sense to a sailor because sail could be shortened and one sail not in use could serve as an awning. They had no spare sail, so they patched the one they had with their shirts. Sometimes they bailed frantically as water came over the sides, suggesting that the craft did not have waterways or side decks. It did have frames along the sides of the hull, constructed so they could secure Indian shields ("targets") in Viking fashion, to protect men at the oars. Vertical thole pins down each side served as fulcrums against which the oars could work.

When the *Godspeed* and *Susan Constant* arrived at the Virginia Capes in 1607, they had aboard a barge to be quickly assembled, a process that would take only a few days. It is likely, but not certain, that this was the boat used in bay exploration. The Virginia Company's instructions also ordered the

ions expected to be shot at sooner or later. Thus we have no detailed population figures on men, women, or children, much less vital statistics about them. Smith was wonderful about writing down the names of as many Indian settlements and districts as he could obtain information about, but he seems not to have asked which settlements belonged to which district leaders. He also obtained only the sketchiest news of rivalries between districts, except for the one (Rappahannock vs. Moraughtacund) in which he personally interfered (see chapter 13). He and his compatriots were selective about directions, too: they asked repeatedly about waterways and lands lying to the west and north (the major rivers of the region run northwest colonists to carry a light skiff; a Thames wherry was recommended, which is an excellent, fast boat that one man can row at a speed of four knots. But these were "fly boats" to run messages or get help, not vessels for voyagers.

A number of writers have speculated on the form the barge actually took, and several period boats such as the shallop built for the *Mayflower* at Plimouth Plantation, the tender of the *Elizabeth II* at Roanoke, and one built for the *Maryland Dove* at St. Mary's City have been put forward as models. All three are stable and roomy, but heavy and difficult to row under adverse conditions.

In 1986, a group of nine historians, shipwrights, and mariners assembled at Calvert Marine Museum and proposed their own design based on the requirements for the barge and on research into small craft illustrated during the seventeenth century. They came up with a much lighter boat, flat-bottomed and knocked down for shipment yet easily assembled. That vessel was never built, but one based on the same concept was launched in 2006 in Deltaville, Virginia.

Meanwhile in 2005–6, Sultana Projects, Inc., of Chestertown, Maryland, built a round-bilged, whole-molded boat with bow and stern sections that joined amidships. A similar boat was built at the same time in Deltaville. The Sultana Projects "barge" was widely exhibited in Maryland and Virginia before being sent around the Chesapeake in a replication of John Smith's expeditions during the summer of 2007. It will be interesting to see how all three will perform in the long run against the rigorous squalls, obdurate tides, and head seas that the real adventurers encountered in the summer of 1608.

to southeast), and they sent south to the Chowan River to inquire after the Lost Colonists. But Smith and the other Jamestowners took so little interest in the lower south side of the James River's mouth that it is impossible to know whether Powhatan wiped out the Chesapeake Indians before or after Jamestown was settled.

Causing a Stir

Smith's two major voyages of exploration around the Chesapeake region in 1608 violated Indian protocol. He may have known this, but it is doubtful that he cared much. During his captivity the previous December, he had supposedly become an ally—a "subject" in Powhatan's view—of the paramount chief of eastern Virginia. Powhatan therefore would have felt entitled to supervise Smith's becoming acquainted with other "subjects" and with neighbors like the Piscataways. The introductions should also have been made through a qualified interpreter, but neither side had one before the autumn of 1608. The inhabitants of Jamestown felt differently: an alliance with a native leader was automatically overruled by the Virginia Company's (and by extension, King James's) orders that they explore the region as soon as they were able. The reason was simple. The Jamestown squatters—they did not ask the Paspaheghs' permission before settling on Jamestown Island—assumed that their king back in England "owned" all of the countryside they were exploring. James I himself assumed as much in the 1606 charter,[32] in which he said "his" land lay between 34° and 45° north latitude in the New World. John Smith seems to have felt in his explorations that he was taking intellectual possession of his own country's still unknown outer territory, in the manner of Lewis and Clark's later exploration of the Louisiana Territory, rather than prying into the nooks and crannies of land owned by another people.[33] He certainly seems to have had little notion of another reason for the hostility he encountered in places: his friends wrote (with his approval) in 1612 that when landing in a "new" town, "our captain ever observed this order to demand their bows and arrows swords mantles or furs, with some child for hostage, whereby he could quickly perceive when they intended any villainy."[34] The demands, especially for children, were not a good way to forge lasting alliances!

English weaponry is often assumed to have been superior to native bows and arrows. It was and it wasn't. European warfare was fought on open fields, not in the woodlands, and the armies came from large populations whose leaders considered foot soldiers expendable, unlike the much smaller Native American populations who strained to preserve every single warrior (of their own, that is). The weaponry used on the two sides of the Atlantic reflected these differing conditions. The Indians used bows and arrows and darted in and out of any cover they could find. The English used guns, many of them big and cumbersome and extremely loud, like a thunderclap. Many native people who heard English guns were terrified by the noise; they remained so until they had learned the guns' limitations—prior to 1607 in the Chesapeake-Nansemond area,[35] after 1608 in the James and York river valleys,[36] and probably after that to the northward.[37]

The Algonquian speakers' bows shot arrows levelly for 40 yards and up to 120 yards "at random." Such weapons, shot at a reasonable distance, could penetrate a wooden English shield "a foot through or better [at least 30 centimeters]." Unburdened by metal armor, the speed with which warriors could jump from cover, let off a volley of arrows, and take cover again, amazed Europeans.[38] The English, on the other hand, were protected by their armor—although less so by plate mail—but were prevented from doing as much damage to their opponents as they wished, especially opponents who did not stand still. Forty- to fifty-caliber pistols only shot accurately up to twenty-five feet (7.6 meters), smaller ones for shorter distances. (That's why at the end of 1607 the captive John Smith broke the cock of his pistol to avoid trying to hit a target the Pamunkeys set up for him "sixscore" paces away![39]) Seventy-caliber guns, called arquebuses, shot accurately for seventy yards (64 meters); 90-caliber ones, properly called muskets in the early 1600s, were accurate for one hundred yards (91.5 meters) and could still do considerable damage at three hundred yards (274.5 meters), much farther than arrows could travel. The muskets, however, were so heavy that they required the setting up of a fork-rest for shooting. Pistols had an efficient wheel-lock mechanism that made for quick firing, but it took two hands to load them, so that many soldiers carried two or three pre-loaded pistols on their persons. Most of the other firearms in use before the 1620s were matchlock rather than snaphaunce affairs—a separately carried "match" or taper had to be kept alight somehow and applied to the powder for firing—so that loading the powder and wadding down the barrel was also cumbersome.[40] The armorer at Jamestown Settlement estimates that in the time it took to load and fire an arquebus (the weapon fired for the benefit of tourists visiting the fort exhibit at Jamestown Settlement), a Native American man could release five arrows. It took the soldiers' going out prepared to fire off multiple, scattered shots (then called "pistol shot" rather than "shotgun") to make up the difference. Little wonder that before long, familiarity bred a certain amount of contempt in Indian men who took on the English—although that did not prevent them from laying hands on guns whenever possible.

Looking Ahead to Land Matters

Land transfers to settlers, at a meager three acres (1.2 hectares) per individual, began in 1614. That year turned out to be pivotal, for it saw the first barrels of Virginia-grown tobacco shipped back to England. By 1616, when the London Company began to offer one hundred acres (40.4 hectares) of land

Early Colonial Plantation Houses

Tourists visiting "Olde Virginia" plantations such as Shirley, Westover, and Berkeley usually assume that those are the really *old* plantations they are seeing. Well, they are, and they aren't.

"Plantation" refers both to buildings and farmland. The farmland of Virginia plantations does date back to the early seventeenth century, and parts of it were small, shifting, Indian-cleared fields before that (the soil is prime for corn growing). But the impressive brick houses we see today date from the 1700s, when the Virginia Colony's "first families" had had a century or more to consolidate their landholdings and amass the wealth and slaves that built the houses.

Plantation houses in the 1600s were nearly all small wood-and-daub affairs; since the word "plantation" applied even to small farms, that meant very small houses indeed. (Think of houses like the ones in Jamestown Settlement's English fort standing alone in a small, newly cleared field.) And since tobacco cultivation was so labor-intensive, many "planters" put a minimum of effort into building and maintaining their homes. That is why there are so few authentic seventeenth-century dwellings remaining in either Virginia or Maryland. The rare exceptions, such as Bacon's Castle, were large for their time—mansions, compared to other people's dwellings—although they seem rather cramped to us today. But those houses and their chimneys were built of expensive, handmade bricks, so they were less vulnerable to the fires that obliterated so many of the region's houses.

to anyone who paid for transport to the colony, the annual tobacco export had risen to 2,500 pounds (nearly 1,000 kilograms). That large an incentive worked. In response to the new economic opportunities, over 4,500 English people took the risk of venturing to Virginia between 1619 and 1624. They took up land in an uncontrolled land-grab, exporting over 1 million pounds (about 400,000 kilograms) of tobacco by 1628.[41] It is little wonder that the Powhatans attempted in 1622 to push this expanding population back toward Jamestown, killing a quarter of the colonists on the opening day of a ten-year war (1622–32). Of the estimated ten thousand English who arrived in the Chesapeake between 1607 and 1622, only 20 percent were still alive and in Virginia in 1622.[42]

England's agricultural system was based primarily on the seed crops of wheat and barley, supplemented with the meat of domestic animals—pigs, cows, and chickens. The English expected men to cultivate crops, so they perceived the Algonquian practice of women doing that work as a situation of lazy Indian men exploiting native women. Under the leadership of John Smith, the colonists managed to plant thirty acres (12 hectares) of corn in the spring of 1609. When those crops failed, the English desperately resorted to hostile seizure of crops that the native people had harvested and stored to support their own population through the winter. After 1616, when English farming turned almost exclusively to tobacco as a money crop, laws had to be passed requiring each farmer to grow two acres (.8 hectare) of corn, sufficient to sustain an individual's basic needs. But the boom years of tobacco had a long-term detrimental effect: they increased the demand for indentured servants to do the hard labor, a practice that made humans into little more than property. Unlike the Spanish, the English were unable to enslave the native peoples of the Chesapeake as an effective local work force. But beginning in 1619, Africans were imported as servants or slaves (the records are unclear). After the First Anglo-Powhatan War (1622–32), English policy became one of territorial expansion by expelling and killing the neighboring Algonquian peoples while continuing friendly trade relations with more distant chiefdoms. This scheme satisfied the profit-driven desire for more tobacco-growing land while providing large quantities of captured Indian stored foods; it also reduced the number of Indian men hunting in the forest where cattle, pigs, and other domesticated animals were now left to roam free.[43]

In 1607–9, the Algonquian speakers in what is today Virginia had no idea that any of these things were coming, notwithstanding the prophecy of their priests that a people from the east would one day threaten them. They seem to have thought that the prophecy pointed to the Chesapeakes in what is now Virginia Beach, not to a few dozen visiting Europeans. Thus during much of John Smith's time in Virginia, the native people were generally wary but hospitable. Real animosity between the English and the Indians broke out in the James River valley in the summer of 1609 and gradually moved northward thereafter (see chapters 6–13). For their part, the English knew that they intended to occupy the Chesapeake region permanently; anticipating that the native people would quickly discover their intentions, they acted defensively from the very beginning.

The English who came to Virginia in 1607–9 had a worldview, a class system, an economy, and a profit motive that would require years of adaptation to the Chesapeake world before their colony could be called a success.

Where Pocahontas Fits In

Most of what we "know" about Pocahontas is legend that grew up long after she died. She was not a prominently powerful diplomat among her own people, being first the noninheriting female child of a male chief and later the wife of Kocoum, a mere "private captain" rather than a chief in his own right. Her second marriage was to an English gentleman, John Rolfe, who left few writings that even mention her, and when she went to London as the guest (and the exhibit) of the Virginia Company of London, she was a flash-in-the-pan celebrity that hardly anyone bothered to write about. Her father had taken another daughter as his favorite after Pocahontas married among the English.

The only portrait of her created in her lifetime was an engraving, not a painting, and it certainly does not resemble the Europeanized image she has been given by artists since then. The tradition that the king of England made much of her, even being miffed with poor Rolfe for daring to marry "royalty," is just that: tradition. Its nucleus began with John Smith's 1624 account and blossomed thereafter. Indeed much of the legend of Pocahontas began with Smith's 1624 embroidery on his more matter-of-fact 1612 account. (For a biography of Pocahontas based on both the contemporary documents and Powhatan culture—with remarks on Smith's embroideries—see Rountree [2005].)

The facts that contemporaries recorded about Pocahontas and the places in Virginia where she is known to have set foot are very few. No one seems to have asked where she was born (probably in 1596) or who her mother was, but if Henry Spelman was correct about Powhatan's children living away, in their mothers' hometowns, for their first several years, then we have no idea where she lived as a child. Later in her childhood she joined her father and his household, which by that time was probably at Werowocomoco on the York River (his earlier capital being Powhatan town, near modern Richmond). There she was living when John Smith was introduced as a captive, when he and Christopher Newport and an entourage made formal visits in the late winter and fall of 1608, and finally when he returned with a force of soldiers to take her father's winter stores of corn. (In all fairness, it should be noted that Powhatan had planned to ambush Smith as well.) That incident served to break the alliance between Powhatan and the English, which had been shaky since the late spring of 1608. It is most likely that Pocahontas made her visits to the Jamestown fort in that spring, while relations were good.

After becoming the ambushee instead of the ambusher in January 1609, Powhatan moved his capital, and Pocahontas with it, to a new site called Orapax in the swampy headwaters of the Chickahominy River near where

Interstate 64 crosses it today. That location was not tenable as a political center for a powerful man, so by 1614 the capital—and Pocahontas's home—was at Matchut (another Matchut), on the upper Pamunkey River near today's U.S. 360 bridge, beyond the reach of English watercraft. Pocahontas was married by then, but she seems to have been living close to or with her father, for she had remained his favorite child.

Pocahontas was captured on the Potomac River in early April 1613 by Samuel Argall. No one recorded what she was doing there, other than Ralph Hamor saying later that she was visiting "friends." She was not visiting the chief, though: she was visiting Iopassus (Japazaws), the ruler of one of his satellite towns, located on Passapatanzy Creek. Kocoum may have been absent, for he was not mentioned.

Instead of taking Pocahontas at once to her father's capital to bargain for her exchange, Argall took her to Jamestown, where she remained for almost a year while her father dithered. During that time, as an honored and evangelized captive, she and John Rolfe fell in love, and she converted to English culture and religion. In late March 1614, the Jamestown governor took her away again, all the way to Matchut by boat, to force her father's hand, and it was there that she and Rolfe revealed their desire to marry. Powhatan consented. The couple and the governor returned to Jamestown, where the marriage

took place in early April. Several of her relatives—although not her father—were in attendance.

Tradition holds that, after marrying, the Rolfes settled at Varina, several miles down the James from modern Richmond; the same tradition asserts that they married there, too. But there is no documentary proof of these events. On the other hand, John Rolfe had claimed and begun to farm land across the river from Jamestown (now called Smith's Fort), on a creek then called Rolfe's Creek and now called Grays Creek. That would be a very likely place for the Rolfes to have lived. Also missing is a contemporaneous record about where and when the couple's only child, Thomas Rolfe, was born.

Pocahontas went to England, the cost of her tour underwritten by the Virginia Company of London, which touted her conversion to Christianity and English ways. She died there, and her widower returned to Virginia, leaving his sickly son to grow up among the Rolfes as an Englishman and then follow him to Virginia nearly twenty years later.

Sources: Argall's letter, in Brown 1964 [1890]; Haile 1998; Hamor 1957 [1615]; Kingsbury 1906–35; McClure 1939; Purchas 1617 and 1904–6 [1625]; J. Smith 1986c [1624]; Spelman 1910 [1613?]; Strachey 1953 [1612].

The Maryland colony, begun in 1634, would build upon what had already been learned the hard way. The English ultimately had to learn the Algonquian speakers' gardening techniques (shifting fields, hoe agriculture) before they could raise corn to feed themselves. They had to learn the Indians' methods of shellfishing and catching fish in weirs to supplement the limited numbers of pigs, chickens, and cattle they raised for food (most of their labor being expended on tobacco). In the interim, thousands of them would die, mostly of local microbes, sometimes from famine, and sometimes at the hands of the native people they were crowding off the land. Their own leaders were usually not sympathetic in the early years: when colonists died, the bosses sent home for more, and when starving colonists ran away to the Indian towns, the leaders meted out severe punishment to those they managed to recover.

The preoccupation of John Smith and his compatriots with obtaining enough to eat, as well as carrying out the rather narrow orders of the Virginia Company, meant that the early historical records about the Chesapeake region are full of accounts of the English colony's tribulations. In order to know more about the environment of the Chesapeake region, its lands, waters, plants, animals, and people as it appeared to the Indians and the English in what archaeologists call the "Contact period," we must turn to other academic disciplines: geology, hydrology, botany, ichthyology, zoology, ecology, archaeology, and cultural anthropology. The lenses of these various "ologies" provide a more powerful instrument for looking back into this fascinating period in time.

4

John Smith's First Voyage up the Chesapeake Bay: June 2–July 21, 1608

Wayne E. Clark, Kent Mountford, and Edward Haile

FOR WELL OVER A CENTURY, the two great English voyages of exploration around the bay,[1] as well as the resulting maps,[2] have been studied by historians, anthropologists, environmentalists, and the descendants of both the English and the Algonquian speakers in the region. Our understanding of the past improves with each generation as we gather more corroborative evidence by way of archaeology, analysis of drilled cores from the bay's floor, and so forth. Social historians' recent study of how the Jamestown explorers fitted into the larger European colonial enterprise has also helped us understand some of the peculiar gaps in Smith's itinerary in the first expedition.[3]

Authors' Working Assumptions: Interpreting Smith's Map

- Direct statements about dates or places visited are never contradicted.

- Aside from Smith's written account, if a feature appears on his map, Smith went there (unless the feature is in the mountains or deep in the Piedmont—information that came to him by hearsay).

- If a feature does not appear on the map, Smith was on the other side of the estuary.

- Descriptions have been first related to the lay of the Smith map, after which they were transferred to a modern map, rather than vice versa.

- Crosses were placed by parties that included Smith, but the parties may have reached those locations on foot or by canoe, not necessarily on the barge.

- Smith visited all the "kings howses" as he passed, except for Accohannock. As a corollary, chiefs' houses likely represented overnight stays, given Native American hospitality customs.

- No one hurried. Long travel days, when they occurred, were the result of favorable weather and were always on the open Chesapeake Bay.

- Night travel—other than the documented night of August 22–23 on the Rappahannock River—would have been on the bay, not on a river.

The Mission

The Virginia Company ordered Smith and his compatriots to explore the region with certain goals in mind. England fully intended to colonize the Chesapeake, whether or not the native people wanted them to and—more salient in English minds—whether or not the king of Spain liked it. Spain had claimed that part of North America for nearly a century, so native people apart, the English were aware that, in the minds of others, they were "trespassing." They wanted to plant numerous outposts around the Chesapeake to consolidate their hold on the region (which they did by the 1630s), and these outposts needed to be defensible sites well away from the Virginia Capes, preferably near exportable mineral deposits or native people with furs to trade.[4] In 1608, the English also had high hopes that North

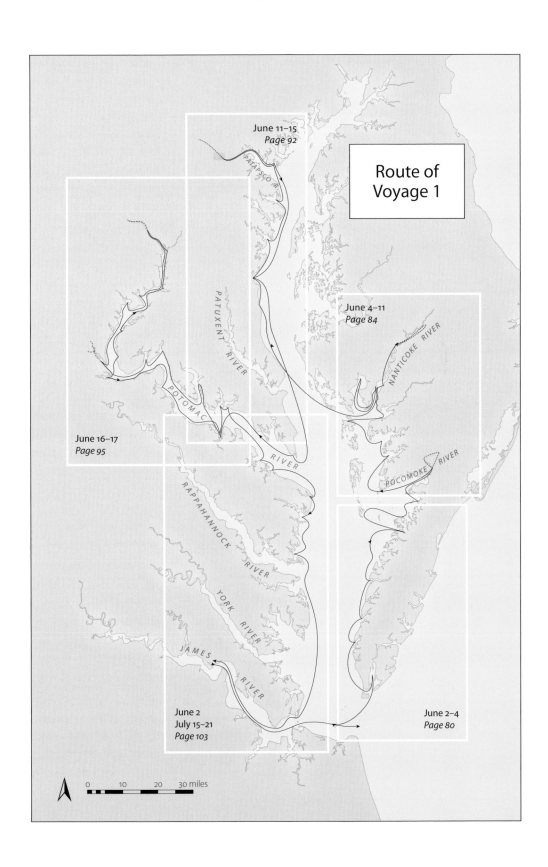

Route of
Voyage 1

June 11–15
Page 92

June 4–11
Page 84

June 16–17
Page 95

June 2
July 15–21
Page 103

June 2–4
Page 80

PATAPSCO R.

PATUXENT RIVER

POTOMAC

RIVER

RAPPAHANNOCK RIVER

YORK RIVER

JAMES RIVER

NANTICOKE RIVER

POCOMOKE RIVER

0   10   20   30 miles

Members of the First Voyage up the Bay

Captain: John Smith*

Gentlemen (familiar with firearms): James Bourne, William Cantrill, Richard Fetherstone, Thomas Momford, Ralph Morton, Michael Sicklemore

Medical doctor: Walter Russell

Carpenter (boat repairman): Robert Small*

Tailor (sewer of clothes and canvas [tarpaulins and sails]): John Powell

Blacksmith: James Read*

Fisherman/sailor: Jonas Profit*

Fish merchant (knew about various edible fish): Richard Keale

Laborer/soldier: James Watkins

Soldier: Anas Todkill*

* Arrived as original colonist and was "seasoned" by summer of 1608. Arrival status of Bourne, Momford, and Keale is uncertain.

Sources: Haile 1998; J. Smith 1986b [1612]; J. Smith 1986c [1624].

America would turn out to be a narrow continent crossed by a "Northwest Passage" to the Pacific Ocean, on the other side of which lay the riches of China. Thus John Smith's eyes were already trained on the northern and western parts of the Chesapeake basin when he left the shore at Jamestown.

The voyage had to be made in a shallow-draft boat, as described in the text box on p. 66. Smith expected to go ashore frequently to ask questions of the local people, who might become allies of the English and who would know where the major rivers led, where the glittery minerals were, and so on. If the people were hostile, the boat would have to be capable of a quick getaway in any weather. That dictated a rowboat, albeit one large enough to hold the necessary crew for such an undertaking. The vessel used was therefore a "barge," or shallop, which in 1608 described a largish wooden boat that could be sailed or rowed. Europeans of that day recorded only the carrying capacity of vessels: this craft's "burthen" was two to three tons, which indicates that it was some thirty feet (9 meters) long.[5] Scholars disagree about whether its hull was round-bilged or flat-bottomed; both have some sort of keel.[6] It was rib-framed and open to the weather, requiring a canvas tarpaulin to be brought along, and its gunwales were strengthened inside by a stringer (a horizontal wooden slat) and on the outside by a rail—which would come in handy for fooling some hostile locals on the second voyage.

John Smith's Chesapeake Voyages, 1607–1609

Its sail may have been a square lugsail that could be hauled quickly up the single mast. Such a craft would not have been a smart handler unless the winds were favorable, but it would give sick or exhausted men a respite if they needed one. The bow and stern were relatively high, judging from the sketch on John Smith's map, which would lessen overwash when sailing downwind with heavy following seas.

The crew for the voyage was diverse, reflecting the various skills that might be needed in the coming weeks (see box listing the members of the first expedition). The "gentlemen," presumably with military experience behind them, would serve ashore either as Smith's entourage or his body-guards. No one wanted to be wounded or fall ill, but it only made sense to include a doctor. Likewise, no one wanted to see the boat or sail damaged, but only fools would have embarked without taking a ship's carpenter along. Finally, the limited space after fifteen people had boarded meant limited food and water for the journey, so provision was made to catch fish to eat along the way. The voyagers hoped to find freshwater as they proceeded. Finally, Smith expected to map the region, so he would have brought along writing materials, a compass, and an instrument to measure latitude.[7] Measuring longitude was still a matter of educated guesswork, and would remain so until reliable portable chronometers appeared over a century later.

The supplies have been loaded and the men are aboard. Let the voyage begin.

June 2, 1608: Jamestown to Cape Charles (Map Stop 6.2-1)

John Smith says little about this leg of the journey,[8] but the passage down the James could be a long, difficult one unless wind and tide cooperated. Smith's barge and one of the First Supply ships, the *Phoenix,* bound for England, left Jamestown together; we assume the *Phoenix* with its much greater sail-power was towing the barge (which would have slowed its maximum speed to about six knots [6.9 mph or 11.1 km/hr]). The departure may have been carefully timed. June 2 of that year (it would be June 12 by our modern calendar)[9] fell at the new moon, which (like the full moon) is a time of higher-than-normal "spring" tides[10] and faster currents. Mariners in those days normally chose to leave riverside ports just after high tide peaked, so that the current would carry the vessel downstream (hence the phrase "falling down the river"). The current would be 25–30 percent swifter in a spring tide than in one occurring a week later, between new and full moon. Such a current would help immensely if the wind were weak or in

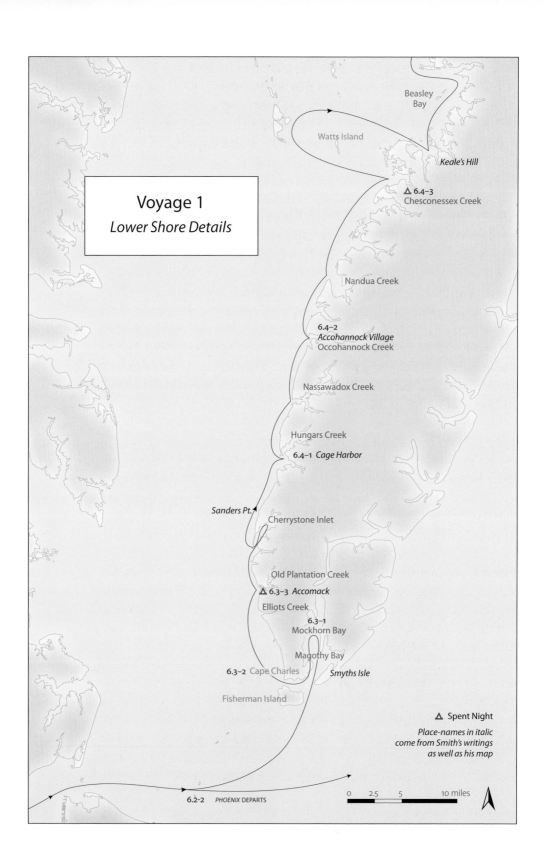

Voyage 1

Lower Shore Details

Beasley
Bay

Watts Island

Keale's Hill

△ 6.4–3
Chesconessex Creek

Nandua Creek

6.4–2
Accohannock Village
Occohannock Creek

Nassawadox Creek

Hungars Creek

6.4–1 *Cage Harbor*

Sanders Pt.

Cherrystone Inlet

Old Plantation Creek

△ 6.3–3 *Accomack*

Elliots Creek

6.3–1
Mockhorn Bay

Magothy Bay

6.3–2 Cape Charles   *Smyths Isle*

Fisherman Island

△ Spent Night

*Place-names in italic
come from Smith's writings
as well as his map*

6.2–2   *PHOENIX* DEPARTS

0   2.5   5   10 miles

the wrong quarter. And with the bends and turns of the lower James and the inability of English watercraft of that day to sail as close to the wind as modern vessels can, the wind was often in the wrong quarter.

The *Phoenix* made such good time down the James to Cape Henry that Smith recorded nothing about that part of the journey. It would seem then that the wind was a brisk westerly one, favorable for all the distance to be traversed.[11] Any more southerly wind would have made the north-south reach between Hog Island and Newport News impossible. We estimate that the two craft, one towing the other, made four knots (4.6 mph or 7.4 km/hr). They likely started bucking an unfavorable tide in a few hours, but when it turned, in passing Newport News and Hampton, where the channel is fairly narrow, the ebb tide would run 1.1 to 1.7 knots (1.2–1.9 mph or 2–3.1 km/hr), increasing the ship's speed by almost 40 percent.[12]

Arriving that night off Cape Henry, the *Phoenix* put the adventurers aboard the barge, dropped the tow, and headed out to sea, incidentally carrying with it John Smith's manuscript for the "True Relation."[13] Smith's party could have spent the night there (*Map Stop 6.2-2*), but we propose that they sailed northward, using the stars or their compass to arrive around dawn at Fisherman Island.

June 3, 1608: Cape Charles to Accomack Town

The barge had steered for Cape Charles, but a second ebbing tide had carried it northeast.[14] That gave the party a chance to explore the lower barrier islands, as shown on Smith's map. He seems to have explored to the end of Magothy Bay, with a route favoring the mainland's shoreline (*Map Stop 6.3-1*). When the tide turned, and as the frequent southerly sea breeze rose, they rode the current back to Fisherman Island, where they saw some Indian men fishing with bone-headed spears (*Map Stop 6.3-2*). The fish that were so abundant that they could use the spearing method were supposedly cod, which today rarely visit the Chesapeake and then not in June.[15] It is more likely that the quarry was kingfish or sea trout.[16] Defensive at first, the fishermen eventually directed the Smith party to their chief, who was the proper person to answer foreigners' questions. So the barge made its way to Accomack, in the vicinity of Elliots Creek.[17] This was probably done expeditiously by a combination of rowing (making about 3 knots [3.5 mph or 5.5 km/hr]) and using the flood tide running past the cape and up the bay (with a maximum assist of 1.2 knots along Old Plantation Flats).

At Accomack (*Map Stop 6.3-3*), Smith and his fellows met a friendly reception. There being no qualified interpreters yet (there would be none un-

Accomac men spearfishing as the English expedition barge approaches on June 3, 1608. (Pen and ink illustration by Marc Castelli for the Captain John Smith Four Hundred Project)

til the following autumn), John Smith used the words he had picked up as a captive the previous winter to interview the chief and ask him what lay to the north. The answer was "good harbors for canoes [but not for ships]" for a long way north. At that point, Smith seems to have lost interest; he asked little more and did little exploring. Thus he missed numerous Indian towns on the Virginia Eastern Shore (see chapter 8). The only exception was Accohannock on Occohannock Creek,[18] and that may have been because the chief there may already have been a close ally of the Accomac chief, so that he would have come up in conversation; in 1621, the two chiefs (the same encountered in 1608?) were brothers and co-rulers.

Since chiefly hospitality among the native people involved feasting, orations, and honoring dances, Smith and his men would have spent the night.

June 4, 1608: Accomack Town to Chesconessex Creek

Leaving Accomack in the morning,[19] Smith moved north along the shore, exploring Old Plantation Creek and then Cherrystone Inlet (*Map Stop 6.4-*

1), passing the mouths of the Gulf and of Hungars Creek and then going up either Nassawadox or Occohannock creek (*Map Stop 6.4-2*). Passing the other creeks, with the tree-covered hummocks of Watts and Tangier islands now in sight on the horizon, Smith missed not only their human inhabitants but also multiple chances for taking on more drinking water, which would have saved him and his crew a good deal of misery the next day. He headed north as far as Nandua Creek, where to the north-northeast the outline of islands (the tree-covered hummocks of Watts or Tangier) came into view on the horizon. At the moment, the islands were where he wanted to go, with their promise (he hoped) of higher, more useful lands beyond. They had a following southwest wind, sometimes (unknown to them) an indicator of an impending afternoon thunderstorm. Haze apparently concealed the severity of coming weather until it was almost on top of them.

There would hardly have been time to lower the mainsail,[20] to prevent it from being knocked down. When the thunder squall hit from the southwest, shifting to northwest, it was amazingly violent. Such storms in the Chesapeake easily achieve 60-mile-per-hour (96.5-km/hr) winds (nearly 100 mph [160 km/hr] has been recorded),[21] four-foot (1.2–meter) waves only several yards apart and arriving every few seconds, and a cascade of rain. Smith and his men had to shelter as best they could under their tarpaulin, ready to bail the boat out if too much water was shipped over the rail. If any sail was still shown in this blow,[22] the barge could have heeled until solid water was taken over the lee rail. The bailers would be overwhelmed. It was an anxious time for all concerned—but being a typical squall, it might have been over in a half hour. With the wind then being from the northwest, an unfavorable direction for going out to the midbay islands, they fell off before the wind and sought a lee in which to anchor for the night. Their haven could have been Chesconessex Creek (*Map Stop 6.4-3*); to the southeast is the highest elevation on the Virginia Eastern Shore, near modern Onley, a rise that may be "Keale's Hill" on Smith's map.

June 5, 1608: Chesconessex Creek to Wighcocomoco Town

After the previous day's storm, the morning would likely have brought gentle winds; the mariners may have rowed with the tide up Tangier Sound[23] and spent time exploring Watts and Tangier islands, which Smith named Russells Isles in honor of the expedition's doctor (*Map Stop 6.5-1*). It could have been very hot, with the journey involving a good deal of rowing; in addition, the crew was running out of drinking water. But at that season no freshwater was to be found on the low-lying islands around them. He sailed

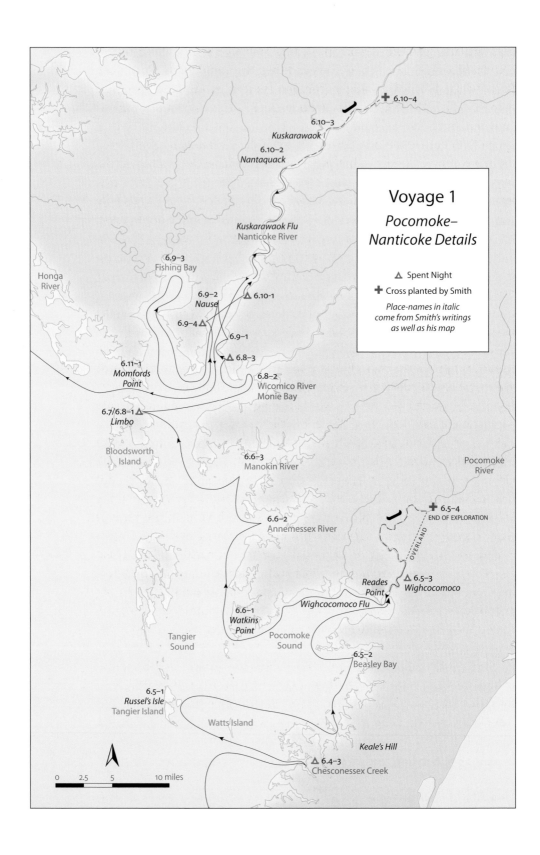

6.10-4

6.10-3

Kuskarawaok

6.10-2
Nantaquack

Voyage 1

*Pocomoke–
Nanticoke Details*

△ Spent Night

✚ Cross planted by Smith

*Place-names in italic
come from Smith's writings
as well as his map*

Kuskarawaok Flu
Nanticoke River

Honga
River

6.9-3
Fishing Bay

6.9-2
Nause

△ 6.10-1

6.9-4 △

6.9-1

6.11-1
*Momfords
Point*

△ 6.8-3

6.8-2
Wicomico River
Monie Bay

6.7/6.8-1 △
Limbo

Bloodsworth
Island

Pocomoke
River

6.6-3
Manokin River

6.5-4
END OF EXPLORATION

6.6-2
Annemessex River

OVERLAND

*Reades
Point*

△ 6.5-3
Wighcocomoco

Wighcocomoco Flu

6.6-1
*Watkins
Point*

Tangier
Sound

Pocomoke
Sound

6.5-2
Beasley Bay

6.5-1
Russel's Isle
Tangier Island

Watts Island

Keale's Hill

△ 6.4-3
Chesconessex Creek

N

0   2.5   5   10 miles

eastward and searched Beasley Bay (*Map Stop 6.5-2*), after which he encountered a large marshy peninsula and then the mouth of the Pocomoke River, which he called the Wighcocomoco. (In 1670, Augustine Herrmann's map would label it "Wighco alias Pokomoake R.") This river's size promised a higher, better-watered land.

The residents of the first downriver town they encountered (*Map Stop 6.5-3*) were initially hostile, but peace was soon made; the Wiccocomicos were outside Powhatan's domain and spoke a different Algonquian dialect.[24] Smith's men were able to fill a few kegs ("barricoes") with unpalatable water. The party then explored upriver overland with a guide or by canoe, according to Smith's map reaching as far as the site of Pocomoke City today (*Map Stop 6.5-4*). Here they may have found freshwater at Town Creek. But as the barge would have remained downriver, they probably filled their water barrels from the smaller Cedar Hall Creek. After that longish hike or canoe trip,[25] they returned downriver, resting for the night and enjoying the hospitality of the Wiccocomico chief.

June 6, 1608: Wighcocomoco Town to Limbo Isle (Bloodsworth Island)
The barge left the Pocomoke River and headed west, likely taking advantage of the prevailing southerly wind blowing up Tangier Sound.[26] Such a wind allowed east-west travel there: Smith went fourteen miles (22.5 kilometers) along the northern, salt-marsh shore of Pocomoke Sound, noting Marumsco, East, and Ape Hole creeks as he went. They rowed past today's Great Fox Island and into Tangier Sound (*Map Stop 6.6-1*). The broad but low marshlands did not interest him, except as a place "good to cut hay in summer and to catch fish and fowl in winter." The mainland beyond was wooded but too low to be very promising. Heading north up Tangier Sound, the explorers visited the wide part of the Annemessex River (*Map Stop 6.6-2*) and sailed around the wider section of the Manokin River, noting Deal Island (*Map Stop 6.6-3*). This cursory exploration bypassed the people known from later records to have lived along them (see chapter 9). From there they went on toward the island they were to call "Limbo," the present-day Bloodsworth Island.

The day was ending, and another storm blew in. This one, which appears to have presaged a nor'easter setting in, tore away the mast and sail both, so that the barge could not be sailed. Smith and his men had to bail to keep from being swamped.

June 7–8, 1608: Limbo Isle (Bloodsworth Island)

Smith and his men were stranded ashore for a day and a half (*Map Stop 6.7/6.8-1*)[27] until their tailor, John Powell, could mend the foresail using the men's shirts. The island's small wooded ridges may have provided a new mast or the original spar may have been recovered. It was a deeply discouraging time, exacerbated by the lack of drinking water,[28] and it is no wonder they named the island as they did: Limbo was believed to be the region in the next world, being neither heaven nor hell, to which unbaptized babies were consigned.[29] The explorers' account sounds as if an additional or continuing storm hit the next day, making them even more uncomfortable. They could have rowed east, but the wind, if northeast, would have prevented it. In any case, Smith seems to have been unwilling to depart until they had a functional rig on the barge. The location of their camp on the island is uncertain, due to significant changes in the shoreline over the past four centuries; the site may well be underwater today.

June 8, 1608: Limbo Isle (Bloodsworth Island) to the Mouth of Nanticoke River

Once under way again in the afternoon, Smith and his men made for the Eastern Shore mainland,[30] sailing up the Wicomico River to the divide at Monie Bay (*Map Stop 6.8-2*). The area was all salt marsh, so they gave up before encountering the interior uplands where Indian towns are known to have existed later (see chapter 9). They then followed the Eastern Shore to the north-trending Kuskarawaok River, now called the Nanticoke. They must have felt encouraged by the wooded uplands they saw coming down to the river's edge, offering the promise of dry land, drinking water, and human habitations.

By the time they passed Roaring Point, the local people were ready, shooting arrows at them from trees. Smith kept the barge anchored in midstream, beyond the reach of arrows, trying to convince his attackers he was not an enemy. Nothing worked, so there the barge remained for the night, probably south of Ragged Point (*Map Stop 6.8-3*).

June 9, 1608: Mouth of the Nanticoke River

The next day,[31] Smith forced matters by approaching the shore, where the people stood unarmed, laden with baskets of goods to trade and beckoning him to land. Suspecting an ambush, he had his men discharge a volley of shot into the crowd, which dispersed. He saw that armed warriors were hiding in the marsh on the point, ready to attack if he landed, so he

The barge anchored beyond the range of arrows from the Nanticoke River natives, whose initial response to the expedition was defensive and nonwelcoming. (Pen and ink illustration by Marc Castelli for the Captain John Smith Four Hundred Project)

returned to midriver to wait out the situation. That evening he had the barge steered near shore again and had another volley fired into the reeds, but no one was there (*Map stop 6.9-1*). Seeing smoke on the opposite bank, the English rowed there to find two or three houses that were probably the summer fishing camp of Nause (*Map Stop 6.9-2*). The residents had fled, so Smith left trade goods there before going back out the river's mouth and into Fishing Bay (*Map Stop 6.9-3*), where they explored past Elliott Island. They noted the Transquaking River heading off to the north but missed the people who may have lived there. The land was marsh and upland woods without streams, so they found no drinking water. After dark they returned up the Nanticoke and anchored adjacent to Nause again (*Map Stop 6.9-4*).

June 10, 1608: Mouth of the Nanticoke River to Broad Creek and Back
Early the next morning, four Nanticoke men came paddling upriver, unaware of the previous day's imbroglio because they had been out fishing.[32] Smith treated them kindly, and they left to confer with their neighbors, twenty of whom came out to trade. Word spread rapidly upriver and hun-

dreds of people came down to meet the strangers ashore, probably between the modern settlements of Bivalve and Tyaskin (*Map Stop 6.10-1*). Trading was fast and furious for a while, and given the number of people involved, it is likely that the *tallak* (paramount chief) himself was there; at some point, he and Smith would have formally interviewed one another. Smith noted that the Nanticokes had plenty of furs to trade; later he wrote that those were the highest-quality furs he had seen anywhere in the Chesapeake. The reason was not that the Nanticokes' hunting territory was exceptional; it was that the people there made great quantities of shell beads, with which they purchased furs from other, unspecified Indians.[33]

Smith may not have taken enough time to explore the river, including Marshyhope Creek, as thoroughly as his map indicates. (He supposedly placed crosses at the farthest extent of his explorations.) The map shows him traveling up the Nanticoke past the village Nantaquack, in the area of the present-day town of Vienna (*Map Stop 6.10-2*), not to mention the paramount chief's town of Kuskarawaok just north of present-day Vienna (*Map Stop 6.10-3*),[34] about fifteen miles (24 kilometers) upstream from Nause. From Kuskarawaok to the end of exploration just upriver of Broad Creek was another ten miles (16 kilometers), making a round-trip exploration of fifty miles (80 kilometers) that day. That was a good many miles of river to cover, supposedly in one day, even in an energetically paddled canoe taking advantage of flood and ebb tides. Moreover, etiquette would have required at least one more long upriver stop at the *tallak's* town, where the visitors would have been feasted again. It is likely, given Smith's orders to find a Northwest Passage, that at least part (and perhaps all) of what Smith learned came from interviewing the Nanticoke paramount chief and his councilors on the shore opposite Nause and having them draw a map in the dirt. The native people of the Chesapeake were perfectly capable of drawing maps; Powhatan himself would "draw plots upon the ground" for Smith the next time they met.[35]

There were several towns upriver, but no promise of minerals or a passage to the Pacific. Far from it: the land was but "a ridge of land betwixt the [Chesapeake] bay and the main [Atlantic] ocean." (That bit of information could only have come in an interview.) The Nanticokes did say something, however, that made Smith prick up his ears: they told of "a great nation called Massawomecks" who could be found farther up the Chesapeake. Smith would already have learned during his captivity that those fearsome people came from a land to the northwest. Now he would get somewhere if he could talk to some of them. So Smith and his men probably spent that night at the two-mile-wide (3.2-kilometer) section of the lower Nanticoke River's mouth, ready to push onward the next day.

June 11, 1608: Nanticoke River to Randle Cliff

The voyagers sailed past Fishing Bay and through Hooper Strait.[36] Bypassing the Honga River, Smith reached Momfords Point (now called Nancy Point) on Lower Hooper Island (*Map Stop 6.11-1*). From there, he was able to look across the Chesapeake and see great high cliffs barely rising above the horizon, yellow in the morning sunlight. What he was seeing were the eroding cliffs from Drum Point to Little Cove Point, which shine brightly in the morning sun. That was the mainland, and he made straight for it. He could also have caught a flood tide, which flows through Hooper Strait toward the bay at eight- or nine-tenths of a knot (about 1 mph or 1.6 kph). Further, at that time of year the winds are usually southwesterly, which would have impeded any attempt to take a more westerly or southerly course. Sailing with the wind, the flood tide could have carried Smith across the bay to Calvert Cliffs, where the continuing flood impeded entry to the Patuxent, which he could have seen clearly on the port (left) side. In any case, Smith was eager to head north to find the head of the bay and contact the Massawomecks. Calling the cliffs "Rickards Cliffs," after his mother's maiden name,[37] Smith continued on the favoring tide up the bay along its western shore. On his map he noted Plum Point Creek, at Breezy Point, and Fishing Creek, at Chesapeake Beach. Near sunset the thermally driven winds would likely have failed, and the party probably spent the night between Fishing Creek and Randle Cliff (*Map Stop 6.11-2*).

June 12, 1608: Randle Cliff to Sillery Bay on Patapsco River

The next morning Smith and his party once again headed north,[38] probably leaving near slack water to take advantage of another flood tide. Smith noted that the smaller tidal rivers north of Rickards (Calvert) Cliffs were "all along well watered," thick with woods and underbrush, and well stocked with wild animals, but those tributary valleys had no human inhabitants to make him stop and ask questions. The voyagers entered Herring Bay (*Map Stop 6.12-1*), the mouth of the South River (*Map Stop 6.12-2*), and sailed past the wide mouth of the Severn River and White Hall Creek before exploring the Magothy River at least to Sillery Bay (*Map Stop 6.12-3*). Then they proceeded to the mouth of the Patapsco River, which Smith called the Bolus River, in one day's sail (*Map Stop 6.12-4*). Taking advantage of both the southerly wind[39] and the strong northward tidal current (of almost

Calvert Cliffs on Maryland's Western Shore. This portion of the cliffs, Rocky Point, is about 130 feet high. It drew Smith from the Straits of "Limbo" on the Eastern Shore to continue his exploration of the Western Shore. (Photograph by Kent Mountford)

a knot), which during the flood tides expedited their progress, may have caused them to keep moving along the western shore rather than exploring it thoroughly. Across the bay, the islands along the Eastern Shore (much diminished by erosion since 1608) may have blocked his view of rivers like the Choptank (his map shows—and his text indicates—only a wooded interior), so that he missed several more groups of people and remained focused on finding (nonexistent) west-side people to interrogate.

Smith's account says nothing about where they stopped for the night, but a likely place was the mouth of the Patapsco River, either at Bodkin Point or across the river at Old Road Bay (*Map Stop 6.12-4*), which the map shows he explored. The former is more secure during thunderstorms, while the latter would be logical as a shelter later from northeast winds.

June 13, 1608: Old Road Bay to Elkridge and Back, on the Patapsco River

Smith explored the Patapsco thoroughly[40] by barge as far as the colonial port and modern town of Elkridge (*Map Stop 6.13-1*),[41] and on foot past the first falls of the river near where I-95 crosses it today, a place he named "Downs Dale" (*Map Stop 6.13-2*). His map indicates that he and his men took time to climb past the 360-foot (110-meter) elevation of the fall line, a half mile (less than a kilometer) north of Avalon, to place a brass cross claiming the valley for the English (at "Blands C"). They also searched (in vain) for minerals. This part of the trip required eighteen miles (29 kilometers) of rowing and two miles (3.2 kilometers) of overland exploration; they may have taken advantage of an ebb tide on their return downstream.

In the lower Patapsco valley, which looked like good farmland (now covered over by the city of Baltimore), there were no human habitations at all—no one to entertain, feed, or inform them. Hindsight tells us that any local Algonquian speakers had abandoned the area due to raids from the Susquehannocks and Massawomecks (see chapter 10), but at the time Smith was simply mystified. In addition, it had become plain that the river was not a major route into the interior. One potentially exportable commodity, however, was found in outcroppings of bole armoniac, a reddish-brown-yellow clay that Europeans imported from Armenia because of its reputed medicinal properties. This type of clay is no longer exposed today, being buried by development and landfill along the much built-up Patapsco. On the other hand, Federal Hill in today's Inner Harbor of Baltimore is made up of sands formerly mined for glass manufacture. Smith explored up the Northwest Harbor and Middle Branch to the head of tide.

The return trip down the Patapsco took them back to the tidal basin in what is now Baltimore, where Smith noted that Old Road Bay was an open bay; it may have been where the party sheltered in the ensuing days (*Map Stop 6.14*). They continued searching for minerals, and though the natural ironstone deposits mined so extensively in the eighteenth and early nineteenth centuries near Deep Run and Stony Run were noticed at the time, Smith wrote elsewhere only of minable iron in what is now Virginia. Most of their progress would have been achieved by rowing, for winds on the Patapsco can be variable, and the weather may well have remained hot and humid.

After a full day of rowing and walking, even though they were no longer dying of thirst, the crew were thoroughly discouraged and out of sorts. Fifteen grown men had been crammed into the barge for "12 or 14 days,"

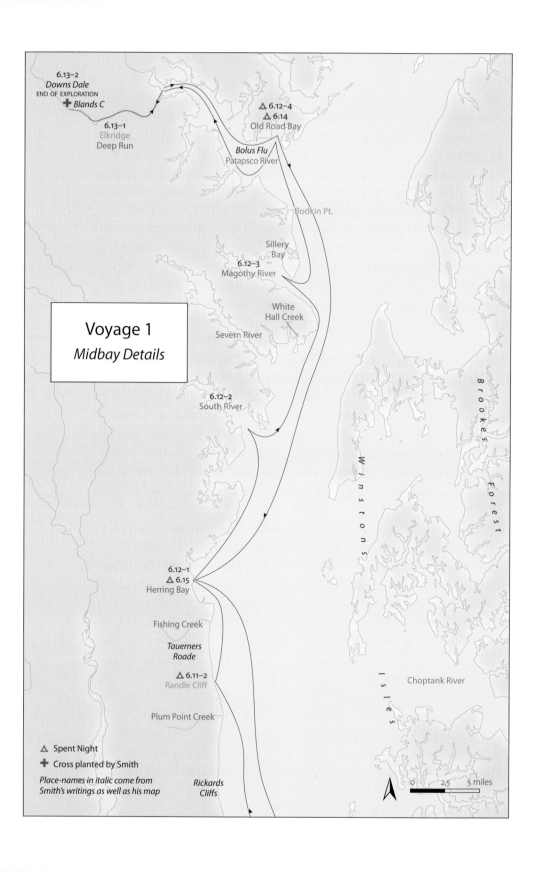

6.13–2
Downs Dale
END OF EXPLORATION
✝ *Blands C*

6.13–1
Elkridge
Deep Run

△ **6.12–4**
△ **6.14**
Old Road Bay

Bolus Flu
Patapsco River

Bodkin Pt.

Sillery
Bay

6.12–3
Magothy River

White
Hall Creek

Severn River

Voyage 1
Midbay Details

6.12–2
South River

W i n s t o n s

B r o o k e s

F o r e s t

6.12–1
△ **6.15**
Herring Bay

Fishing Creek

*Tauerners
Roade*

△ **6.11–2**
Randle Cliff

Plum Point Creek

I s l e s

Choptank River

△ Spent Night
✝ Cross planted by Smith

*Place-names in italic come from
Smith's writings as well as his map*

*Rickards
Cliffs*

0   2.5   5 miles

and the bread they had brought along had rotted after getting wet in the storms.

Fed up with these working conditions, and with no native people to feed them, they wanted to return to Jamestown. John Smith had all he could do to convince them that they should not give up looking for the Massawomecks and the mouth of the Potomac River. "As for your fears that I will lose myself in these unknown large waters, or be swallowed up in some stormy gust, [you should] abandon these childish fears, for worse than [has] passed is not likely to happen [again], and there is as much danger to return as to proceed."[42] Before long, however, he had to change his tune.

June 14, 1608: Patapsco River
When the barge tried to leave the Patapsco, it was held up for a time by "wind and weather," probably meaning unfavorable winds and constant showers.[43] This may have been a nor'easter,[44] whose chilly winds and nasty chop would have prevented the party from going upbay even if they had had the will to do so. As it was, the fishermen in the barge seem not to have done any fishing, and now hunger and illness stalked the men in earnest. Several crewmen fell ill. The Patapsco River was a decent haven, so they stayed there until the bad weather passed.

June 15, 1608: Patapsco River to the Mouth of Herring Bay
When the weather cleared, the winds shifted northwest, the mariner's cue to depart southward. In addition, it was three days past the new moon, and tidal currents, if played correctly, could be more helpful than usual in getting around. An ebb tide coupled with a northerly wind could have sent the barge down the bay at up to six to seven knots (7–8 mph or 11–13 km/hr). At that rate, they could have traveled the thirty-three statute miles (53 kilometers) from the Patapsco River to Herring Bay (*Map Stop 6.15*) in one easy day, perhaps in a single long morning or afternoon. Sailing for a change and heading south, and having enjoyed a good night's rest, probably began to restore the men's health and spirits.

June 16, 1608: Herring Bay to Cornfield Harbor
Having explored the western shore's cliffs on the trip north, the mariners sailed out into the bay and headed south for fifty-six miles (90.1 kilometers) to reach the Potomac.[45] Although they must have seen the mouth of the Patuxent River, they sailed past it, possibly because of strong ebb currents running at the time out of the river as well as the favorable winds for con-

tinued southern progress. After such a long day's sail, even with favorable winds, they probably rounded Point Lookout and rested for the night at Cornfield Harbor (*Map Stop 6.16*).

June 17, 1608: Cornfield Harbor to Nomini Creek

The next day the northwest wind could have been dying or gone, gradually replaced by seasonal light upstream breezes. Leaving the northern mouth of the Potomac, and heading southwest across the seven-mile-wide (11.3-kilometer) river, the barge sailed along the southern bank of the Potomac.[46] Here, once again, Smith saw no human habitations, but he soon found out that he had missed some. As discussed in chapter 12, the Potomac is wide enough and the winds crossing it are strong enough that the native people preferred to live well up the tributaries. Raids down the river by the Massawomecks may have reinforced that decision. So no Indian houses would have been in sight as Smith and his men went upriver, and he bypassed the Sekakawons.[47] The Sekakawons, however, saw *them* and spread the word.

At Nomini Bay, Smith saw two men, who would logically have been in a canoe. They were also there as bait, to entice the English into a trap. Accepting the invitation to go up Nomini Creek (*Map Stop 6.17*), they ran into an ambush manned by so many warriors that it must have involved the Sekakawons and perhaps also—if there had been enough time to summon them—the Wiccocomicos. Smith and the gentlemen replied with gunshots, aimed low to avoid harming anyone, and the noise and ricochet of shot on the water caused the attackers to lay down their arms and agree to an exchange of hostages. The English hostage, soldier James Watkins, was taken "six miles [nearly 10 kilometers] up the woods to their king's habitation" (probably, at that season, a foraging camp), after which there was a parley. The ambush, the chief explained, had been carried out on Powhatan's orders, for Powhatan was their overlord. Smith added snidely in his account that the malcontents at Jamestown had put Powhatan up to it, but that may not be the whole story. After receiving a report from his subjects the Accomacs, Powhatan would have been sufficiently piqued on his own account, since John Smith was supposedly a war captain under himself (an outcome of Smith's captivity) and yet was ranging the Chesapeake without permission.

Peace was made all around. Smith and his men probably spent the night either with the Onawmanient chief or in the barge anchored in Nomini Bay.

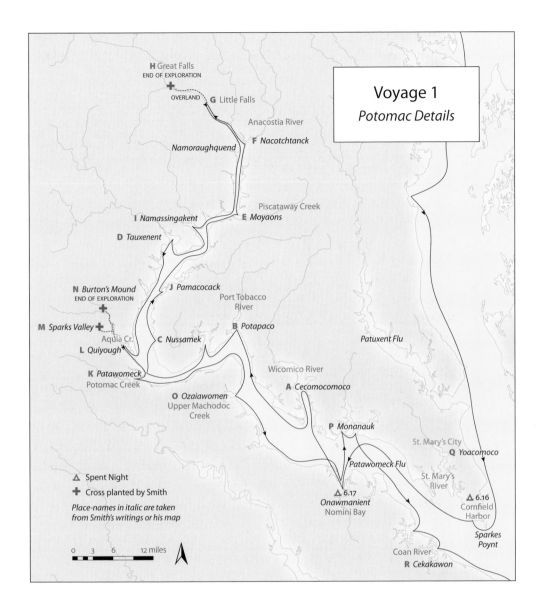

Voyage 1
Potomac Details

H Great Falls
END OF EXPLORATION
OVERLAND   G Little Falls
Anacostia River
F Nacotchtanck
Namoraughquend
Piscataway Creek
I Namassingakent   E Moyaons
D Tauxenent
N Burton's Mound   J Pamacocack
END OF EXPLORATION
Port Tobacco
River
M Sparks Valley   B Potapaco
Aquia Cr.   C Nussamek
L Quiyough   Patuxent Flu
Wicomico River
K Patawomeck   A Cecomocomoco
Potomac Creek
O Ozaiawomen
Upper Machodoc
Creek
P Monanauk
St. Mary's City
Q Yoacomoco
Patawomeck Flu
St. Mary's
River
△ 6.16
△ 6.17   Cornfield
Onawmanient   Harbor
Nomini Bay
Sparkes
Poynt
Coan River
R Cekakawon

△ Spent Night
✝ Cross planted by Smith
*Place-names in italic are taken
from Smith's writings or his map*

0   3   6   12 miles

June 18 to July 15, 1608: Nomini Bay to Great Falls and Return to the Mouth of the Potomac

It is more difficult to reconstruct John Smith's chronology after his stay in Nomini Bay, for he covers four weeks' explorations in a relatively few pages (what a pity!) without indicating times or sequences.[48] He did include one episode from those explorations in the account of his second voyage, in a sort of flashback. Therefore at this point we shall switch from accounts of

Hypothetical Log: Days Spent on the Potomac River

June 16 Pass Sparks Point and arrive at Cornfield Harbor to spend night.

June 17 Cornfield Harbor to Nomini Creek: 34 miles (54.7 km) to Onawmanient Village. Mosco from village of Wighcocomoco joins barge as guide and ambassador. Given hostile receptions planned on the south shore of the Potomac, he directs crew to the north shore beyond Powhatan's influence.

June 18 Nomini Creek to Cecomocomoco: 19 miles (30.6 km), southerly winds to north shore: Cecomocomoco to Potapaco. 18 miles (29 km) to head of tide Port Tobacco Creek.

June 19 Potapaco to Nanjemoy Creek, stop at Patawomeck where Mosco stays, and then spent night at Nussamek, weroance village of the Nanjemoy chiefdom: 34 miles (54.7 km).

June 20 Nussamek to Pamacocack on Mattawoman Creek to Occoquan Bay and chiefdom of the Tauxenent where spent friendly night at Tauxenent: 19 miles (30.6 km).

June 21–22 Tauxenent to Cinquaeteck, back to Pohick Bay and end at Moyaons: 22 miles (35.4 km); spent next day and night at Moyaons as guest of tayac of Piscataway chiefdom.

June 23 Moyaons to head of tide of Piscataway Creek, to Nacotchtank: 18 miles (29 km).

June 24 Nacotchtank to 2 miles (3.2 km) up Anacostia River to Little Falls: 15 miles (24.1 km).

June 25 Little Falls overland to Great Falls: 10 miles (16 km) on foot for part of crew.

June 26–27 Great Falls to Little Falls; search for minerals for part of crew: 10 land miles (16 km).

June 28 Little Falls to Nacotchtank to Assaomeck on western shore: 14 miles (22.5 km).

June 29 to June 30 Assaomeck to Moyaons to Dogue Creek to Tauxenent, spent next day and night at Tauxenent: 24 miles (38.6 km).

separate days to accounts of separate areas of the Potomac valley, and the map stops will be labeled in sequence with capital letters A through R, rather than by date.

John Smith's Chesapeake Voyages, 1607–1609

July 1 Tauxenent to Powells Creek to Quantico Creek at Pamacocack: 14 miles (22.5 km).

July 2 Pamacocack back to Patawomeck: 19 miles (30.6 km).

July 3 Patawomeck to head of tide on Aquia Creek and by land to last village: 10 miles (16 km) by water and 10 miles (16 km) on foot with hostages and guides.

July 4–5 Exploration of antimony mine in Sparks valley to south, and look for minerals to Burtons Mount to north of Beaverdam Run: 17 miles (27.4 km) overland.

July 6 Transport of minerals on foot to Quiyough and then by barge to Patawomeck: 10 miles on land (16 km) and 10 miles (16 km) by barge.

July 7 Day of rest as guest of Patawomeck.

July 8 Patawomeck along southern shore to Ozaiawomen: 27 miles (43.4 km).

July 9 Ozaiawomen past Mattox Creek to Wicomico River: 23 miles (33.8 km).

July 10 Wicomico River to Onawmanient: 10 miles (16 km).

July 11 Onawmanient to St. Clements Bay (Monanauk) and back to Lower Machodoc Creek: 25 miles (40.2 km).

o Lower Machodoc Creek to Yeocomico River Mouth to Coan River to spend night at Cekakawon: 22 miles (35.4 km).

July 13 Cekakawon to Wighcocomoco to return Mosco to his village: 13 miles (20.9 km).

July 14 Wighcocomoco; spent day and next night.

July 15 Wighcocomoco to Great Wicomico River to Ingram Bay: 21 miles (33.8 km).

Note: Given the vagueness of Smith's text, the days with their distances presented here, estimated mainly by Edward Haile, reflect only one possible scenario for the journey. Modern boaters may follow any of several other possible scenarios in retracing Smith's route.

Lower Potomac, Ascending the River

Smith wrote little about this leg of his journey except his map, showing Indian settlements, and his later flashback.[49] Smith said he and his men encountered a hostile reception at Patawomeck and "Cecocawonee," both presumably by the same order from Powhatan as the Onawmanients had received. The mention of Sekakawon here seems to indicate a reversal of course back down the Potomac to contact the town there, which would have been easy if a southerly wind was blowing again. However, it is equally plausible that they continued upriver from Onawmanient (see box detailing a hypothetical log). Early in his Potomac exploration, probably at Onawmanient, Smith met the Wiccocomico man Mosco, whose heavy beard indicated European ancestry.[50] The man had probably been teased about his hairiness since puberty, since traditional Indian humor often included teasing.[51] Now he was overjoyed to see—for the first time—other men as hairy as himself. He welcomed the English as fellow-countrymen and promptly constituted himself the expedition's guide and facilitator, both on the trip up to Patawomeck and on the Rappahannock River portion of the second voyage.[52]

Mosco went as far as Patawomeck with them and then insisted on staying there, for reasons unknown (*Map Stop K*). In his initial enthusiasm, Mosco also offered, as they set out from his hometown, to induce his fellow villagers to tow the barge upriver if necessary, "against wind or tide, from place to place." That presumably meant a dugout canoe towing the barge; apparently the offer did not have to be accepted. Interestingly, Mosco did not guide Smith across the Potomac to St. Mary's River, so the Yoacomocos—who were friendly with the south bank people—are missing from Smith's map.

Knowing that south-shore people under Powhatan's influence were apt to be hostile, Mosco probably directed the mariners to the north (Maryland) shore of the Potomac; the return of southerly winds would have aided such an itinerary. Due north of Nomini Bay is St. Clements Bay, where the map shows a visit (*Map Stop O*); next came the Yeocomico River (*Map Stop A*), and then, back on the Potomac, the chief's town of Cecomocomoco. After that came the Potopacos on the Port Tobacco River (*Map Stop B*), an outlier of the Piscataway paramount chiefdom; establishing friendly relations with them would have opened up the rest of the Potomac's left (north/east) bank to the English, all the way to the fall line. The next stop would have been at Nussamek, capital of the Nanjemoy chiefdom (*Map Stop C*), and then came the Patawomecks.

John Smith had heard, presumably from Indian people in the James or York river valleys, about a desirable mineral that they purchased from these Patawomecks. Since finding minerals was one of the major goals of the whole voyage around the Chesapeake, once hostilities had died down, Smith probably asked the Patawomeck chief to lead him to the mine and was refused (otherwise the mine-seeking jaunt would have taken place earlier). Bidding his new but still wary friends farewell, Smith left the town and proceeded upriver. Mosco preferred to stay behind, and Smith knew that he would soothe the chief's fears, which would be useful later.

Upper Potomac below the Falls

The English party continued upriver,[53] receiving a friendly welcome from the Tauxenents ("Toags," or Dogues) (*Map Stop D*), who were supposedly a "fringe" part of Powhatan's domain.[54] There was similar hospitality to sample at Pamacocack (*Map Stop J*), Moyaons (Piscataway) (*Map Stop E*), and Nacotchtank (*Map Stop F*). As with other regions of the Chesapeake, John Smith never specifies how many of the towns and villages on his map he actually visited, but he definitely stopped at these capitals, and probably also a few villages along the way, to ask where the local people's chiefs lived. Indian guides may or may not have joined the explorers: Smith is silent about all except Mosco. On this stretch of the river, Smith took careful note of the tributaries and human habitations along them—within reason. One could wish, though, that he had explored up the Occoquan River, whose headwaters are in the Bull Run Mountains; he may have missed more villages.

Pressing on past Nacotchtank, Smith soon encountered the Little Falls of the Potomac, a mile (1.6 kilometers) above the boundary of modern Washington, D.C. (*Map Stop G*). At last! Rocks to examine! The ones in the falls had "divers tinctures," which raised their hopes of finding valuable minerals, and they took samples. The repeated emphasis on the Potomac as a source for special metals may have motivated a landing party to continue upriver on foot, to Great Falls (*Map Stop H*). It was in that area that the explorers met a number of men in canoes that were "well loaden with the flesh of bears, deer, and other beasts, whereof we had part." The identity of these people is uncertain, although if they had been Massawomecks from farther upriver, Smith would surely have said so. They were probably locals who had been hunting in the Piedmont, then a buffer zone between Algonquian speakers and the Massawomecks. Smith did not record what, if anything, he learned from them about who or what was upriver. At the falls, sediments from the river had collected in low places along the rocky shore, and here they found spangled layers of gilded soils (probably mica-rich sediments common today at this location). They hiked above the river into the valley slope to look for silver or gold and found "a clay sand so mingled with yellow spangles as if it had been half pin-dust" (brass filings, so probably iron pyrite is meant here).

Still "ignorant" of mines but with furs bought from the men in the canoes, Smith and his men turned back down the river. Their progress may have been assisted by the ebb of the spring tide associated with the new moon, which occurred around July 12. Rowing early in the day while it was still cool, and before upstream winds developed, would be a good strategy to follow.

Lower Potomac, Descending the River

Left at Patawomeck, Mosco had persuaded that district's chief to let the English know, upon their return downriver, where to find one of his people's great treasures: *matchqueon,* a black ore with silvery glitters in it. The finer grains and glitters were washed out of the ore in a nearby stream, then bagged and traded over long distances, so that people could add grease to make a face paint that "makes them look like blackmoors dusted over with silver." John Smith was eager to know whether this stuff contained silver, and now with the Patawomeck chief's cooperation he and his men went to a great deal of trouble to obtain some at the source, which was way up in the headwaters of Aquia Creek.[55]

Smith, six crew members, and several Patawomeck volunteers ascended Aquia Creek (*Map Stop L*) as far as possible in the barge, probably a distance of thirteen miles (20.9 kilometers), after which they traversed the remaining eight miles (12.9 kilometers) on foot. The Patawomeck men were led as "hostages in [holding] a small chain they were to have for their pains, being proud so richly to be adorned"—indicating that the guides may have had mixed feelings about their mission. The mine seems to have been located up one of the tributary headwaters of the creek, perhaps Beaverdam Run. Smith explored the surrounding area as well (*Map Stop M*), calling it "Sparks Valley." He may have been deliberately vague about its location in his narrative, which was for general readers.[56] The location and meaning of "Democrites tree"[57] and "Burtons Mount" (*Map Stop N*) are also left unexplained.

Then the party returned downstream, first on foot and then by barge, with Smith and his men carrying a large quantity of ore. The junket, allowing for travel and then gouging out ore with "shells and hatchets," must altogether have required several days. The ore was subsequently taken to England, assayed, and found to contain no silver at all.

As he returned downriver from Patawomeck, Smith may have revisited places or picked up loose ends, such as the town of Ozaiawomen on Upper Machodoc Creek (*Map Stop O*) and, if he had not visited them earlier, the Sekakawons on the Coan River (*Map Stop R*). But he still altogether missed the Yoacomocos (*Map [non-]Stop Q*), possibly indicating that he was impatient to go on to the next river, the Rappahannock, and find out how far inland that one led.

Smith wrote later about the Chesapeake in general—but probably about the fresher reaches of the bay and its tributaries, including the Potomac's mouth—that he and his men had seen an abundance of "fish lying so thick with their heads above the water as for want of nets (our barge driving amongst them) we attempted to catch them with a frying pan, but we found it a bad instrument to catch fish with." One wonders what equipment Jonas Profit *had* brought with him,[58] for Smith recorded that his crew was running out of food again as they left the Potomac River. (For all they knew, they could have traded for some from the Yoacomocos.) The attempt to catch fish may have occurred on the upper tidal Potomac, based on the names of several villages noted on Smith's map. The translations of the village-names of Namassingakent (*Map Stop I*) and Namraughquena are "fish—plenty of" and "fishing place."[59]

July 15, 1608: Mouth of the Potomac to Ingram Bay

The explorers headed south, probably hindered by a southwesterly wind so that the barge had to hug the shoreline, in the lee, with the crew rowing. Once the tide was on the ebb, they would be assisted by that southward-moving current, which runs somewhat faster than it does along the Eastern Shore thanks to the Coriolis effect. That was useful for exploring the creeks indenting the eastern end of the Northern Neck and for visiting Wighcocomoco on the Little Wicomico River (*Map Stop 7.15-1*) and the outlying village of Cinquack (*Map Stop 7.15-2*). Smith and his men probably spent the night nearby in Ingram Bay.

Logically, Smith would have done his exploring during the flood tides and moved south on the ebbs, though his account says nothing at all of his movements between the Potomac and the Rappahannock rivers' mouths.

July 16, 1608: Ingram Bay to Fleets Bay

Smith and his men continued sailing and rowing their way south,[60] probably using the current supplied by an ebbing tide. They rowed up Dividing Creek (*Map Stop 7.16-1*) and then sailed into Fleets Bay, perhaps thinking it

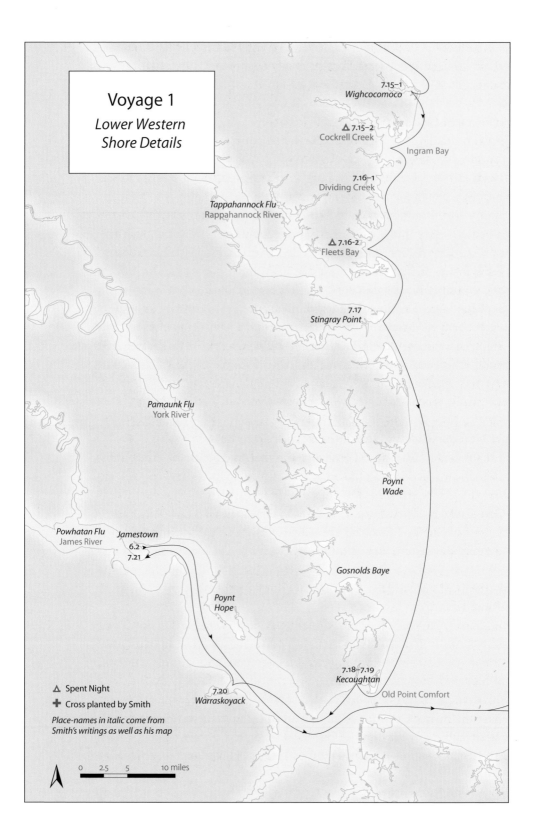

Voyage 1
*Lower Western
Shore Details*

7.15–1
Wighcocomoco

△ 7.15–2
Cockrell Creek

Ingram Bay

7.16–1
Dividing Creek

Tappahannock Flu
Rappahannock River

△ 7.16–2
Fleets Bay

7.17
Stingray Point

Pamaunk Flu
York River

*Poynt
Wade*

Powhatan Flu
James River   *Jamestown*
6.2 ▶
7.21 ◀

Gosnolds Baye

*Poynt
Hope*

7.18–7.19
Kecoughtan

Old Point Comfort

△ Spent Night

✚ Cross planted by Smith

7.20
Warraskoyack

*Place-names in italic come from
Smith's writings as well as his map*

0   2.5   5   10 miles

the mouth of the Rappahannock River, and entered three of its tributaries without seeing any villages. They probably anchored for the night off the south shore of Fleets Bay (*Map Stop 7.16-2*).

July 17, 1608: Fleets Bay to Stingray Point

The next morning they seem to have taken advantage of ebbing currents to progress southward.[61] In the mouth of the Rappahannock, shoal water extends eastward for a long way, and there they ran aground (*Map Stop 7.17*) somewhere out on the wide, sandy flats at the mouth of the Rappahannock; it seems to have been low tide or nearly so. They would have to wait several hours for the tide to rise again before they could start upriver. Meanwhile, they went after the thrashing fish in the shallow, a venture that appeared productive but soon proved to be a mistake.

Cownose rays feed on mollusks and are common in July in the river and grass beds around Stingray Point and in the grass beds formerly present off the point; anyone grabbing the tail of one is at risk of being impaled. That is what happened to John Smith. He and his men were "fishing" with their swords, which was possible as the fish milled in schools. But none of them knew this species, and Smith speared one and then tried to remove his sword while pushing the ray away with his free hand. The tail spine went deep into his wrist, releasing as it did a toxin that not only causes terrific pain but also sends some of its human victims into anaphylactic shock.[62] Smith's arm, shoulder, and chest swelled so horribly in the next four hours that his life was despaired of. But Dr. Russell probed the wound and applied an oil (no description recorded), and eventually the swelling subsided. By evening, after perhaps eight hours, Smith was well enough to eat his supper—which consisted of the cownose ray. Smith triumphantly named the place where it all happened Stingray Point.

July 18–19, 1608: Stingray Point on the Rappahannock River to Kecoughtan

With Smith still a bit under the weather, a decision was made to head back to Jamestown.[63] The Rappahannock River, like the head of the Chesapeake Bay and a meeting with the Massawomecks, would have to wait. The barge had been refloated, and now the mariners seized this ebb tide to set off southward again, even though it was night and they had to steer by dead reckoning (no stars are mentioned). The wind was probably west to southwesterly, which would help them initially but slow them down (forcing them to tack) once they were out in the bay, making them dependent on

Modern Equivalents of Geographic Features on Smith's Map: Voyage One

James River (explored on other expeditions)
Cedar Isle = Mulberry Island
Mortons Bay = Lynnhaven Bay
The New Forge = Smith's Fort, on Grays Creek
Point Comfort = Old Point Comfort
Point Hope = Newport News
Sharps Isle (on Nansemond River) = Dumpling Island

York River (explored on other expeditions)
Gosnolds Bay: mouth of Poquoson and Back Rivers
Point Warde = New Point Comfort
Tindals Point = Gloucester Point
Wiffins Point = eroded marshes east of Hog Island

Eastern Shore
Cage Harbor = Cherrystone Inlet
Keale's Hill = Onley, Va.
Limbo = Bloodsworth Island
Limbo Strait = Hooper Strait
Momfords Point = Nancy Point, on Lower Hooper Island
Rappahannock Flu = Honga River

ebb tides and rowing to make much progress. At least they would avoid running into choppy water if they stayed fairly close to land, at least as far as the mouth of the York. Before nightfall on July 18, they rounded Old Point Comfort and put in at Kecoughtan (*Map Stop 7.18-7.19*).

There they caused a sensation: Smith and his men must have made war on somebody up north! Look at all those "bows, arrows, swords [warclubs], shields, mantles, and furs!" Smith was mobbed by native people demanding to know with whom he had been fighting. His protestations about having bought the goods fell on deaf ears. The Kecoughtans, like most of the Powhatans, had a genuine and well-founded fear of Massawomeck raiders (see chapter 10). Before long Smith gave in and said yes, it was the Massawomecks he had encountered. At that point the "moccasin telegraph"[64]

Reades Point = Williams Point
Russels Iles = Tangier, Goose, and Watts islands
Sandersons Point = the point just south of Cape Charles harbor
Smith Isles = Smith and Mockhorn islands
Warnfords Point = uncertain
Washeborne C: ["C:" = claim? Climb?] = near modern Wachapreague
Watkins Point = Watkins Point
Winstons Isles = Kent and Tilghman islands

Calvert Cliffs to Patapsco River
Blands C: = hilltop (elevation 360 ft.) north of Avalon
Bolus River = Patapsco River
Downs Dale = Patapsco River above the fall line
Rickards Cliffs = Calvert Cliffs
Taverners Roade = higher elevations of Western Shore on coastal plain

Potomac River
Burton's Mount = Independence Hill
Democrites Tree = uncertain
Sparks Point = Point Lookout
Sparks Valley = Piedmont section of Aquia Creek valley

went into overdrive to spread the news. There must have been tremendous rejoicing that night and into the next day and night, while Smith and his men rested and joined in the celebrations.

July 20, 1608: Kecoughtan to Warraskoyack

The next day the travelers began working their way up the James River.[65] Any southwest wind would have been against them until they had rounded Newport News, and they only managed the fifteen miles or so (about 24 kilometers) to Warraskoyack, near modern Smithfield (*Map Stop 7.20*). There they were treated royally, as victors over the Massawomecks. None of the mariners disagreed.

July 21, 1608: Warraskoyack to Jamestown

The last legs of the journey up the winding James River took another day,[66] using the tides and perhaps a wind that had backed to south or southeast, following the course of the James. But Smith and his party were in high enough spirits that they decided to play a practical joke on the inhabitants of Jamestown Fort. All the English had been living in fear of a Spanish military strike in the territory the king of Spain considered his own. So the mariners trimmed their barge's rigging with "painted streamers and such devices as we could,"[67] so that the color scheme would look "Spanish" rather than "English." The ruse worked: "We made them at James town jealous [afraid] of a Spanish frigate [following the scouting boat]."

Thus, on his first voyage around the bay, John Smith covered a great deal of territory, though not as much as he would have liked. And he brought all his men back in good health. He would not be so fortunate the next time around.

John Smith's Second Voyage up the Chesapeake Bay: July 24–September 7, 1608

Wayne E. Clark, Kent Mountford, and Edward Haile

THE RETURNEES FROM JOHN SMITH's first voyage[1] found the Jamestown fort in disarray and in sore need of being put to rights. Among other things, the president, John Ratliffe, had feathered his own nest at others' expense, allocating much of the food to himself and his friends and putting the others to work building him a fancy house outside the fort. Feeling was so strong against him that the colony deposed him and elected in his stead the newly returned, obviously successful John Smith. Smith took charge within three short days, seeing to it that work on the new house was abandoned and the men were properly fed. Then, appointing Matthew Scrivener his stand-in, he prepared to set forth again and finish the rest of his program in the Chesapeake. He took along some of the same men, while he replaced others.[2] There were only twelve people in the barge this time, and it seems that a greater proportion of them were relatively new arrivals in Virginia, having come with the First Supply a few months before. The summer heat and the still-unfamiliar microbes would wreak havoc on the expedition at a crucial time. Except for its slightly reduced crew, the expedition would use the same plank-and-frame barge and equipment as before. Smith planned to return by September 10, 1608, at the end of the term of deposed President Ratliffe, so he could assume the role of president at the start of the next term for that office. This allowed him seven weeks to complete his explorations.

July 24, 1608: Depart from Jamestown

Smith was now focused on certain areas in the Chesapeake, namely the head of the bay and the Rappahannock River, in which he hoped to find minerals and meet Massawomecks, who could tell him how far to the west the larger rivers led. He would not return to the Eastern Shore or the Potomac. His eagerness to secure answers for the Virginia Company (and, of course, for England) led him to depart from Jamestown after only three days in port,[3] where the internecine fighting was at such a pitch that the unknowns of the upper Chesapeake Bay seemed minor by comparison. Another trigger for his departure may have been a favorable wind from the southwest to speed him down the James. The tide was probably yet another factor: the last week of July was a time of spring tides, for the full moon fell on July 27.

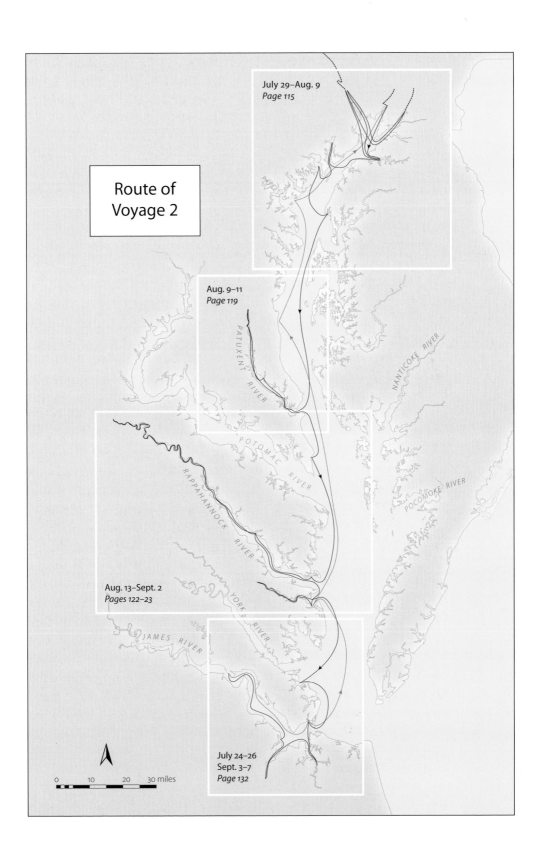

Route of
Voyage 2

July 29–Aug. 9
Page 115

Aug. 9–11
Page 119

PATUXENT RIVER

NANTICOKE RIVER

POTOMAC RIVER

POCOMOKE RIVER

RAPPAHANNOCK RIVER

Aug. 13–Sept. 2
Pages 122–23

YORK RIVER

JAMES RIVER

July 24–26
Sept. 3–7
Page 132

0   10   20   30 miles

July 25–26, 1608: Staying at Kecoughtan

Apparently because of a weather system coming up the coast, the winds changed the next day, and for two days held east or northeast, which for any seventeenth-century sailing vessel was an unfavorable direction for northerly progress. This development meant that the barge could not be sailed past Old Point Comfort and out into the bay. So Smith and the crew stayed "two or three days" with the Kecoughtans (*Map Stop 7.24-7.26*),[4] who were convinced that Smith was now heading north to assault their enemies the Massawomecks. Smith let them believe what they wished. One evening he had some aerial rockets (flares) fired off to impress his hosts. Having never seen anything like it before, they were terrified, and more convinced than ever (or so Smith understood through his beginner-level Powhatan) that these were indeed the people to face those dreaded warriors from the northwest.

July 27, 1608: Kecoughtan to Stingray Point

Once the nor'easter passed, the sky cleared and the wind shifted north, then west to assist his departure,[5] Smith wasted no time: he went straight up the bay for forty-five miles (72.4 kilometers), making about six knots (11 km/hr), and perhaps seven knots (13 km/hr) during the times of favoring tide. The barge lay at Stingray Point the first night out (*Map Stop 7.27*).[6]

July 28, 1608: Rappahannock River to Cove Point

The next day, the westerly probably failed,[7] becoming with fair weather a southerly breeze. Smith and his crew crossed the Potomac and Patuxent river mouths, possibly to spend the second night near Cove Point (*Map Stop 7.28*).

July 29, 1608: Cove Point to Mouth of Patapsco River

With favorable southerly wind and a flood tide behind them, the next day they continued toward the head of the bay.[8] Trouble was brewing, however, for by now all of the men who had come to Virginia in the First Supply were falling "sick almost to death until they were seasoned to the country." They would hardly be able to sit up, much less row; only six men, including Smith, remained active. However, the expedition could continue to move under sail. With the men ill, the goal would be to sail northward without exploring the smaller tributaries along the bay's Western Shore. With a southerly wind, plus two flood tides and a contrary ebb between, they could average five or six knots (5.8–6.9 mph or 9.3–11.1 km/hr), and they would be able to clear Bodkin Point at the mouth of the Patapsco before nightfall. They may have anchored in the lee of Bodkin Point at the mouth of Bodkin Creek[9] or else continued to the opposite shore to spend the night in Old Road Bay (*Map Stop 7.29*). They believed from their previous voyage that the area had no inhabitants to threaten them. They probably replenished their water supply there, at a spring found on their previous exploration.[10]

July 30, 1608: Patapsco River to Head of North East River

Sailing north, they would see the openings of the Gunpowder and Bush rivers.[11] Beyond Worton Point, the Sassafras River opens to starboard, and they could "see the bay divide in two heads, and arriving there [at today's Turkey Point] we found it [the bay] divided in four, all of which we searched as far as we could sail them." Because the Elk River headed northeast, they probably headed for it with the wind behind them. Having sailed into it to the head of tide, from which a small stream issued, they rested for the night (*Map Stop 7.30*).

The ensuing exploring work would be slow, with so many men out of commission. Light bay-breeze winds develop through the morning and tend to blow directly up each of the head-of-the-Chesapeake rivers, drawn in on many sunny days by the vacuum created as warm air rises from the warming land. That would have helped the barge ascend those rivers a little faster. They could have rowed downstream with the tide either before winds came up or late in the day when they fell calm. Smith probably saved the Susquehanna until later, though thanks to the vagueness of his account, his itinerary remains uncertain. We will assume below that the mapping of the minor rivers, exclusive of the Sassafras, took three days.

July 31, 1608: North East River to Sassafras (Tockwogh) River

Having spent the night without seeing anyone, they may have felt safe enough to leave the sick crew with a few able-bodied sailors and send a small land party to walk six miles (nearly 10 kilometers) up Little North East Creek until it divided into two smaller tributaries. Here they placed a cross to claim the head of the bay for the English nation (*Map Stop 7.31-1*) before returning to the barge. They headed down the North East River, perhaps with the wind light, the tide favorable, and a few men at the oars, and continued around the head of the bay over what are now the Susquehanna Flats.[12] They later discovered the true source of the Chesapeake Bay to be the impressive Susquehanna River. But with its out-flowing current and the diminished crew unable to row up it, they bypassed the mouth for the time and probably continued counterclockwise around the Susquehanna Flats.[13] With a light southerly wind and no waves to contend with, they passed Spesutie Island, Sandy Point, and Turkey Point and headed toward the Sassafras (Tockwogh) River, which they had not explored the day before (any favorable southerly winds being lost upon entering the river, with its high cliffs along the waterside). Then, just as they were about to enter the Sassafras, they spotted seven or eight canoes coming out towards the bay—light, fast, birch-bark canoes, meaning the occupants were Massawomecks.[14]

The Massawomecks, whose identity remains uncertain (see chapter 10), made ready to fight. That put the explorers in a terrible predicament: seven of the thirteen men were too incapacitated to defend themselves. John Smith was a quick and canny thinker, however. He had the healthy crew leave off rowing while the enemy was a good distance off and hide the sick under the tarpaulin. Then he had sticks inserted into the spaces made by the boat's frame heads and the rail-and-stringers that formed the gunwales; atop each stick he ordered the placement of a hat from one of the sick men. Between each pair of sticks, he placed a man with two muskets, giving the impression of many more armed men than the barge actually carried. When the Massawomecks were close enough to see the "men" and guns clearly, they retreated and paddled to shore, "and there stayed, staring at the sailing of our barge till we anchored right against [opposite] them." The English made friendly signs, but the warriors would not move, and there matters remained for a while. The place may have been in calm, sheltered water along the high cliffs east of Howell Point ("Point Pisinge") (*Map Stop 7.31-2*) or just past the cliffs, in the lower ground near Betterton.

Finally two unarmed warriors paddled out, with the rest boarding their canoes in case of trouble. But there was none: instead the emissaries received metal bells, which were a novelty to them. That broke the ice, and a brisk trade followed in which Smith was able to acquire not only fish, venison, bear meat, and bear skins but also Massawomeck weapons (bows, arrows, and war clubs) and—quite useful later—shields ("targets," in Smith's parlance). In spite of the language barrier, the warriors made it plain that they had been fighting with the Tockwoghs, displaying their fresh wounds. The trading and questioning (largely fruitless, judging by the vagueness of Smith's map in the northwest) went on until nightfall. Smith expected to see them again in the morning, but they were gone. He understood later that they had gone up the Bush River.[15]

Braced for meeting the Massawomecks, Smith tried to give the impression that his cadre of armed men was larger than the five crew members who were still healthy enough to defend the barge. (Pen and ink illustration by Marc Castelli for the Captain John Smith Four Hundred Project)

August 1, 1608: Up the Sassafras (Tockwogh) River

Having learned of the Tockwoghs from the Massawomecks, Smith moved slowly up the Sassafras River.[16] The going was probably slow because of the high cliffs to the south and the fact that most of his men still could not row. As they progressed up the river, an alarm conveyed to the Tockwogh village brought the men downriver in canoes to surround and attack the barge. Smith used his best Powhatan language skills to convey his friendly intentions to trade, but the Tockwoghs spoke a different Algonquian language.[17] As it happened, one of the Tockwoghs was bilingual, speaking Tockwogh and Powhatan. He conveyed Smith's friendly intent to his compatriots, and both sides then met in the river, where the Tockwoghs saw the distinctive Massawomeck weapons. As he had done at Kecoughtan, Smith allowed these people to think that he had bested those ferocious warriors, which the local men welcomed as good news and escorted the barge seven miles (11¼ kilometers) upriver to their palisaded town. The fortifications consisted of upright poles with interwoven branches and formal breastworks. The village was probably sited on the headland that jutted out the farthest on the south side (*Map Stop 8.1*).

The Englishmen observed that the Tockwoghs had iron cutting tools and pieces of brass, so Smith immediately asked how they had acquired them. The answer: from the Susquehannocks, who were their allies and who lived two days' journey above the falls in the Susquehanna River. Now, that was another group of people that the Virginia Company would want Smith to question! So he persuaded the Tockwogh speaker of Powhatan to take another bilingual Tockwogh, who spoke Susquehannock, and go to the Susquehannocks' town to invite them to a meeting. Smith and his men then relaxed and enjoyed the local hospitality.

August 2, 1608: Tockwogh to Smith's Falls on the Susquehanna River

Having feasted and rested, the crew and two Tockwogh interpreters sailed the barge down the Sassafras River, likely with persisting south winds, continuing across the Susquehanna Flats to the mouth of the Susquehannock and then up that river to the head of tide at Smith's Falls (*Map Stop 8.2-1*).[18] The two interpreters disembarked and told the English that the trip to and from the lowest downriver village, Sasquesahanough, would take from three to four days. Smith promised to return to the falls in three days to wait for them. After the interpreters left, he had his men plant a cross at Smith's Falls to claim the river for the English. The rest of the day they went down the river with the currents, exploring various islands in the river valley (as noted on the Smith map). Meanwhile, the two interpreters traveled twenty miles (32 kilometers) to the area of the York barrens in Pennsylvania, before resting for the night (*Map Stop 8.2-2*).[19] The barge could have returned to Susquehanna Flats to spend the night (*Map Stop 8.2-3*).

August 3, 1608: Susquehanna River to Head of Elk River

With a day to explore, Smith probably decided to sail across the Susquehanna Flats and pass the North East River to Turkey Point, so they could turn north to explore the Elk River to the head of tide. Trending to the east, Smith neglected the Bohemia River, whose mouth he could see plainly, and omitted showing it on his map. At the head of the Elk, the party spent the night (*Map Stop 8.3/8.4-1*). Meanwhile, the two Tockwogh interpreters reached the village of Sasquesahanough on the east side of the river in the area of today's village of Washington Boro, which also happens to be the name of the archaeological site found there.

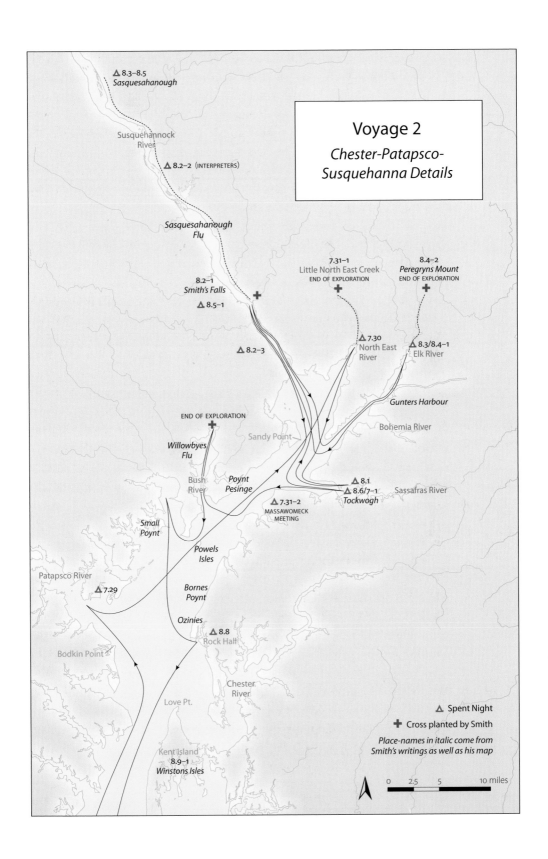

△ 8.3–8.5
Sasquesahanough

Susquehannock
River

△ 8.2–2 (INTERPRETERS)

*Sasquesahanough
Flu*

7.31–1
Little North East Creek
END OF EXPLORATION

8.4–2
Peregryns Mount
END OF EXPLORATION

8.2–1
Smith's Falls

△ 8.5–1

△ 8.2–3

△ 7.30
North East
River

△ 8.3/8.4–1
Elk River

Gunters Harbour

Bohemia River

END OF EXPLORATION

*Willowbyes
Flu*

Sandy Point

Bush
River

*Poynt
Pesinge*

△ 8.1

△ 8.6/7–1
Tockwogh

Sassafras River

△ 7.31–2
MASSAWOMECK
MEETING

*Small
Poynt*

*Powels
Isles*

Patapsco River

△ 7.29

*Bornes
Poynt*

Ozinies

△ 8.8
Rock Hall

Bodkin Point

Chester
River

Love Pt.

Kent Island
8.9–1
Winstons Isles

Voyage 2
*Chester-Patapsco-
Susquehanna Details*

△ Spent Night

✝ Cross planted by Smith

*Place-names in italic come from
Smith's writings as well as his map*

0   2.5   5   10 miles

August 4, 1608: Head of Elk River to Big Elk Creek

Those of Smith's crew who were still sick were left on the barge with some healthy sailors while a small shore party walked up Big Elk Creek, a distance of eight miles (nearly 13 kilometers), probably searching for minerals as they went. Here the creek splits into two tributaries. They left the stream to climb the 250-foot-plus-high (76-plus-meter) "Peregryns Mount" (in what is now the Fair Hill Natural Resource Management Area), upon which they placed a metal cross to claim another river for England (*Map Stop 8.4-2*). From the hilltop, they looked eastward down the headwaters of the Christina River valley. They may have observed the Delaware Bay as a vague body of water in the far distance, as noted on Smith's map. Returning to the barge with news of their discovery, they rested from their eight-hour hike up and down the Big Elk Creek.[20]

Up at the village of Sasquesahanough, the two Tockwogh interpreters rested and answered questions while waiting for the local leadership to assemble at the village. They all enjoyed feasting and dancing that evening at the news of the defeat of the Massawomeck raiding party.

August 5, 1608: Elk Creek to Smith's Falls on Susquehanna River

The barge departed the head of the Elk River to recross the Susquehanna Flats and go up the river itself to Smith's Falls, where they waited for the return of the interpreters the next day. The sky may have been showing, unknown to them, the clouds that presaged a warm front, which would be preceded by strong winds up the bay. Meanwhile, at the village, the assembled leadership of the Susquehannocks conferred all day to come to a collective decision to meet with the English, to pick the warriors who would attend, and to select the trade goods and load them in the canoes for the half-day trip downriver the next morning.[21]

August 6, 1608: Smith's Falls to Tockwogh Village

Early in the afternoon, the English saw the Susquehannock fleet of canoes coming downriver with sixty people and a cargo of presents and trading goods: "venison, tobacco pipes . . . baskets, targets [shields], bows, and arrows."[22] Five of the leaders "came boldly aboard us" (the barge) to be taken "across the bay for Tockwogh." The rest stayed behind for the time being, "the wind being so high they durst not pass." That was not a thunderstorm, which would have kept the English where they were, too. It was probably the winds before a warm front, south and southwest ones that can blow hard and sustained in the upper bay, creating a short, nasty chop. The Indians' heavy canoes (presumably dugouts; only Massawomecks are mentioned as having bark canoes) would have taken the waves broadside and been swamped out on the flats. The barge, with its rectangular mainsail and jib, could shape a course (they were likely on a high reach) toward the Sassafras River's mouth and push through some of the chop. After the front passed, the subsequent wind shift allowed them to proceed up the Sassafras River to the village of Tockwogh, where feasting and dancing took place that evening (*Map Stop 8.6-8.7*)

August 7, 1608: Tockwogh Village

Smith wrote that the Susquehannocks were gigantic in stature, which has since been belied by the archaeological evidence in their homeland. Tall men may have been deliberately chosen to overawe Smith. Smith in turn wanted to impress them, as well as interview them. He inadvertently found that one of his and his crew's practices served the purpose, after the arrival back at Tockwogh. Most English people in those days held daily morning prayer services[23] that included an Old Testament psalm, which was chanted.[24] In the hearing of the Susquehannock leaders (and the Tockwoghs), Smith led his men in a service. The singing struck a chord with the Susquehannock leaders. Were they being honored by a song? Was this part of the trade and friendship ritual of the foreigners? After a consultation among themselves, they reciprocated with a song of their own, apparently calling upon their deity (represented by the sun) to bless Smith (whom they embraced, to his embarrassment). A passionate oration followed, after which they presented Smith with a great many of the things they had brought, including a "great chain of white beads" (a wampum belt).[25] Smith understood—or thought he did, through two interpreters and his own shaky Powhatan—that the Indians were making him their "governor" in exchange for his protection against the Massawomecks. It is more likely that they were simply making a formal alliance with him, for the Tockwoghs had confirmed what the interpreters had told them at the outset: these foreigners had defeated their mutual enemies. Another afternoon and evening of entertainment followed, providing much-needed food and rest for Smith's crew. They were probably feeling much better by this time and ready to travel with the return of good winds and tide.

August 8, 1608: Sassafras (Tockwogh) River to Rock Hall Area, Mouth of Chester River

Smith's observations and conversations had shown that the bay's headwaters were not the famed Northwest Passage, but rather another river (the Susquehanna) that headed north into the territories of mountain-dwelling people with whom the Susquehannocks traded for European goods from Canada. Having established trade relations and alliances with the native peoples, and learning of the Ozinies to the south on the Eastern Shore, it was time to return to Jamestown. The wind may also have shifted to the northwest, brisk, cooler—a "favorable" wind to run down the narrow part of the bay that no decent sailor would pass up, since at that season it would only last for a day or so. The Susquehannocks were reluctant to see their new ally go, but Smith promised to return the next year, a promise he could not keep.[26] It would have been a speedy trip down the bay, with the tide helping; Smith may have checked out creek mouths for potential settlement sites and perhaps looked into the Bush River where the Massawomecks had gone.[27] Then he visited the village of Ozinies, learning their strength in war (see chapter 10) and mapping Swan Point (his Bornes Point) and Rock Hall Bay. He may have anchored in the latter for the night (*Map Stop 8.8*), or, wanting to continue south, he may have continued on the following ebb to get clear of today's Sandy Point, where the flood tide stops progress by slower vessels.

August 9, 1608: Chester River to Patuxent River

At this point, Smith wrote merely that he and his crew "returned to discover the River of Pawtuxunt,"[28] but it is probable that he learned whatever he put on his map about the upper Eastern Shore during August 8 and 9. Leaving on August 9 from the Rock Hall area, he must have sailed somewhat southwest to clear Love Point at the northern tip of Kent Island (*Map Stop 8.9-1*), implying a northwesterly wind. From that route, he probably got the impression that the Chester was like Tangier Sound, a north-south thoroughfare behind the eastern Winstons Isles (Kent and Tilghman islands) that he had seen in the distance on his three previous passes up and down the bay. Now, heading for the Western Shore for the voyage south, and clearly showing his own focus upon the people and possible mineral riches to the northwest, he once again left the Chester, Wye, Miles, and Choptank rivers for later English mapmakers to record.[29]

Crossing the bay, Smith reached the mouth of the Patuxent River and this time, no longer curious about the upper bay, he entered it, but not

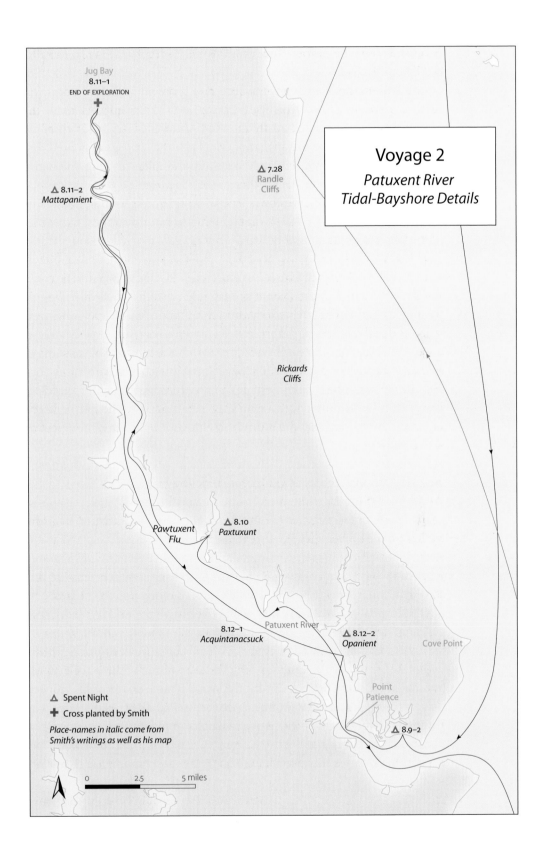

Jug Bay
8.11–1
END OF EXPLORATION

△ 7.28
Randle
Cliffs

Voyage 2
*Patuxent River
Tidal-Bayshore Details*

△ 8.11–2
Mattapanient

*Rickards
Cliffs*

*Pawtuxent
Flu*

△ 8.10
Paxtuxunt

8.12–1
Acquintanacsuck

Patuxent River

△ 8.12–2
Opanient

Cove Point

Point
Patience

△ 8.9–2

△ Spent Night
✚ Cross planted by Smith

*Place-names in italic come from
Smith's writings as well as his map*

0   2.5   5 miles

necessarily very far at first. The favorable northerly wind may have failed by this time; in the next few days, southerly upriver winds together with favorable tides would expedite their journey. But there are strong currents where the river narrows at Point Patience, and they needed a flood tide for an ascent that would not be extremely laborious. Smith's account says nothing of what the tide was doing when he arrived. If he passed Cove Point on the tail of an ebb pushing him south and then quickly caught the succeeding flood into the Patuxent, there need have been no wait. Otherwise, wanting to conserve his men's energy by sailing, Smith would have had to anchor and wait for the tide to turn. Point Patience was aptly named by future generations of mariners! (*Map Stop 8.9-2*)

August 10, 1608: Point Patience to Pawtuxunt Village on Battle Creek
Smith's map tells us most of what he was able to learn about the Patuxent; he says little in his writings except that the channel is sixteen to eighteen fathoms deep in places (thanks to the scouring current) and that the people were "very tractable and more civil than any."[30] The meaning of that phrase and the locations of the towns will be discussed in chapter 11; Smith's voyage upriver will also be reconstructed in more detail. Yet again, Smith either was not much interested, or he knew his readers would not be much interested, in a river that could not be a Northwest Passage. The uncanny accuracy of his map indicates that they ascended the river. The naming of every village mapped suggests he took a local Algonquian guide on the barge to help with the exploration and mapping.[31]

On August 10, the wind would be best later in the day, when the southerly upbay wind penetrated up the river; and it would often weaken the farther upstream he went, because it was late summer and land and water were close to the same temperature, dampening the sea-breeze effect. That would have necessitated rowing and canny use of the tidal currents, which were peaking in velocity with the new moon that night. At Point Patience, the tidal current reaches a velocity of one knot (1.15 mph or 1.85 km/hr) or perhaps a little faster. The party would have done well to cover ten miles (16 kilometers) a day, for during the ebb (traveling upstream) or the flood (going downstream) the tide would have been against them. They would have been smart to anchor during the peak of such adverse tides (about two hours).[32] This first day on the river, they sailed along its eastern shore and noted two villages, perhaps stopping at one to establish friendly relations and to ask for directions to the weroance village to trade and establish friendship. They would have been directed to the weroance village of Pawtuxunt on the eastern shore of Battle Creek, where they would have spent the night with feasting and festivities (*Map Stop 8.10*).

August 11, 1608: Pawtuxunt Village to Mattapanient Village

Fortunately for the explorers, the Pawtuxunt weroance was the most important chief in the valley, so good relations with him ensured a warm reception by all. Probably with a guide on board, the barge then sailed along the eastern shore, mapping two more villages of the Pawtuxunt chiefdom before they came to a ten-mile-long (16-kilometer) stretch that their guide may have explained to them was the hunting territory between chiefdoms (see chapter 13). They then began noting a series of villages on the narrower upriver section.

Smith did not place a cross mark at the end of his exploration, but his map indicates that he noted the curves in the river as far north as the tip of today's Merkle Wildlife Management area, south of Kings Branch on the eastern shore (*Map Stop 8.11-1*). After this point, the river narrows before expanding again at Jug Bay. Since Smith did not note Jug Bay, he never reached that far before turning back. He might have stopped at the weroance village of the upper chiefdom to satisfy protocol and spend the night, even though he does not show which of the villages was the chief's. In the 1630s, the weroance resided in the village of Mattapanient, and as Smith calls this upriver chiefdom "Mattpanient," we can assume the same applied in 1608 (*Map Stop 8.11-2*).

August 12, 1608: Mattapanient Village to Acquintanacsuck Village

With the end of the flood tide, the voyagers rowed downriver, assisted by the current and noting the mouths only of the many tributaries. Custom required a visit and trading session with the weroance of the Acquintanacsuck chiefdom, at the village of the same name (*Map Stop 8.12-1*). After trading and being entertained by the Acquintanacsucks, they may have traveled downriver to the eastern-bank village of Opanient (*Map Stop 8.12-2*), to return their guide and position themselves for the next day's run past Point Patience.

August 13, 1608: Patuxent River to St. Jerome Creek below Point No Point

Smith provides no details of this part of the journey,[33] but given the season and the "spring" tides surrounding the new moon that had occurred three days before, the winds if southwesterly would have permitted sailing down the river and clearing today's Cedar Point. The barge could also carry sail, at least to Point No Point and possibly to Point Lookout, making a day's run of just twenty-eight miles (45 kilometers). A slow run to the Potomac River's mouth rowing at three knots (3.5 mph or 5.5 km/hr) would only cover about ten miles (16 kilometers) a day, with two ebb tides helping. So the barge crew probably supplemented their rowing by simultaneously sailing close to the wind. They probably did not try rowing against the flood tides. Presumably they anchored and rested in St. Jerome Creek, to put them in a good position to tackle the conditions of the mouth of the Potomac the next day (*Map Stop 8.13*).

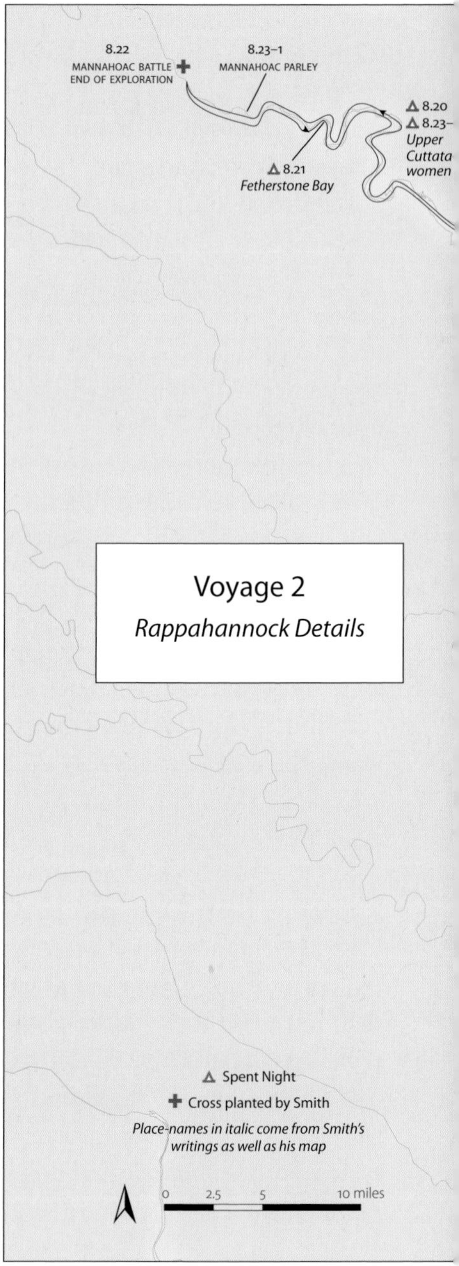

August 14, 1608: Potomac River to Rappahannock River

Whenever the wind "backed" again to the south or southeast, their run to the Rappahannock River would more easily allow Smith and his men to counteract adverse Potomac currents and navigate past the smaller rivers and creeks on the east end of the Northern Neck and past Cedar Point, coming to anchor at the northern shore of the mouth of the Rappahannock River. Having explored the neck's eastern waterways on the first voyage, they did not

8.22
MANNAHOAC BATTLE
END OF EXPLORATION

8.23–1
MANNAHOAC PARLEY

△ 8.20
△ 8.23–
Upper
Cuttata
women

△ 8.21
Fetherstone Bay

Voyage 2
Rappahannock Details

△ Spent Night
✚ Cross planted by Smith
Place-names in italic come from Smith's writings as well as his map

0   2.5   5   10 miles

need to do so now. Their goal was exploring the Rappahannock River, an "excellent, pleasant, well inhabited, fertile and a goodly navigable river."[34]

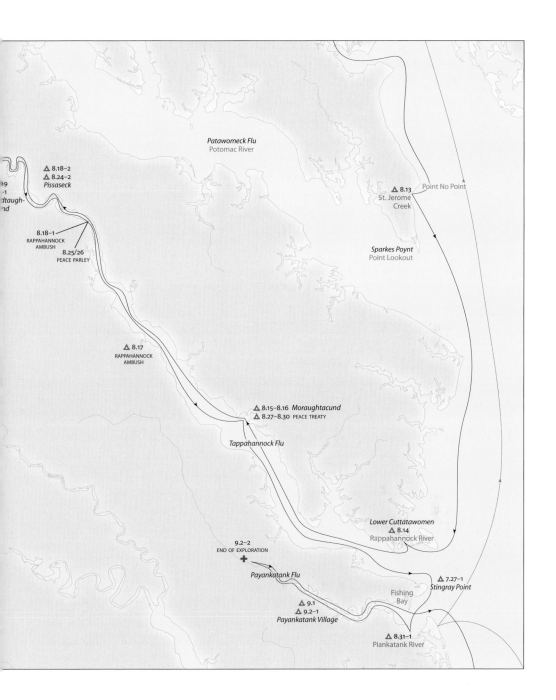

△ 8.18–2
△ 8.24–2
Pissaseck

19
–1
*ttaugh-
nd*

8.18–1
RAPPAHANNOCK
AMBUSH

8.25/26
PEACE PARLEY

△ 8.17
RAPPAHANNOCK
AMBUSH

Patawomeck Flu
Potomac River

△ 8.13
St. Jerome
Creek

Point No Point

Sparkes Poynt
Point Lookout

△ 8.15–8.16 *Moraughtacund*
△ 8.27–8.30 PEACE TREATY

Tappahannock Flu

Lower Cuttatawomen
△ 8.14
Rappahannock River

9.2–2
END OF EXPLORATION
✚

Payankatank Flu

△ 7.27–1
Stingray Point

*Fishing
Bay*

△ 9.1
△ 9.2–1
Payankatank Village

△ 8.31–1
Piankatank River

August 15–16, 1608: Mouth of River to Moraughtacund Village

Arriving at Moraughtacund (*Map Stop 8.15-8.16*)—there is no mention of visiting the downstream Cuttatawomens, though he probably did so—

Smith was reunited with the bearded Wiccocomico man Mosco, who probably intercepted them there after hearing that the English party was making its way (at a snail's pace) past the Northern Neck and into the Rappahannock. Smith's subsequent adventures, with Mosco assisting, were described in infinitely more detail than any other part of his voyages; they were also written from memory in 1624. In 1612, next to nothing is said about the Rappahannock exploration, other than that Smith subdued the Rappahannocks themselves. Mosco probably went to Moraughtacund to intercept his English friends, and the weroance there treated the English with great kindness. They probably spent an extra day learning of the river's layout, peoples and politics, with feasting and resting prior to proceeding into hostile Rappahannock territory.

August 17, 1608: Moraughtacund to Rappahannocks' Ambush at Cat Point Creek

Mosco informed Smith that because he had accepted Moraughtacund hospitality, the Rappahannocks would now be enemies to the English. The reason was that the Moraughtacund chief had stolen three of the Rappahannock chief's wives, an insult not lightly forgiven. If the English were to go there, Mosco warned, they would run into trouble. Smith suspected that Mosco was trying to help the Moraughtacunds keep all the English trade goods for themselves, "so we crossed the river to the Rappahannocks."[35] It turned out, however, that Mosco had been right. On the north shore of the river, possibly near the mouth of Piscataway Creek (*Map Stop 8.17*), a dozen or so Rappahannocks beckoned the English ashore with baskets of goods to trade, and once hostages had been exchanged, mounted an attack. The two hostages began making their way back to the barge through a barrage of arrows, while Smith had his other men set up the Massawomeck shields around "the fore part of our boat like a forecastle." Using this barrier for cover, he and the gentlemen let loose musket fire that drove the warriors back into the woods; holding the shields on their arms, they then rescued Anas Todkill, the English hostage. The attackers had left their dead, their arrows, and their four canoes behind; Smith had the arrows broken to prevent reuse, except for some he kept for Mosco. Mosco also received the canoes, making him instantly a wealthy man. The party returned to Moraughtacund territory, where Smith and his men spent the rest of the day working on the barge, setting up sticks so that the Massawomeck shields could be fastened around the gunwales to serve "as waistcloths." There was a triumphant feast in town that night.

Oars shipped and Massawomeck shields on the Smith expedition's barge, a tactic Smith employed upon the advice of his Algonquian interpreter Mosco. As a result, the entire crew survived barrages of Mannahoac and Rappahannock arrows. (Pen and ink illustration by Marc Castelli for the Captain John Smith Four Hundred Project)

August 18, 1608: Cat Point Creek to Pissaseck

The next morning Smith headed upriver,[36] and when Mosco ran to catch up with the departing barge, they took him back aboard. The explorers had left without this ally of the Moraughtacunds in hopes of passing through the Rappahannocks' territory with favorable tide and light and without further trouble. The barge probably hugged the southern shore now, because all the Rappahannock villages were located along the northern shore.

At first, this leg of the journey seems to have been uneventful. Given the Rappahannocks' hostility, Smith did not visit any of their settlements and inquire about which town was the capital and what the towns' names were; Mosco may have been able to fill him in (otherwise that information would have had to wait until later, when peace was made). There may have been no one in the towns to attack him, however, for the men had gone upriver on foot to set the next ambush. By the time the explorers passed the villages of Pissacoack, Matchopick, and Wecuppom, they thought they were in friendly territory again. Reaching Beverley Marsh opposite Carters

Wharf (*Map Stop 8.18-1*), they had become both tired and vulnerable. The river not only narrows there but turns left toward what is now Leedstown. Smith's crew would have been rowing, with the wind probably unfavorable and decreasing that far upriver. So this site, naturally, was where thirty or forty Rappahannocks (as Mosco reported) let fly a hail of arrows from the bushes along the riverbank. Smith had a musket volley shot off, which made the attackers take cover, although they appeared afterward, when Smith was a half mile (almost a kilometer) away, "dancing and singing very merrily" (in derision). The voyagers pressed on another five miles (8 kilometers) upriver, to spend the night at Pissaseck (*Map Stop 8.18-2*), whose weroance welcomed both them and their exotic trade goods.

August 19, 1608: Pissaseck to Nandtaughtacund Villages
Smith noted only that the people farther upriver—Pissasecks, Nandtaughtacunds, and Cuttatawomens—were friendly.[37] These people appealed to Mosco as an intermediary to get the English to come ashore, visit, and trade. Smith does not say how many days he spent in this part of the river, but each stop would have been time-consuming, however pleasant, for the Algonquian-speakers' ideas of hospitality involved elaborate feasting, oratory, and dancing to honor the guests. Besides, the upstream rowing between stops (the winds being negligible for sailing and the river meandering) would have made long visits welcome.

The next weroance's village was located on the southeast side of the broad Portobago Bay. They would have spent the night there, at Nandtaughtacund (*Map Stop 8.19*).

August 20, 1608: Nandtaughtacund to Upper Cuttatawomen Villages
The expedition members must have been pleased to be in friendly territory now, where the river became increasingly narrow and forced them to row upriver with the flood and slack tides. At the head of the oxbow of Skinkers Neck, they arrived at the weroance's village of Cuttatawomen, near modern Hopyard Landing (*Map Stop 8.20*). They would have kept their concerns about one seriously ill crewmate to themselves, as they participated in the festivities that evening.

August 21, 1608: Cuttatawomen Village to Fetherstones Bay
Richard Fetherstone, a gentleman member of the crew, was very sick indeed, either from the same bout of the malady (possibly malaria) that had struck the First Supply men three weeks before or perhaps from heat stroke, which

threatened all the rowers in that hot weather. Everyone else had recovered, but now poor Featherstone died when the barge was somewhere between Secobeck and Massawoteck. The company gave him a formal burial, either overboard or in the marsh, "in a little bay we called 'Fetherstones Bay'" (*Map Stop 8.21*), concluding the service with a volley of shot. Fetherstones Bay may have been on the northeast side of Moss Neck, with the swamp in that area shown on Smith's map as an island. Depressed and reflective, the survivors probably spent the night there, with no desire to put on the public face that would be required if they stopped for a feast at the next village.

August 22, 1608: Fetherstones Bay to the Fall Line to Hollywood Bar
Smith and his men continued on upriver,[38] going "as high as our boat would float." The barge may have run aground a mile or two (a few kilometers) short of the fall line,[39] in a shallow stretch of the river just below modern Fredericksburg (*Map Stop 8.22*), in the area of today's Chatham Bridge (Virginia Route 2). The explorers went ashore, "digging in the earth, looking of stones, herbs, and springs." After an hour, the attack came: one hundred Indian men shot at them while "skipping from tree to tree." Smith and his men began doing the same (this was not the time to stand upon his dignity, with European ideas of "bravery"), with Mosco taking a particularly enthusiastic part, and after a half hour the warriors withdrew up the river. They left a man behind, however, unconscious rather than dead. John Smith had him carried to the barge, over Mosco's vehement protests (he's an enemy! kill him!), and had the physician treat him. Smith appeased Mosco by having the other crewmen gather up the enemies' arrows and give them to him, "an armful." Given that each arrow took most of a day to make, they were decidedly valuable to a professional bowman. Mosco was becoming wealthier yet.

Mosco now made himself useful in another way: he was able to communicate with the captive, named Amoroleck, either by signs or by some knowledge of the language he spoke (Smith does not say). Once again John Smith interviewed someone from beyond the fall line, this time through only one interpreter plus his shaky knowledge of Powhatan. He found that Amoroleck was from one of the Mannahoac towns, Hassinunga, on the upper Rappahannock (see chapter 13). But the man did not know what was beyond the mountains: only that mountains lay to the west.

Smith gave his erstwhile prisoner many presents and tried to get him to return downriver with the party. Amoroleck, knowing that his people's Algonquian-speaking enemies would put him decidedly at risk, no matter what Smith told them, argued instead for the explorers' staying where they were; his fellow warriors would surely return to take care of their dead. That disturbed Mosco, but Smith overruled him. The party would stay, but remain on guard. As night fell, they boarded the barge, set up the Massawomeck targets as a sort of deck, and anchored in midriver, the river being dangerously narrow, with a cliff on one side. It was three days before the full moon, so the enemy could see them dimly until the wee hours of the morning.

After a time (Smith was not precise), arrows began "dropping on every side [of] the boat": the Mannahoacs were back, apparently with reinforcements, making such loud war cries that Amoroleck's shouts to them could not be heard. Smith had the anchor weighed to let the barge drift downstream; someone probably manned a couple of muffled oars to keep it at midriver and assist the current. The Mannahoacs followed, shouting taunts while the English occasionally shot at them. Thus it went for Smith's estimate of twelve slow miles, probably nine miles (14.5 kilometers) in reality as that was still in the buffer zone. By daybreak the barge had reached a broad bay and could anchor safely so the occupants could have breakfast (*Map Stop 8.23-1*). This pause was probably off the downstream end of Hollywood Bar.

August 23, 1608: Hollywood Bar to Cuttatawomen

Once the sun was up, the English untied the shields and let themselves and their Native American passengers be seen. That reassured the Mannahoacs on the shore: Amoroleck was not being held by enemies after all. The man himself shouted to his countrymen that the foreigners were good people, in fact having preserved him from a "Patawomeck" (Mosco) who had tried to kill him. They would bring Amoroleck ashore and free him if his compatriots would disarm. Harming the explorers was impossible anyway, he said— which was probably true, given their use of the Massawomeck shields. This argument convinced the Mannahoacs. They hung their weapons on trees, while two of them swam out to the boat with a bow and a quiver of arrows (held on their heads) to present formally to John Smith on behalf of the Hassinungas. Smith rewarded them but demanded the same from the leaders of the other Mannahoac towns; that demand also was met.

The barge then anchored at a low marshy point, and a friendly meeting was held in which John Smith probably queried the leaders to find out if they knew more about the lands to the west than Amoroleck did. They did not. A certain amount of trading went on, though the Mannahoacs had only weapons, tobacco bags, and pipes with them and the English would not part with any of their pistols (which the warriors took to be fancy pipes). Finally the English departed, leaving their new friends "making merry."

Exhausted now, they were hard-pressed to row down to Cuttatawomen (*Map Stop 8.23-2*), but had no choice in the matter because the weroance would expect a firsthand report on their victory.

August 24, 1608: Cuttatawomen to Pissaseck Villages
The explorers' progress downstream was slow, not so much due to unfavorable wind (which was probably southwesterly) and the winding river as from the celebrations they were given ashore as "conquerors" of the Mannahoacs.[40] Every district they passed would have wanted to play host to such powerful allies, and proper hospitality in the Indian world took time. They may have stopped at Nandtaughtacund (*Map Stop 8.24-1*) and then continued downriver with an escort of celebratory weroances and warriors. At the village of Pissaseck (*Map Stop 8.24-2*), the weroances of that village and Nandtaughtacund insisted that the English make peace with the Rappahannocks.

Smith countered this demand with the fact that the Rappahannocks had attacked him twice as he came upriver, and his conditions for making peace were stiff: the Rappahannocks would have to come unarmed into his presence, agree to make peace with the Moraughtacunds, present himself with the chief's own bow and arrows, and turn over the chief's son as a hostage before any meeting took place. (How very like a chief Smith sounds! Powhatan must have been furious when he was told—and he would, as overlord, receive a report.) The upriver chiefs agreed, probably after some haggling, to send word of the offer to the Rappahannocks, along with their assurance that they themselves would be present as intermediaries. The Rappahannocks agreed to a parley at the same creekside place where they had previously ambushed the English. After this message came back up the river, the night at Pissaseck was spent in planning mixed with feasting.

August 25, 1608: Pissaseck to Rappahannocks' Ambushing Place at Piscataway Creek
The parley went well.[41] The Rappahannocks met all but one of Smith's demands. As the chief could not bear to give up his one and only son, he made a counteroffer: he would give up his claim to the three wives the Moraughtacund chief had abducted—and give them to John Smith instead. That saved face for himself and put Smith in a delicate position. He wanted to be counted as a chief, but he did not desire any wives.[42] Smith accepted the offer, however, for he knew of a custom among the people that he could utilize.

August 26–29, 1608: Shuttle Diplomacy

Mosco, Smith and his crew, and perhaps also the chiefs of Pissaseck and Nandtaughtacund, spent the next several days sounding out the Moraughtacund chief about giving up his claim to the wives in the interest of peace, securing his acceptance and his consent to meet with the Rappahannock chief, and reporting back to the Rappahannocks. Word was then sent to towns up and down the river so that the men in them could go after deer and the women could begin collecting what they needed for a grand feast, to be cooked and eaten at Moraughtacund. People gathered from far and wide.

The three wives were presented to John Smith, and as the two chiefs' claims to them were now void, there was no longer any official reason for enmity. Smith then played Solomon with his new "possessions": he gave each woman a chain of beads, and, using a chief's prerogative, he gave away all three women. (The women were not consulted, but marriage to a chief may have been as temporary as marriage to Powhatan himself was: have a child, then be divorced or reassigned to another man.[43]) Smith first had the Rappahannock chief choose the woman he wanted to keep, then the Moraughtacund chief selected the one he preferred of the two remaining, and Mosco (now a VIP in the Indian world) received the third. Smith preserved his option to take a Christian wife in the future—something else, like fighting the Massawomecks or returning to Tockwogh, that he never did.

The rest of the day was spent celebrating with the townsmen and the visiting Rappahannocks. Mosco was a featured player and announced that after his great adventure, he had changed his name to *uttasantasough*, meaning "stranger" or Englishman. The name change was done to honor John Smith and his crew; new names also meant a change, usually an elevation, in one's status among that native people.[44]

August 31, 1608: Moraughtacund to Piankatank River

On or around the last day of August, John Smith and his crew set off well before the festivities were over (in the Indian world, they could go on for days).[45] Smith had to be back at Jamestown by September 10, and he might be fighting the prevailing south/southwesterly winds for much of the way. The expedition had to get under way, especially since there was another small river yet to explore to complete Smith's map. Although he had not found minerals or a Northwest Passage up the Rappahannock, the people on that river were now so friendly that they had promised to plant extra corn for the English the following year (or so Smith claimed), and he was ready to move on. So with shouts of farewell from shore and a volley of shot

John Smith's Chesapeake Voyages, 1607–1609

fired into the air by his men, Smith set out. He made good enough time that the barge was anchored in the Piankatank River by nightfall, probably at Fishing Bay (*Map Stop 8.31*).

September 1–3, 1608: Exploring the Piankatank River

In his writings, Smith glosses over the Piankatank except to say that he explored it and, in his 1624 version, that he saw few people, for most able-bodied persons were "a-hunting, save a few old men, women, and children that were tending their corn."[46] It was a dry year,[47] and the corn may have been the first (and only) crop that would come that year; thus the adults would still have been out foraging and unavailable to greet visitors.

Meanwhile, Smith mapped the Piankatank, which at that season and in that narrow, troughlike river valley meant a good deal of either tacking or rowing. His first stop, and where he probably spent the night of September 1, was the weroance's village of Payankatank (*Map Stop 9.1*). The chief was probably off hunting with his warriors, so the next day Smith's party went farther up river in search of them. His map indicates that he got as far as Dragon Run, possibly as far as the straight section past the bends (*Map Stop 9.2-1*).[48] He may also have taken his time in hopes that the chief and his councilors would return from hunting, but apparently that did not happen. The party would have spent the night again at the weroance's village. The few people in the towns promised Smith a share of the corn crop "when we would fetch it"—an arrangement that apparently angered Powhatan when he heard about it. (Here, on his back doorstep, his subjects were promising those interlopers what in a dry year would amount to *his* tribute.) By winter, Powhatan had set up an ambush that obliterated them: most of the men were killed, and the chief, women, and children were taken as captives to Werowocomoco.[49]

September 3–4, 1608: Piankatank River to Point Comfort

The morning of September 3, the explorers began what would be a slow passage back to Jamestown.[50] There was no wind for sail, so they had to row. They probably spent most of their energies during the ebb of the tide and rested during the peak of the flood. This day saw the only co-occurrence during either voyage of syzygy and perigee tides,[51] so the unusual ebb currents would have helped them southward. By nightfall they managed to pull into shelter in the mouth of the Poquoson River ("Gosnold's Bay") (*Map Stop 9.3*). Before long, however, a thunder squall came roaring in and the mariners suddenly found themselves bailing instead of sleeping. Smith

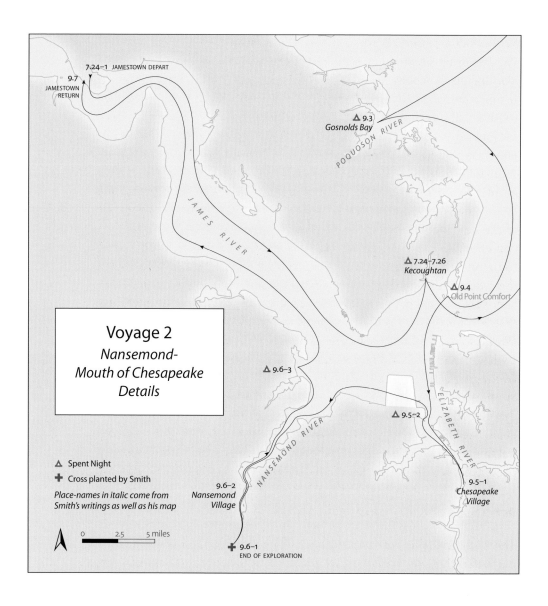

Voyage 2
*Nansemond-
Mouth of Chesapeake
Details*

△ 7.24–7.26
Kecoughtan

△ 9.4
Old Point Comfort

△ 9.3
Gosnolds Bay

POQUOSON RIVER

JAMES RIVER

7.24–1 JAMESTOWN DEPART

9.7
JAMESTOWN
RETURN

△ 9.6–3

△ 9.5–2

ELIZABETH RIVER

NANSEMOND RIVER

△ Spent Night
✚ Cross planted by Smith

*Place-names in italic come from
Smith's writings as well as his map*

0   2.5   5 miles

9.6–2
*Nansemond
Village*

9.5–1
*Chesapeake
Village*

✚ 9.6–1
END OF EXPLORATION

decided to take advantage of the strong wind shift to northwest, which was exposing them on a lee shore in Gosnolds Bay, and head south again. The nearly constant lightning enabled them to see land and avoid the shoals on Poquoson flats. The explorers made a run for Point Comfort (*Map Stop 9.4*) and took shelter in its lee. Exhausted from the long night with little or no sleep, they spent the rest of September 4 relaxing, recovering and probably drying their clothes.

September 5–7, 1608: Point Comfort to Jamestown

The last three days (by our estimate) of the voyage were most likely spent working up the James against a northwesterly wind (following the storm); within a day or so, that wind would have died out and been supplanted by southerly upriver breezes. Smith's 1612 record says nothing about that leg of the journey except that they sheltered at Point Comfort and arrived back at Jamestown on September 7.

In 1624, however, John Smith wrote that he explored not one but two more rivers before reaching Jamestown.[52] He says that on September 5 he traversed the mouth of the James and explored up the Elizabeth River to the new Indian town of Chesapeack, returning to spend the night anchored off Craney Island. The next day he has the voyagers proceeding to the mouth of the Nansemond, where they met fishermen who invited them up the river and into a prearranged ambush. Smith claimed, in that later version, that he had a humdinger of a running sea battle in this, his first encounter with them—in spite of the neighboring Kecoughtans' and Warraskoyacks' alliance with the "conqueror" of the Massawomecks. It is a wonderful "read," like the rest of Smith's adventures, but the major problem with it is that in 1608, when the memory was only a few months old, Smith wrote that he had gone up the Nansemond River (and probably also the "Chesapeake" [Elizabeth]) while seeing Christopher Newport off for England back in April.[53] This earlier version portrays the participants as wary but not nearly as violent—which is probably closer to the truth. By the end of September 7, 1608, the barge made its safe return to Jamestown Island.

Reflections on the Second Voyage

The barge made its way back to Jamestown loaded with notes and draft maps and the gifts of the Tockwoghs, Susquehannocks, Massawomecks, and Patuxent-Rappahannock-Piankatank River chiefdoms. What we would give today for Smith to have sent this ethnographic treasure trove back to England to reward the backers in the Virginia Company! The records are silent as to what happened to these Algonquian, Iroquoian, and Siouan artifacts from the summer of 1608. One suspects that the nonperishable parts of the gifts might soon be found in the English trash pits within James Fort, currently being uncovered by the Jamestown Rediscovery crews of the Association for the Preservation of Virginia Antiquities.[54]

The twelve surviving members of John Smith's crew had journeyed over one thousand miles (1,600 kilometers) under conditions of frequent hard-

Modern Equivalents of Geographic Features on Smith's Map: Second Voyage

Head of the Bay
Bornes Point = Swans Point
Broade [Creek] = uncertain
Brookes Forest = mainland of Maryland Eastern Shore
Downs Dale = Patapsco River above the fall line
Gunters Harbor = North East River
Peregrins Mount = Fair Hill Natural Resource Management Area
Point Pisinge = Howell Point
Smalls Point = Miami Beach Park
Smyth's fales = Conowingo Dam site
Taverners Roade = higher elevations of the Western Shore coastal plain
Willoughby's River = Bush River

Patuxent River
The map shows only Algonquian place-names.

Rappahannock River
Boolers Bush = oxbow marsh south of Graves Corner (name of river bend)
Fetherstones Bay = Moss Neck
Stingray Isle = Stingray Point

ship. When John Smith polished and added to his friends' 1612 account (which he approved but did not write), he added some lines of poetry that capture the explorers' feelings of adventure, fear and accomplishment:

> But to this place to come, who will adventure
> With judgment's guide and reason now to enter
> Finds in this world's broad sea with wind and tide
> There's safer sail than anywhere beside.
> But 'cause to wanton novices it is
> A province full of fearfulness, I wish,
> Into the great, vast deep to venture out,
> Those shallow rivers let them coast about,
> And by a small boat learn there first and mark
> How they may come to make a greater bark.[55]

In response, as a way of providing the Algonquian perspective, below is Powhatan's conciliatory and prophetic speech to Smith in 1609:

> But this bruit from Nansamund that you are come to destroy my country so much affrighteth all my people as they dare not visit you. What will it avail you to take that by force [which] you may quickly have by love? Or to destroy them that provide you food?
>
> What can you get by war when we can hide our provisions and fly to the woods? Whereby you must famish by wronging us, your friends. And why are you thus jealous of our loves, seeing us unarmed, and [who] both do and are willing still to feed you with that [which] you cannot get but by our labors?
>
> Think you I am so simple not to know it is better to eat good meat, lie well, and sleep quietly with my women and children, laugh, and be merry with you, have copper, hatchets, or what[ever] I want, being your friend, than be forced to fly from all?—to lie cold in the woods, feed upon acorns, roots and such trash, and be so hunted by you that I can neither rest, eat, nor sleep. . . .
>
> Let this therefore assure you of our loves, and every year our friendly trade shall furnish you with corn.[56]

As Jamestown's president, Smith would apply many of the lessons learned in diplomacy, trade for corn, and dispersal of the colonists during the following spring's food deficiency. The interplay and struggle between Smith and Powhatan continued until the arrival in the summer of 1609 of new orders removing him as president and decreeing new orders from the Virginia Company. This change set the English at each other, with the pro-Smith and anti-Smith forces almost coming to arms on the upper James in the autumn of 1609. On his return from that confrontation, his gunpowder bag "ignited" while he slept, setting him afire and causing him to jump overboard to douse the flames. In great pain, Smith took the next ship back to England. His rivals, in power once more, told the Powhatan that Smith died in England. The hard-won English relations with the Indians turned to dust, and the Powhatans began a war on the English that lasted from 1609 to 1612,[57] leading to starving times and a horrific death toll among the colonists. John Smith's 1608 voyages of exploration showed the English horizons how vast and valuable the Chesapeake estuary could be, if only they could win it from their Algonquian hosts and defend it from the Spanish.

6

The Powhatan River,
Becoming "King James His River,"
and Hampton Roads

THREE ENGLISH SHIPS PASSED between the Virginia Capes in April 1607. They were by no means the first European visitors to the region, nor were they the first Europeans intent upon founding a colony (see the box on p. 54). The Spanish had been there before them and still claimed the territory. The English therefore knew that they had better settle well away from the capes, if possible. They had another requirement for a place to settle: it had to be on a relatively low terrace (neither a marsh nor a bluff, the same preference the Indians had) with a deepwater anchorage immediately adjacent. That combination was not easy to find along the James.

The James River and Environs

The James River is about 335 miles (540 kilometers) long. Its drainage, covering some ten thousand square miles (25,900 square kilometers), lies wholly within the modern boundaries of Virginia. Since its headwaters lie far up in the Appalachian Mountains, it brings great quantities of freshwater down to the Chesapeake Bay. In the process, the river passes through a gap it has made in the Blue Ridge, after which it follows a broad and fertile valley where a mixture of forests and more open grasslands, and later agricultural fields, have fostered grazing wildlife.

The River and Its Surroundings

The land along the mouth of the James is low, with dune-fields and sandy peninsulas (incipient barrier islands) along the southern and western rim of the bay itself.[1] Such areas were not desirable beachfront back then. The Native Americans found them useless, though offshore shallows were fine for fish traps (see chapter 8); the English called them "deserts" because they could not be farmed.

Oxbows, or deep recurvatures, in the river's course made exploratory trips upstream a long passage for men rowing and were a difficult course to sail because on every turn some portion would be into the wind. There are long curving reaches at Hog Island, Weyanoke Point, Presque Isle, Jones Neck, and Hatcher and Farrar islands. These features echo the James River's ancient geological history as a meandering coastal plain river. Today most of the meanders remain in the freshwater zone, making for great riches of aquatic resources. The cliffs exposed by erosion along the riverfront are of varying ages, with Pleistocene wind- and rain-deposited layers on the top. At both Kingsmill and Claremont, the lower layers are late Miocene through early Pleistocene (1.5–8 million years old); at Grays Creek, across from Jamestown Island, they are late Miocene (6–8 million years old); around Hopewell they are Paleocene (55–65 million years old), and opposite Hatcher Island they are much older (Patuxent formation, 106 million years old).[2]

From Weyanoke Point upward, the river narrows remarkably and tidal currents become stronger and very important to navigation. "Tidewater," the appellation applied to all the Chesapeake's lower rivers, was exactly that; and the tide, more specifically tidal currents, was a major factor in how people got around before the introduction of steam and internal combustion marine engines.[3] The James ceases to be navigable for any craft larger than a canoe at the fall line, where the river's course intersects the older, hard-rock geology of the Appalachian foothills. Here major rapids, punctuated by large rocks and turbulent eddies, signal higher terrain beyond. For many years that terrain would be inaccessible to waterborne trade unless cargoes were offloaded to smaller vessels such as canoes or colonial-era bateaus, until canals eventually bypassed and opened new routes in the

The Powhatan River

nineteenth century. This disjunct in navigation was the basis upon which the city of Richmond, current capital of Virginia, was founded; the city of Fredericksburg on the Rappahannock River has the same origin.

The emergence of rock substrates at the fall line later became the basis for efforts to extract iron and operate foundries. Only small amounts of copper were ever found in Virginia, most of it in the Piedmont and the rest in the mountains. Native Americans greatly valued copper, and its scarcity made it an opportunistic item for early trade by the English colonists. Gold, which the Virginia explorers were mandated to seek, was also elusive, although small amounts were eventually found in the Piedmont portion of the James basin.[4]

The Waters

Water is a river's life, so drought may seriously affect the James. Cypress tree growth rings reflect rainfall throughout the trees' life, and specimens along the Nottoway River, just outside the Chesapeake drainage, are the basis for the conclusion that severe drought occurred during the North Carolina Roanoke settlement period (circa 1585) and the founding of Jamestown (circa 1607–9).[5] From an environmental standpoint, two estuarine features made Jamestown Island a poor choice for English settlement. First, in drought years the salt front of the estuary moves upstream without the countervailing pressure of freshwater flowing downstream from the interior. As a result, the waters of the lower James were frequently brackish. By September, the salt front could easily have reached Jamestown Island. Second, without major freshwater input, tides tended to ebb and flow in this section of the river without a major exchange of fresh and salt water. Furthermore, this region could have been in what oceanographers call the "turbidity maximum," which develops as freshwater bearing dissolved organic materials and particulates from upriver encounters salt water. Many of these materials tend to aggregate into minute particles, or to adsorb (stick) to clay and silts that become suspended in the water column. The result is more-turbid water that is circulating less. Colonists using the river to wash, drink, and carry off their wastes thus were exposed both to pathogens and to brackish water that was difficult for their bodies to process and unhealthy to consume.[6]

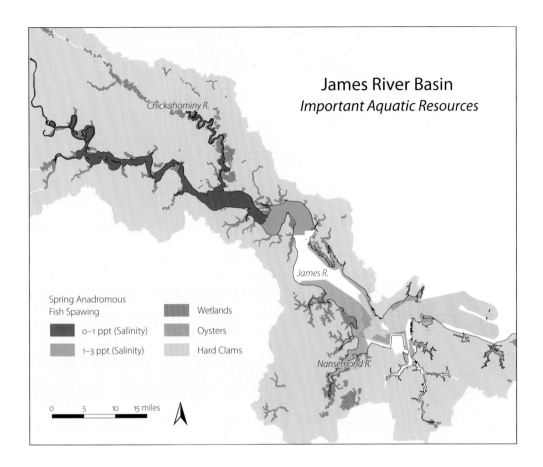

James River Basin
Important Aquatic Resources

Chickahominy R.

James R.

Spring Anadromous
Fish Spawing

0–1 ppt (Salinity)

1–3 ppt (Salinity)

Wetlands

Oysters

Hard Clams

Nansemond R.

0   5   10   15 miles

Wetlands

The James and, to a greater extent, its tributaries, are densely lined with marshes from the Hampton Roads area up to about Hatcher Island,[7] where the river turns north to run straight and on a parallel with the fall line for approximately twenty miles (32 kilometers) before crossing it at Richmond. In that last stretch, there is little marsh, although the islands that existed there before industrial activities obliterated them may have been an exception. Below Hatcher Island, the James has some spectacular meanders that have been cut off to facilitate shipping traffic, and farther down, where the river only curves gently, its old floodplain shows how it meandered there as well in ancient times. Only the Chickahominy River has a more sinuous course, nearly all of its meanders containing marshes and, farther up, a combination of marsh and swamp forest. It is these meanderings of the James and Chickahominy that contain the largest expanses of emergent plants.

Depleted Already: Nansemond River Oysters in the 1830s

Today we hear of oysters being in short supply, but that is not entirely a modern phenomenon. By the mid-1830s in the lower James River valley, the supply of oysters had become so depleted that citizens of Nansemond County (now the City of Suffolk) had a bill introduced in the state legislature. The idea was to prohibit oystering between May 1 and September 1 in parts of the Nansemond River and Chuckatuck Creek. Even oyster "reefs" were to be left alone during that time. Two years later, the citizens of the same county wanted oystering prohibited to "Yankee" vessels for most of the year: Virginia oysters were being transplanted to northern states' waters, to the detriment of the local industry. They also wanted dredging—supposedly for terrapins but also for oysters—prohibited to everyone. The controversy over who could take oysters for how much of the year continued into the 1850s.

Sources: Commonwealth of Virginia, Legislative Petitions, Nansemond County, Jan. 4, 1836; Jan. 5 and 13, 1838; March 1, 1843; Feb. 22, 1849; Jan. 17, 1851.

Bald cypress trees occur along the James from Kennon Marsh down to Jamestown Island, after which one finds them only in tributaries' headwaters (for example, Cypress Swamp in the Pagan River). Cow lily is common only in the middle reaches of the Chickahominy River. Tuckahoe (arrow arum) is a tough, deep-growing plant that tolerates slightly brackish water. Accordingly it is found in small quantities in the headwaters of even the direct tributaries of Chesapeake Bay (such as the Northwest Branch of Back River, in Hampton, Virginia) if they go far enough inland. Along the James, the plants are found from the headwaters of the Nansemond River upward, first appearing along the James itself around Jamestown Island. Meandering tributaries often have large, almost pure expanses of tuckahoe, the most easily visible being Halfway and Powhatan creeks along the Williamsburg-Jamestown leg of the Colonial Parkway. On the other hand, cattail marshes are decidedly limited today in the James River valley. Several edible seed-producing emergent plants appear in the headwaters of Nansemond River in Suffolk and Deep Creek in Newport News and become more widespread upriver: wild rice and water hemp; wild millet begins in the headwaters of Lower Chippokes Creek. The latter two begin to grow along the James

John Smith's Chesapeake Voyages, 1607–1609

River proper around its junction with the Chickahominy River, while wild rice shows up on the riverside farther up, around Powells Creek.

Shellfish

The oyster resources of the lower James were enormous four centuries ago, collectively representing the greatest single biological feature of the tidal section of the river. Abundant oysters formed living reefs, and John Smith would later write of Englishmen living on oysters during the "starving time" of 1609–10. People would do so again during the American Civil War.[8] Several clusters of dots, probably representing oyster reefs, appear on Robert Tyndall's draft map of 1608. The extraordinary ability of huge oyster beds to filter nutrients from the water column played a significant role in keeping the pre-European Chesapeake a relatively clear water environment, at least in the saltier parts where oysters live.[9]

Crabs, notably the Chesapeake blue crab, were easily seen and captured in the shallows along the river, often moving upstream almost to freshwater in summer. When "doubling" as part of their reproductive process, crabs in pairs could be dipped from the surface with a hand net.

Fishes

The James itself had abundant fishery resources, although the English, with the few and poorly maintained nets they brought and with their recognition of the region's seasonality but not its ecological features, could well have starved in the presence of periodic plenty. The anadromous fish passing Jamestown tended to stay in deep water until they arrived in small tributary streams; there they could be easily scooped up with hand nets. Native Americans also used shallow-water weirs, consisting of fences of thin stakes used to guide fish into a trap at the deep end, but while they tried to teach this technique to the English in the early spring of 1608, the newcomers did not immediately employ it.[10] In spring, sturgeon move upstream to feed, at which time the females are rich with roe (eggs otherwise known as the delicacy caviar) and intent on spawning. Sturgeon are relatively sluggish swimmers, and if approached cautiously in shallow water they could be captured by Native American fishers who could literally wrestle the massive fish ashore or by looping a noose about the tail.[11] Colonists could use these techniques, a harpoon, or musket, and the sturgeon became a life-saving resource at Jamestown.[12]

The Sturgeon

Imagine a fish rivaling the size of some of the sharks that course through the bay. Then imagine this fish with a spadelike, upturned snout and bony plates that armor its sides and you have a link to the past; a fish whose heritage dates from some 200 million years ago. The Atlantic sturgeon was once quite common in the Chesapeake Bay and was the first "cash crop" at Jamestown. These primitive-looking fish can grow to ten feet (3 meters) or so and weigh several hundred pounds (over 300 kilograms)—yet these lumbering giants have been known to spring from the water and then flop back with a tumultuous splash.

Read the words of Nathaniel Hawthorne, who saw a sturgeon clear the water in Maine in 1837 and wrote: "I saw a great fish, some six feet long and thick in proportion, suddenly emerge at whole length, turn a somerset, its fins all spread, and looking very strange." Perhaps the Native Americans in Chesapeake Bay saw the same phenomenon. Another nineteenth-century writer recalled that "On the Potomac, during the Revolutionary war, one large sturgeon leaped into a ferry boat at Georgetown, coming down on the lap of an American officer with such violence as to break his thigh; the injury later resulted in death."

Henry Wadsworth Longfellow immortalized the sturgeon in his memorable poem about the mythical Ojibway man, Hiawatha.

> ... On the white sand of the bottom
> Lay the monster Mishe Nahma,
> Lay the sturgeon, King of fishes;
> Through his gills he breathed the water,
> With his fins he fanned and winnowed,
> With his tail he swept the sand floor.
> There he lay in all his armor;
> On each side a shield to guard him,
> Plates of bone upon his forehead,
> Down his sides and back and shoulders ...

Source: Eliot 1830.

Land Mammals

White-tailed deer were common in the James River basin, serving as a major source of meat for Native Americans and colonists alike. In the lower basin, deer were overhunted because the "necks" of land were narrower[13] and the human population was greater;[14] the animals were more abundant upstream, especially in the "no-man's-land" (buffer zones) between territories dominated by the Powhatans and the inland Monacans, who were often in conflict with each other. Elk were apparently present in the Piedmont. Far into the Appalachian valleys drained by the rivers were scattered populations of Eastern Woodland bison, which left their names on James tributaries such as the Bull-, Cow-, and Calfpasture rivers. Apparently the Jamestown colonists never encountered them in the watershed, although they are mentioned elsewhere. They were likely never abundant and were driven extinct before 1800.[15]

Trees

The sandy soils at the mouth of the James would seem not to be a good venue for forest. They do, however, support a southern dune forest that in Virginia Beach includes yaupon holly (almost at its northern limit in the United States) and, in the Hampton Roads area plus Cape Charles in Northampton County and near New Point Comfort in Mathews County, live oak (also reaching its northern limit in the United States). A little way inland, in what is now First Landing State Park, were pockets of freshwater among the dunes, and there bald cypress trees still flourish, festooned on their lower branches, below the reach of winter winds, with Spanish moss. This moss species also reaches its northern limit today in the Hampton Roads area;[16] the cypress trees fade out on the upper Eastern Shore (see chapter 10).

In its middle reaches, above Jamestown Island, the banks of the James and its tributaries usually have shallow shoulders; the water is fresher than it was four centuries ago thanks to heavier runoff from the land (see chapter 1), so large stands of bald cypress have survived slowly rising sea level. Cypress resists checking or cracking with frequent cycles of wetting and drying, an important quality for maintenance of a leak-free canoe hull. Accordingly, along with equally large, straight-growing pines and tulip poplars, the bald cypress was highly favored by Native American and English boatbuilders alike, whenever they could get it. Cypress trees attain a very large size in the Chesapeake region, with individuals several hundreds of years old still extant in spite of a logging "boom" in recent centuries.

The People

Circa 1607 the coastal plain in the James River drainage was occupied by eleven Algonquian-speaking groups, with the Piedmont being held by the Monacans (see chapter 13). Of those eleven, which are listed below, all but two belonged to the paramount chiefdom of the man Powhatan, who took his name from his hometown;[17] modern scholars bestow it upon his subjects' language and political organization as well. Two groups resisted being absorbed into that organization: the Chickahominies, who were governed by elders and were populous enough to remain autonomous, and the Chesapeakes, who, as described later, were overrun sometime around the time Jamestown was founded.

The Powhatan towns along the James[18] were mainly dispersed-settlement towns: scatters of houses, gardens, and groves of trees along the banks of streams. The known exceptions mentioned here were in frontier areas—near the Virginia Capes and near the fall line, where attacks from the Monacans (probably returned by the Powhatans) were an annual occurrence.

Chesapeake

This group consisted of three towns with an estimated 425 people, including 100 warriors (Smith); the chief's name was not recorded. The towns were: *Chesipiuk,* shown on Lynnhaven Bay on Theodor de Bry's map of 1590[19] and on Elizabeth River on the Smith map of 1608 (both maps are vague about geography, showing limited English exploration of that area at the time); *Apasus* nearby on Lynnhaven Bay; and *Skicoak* on the Elizabeth River.

A major nucleated, palisaded, Late Woodland site has been partially excavated on Broad Bay, a tributary of Lynnhaven Bay.[20] It presumably represents the Chesapeakes' capital town of the 1580s.[21] Several other contemporaneous sites in the northern Lynnhaven Bay area, with a dispersed-settlement pattern, may represent the village of Apasus.[22] On the other hand, along the Elizabeth River, industrial development has wiped out any remains of Late Woodland sites.

Excavated ceramics indicate that the Chesapeakes (and their neighbors) had close ties to Algonquian speakers in the Carolina sounds.[23] Thus it is no surprise that the first English colony on Roanoke Island sent some of its people to stay with the Chesapeakes in the winter of 1585–86.[24] Both David B. Quinn and Helen C. Rountree have suggested that part of the second, or "lost" colony, took refuge with the Chesapeakes in 1587–88, although their eventual fate is unknown.[25] The Chesapeakes were eliminated as an

Posthole pattern of a chief's large house with rounded ends excavated at the Great Neck site on Lynnhaven Bay, Virginia. (Virginia Department of Historic Resources)

independent polity by Powhatan around 1607, so that when John Smith explored the Elizabeth River in the spring of 1608, he found little evidence of human inhabitants.[26] Apparently the territory was taken over by the Nansemonds.

Nansemond

This group of four towns had an estimated 850 people, including 200 fighting men; the chief was Weyhohomo, with satellite town chiefs Amapetough, Weywingopo and Tichtough under him.[27] To date there have been no major archaeological excavations. The towns were: *Nandsamond,* on the three points where the Nansemond River splits; *Mantoughquemend,* on the east side upriver; *Teracosick,* farther upriver on the west side; and *Mattanock,* uncertain location somewhere downriver on the west side.

Sites revealed by archaeological survey and of the correct age are Mattanock and part of Nandsamond.

Kecoughtan

The Kecoughtan group consisted of an estimated 180 people including 20 fighting men; the chief was Pochins. There was a single town, Kecoughtan, located where the Veterans Administration Hospital complex (until recently still called "Kecoughtan") is in the city of Hampton. Small-scale excavations have been carried out.[28]

Warraskoyack

This group consisted of three towns with an estimated 210 people including 40 warriors; the chief was Tackonekinaco. The towns were: *Warraskoyack,* on the west bank of Jones Creek (a tributary of Pagan River); *Mokete,* probably near Rescue; and *Mathomauk,* near Tormentor Creek (another tributary of the Pagan River).

Known archaeological sites in the territory do not include any of these towns.

Paspahegh

This group consisted of seven towns with an estimated 120 people including 40 warriors; the chief was an outstanding warrior named Wowinchopunck.

There are two maps of this area, both originally drafted in 1608 by John Smith himself, which do not entirely agree with each other; presumably they represent different stages in his learning about the country.[29] Working upstream, the towns are: *Namquosick,* about halfway between Jamestown Island at the mouth of Chickahominy River; "*Paspahegh*" (unnamed on the published Smith map), at Barretts Point; *Cinquactock,* north of Barretts Point; *Marinough,* a short distance up the Chickahominy on the east side; a town of unknown name, around Dancing Point on the west side of the mouth of the Chickahominy; [a second] *Paspahegh,* around Tettington, just west of Sandy Point (Smith's map shows this to have been the district capital); and a town of unknown name, farther up the James.

There are several likely Late Woodland Period sites in the vicinity of the Paspahegh capital. However, the only comprehensive excavation in the Paspaheghs' territory has been the one at Barretts Point (now the development Governor's Land at Two Rivers) in the early 1990s. There the central part of a town was uncovered.[30] Besides several dozen house outlines, the archae-

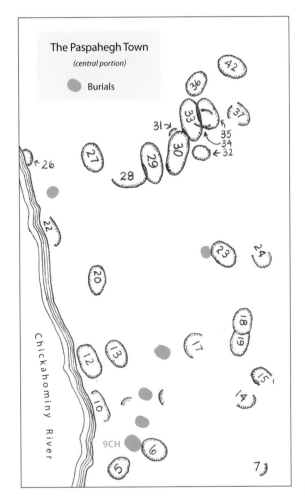

The Paspahegh Town
(central portion)

● Burials

Locations of Algonquian house patterns and other elements of a Paspahegh town, possibly the one called Cinquactock on the Zuñiga map, as revealed by archaeological excavation. Excavated houses are marked by numbers in full or partial ovals. The feature marked "9CH" was a high-status burial, possibly of a chief. (Helen C. Rountree, based on site map by James River Archaeology, Inc.)

ologists found numerous burials; after analysis, the bones and associated grave goods were ceremonially reburied by members of the modern Virginia Indian tribes on nearby land donated by the developers. Numerous other Late Woodland sites, such as the one farther east at Carter's Grove, have also been excavated; they were probably inhabited and abandoned before 1607.

Chickahominy

The Chickahominy group encompassed an estimated 1,500 people including 200–300 fighting men (Smith, Strachey) or 500 (Hamor). This tribe was independent of Powhatan's organization and preferred to be governed by eight elders.[31] Again, the two maps disagree: Smith's map shows nine

Chickahominy towns south of the river and seven north of it, while the "Zuñiga" map adds another four hamlets, three of them north of the river. An extensive survey of the district was carried out in 1967–71, with candidates for six of the towns emerging,[32] but as of this writing little excavation has been done.

Moving upstream along the south bank of the Chickahominy (Charles City County) the towns were: *Mansa,* on Old Neck, between Sunken Marsh and Mount Airy; *Opahock,* same location; *Menascosic,* opposite the mouth of Diascund Creek; *Paspanigh,* a short distance upstream; *Mamanahunt,* on Wilcox Neck; *Chosicks,* around Graves Landing, opposite Chickahominy Shores; *Paspanegh,* on Matahunk Neck; *Roghtacut/Righkahauk,* near Cypress Bank Landing; *Nechanicok,* a short distance upstream; and *Mattahunt/Mattalunt,* near Tonyham Swamp.

Moving upstream, in James City County and then New Kent County, the towns were: *Mattapanient,* around Shipyard/Yarmouth Creek (this town was far enough downriver that it may actually have been a Paspahegh town); a town of unknown name, a short distance upstream; *Ozenick/Oranieck,* at a bend near Uncles Neck and Hog Neck Creeks (this would be the last seventeenth-century town occupied by the Chickahominies); *Werawahon,* at Chickahominy Haven; *Askakep,* on the north side of the mouth of Diascund Creek; a town of unknown name, a short distance up Diascund Creek from Askakep; *Moysonec,* in a bend formed by Diascund Creek and the Chickahominy River;[33] *Quosaugh,* west of Wilcox Point, perhaps on Turner Neck; *Attamuspinck,* just downriver from Apocant; and *Apocant,* a short distance above Providence Forge.[34]

Much farther upstream was the settlement of Orapax, established in early 1609 when Powhatan moved his center of government away from the York River to avoid the English. Historical records indicate that it was in the headwaters of the Chickahominy.[35] Its likely location was near Bottoms Bridge; the building of Interstate 64 there destroyed a large Late Woodland site—in a swampy area where such a large settlement would ordinarily have been anomalous.

Quiyoughcohannock

This group consisted of four towns with an estimated 255 people, including 25 fighting men (Smith) or 60 (Strachey); the chief was Tatahcoope, a boy whose mother, Oholasc, governed as regent. The former chief, Pepiscunimah (Pipsco), had been deposed,[36] and his brother Chopoke (Chippokes) was de facto co-ruler with Oholasc. The towns were: *Quiyoughcohanock,* east of Claremont; *Chawopo*, at Claremont; *Nantapoyac* ("Tappahannah" to the English at first), opposite the mouth of the Chickahominy River; and village of unknown name, east of the upper reaches of Upper Chippokes Creek.

To date no likely candidates from archaeological survey have been located.[37]

Weyanock

This group consisted of seven towns with an estimated 530 people including 100 warriors (Smith) or 150 (Strachey); the chief was Kaquothocum, with Ohoroquoh governing the sector south of the James. This far upriver the James is narrow enough that it did not constitute a barrier between tribes; thus the Weyanocks and all the groups upriver from them had their villages on both sides of the river.

South of the James, heading upriver, the towns were: two towns of unknown name somewhere between Brandon and Upper Chippokes Creek; "Weyanock" at Flowerdew Hundred; excavated in 1980s;[38] and a town of unknown name at Jordan's Point, at the south end of the Virginia State Route 156 bridge; excavated in the 1990s.[39]

North of the James, heading upriver, the towns were: a town of unknown name somewhere between Queens Creek and the east end of Eppes Island; another *Weyanock,* the district capital, somewhere between that town and Shirley Plantation; and one town of unknown name farther upriver.

Several promising Late Woodland Period sites have been found on the north bank of the James but have not been excavated. Yet another Late Woodland site, located well up Powell Creek on the east side, apparently representing a mid-seventeenth-century Weyanock town, has been excavated.[40]

Appamattuck

The Appamattuck group consisted of five towns with an estimated 380 people including 60 fighting men (Smith) or 120 (Strachey). This was one of Powhatan's original inherited territories.[41] The chief was Coquonasum, whose sister Opussonquonuske acted as deputy ruler in the satellite town at the mouth of Appomattox River, commanding 20 of the 120 men. Town sites have been difficult to locate due to the expansion of the city of Petersburg. The towns were: *Appamattuck,* on the north bank of what is now Swift Creek; a town of unknown name at Bermuda Hundred (ruled by Opussonoquonuske); and three towns of unknown name somewhere up the Appomattox River below its falls.

Several archaeological sites may be the settlements indicated on Smith's map, but further testing is needed to verify them as such.

Arrohateck

This group consisted of five towns with an estimated 255 people including 30 warriors; the chief was Ashuaquid. This was one of Powhatan's original inherited territories.[42] Much of the river's shoreline in this territory has been obliterated by sand and gravel mining.

East of the James, going upriver, the towns were: a town of unknown name northeast of Hatcher Island; a town of unknown name near Varina; and *Arrohateck,* near the intersection of Kingsland Road and Osborne Turnpike.

West of the James, going upriver, the towns were: a town of unknown name on Kingsland Creek; and a town of unknown name, its location uncertain.

Further testing is needed to verify whether the archaeological sites located in this area are in fact the towns listed.

Powhatan

The Powhatan group consisted of five towns with an estimated 240 people including 40 fighting men; the chief was Parahunt, a son of Powhatan. Powhatan himself lived there when he first came to power, so that his neighbors called him by the town's name (his personal name was Wahunsenacawh).[43] Industrial development has disturbed much of the river's shoreline in this territory.

East of the James, going upriver, the towns were: two towns of unknown name, the locations uncertain; and *Powhatan,* a few miles below the falls. As a frontier settlement, the latter consisted of a dense cluster of houses surrounded by a palisade.[44] Thus far one promising archaeological site has been discovered but has not been excavated. It is on private property that is currently threatened by development pressure from every direction.

West of the James, going upriver, the towns were: a town of unknown name at Falling Creek; and a town of unknown name, its location uncertain.

Interplay between People and the Environment

Only a small fraction of the oyster resource so useful to Native Americans was actually accessible to them. Oysters can live in the intertidal zone, but they really flourish at depths of eight to twenty-five feet (2.4 to 7.6 meters).[45] The Indians did not make long-handled tongs to reach such submerged reef sections; instead they were limited to sections they could reach with their short-handled rakes and by diving (and how long they could stay underwater).[46] It was the same for the English for over two centuries, until they developed the technology to harvest and subsequently mine the resource—technology that ultimately reduced it to a small fraction of its precolonial abundance.

Nonetheless, many oysters ended up in Indian hearths, where they were heated or steamed to make them open. The shells are found in many archaeological sites, sometimes in amazing quantities. Freshwater clams are also found, as evidenced by the middens at Maycocks Point.[47] In that part of the James, the people were using shellfish as a substantial part of their diet.[48] It is likely that Powhatan groups like the Nansemonds, who had a big population but no tuckahoe (arrow arum) to fall back on in poor crop-years, relied at times upon the abundant shellfish they did have at hand to keep from starvation. Shellfish contain not only protein and iron but also calories to keep people up and moving about.[49] The shellfish need not be the obvious large ones, either. At one summer/fall fishing camp near the 1580s site of Chesipiuk, archaeologists found not only oysters, tagelus clams, and softshell clams but also huge numbers of little marsh periwinkles. (The site also yielded not only evidence of sea trout, Atlantic menhaden, spot, and croaker, but also a few bones of deer, wild turkeys, and box turtles.)[50]

Numerous shellfish species produce pearls when bits of grit get into them and irritate them sufficiently. Pearls were reported before and after 1600 as being plentiful among the people of the Hampton Roads area and the Weyanocks, respectively.[51] Being lustrous[52] and stringable when drilled, they were an obvious choice for valued jewelry, though Native American methods of extraction and drilling "spoiled" them in English eyes.[53]

There was something else in Virginia Beach that the people there gathered and exported: the leaves of yaupon holly. These contain caffeine, and when boiled long enough they yield the famous "black drink" of the Southeastern Indians. The brew contains enough caffeine to cause vomiting—hence the tree's Latin name, *Ilex vomitoria*—and the Virginia Algonquians, at least, are known to have used it as a purge in the spring.[54] The people John

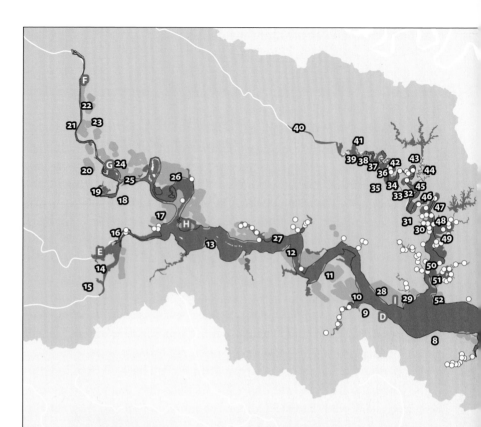

King's House

A Chesapeack
B Nandsamund
C Warraskoyack
D Quiyoughcohanock
E Appamattuck
F Arrohateck
G Powhatan
H Weanock
I Paspahegh
J Kecoughtan

Ordinary Town

1 Chesipiuk (1580s)
2 Apasus (1580s)
3 Mantoughquemend
4 Teracosick
5 Mattanock
6 Mokete
7 Mathomauk
8 Nantapoyac/ "Tappahanna"
9 Chawopo
10 Unnamed Settlement
11 Unnamed Settlement
12 Weanock

13 Unnamed Settlement
14 Unnamed Settlement
15 Unnamed Settlement
16 Unnamed Settlement
17 Unnamed Settlement
18 Unnamed Settlement
19 Unnamed Settlement
20 Unnamed Settlement
21 Unnamed Settlement
22 Unnamed Settlement
23 Unnamed Settlement
24 Unnamed Settlement
25 Unnamed Settlement
26 Unnamed Settlement
27 Unnamed Settlement
28 Unnamed Settlement
29 Unnamed Settlement
30 Opahock
31 Mansa
32 Menascosic
33 Paspanigh
34 Mamanahunt
35 Chosicks
36 Paspanegh
37 Righkahauk
38 Nechanicok

39 Mattahunt
40 Apocant
41 Attamuspinck
42 Quosaugh
43 Moysonec
44 Unnamed Settlement
45 Askakep
46 Werawahon
47 Oranieck
48 Unnamed Settlement
49 Mattapanient
50 Marinough
51 Cinquactock
52 Paspahegh
53 Namquosic

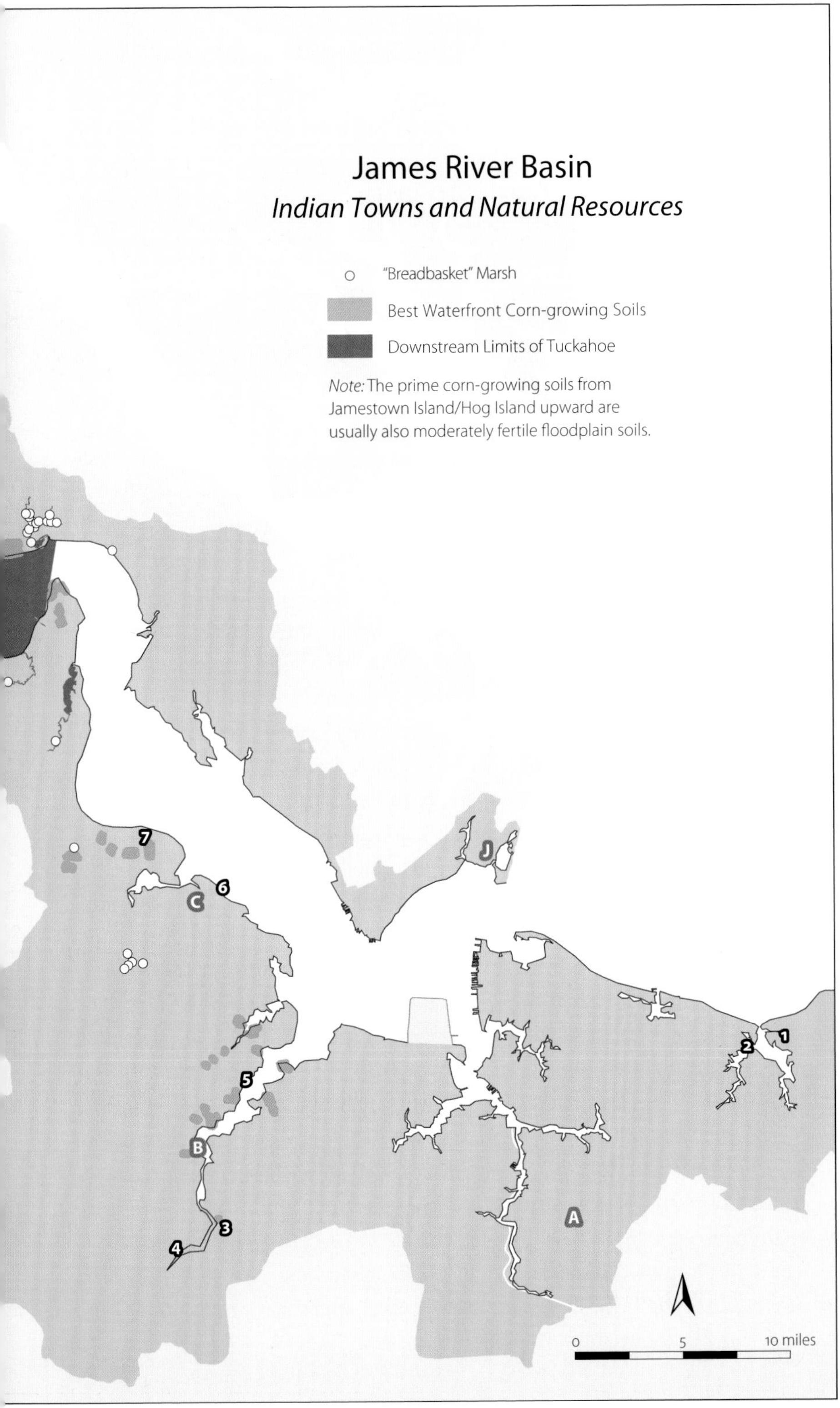

James River Basin
Indian Towns and Natural Resources

○   "Breadbasket" Marsh

▨   Best Waterfront Corn-growing Soils

▦   Downstream Limits of Tuckahoe

Note: The prime corn-growing soils from
Jamestown Island/Hog Island upward are
usually also moderately fertile floodplain soils.

7

6

C

5

B

3

4

D

2   1

A

0   5   10 miles

Smith saw doing that must have traded for the yaupon leaves, for none of Smith's voyages were to what is now Virginia Beach. Only in one other place in the Chesapeake region, namely Mockhorn Island off the Eastern Shore (see chapter 8), could the native people gather yaupon leaves for export.

Village Placement

There were far more Native American villages up the James from Jamestown Island than below. The people were not avoiding the Spanish, as the Jamestown English did. Instead they were seeking out the best food-producing resources in their valley, resources that consisted of prime farmland and wild tuber- and seed-producing marshes. The majority of places where the people were living in John Smith's time were on the former and near the latter. And the farmland not occupied in 1607–9 would have been occupied at some previous time, given the people's custom of slash-and-burn farming noted in chapter 2.

There are good farming soils all up and down the James River valley today, thanks to draining and fertilizer use. But in Indian times, the really good soils were the naturally occurring ones: level or nearly so (to avoid erosion), well-drained (so the roots of crop plants didn't drown), and easy to work (with digging sticks)—the criteria for what agronomists call Class I soils. But there is evidence that the Indian women had developed an additional criterion for prime farmland: a low water table so that a field warmed up early in spring (for the first of the several staggered planting efforts). The women did not, of course, actually test the water table; they had learned where they could do early planting by trial and error across several centuries. These "warm" Class I soils correlate closely with the positions of Indian towns on John Smith's map. The very best soils were also naturally fertile; being river-deposited rather than marine in origin, they occur in the inner coastal plain, usually in patches surrounded by other soils of near-comparable quality. In the James River valley, the preferred farmland was Pamunkey loam, sandy loam, or fine sandy loam; it fades out around Jamestown Island and Hog Island, below which even good "warm" soils are not common.[55] The densest concentrations of Indian towns were in those upper parts of the James; so were—and are—the great colonial plantations such as Shirley and Westover. No surprise: English settlers preferred to take over already-cleared Indian lands, and they soon realized that the best soils were there as well.[56]

The women also paid close attention to where the best marshes were, which we call "breadbaskets" in this volume: marshes large enough and rich enough in tuber-producing tuckahoe (arrow arum) and spatterdock/ cow lily and seed-producing wild rice that several extended families could be fed for weeks if not months on the harvest.[57] All three of these plants are freshwater species, so they are to be found in the inner coastal plain where salty water does not reach.[58]

In the whole Chesapeake basin, one of the clearest examples of village locations correlating with the relative abundance of tuckahoe and other emergent food plants is the Quiyoughcohannock territory. All three settlements in that district had ready access to "breadbaskets" of tuckahoe in Grays, Crouch, and Upper Chippokes creeks, as well as of wild rice in Grays and Upper Chippokes; the downriver creeks lack such riches. At first glance on the Smith map, those downriver creeks resemble a "buffer" zone between the Quiyoughcohannocks and the Warraskoyacks, who also used somewhat different pottery styles. It has been said that there may have been a social as well as geographic buffer, indicating limits on social interaction, in the late 1500s when the Quiyoughcohannocks joined Powhatan's political organization before the Warraskoyacks downstream did.[59] However, the location of "breadbaskets" is just as good an explanation for the dearth of settlements in that "buffer zone." On the other hand, the Quiyoughcohannocks lacked prime farmland, besides having to live on the top of bluffs; so even with the marshes available to them, they had one of the smaller populations in the Chesapeake region.

The most populous tribe in the James River valley was the Chickahominies, who not coincidentally had the most "breadbaskets" in their territory, even if they did lack "warm" farmland for early planting. If they managed to control access to the creeks on both sides of the lower Chickahominy River, rich in both tuckahoe and wild rice, and exclude their neighbors the Paspaheghs, then it would help to explain two observations: their population numbering at least five times that of the group next door, and the presence of the palisade around Mansa, the lowest Chickahominy town on the Charles City County side. There was a historically documented political divide between the two peoples: the Paspaheghs had joined Powhatan's paramount chiefdom, but the Chickahominies, being "a warlike and free people," had managed to remain independent.[60] The divide may have been hostile at times and based upon more than politics.

Enter the English

The first exploration in which John Smith participated was the trip up the James. After tentatively exploring the area around Lynnhaven Bay on April 26–29 and being briefly assaulted by "Chesapeakes" who may have been Nansemonds,[61] he and his crew crossed to (Old) Point Comfort and were relieved to encounter the James River's channel (hence the name "comfort"). There they were received hospitably by the Kecoughtans on April 30,[62] after which they began beating their way up the James; given that it took them four days to go fifty miles (80 kilometers), the wind likely was against them. Word of their progress would have spread for miles, putting everyone on the alert, giving notice of exotic goods for trade. Finally arriving in the vicinity of Jamestown Island on May 4, they got caught in a competition between the Paspaheghs and the Quiyoughcohannocks, both of which wanted to meet the newcomers.[63] The latter were playing host to people who were even more eager to see the *tassantassas,* or strangers: Rappahannocks whose chief had been killed by unidentified Europeans a few years before. Apparently no one in the landing party resembled the assailant; neither did Captain John Smith, who would be taken up to their hometown as a prisoner the following December.[64] The English pushed on, bypassing and thereby giving offense to the Weyanocks, whose town was on the river. They reached the mouth of the Appomattox River, where they were greeted with a defensive reception at the town located at the site of modern Bermuda Hundred. In all that stretch of river, the upriver end of Jamestown Island appeared most workable, so that is where the expedition settled on May 14, 1607. Poor choice! They did not ask permission of the owners, the Paspaheghs, and that group's early efforts to become acquainted with the newcomers also fell flat. Before long the location proved unhealthy for environmental reasons, as described shortly.

Mindful of their orders from London to find a Northwest Passage and also gold or silver mines, a major part of the colony left Jamestown on May 21, before the fort's palisade was even finished, and headed upriver on a week-long jaunt.[65] John Smith did not go along. Bypassing the Weyanocks again, along with the Appamattucks, the expedition entered Arrohateck and Powhatan territory, where their trade goods were a hit and their pointed questions were alarming. No one would take them beyond the river's falls, where the enemy Monacans lived. On the way downriver, the Powhatans and Arrohatecks remained friendly, but the previously snubbed Appamattucks and Weyanocks—both of whom the oblivious English now

Reconstruction of a defensive palisade at James Fort, based on archaeological discoveries and seventeenth-century references on fort construction. Thanks to English metal axes, the trees used in that palisade could be larger in diameter and placed closer together (thus using more wood) than was usual in Indian palisades. (Courtesy of APVA Preservation Virginia)

visited—were hostile until won over with trade goods. A friendly embassy from the Pamunkeys, led by one of Powhatan's brothers, met the foreigners in Weyanock territory and was put off by English wariness. Both sides were touchy. The native people had personally had or known about murderous experiences with Europeans, and the English knew (as the Indians did not) that their plans to settle would antagonize the local people sooner or later.[66]

The Virginia Company's people established a beachhead on Jamestown Island because of its deep-water anchorage close to shore. Unfortunately, the island is in a part of the James River that ranges from essentially fresh and steadily flowing (late winter through late spring) to sluggish and brackish (summer and fall). So in addition to mosquito-borne diseases, the colonists, who as noted earlier had no latrine and did not bother to dig a well until spring 1609, were prey to ills caused by drinking salty, contaminated

Modern Indians

Several Indian tribes live within the James River valley today: the Monacans near Lynchburg, the Chickahominies (two organizations) in Charles City and New Kent County, and the Nansemonds in southside Hampton Roads. All are recognized by the Commonwealth of Virginia, and all but the Eastern Chickahominies put on at least one powwow or other public event annually. The events are announced in the public media. The Nansemonds and Monacans operate small museums, while the Monacans are also partners with Natural Bridge in the Monacan Village there.

water.[67] The dry summers did not help: neither the native people's corn nor that planted by the English under native instruction prospered.

Indian men were fascinated by the Englishmen's exotic firearms and on several occasions chiefs asked their guests to fire a musket. For the uninitiated, the ensuing noise seems to have been the major factor sparking fear. Those who had encountered guns before, such as the "Chesapeakes" who attacked the English near Cape Henry—knew that the sound of a musket shot was more impressive than the guns' range and accuracy.[68]

John Smith got to know the James and its tributaries and people rather well in the following months. He visited the Nansemonds in June 1607, meeting with hostility.[69] In the autumn of 1607, he was the colony's main trader, attempting to buy corn from the Kecoughtans, Quiyoughcohannocks, and Paspaheghs. All three groups resisted parting with the grain, for it had been a dry year.[70] On the other hand, the Warraskoyacks were eager for trade goods,[71] as were the Chickahominies.[72] Smith erred in this regard, however: he pressed his luck with the Chickahominies, making three corn-buying trips within a few December days. By the time he traveled up their river a fourth time, intending only to explore—which the language barrier prevented him from explaining—the Chickahominies and their neighbors were ready to pounce and did.[73] Smith's captivity took him to the York River and Rappahannock River basins (chapters 7 and 13), after which he met Powhatan and became his ally—for a while.

The alliance soon went sour, and Smith's extensive explorations around the Chesapeake Bay in the summer of 1608 did not help. Then, in the late summer and autumn of 1608, the colonists had to carry out diplomatic duties at the Virginia Company's behest, which prevented them from laying in food supplies. Among other things, Powhatan was unwillingly "crowned" and supposedly made a subject of King James, after which the English entered the Piedmont against his wishes and made contact with the Monacans. The alliance with the Powhatans came to an end in January 1609, and John Smith's explorations ceased: he was too busy trying to keep his compatriots fed.

The English began expanding beyond Jamestown in 1609, when they built Smith's Fort up Grays Creek and Fort Algernon near modern Fort Monroe in Hampton and established a livestock station on Hog Island. They also attempted to settle in both Nansemond and Powhatan (town) territory in 1609 but were beaten off by the local people. The people of Powhatan town managed to hold onto their village site until nearly 1700. The Nansemonds' attitude toward the English varied from wary to hostile in the early decades of Jamestown's existence, and that, plus fears of the Spanish, helped to delay English settlement until the mid-1630s.

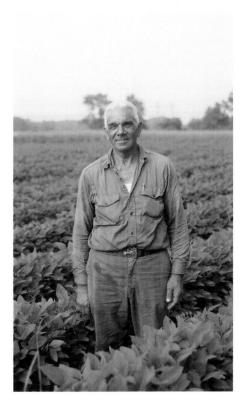

Nansemond Indian Chief Earl Bass in 1971. The Nansemond Tribe is recognized by the State of Virginia. (Helen C. Rountree)

The Nansemonds became factionalized thereafter, and in 1638 the daughter of the pro-English chief married John Bass, an English preacher. Their descendants, who moved to the northeastern rim of the Dismal Swamp in the early 1700s, include the modern Nansemond Indian tribe.

The Jamestowners were more successful elsewhere, although after John Smith left Virginia in October 1609. Kecoughtan was taken over on August 9, 1610, and Paspahegh in 1610–11. The English also managed to gain and keep (until 1622) a foothold at Henricus, which was in Arrohateck territory. All those groups disappeared from the historical record very early.

Once the treasure-hunting phase was past for the Jamestown English, and tobacco became established as a cash crop (by 1617), they wanted the best farmland—which was precisely where the Indian towns were located. The result was a rapid expansion onto Indian farmlands in the James River

English Expeditions on the James, 1607–9
(English dates and Powhatan seasons in parentheses)

Expedition 1 Deciding where to settle (April 26–May 13, 1607; *Cattapeuk*). Cape Henry to mouth of Appomattox River; contacted locals (except Weyanocks) plus Rappahannock visitors.

Expedition 2 Up to the falls of the James and back (May 21–27, 1607; *Cohattayough*). Jamestown Island to the falls of the James; contacted all locals plus Pamunkey visitors

Expedition 3 Trying to trade for food (October–November 1607; *Taquitock*). Kecoughtan up through Quiyoughcohannock.

Expeditions 4–6 Trading up the Chickahominy (Nov. 1607; *Taquitock*). 1st visit: contacted towns as far upriver as Mamanahunt; 2nd visit: to Mamanahunt only; 3rd visit: contacted towns from Mattapanient to Attamuspinck.

Expedition 7 John Smith's captivity (ca. Dec. 9, 1607–Jan. 2, 1608; *Taquitock-*

Popanow). As a captive, John Smith was taken from the Chickahominy's headwaters through Pamunkey Neck, up to the vicinity of Tappahannock, back down to Werowocomoco on the York, and then back to Jamestown.

Expedition 9 Seeing off Christopher Newport (April 10, 1608; *Cattapeuk*). Traveled up Nansemond River as far as capital town.

Expedition 10 First exploration of Chesapeake Bay (June 2–July 21, 1608; *Cohattayough*).

Expedition 11 Second exploration of Chesapeake Bay (July 24–September 2, 1608; *Cohattayough*) (delayed harvest, hence extended Earing of Corn).

Expedition 14 Exploring Monacans' country (fall 1608; *Taquitock*). Direct to the falls of the James, then on foot to two towns above the fall line. Smith stayed in Jamestown.

---

valley, which broke the native people's hold on their territories and sparked the Great Assault of 1622. That attack mainly hit James River settlements.[74] A corollary result was that the great James River plantations that tourists visit today, with houses dating from the 1700s, had their origin in takeovers of the sites of Indian towns. Between 1622 and 1650, the Warraskoyacks and the Quiyoughcohannocks disappeared from the record; as a consequence of the Third Anglo-Powhatan War (1644–46), the Weyanocks moved far south of the James, eventually merging with the Iroquoian-speaking Notto-ways, while the Chickahominies moved to the Mattaponi River area. Their

John Smith's Chesapeake Voyages, 1607–1609

Expedition 15 Trading for food with the Chickahominies (late fall 1608; *Taquitock*). Towns not specified.

Expedition 17 Trading for food at Nansemond (late fall 1608; *Taquitock*).

Expedition 18 Trading for food upriver (late fall 1608; *Taquitock*). To Quiyoughcohannock and Appomattox River, which was explored for first time. Native people were out foraging, so English found few residents.

Expedition 19 Attempt to trade for food elsewhere (early winter 1608; *Popanow*) Scrivener only. No details; Smith stayed in Jamestown.

Expedition 20 Taking corn by force from Powhatan and Opechancanough (Jan.–Feb. 1609, about six weeks; *Popanow;*). Heading upriver, stops at Warraskoyack, Kecoughtan, and Chiskiack. Acquiring corn at Werowocomoco and up Pamunkey and Mattaponi rivers.

Expedition 21 Raiding the Paspaheghs in revenge (probably spring 1609; *Cohattayough*). Paspahegh chief's town, above Chickahominy River's mouth.

Expedition 22 Trying to settle by Nansemond River (Aug. 1609; *Nepinough*). Traveled upriver as far as Nansemond chief's town.

Expedition 23 Trying to settle near the falls (Sept. 1609; *Nepinough*). In and near Powhatan town, downstream.

Expedition 24 Establishing a fort (Ft. Algernon) at Point Comfort (Sept. 1609; *Nepinough*). Near modern Ft. Monroe.

Sources: Archer 1969a [1607]; Haile 1998; Percy 1921–22 [1625?] and 1969 [1608?]; J. Smith 1986a [1608]; J. Smith 1986b [1612]; Smith 1986c [1624]; Spelman 1910 [1613?]; Strachey 1953 [1612]; Wingfield 1969 [1608]; 144–45; Winne 1969 [1608]

descendants ultimately returned to their home territory, where they survive today, with recognition by the Commonwealth of Virginia. By 1700, the Powhatans (then called Powhites) and Appamattucks lived as squatters on English farms, vanishing from the record soon thereafter. The English had filled up the valley, even the uplands away from the river, and had begun pushing into the Piedmont, threatening the Monacans.

The English side of the story has been told for centuries, because the English left the records. Their long-term success in the Chesapeake was due not to physical or cultural superiority, although their firearms were impres-

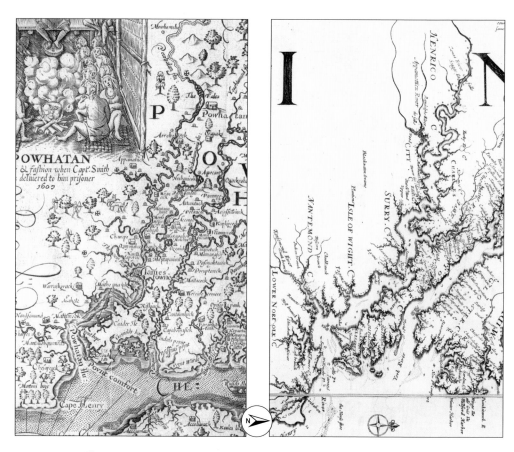

The James River area as mapped by John Smith in 1608 (*left*) and in 1673 by Augustine Herrmann (*right*), showing the transformation from an Algonquian land to one controlled by the English. (The John Carter Brown Library at Brown University)

sive, but to a combination of larger population and the profitable tobacco-raising economy that attracted so many migrants to North America. In 1619, that economy began to bring in other people as well: Africans, initially from Congo and later from other parts of West Africa. In the second half of the seventeenth century, the English hardened their laws to ensure that all incoming Africans arrived as slaves rather than as indentured servants. For several decades, there was a booming trade in human cargo while the Native Americans were pushed out of their ancestral territory, only a few reservations remaining after 1700. This process began in the James River valley (1614) and spread, first to the Virginia Eastern Shore (1620s), then to the York River (early 1630s), then to southern Maryland (including the

Patuxent valley; mid-1630s), then to the Rappahannock and southside Potomac (1640s), and finally, after the fur trade there began to diminish, to the Maryland Eastern Shore (late 1660s).

The English began taking over the York River valley only after establishing themselves on Virginia's Eastern Shore because it was on Pamunkey Neck, the "V" between the Pamunkey and Mattaponi Rivers, that the Powhatan paramount chiefs had had their stronghold since around 1613. John Smith had already seen that part of the Chesapeake, however; he first viewed it as a captive in the last days of the year 1607.

The "Pamunkey":
The York River Drainage

JOHN SMITH FIRST SAW the basin of the York River—which Powhatan and his people called the Pamunkey—while he was a prisoner in December 1607. Although he was in constant fear of his life,[1] he carefully noted what that region and its people were like. Smith need not have worried, for the native people were far too curious about the foreigners to have harmed him—yet.

The Environment

The York River lies across the Virginia Peninsula from the James and passes through similar terrain from the western margin of the Chesapeake Bay to the Piedmont. Yet the environment it presented to John Smith and his compatriots differed in some key ways from the James River country they had already explored. For one thing, the York divides, while still well inside the coastal plain, into two major branches with different names, so the "York River" only exists below West Point, Virginia.

The Waterways

The York's headwaters do not penetrate nearly as far west as those of the James, reaching across only about two-thirds of the Piedmont. With a smaller drainage basin—only 2,670 square miles (6,915.3 square kilometers), or about 12 percent of Virginia's part of the Chesapeake's drainage—the York therefore carries a much smaller volume of rainwater into the bay than the James does. Even that volume has been reduced in recent times by damming along the headwaters of the Pamunkey, and proposals repeatedly surface for additional impoundments to supply growing urban areas. At European Contact, the human population of the York's drainage was under 5,000; in 2000, some 372,488 people lived there.

As with other tributaries of the Chesapeake, the York River's flow changes significantly with the seasons. It is highest in March and April, when it carries snowmelt. The flow shows a secondary "bump" in July, reflecting summer thunderstorm downpours throughout the basin; these may have been rare in the dry years of the early 1600s. The river flow is lowest in October to November, despite occasional hurricanes and tropical cyclones.[2]

The York runs straight and deep (50–80 feet or 15¼–24⅓ meters), which in colonial and modern times has made it a haven for military shipping. At modern West Point, the river bifurcates into two smaller rivers, the Mattaponi on the north and the Pamunkey on the south.[3] These two are both winding rivers so that a fairly long course has to be followed to progress northwestward. On the Mattaponi, twenty-six river miles (42 kilometers) will take a voyager just fifteen miles (24 kilometers) to the modern Hillsboro. On the Pamunkey, a paddler must traverse thirty-eight river miles (61 kilometers) to reach today's Liberty Hall. Since the Pamunkey is especially sinuous across a wide floodplain, the resulting meanders contain great expanses of wetlands downriver and swamp forest upriver.

Wetlands

The York, Pamunkey, and Mattaponi rivers, as well as their tributaries, are all fringed by marshes except where the rivers cut into cliffs.[4] Freshwater emergents like tuckahoe (arrow arum) grow in the far headwaters of long tributaries of the York such as Poropotank River and Kings Creek, moving closer to the creek mouths as one proceeds up the York, but they do not actually appear along the riverfront until well up the Pamunkey and Mattaponi. Cow lily begins above the Mattaponi Reservation on the Mattaponi and around Cousiac Marsh in the Pamunkey; tuckahoe appears around Muddy Point and Hill Marsh, respectively. Water hemp can be found in small amounts along the Mattaponi River from its mouth upward. Both rivers have sizable marshes with wild rice in them, beginning (on the riverfront itself) at about Lester Manor on the Pamunkey and the mouth of Heartquake Creek on the Mattaponi. Some large Pamunkey River marshes lower down have wild rice in their somewhat fresher-water interiors.

The marshes become enormous where the streams meander in the lower reaches of the Pamunkey and Mattaponi. There the river waters are changing from brackish to oligohaline (very slightly salty) to fresh. The most spectacular oxbow in this basin is where the Pamunkey nearly encircles the modern Pamunkey Indian Reservation. Upriver, by the time one reaches the vicinity of Big Island/Elsing Green, the size of marshes along the river and its tributaries decreases considerably. Along the Mattaponi, the major meanders occur in the oligohaline zone, where needlerush and salt-marsh cordgrass are still fairly common; the freshwater marshes upstream are more limited in extent, though some midstream marshy islands compensate somewhat. Cow lily is the common emergent plant there, along with sweetflag. One emergent plant, the duck potato, is rare in Virginia's freshwater streams, but two fairly dense stands (20 percent of two adjacent marshes of six and nine acres [2.4 and 3.6 hectares], respectively) occur nowadays across from the Mattaponi Indian Reservation. (That is the limit of today's freshwater zone, so the stands may not have been there four hundred years ago.) Bulrushes are not common in any of the York basin's waterways, nor is wild millet.

Bald cypress occurs naturally (and is being replanted) along some tributaries of the Mattaponi and Pamunkey. It grows along the creeks from the Goulders Creek area of the Mattaponi upward and the Romancoke area of the Pamunkey upward; bald cypress also can be found along the Pamunkey itself from about the Pamunkey Reservation onward. The clumps are small, as they are at the limit of the species' range today.[5]

Topography

The York River itself is bounded by low, flat land that grades into marshlands near the bay, ascends into uplands on the south, and into gently sloping country rising to uplands on the north. These uplands, which reach fifty feet (nearly 20 meters) above sea level, are clothed mainly in hardwoods, with an understory of holly, wax myrtle (near the bay), mountain laurel, and, in many places, a jungle of briars, Virginia creeper, yellow jessamine, and (today) Japanese honeysuckle. Visitors can experience the uplands at several parks that have been created along the York: Yorktown Battlefields, the Colonial Parkway, and York River State Park. At York River State Park, visitors can rent canoes and paddle along a tributary (saltwater) creek. The river's north bank, where there are fewer and lower cliffs along the waterfront, has always been more attractive to farmers using water transport,[6] and today it is all privately owned.

The cliffs near Yorktown have given their name to the Yorktown Formation (5–1.5 million years ago), with most of the low exposed cliff at the Moore House dating to about 3 million years ago. The fossils in that formation include shark teeth, whale bones, and a wide variety of shellfish. Upriver, below York River State Park, and also farther upstream at Romancoke on the Pamunkey River, the top sediments are Pleistocene but the lower layers are Miocene, dating to 8–6 million years ago. The bottom sediments exposed in the vicinity of the U.S. 301 bridge are Paleocene in age (65–55 million years).[7]

Shellfish and Fishes

The York River's mouth apparently did not have large, emergent oyster reefs, but the shallows around the necks to the north and south would have been fairly productive in pre-Contact times. In summer, blue crabs are still numerous. On the sandy bayfront beaches, horseshoe crabs would have been seen in May and June, coming ashore to spawn above the full-moon tide line. In the autumn, their molted shells would have washed ashore, as they still do.

Chief Powhatan's center of government in 1607 was on Purtan Bay, where the fishing even today is extraordinarily good.[8] Many fish species enter the lower York as part of their life cycle. Menhaden would have been visibly abundant in the seventeenth century, and due to the York's relative proximity (forty miles [64 kilometers]) to the mouth of the Chesapeake, striped bass, sea trout, drum, spot, croaker, and flounder. Up in the Pamunkey and Mattaponi rivers and their headwaters, resident freshwater species would have included bluegill, pickerel, and yellow and white perch, the latter moving down into the upper estuary, where their habitat overlapped that of striped bass.

The seasonal arrival of anadromous fishes would have been a signal event for Native Americans during their hungriest season, the spring (winter stores used up, game animals with their fat used up, no berries available yet). They would have welcomed the shad and river herring fat with roe,

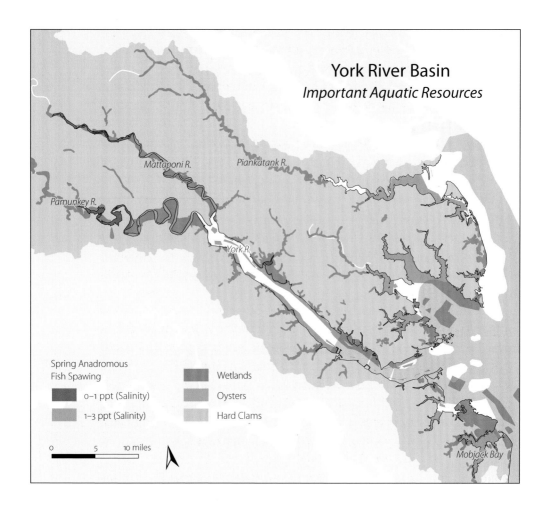

York River Basin
Important Aquatic Resources

Mattaponi R.

Piankatank R.

Pamunkey R.

York R.

Spring Anadromous
Fish Spawing

▮ 0–1 ppt (Salinity)

▮ 1–3 ppt (Salinity)

▮ Wetlands

▮ Oysters

▮ Hard Clams

0   5   10 miles

Mobjack Bay

bent on reproduction, streaming up the rivers and into the smallest fresh-water creeks and rivulets. These species were abundant enough to be easy to harvest and were a rich source of calories as well as protein.

The shad and herring look very much alike: they are thin, deep-bodied, silvery fish with large, smooth scales. Four herring species (two of them called "shad") visit the bay. The largest shad is the American or white shad. Shad roe, the internal egg mass from female shad, is a Chesapeake delicacy. The hickory shad or "tailor shad" are similar in size and shape to the American shad except that the hickory shad has a jutting lower jaw. There are two species of river herring in the bay; the alewife (or big-eye or branch herring), and the blueback herring (also variously called glut herring and alewife). River herring are smaller than the shad and are not as deep bodied. They usually have a single dark spot on their shoulders rather than the series of spots that shad bear. Further, there are two other species of shad that are not anadromous: the gizzard shad and threadfin shad, which are often abundant in brackish and fresh waters. Adults of these species remain in the lower Chesapeake and simply migrate upstream to fresh waters to spawn.[9]

Four centuries ago, an abundance of fishes would have been a boon to humans, plants, and animals alike. In streams surrounded by undisturbed riparian and upland forests, nitrogen for plant and insect growth was at a premium, and the annual flux of large fish populations helped sustain the in-stream communities that fed other parts of the food web. The fish, their eggs, their milt, and their larvae and juveniles were also significant sources of nutrients in smaller upstream tributaries, where a proportion would die or be captured by raccoons, bears, and other predators—which would in turn be hunted by people.

Once the English colonists understood the seasonal fish runs, they began harvesting the bounty as well. Shad are delicious but have abundant fragile bones, a problem for finicky consumers, but they could be smoked or, as later colonists called it, "planked": cleaned of entrails (the roe being separately consumed and a dietary equivalent to caviar from sturgeon) and split open like a book to expose the flesh within. Propped up on a stick or attached to a wooden plank placed close to a well-stoked campfire, the shad would be slowly cooked and eaten freshly roasted or left until they dried and developed a "skin" of sealed tissues that was a barrier to spoilage. Stored carefully, as in the rafters of a pole-built bark lodge, and kept away from rodents and moisture, they would be thus preserved for a substantial time or could be transported for trade.

The People

The York River valley reflected, as no other valley did in the early English records, the three-tier Powhatan political organization. The paramount chief, Powhatan, lived there, first on the York for its central location in eastern Virginia and, after English raids, much farther inland: initially in the Chickahominy headwaters and then, by 1614, on the upper Pamunkey.[10] The names of his district chiefs, including two of his brothers, are known, as are the names of numerous governors of lesser towns overseen by the brothers along what is now the Pamunkey River.[11] In addition, the holiest

Shad Hatcheries on Indian Reservations

Shad have been fished by Native Americans since antiquity, but after European and subsequent colonists became active in the fishery, the indiscriminate use of efficient harvesting technology, combined with the obstruction of spawning streams with dams and road culverts, began to deplete stocks. In the early twentieth century, descendants of the Powhatans started shad hatcheries, employing late nineteenth-century technology. "Ripe" adults were netted and "milked" (squeezed) of their eggs and sperm, these products being mixed in river water as occurs during natural spawning. Then, in a protected environment with aerated water, the many fertilized eggs were allowed to hatch, and the larvae—protected from predators in their most vulnerable life stage—could be released into the river.

While this artisanal hatchery was intermittent, it was later revived. Today, with federal assistance, a modern hatchery laboratory on both the Pamunkey and the Mattaponi reservations produces millions of young fish annually and is receiving its proper public attention.

Pamunkey Indian J. Henry Langston milking eggs from a female shad on the Pamunkey River in 2001. The Pamunkey tribe still operates a shad hatchery. (From the collections of The Mariners' Museum, Newport News, Va.)

temple site in Powhatan's dominions was located on high ground overlooking the Pamunkey near modern West Point.

At this writing, all the towns along the York and its two source rivers on the coastal plain are assumed to be dispersed-settlement towns, rather than densely nucleated towns with palisades.[12] John Smith's map does not specify which towns belonged to which chief—it is possible that loyalties shifted from time to time anyway. The following assignments of towns to territories are therefore our best guess.[13]

Chiskiack

Here a single town, Chiskiack, had an estimated 210 people including 40–50 warriors; the chief was Ottahotin.[14] Chiskiack was located on the south side of the York in a location that today lies on the east bank of Indian Field Creek inside the U.S. Naval Weapons Station. The location was confirmed archaeologically in 2004. Pieces of copper found there are chemically identical with pieces of trade copper unearthed by the APVA/Jamestown Rediscovery project.

Another site, a sixteenth-century Spanish Jesuit mission, may be in this general vicinity.[15] It was established in September 1570 but eliminated by local Indian groups in February 1571. No archaeological traces of the mission have yet been found.

Werowocomoco

This group consisted of six towns with an estimated 200 people including 40 warriors; the chief was Powhatan. The towns were located on the north bank of the York. Traveling upriver these are: *Cantaunkack,* probably at the mouth of Carter Creek, at Shelly; *Capahowasick,* at the modern district of Capahosic; *Wighsakan,* probably around Fox Creek; *Werowocomoco,* on a peninsula extending into Purtan Bay; *Mattacock,* on the east side of Adams Creek; and *Poruptanck,* at the mouth of the Poropotank River. The site of Werowocomoco is confirmed and currently being excavated. It was Powhatan's capital when the English arrived in 1607; he abandoned it in early 1609, moving to Orapax in the Chickahominy River's headwaters near Bottoms Bridge. It was at Werowocomoco that Powhatan first met John Smith.

There are archaeological sites dating from the correct period for all but the Mattacock area, with test excavations at Cantaunkack and Werowocomoco.[16]

Pamunkey

The Pamunkey group consisted of twenty-one towns with an estimated 1,500 people, including 300 fighting men (according to Smith; Strachey says there were many more); the chiefs were Opitchapam and Kekataugh. This was one of Powhatan's original inherited territories.[17] It is difficult to draw boundaries based on John Smith's map, so here we rely on evidence of less-inhabited areas to establish boundaries. The Pamunkey and Mattaponi rivers are narrow enough that tribal territories could encompass two—and in the case of the Pamunkeys, three—riverbanks.

Northeast of the York and lower Mattaponi, heading upriver, the towns were: *Pasaughtacock,* west of Hockley Creek (may have belonged to Werowocomoco); *Mamanassy,* at the mouth of the Mattaponi opposite West Point; and *Matchutt,* between Heartquake and Old Mill creeks.

Northeast of the Pamunkey the towns were: a town of unknown name at West Point; *Cinquoteck,* a short distance upstream from West Point; *Menapucunt,* at modern Romancoke; *Uttamussak,* slightly inland from Romancoke (location of Powhatan people's holiest temple site); *Kupkipcock,* near Sweet Hall Marsh; a town of unknown name a short distance upstream from Kupkipcock; *Accossumwinck,* near Cohoke Mill Creek; *Osamkateck,* on the Pamunkey Indian Reservation; and *Opawunkack,* around Elsing Green.

Southwest of the Pamunkey, heading upriver, the towns were: *Oquonock,* at the mouth of the Pamunkey River below Eltham; *Mattchamins/Matchut,* at Eltham; *Acconoc,* west of the southwestern edge of Lee Marsh; *Potawuncack,* south of or just downstream from Cousiac Marsh; *Attamtuck,* between West Island and Lilly Point Marsh; *Weanock,* opposite southwestern tip of Cohoke Marsh; *Pamuncoroy,* opposite the Pamunkey Indian Reservation; *Righkahauck,* east of the mouth of Black Creek; and *Shamapint,* a short distance upstream from Righkahauck.

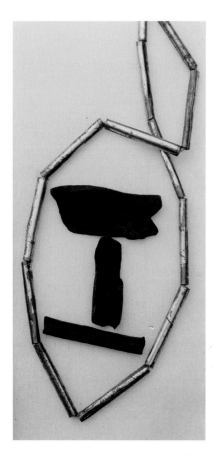

Copper beads excavated at Werowocomoco, surrounded by modern replica beads from Jamestown Settlement Museum. (Helen C. Rountree)

Archaeological survey has located candidates for the towns of Uttamussak, Osamkateck, Pamuncoroy, and Righkahauck, but no in-depth excavations have yet been carried out.

Youghtanund

This group consisted of twelve towns with an estimated 400 people, including 60 warriors; the chief was Opechancanough.

Northeast of the Pamunkey, heading upriver, the towns were: *Askecocack,* at Pampetike Landing; *Cattachiptico,* east of the U.S. 360 bridge, above Manquin Creek's mouth; *Washasatiack,* above the mouth of Mehixen Creek; *Askecack,* east of Sutton Neck, opposite Crump Neck; a town of unknown name, near the mouth of Millpond Creek; and *Enekent,* below the C.R. 614 bridge.

Southwest of the Pamunkey, going upriver, the towns were: *Parokonosko,* around Horseshoe, opposite Pampetike Landing; *Matunsk,* upstream from Parakonosko; *Manaskunt,* in the vicinity of the U.S. 360 bridge; *Youghtanan,* upstream from the U.S. 360 bridge; *Menoughtass,* location uncertain; and *Maskunt,* location uncertain.

Near Cattachiptico, Powhatan would have his final capital, called Matchut (another Matchut), during the last years of his life (1614–18). A number of Late Woodland sites are known from the Youghtanunds' territory, perhaps correlating with Cattachiptico, Parakonosko, Manaskunt, and Youghtanan.

Mattaponi

This group consisted of eight settlements with an estimated 360 people including 30 fighting men (140 according to Strachey); the chief was Werowough. Early English maps show no settlement as being a "kings howse." The settlements designated here as Mattaponi cluster in the middle to upper reaches of the river.

Northeast of the Mattaponi, going upriver, the towns were: *Muttamussinsack,* around modern Rickahock; *Amacauncock,* location uncertain; *Martoughquaunk,* near Walkerton; *Utcustank,* upriver from Walkerton; and a town of unknown name upriver from Utcustank.

Southwest of the Mattaponi, going upriver, the towns were: *Quackcohowaon,* around Horse Landing, above Mantua Ferry; *Myghtuckpassun,* west of White Bank; and *Passaunkack,* above Aylett.

At this writing, there have been no major excavations in the Mattaponi River area, but possible candidates have been found for all the towns except Amacauncock and Myghtuckpassun.

Interplay between People and the Environment

The lowlands next to the bay, consisting of Guinea Neck on the north and Goodwin Neck and Poquoson (the old Powhatan word for "swamp") on the south, have until recently been used mainly by fishermen: Indians in summer fishing camps and postcolonial watermen's communities with near-tribal subcultures of their own. A major facet of the people's way of life was building watercraft. Indian canoes were dugouts, made from single logs (see chapter 2). Early English settlers bought and adapted such canoes or else gouged out their own with metal tools. After the tobacco boom subsided, however, a local "log canoe"–building industry appeared in which the previous design was amplified by the joining of from two to five or more logs, which were then hollowed into a single, well-designed sailing hull. These evolved canoes, built in the York River basin but in many other places as well, were the backbone of the Chesapeake sailing oyster industry well into the nineteenth century, with remnants persisting well into the twentieth century. A number of these craft are still afloat. The log canoes made in Poquoson were considered the most famous of this class. In the 1800s, a European invention, the centerboard—a keel-like piece that could be raised and lowered, depending on sailing conditions—was tried with great success; a log canoe equipped with a centerboard could sail well into the wind without a heavy or fixed keel, an ideal adaptation for the bay's shallow waters. Log canoes were thus the progenitors of the centerboard commercial and pleasure vessels in the Chesapeake.

Location of Indian Towns

Most Native American inhabitants of the coastal plain portion of the York River drainage built their long-term settlements along the Pamunkey and Mattaponi rivers, especially the Pamunkey. When one plots the locations of prime farmland and of the richest wild food resources, the profusion of Indian villages in certain areas makes sense. The native people usually placed their settlements as close as possible to the best arable land and most ample wild food supply. The most powerful chiefs with the most subjects lived along the Pamunkey, which had the richest resources, and when Powhatan occupied his final capital (circa 1614), it was far up that river whose meanders would slow down English boats while runners raced up the trails to warn him.

As discussed in chapter 2, the best soils for raising corn are the "warm" alluvial ones variously called State, Suffolk, Sassafras, Kempsville, Pamunkey, and Wickham, with the latter two having moderate natural fertility.[18] These two soil types can be found within the floodplains of the Pamunkey and Mattaponi, often in curving patches that show the ancient flow of the ancient river that deposited them. Much more often than not, the villages shown on John Smith's map were located on or very near patches of the best soil. Along the Pamunkey, which splits into the North Anna and South Anna rivers just short of the fall line, patches of prime farmland occur up to and beyond the split, much farther than the Algonquian speakers actually settled. Their decision not to live there may have been due more to the narrowness of the river and the dearth of marshes than to fear of Monacan hunters, who lived mainly along the James River's piedmont reaches.

There are no easily reached "breadbaskets"[19] of edible marsh plants in the old territories of the Chiskiacks or Werowocomocos, and those occurring today far up Ware Creek and the Poropotank River (tuckahoe [arrow arum] and wild rice, respectively) may not have existed four centuries ago, when the river was saltier. Those in the territory of the Pamunkeys consist nowadays of large stands of tuckahoe and wild rice near the modern Pamunkey Reservation; they would probably have been present in 1608.[20] The Youghtanunds' territory also contained several excellent stands of wild rice: the largest pure stand of rice on the whole coastal plain is on the south side of the Pamunkey River near the Pamunkey Indian Reservation (and so near Osamkateck). Others are along the mouth of Montague Creek and above Putney's Mill on the south side of the river, and on the north side in the marsh in front of Clayborne Creek, in Jacks Creek (near Opawnkack), in Polkwest Creek (adjacent Shamapint), in Broad Creek near Chericoke, and in the marsh at Piping Tree Ferry. (There may be others upriver.[21]) The Mattaponi River boasts several wild rice "breadbaskets," all of them on the King and Queen County side of the river: two marshes near the Mattaponi Indian Reservation (Mitchell Hill Creek and the island just above the reservation), one marsh in Garnetts Creek, and a riverside marsh next to Rickahock (near Muttamussinsack).

Subsequent Indian Locations

Natural resources also played a role in the native people's choice, as shown by the lands owned by the two surviving reservations. The Pamunkey Indians once owned much of Pamunkey Neck, the land between the Mattaponi and Pamunkey rivers. In 1701, they voluntarily gave up claim to most of that territory as English settlers moved in. The land they chose to keep was a large tract that included the modern reservation, consisting of a peninsula

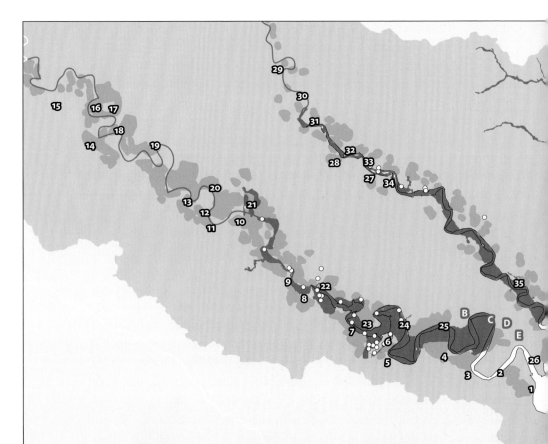

King's Houses

A Chiskiack
B Kupkipcock
C Menapucunt
D Uttamussak
E Cinquoteck
F Werowocomoco
G Payankatank

Ordinary Towns

1 Oquonock
2 Mattchamins/
   Matchut
3 Acconoc
4 Potawunkack
5 Weanock
6 Attamtuck
7 Pamuncoroy
8 Righkahauck
9 Shamapint
10 Parokonosko
11 Matunsk
12 Manaskunt
13 Youghtanan
14 Menoughtass
15 Maskunt
16 Enekent
17 Unnamed Settlement
18 Askecack
19 Washasatiack
20 Cattachiptico
21 Askecocack
22 Opawnkack
23 Osamkateck
24 Accossumwinck
25 Unnamed Settlement
26 Unnamed Settlement
27 Quackcohowaon
28 Myghtuckpassun
29 Passauncack
30 Unnamed Settlement
31 Utcustank
32 Martoughquaunk
33 Amacauncock
34 Muttamussinsack
35 Matchutt
36 Mamanassy
37 Pasaughtacock
38 Poruptanck
39 Mattacock
40 Wighsakan
41 Capahowasick
42 Cantaunkack
43 Unnamed Settlement
44 Unnamed Settlement

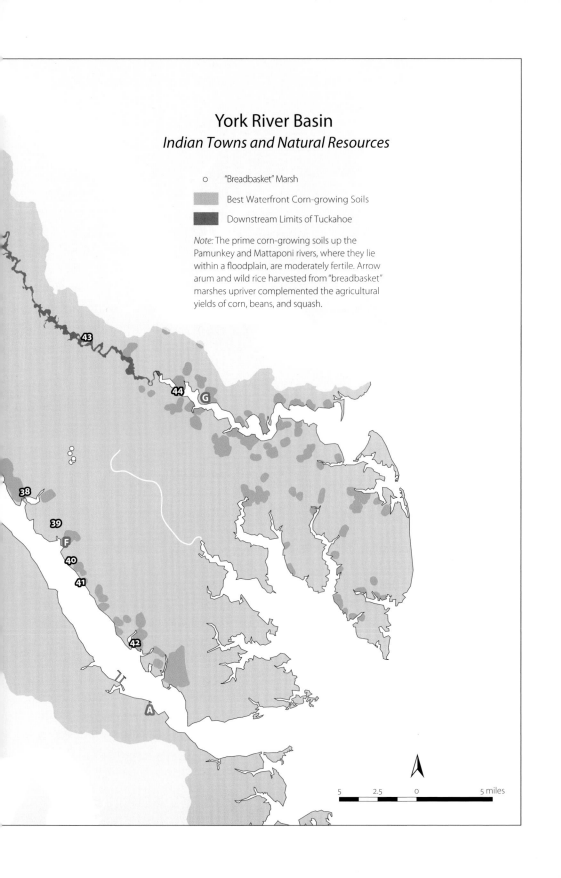

York River Basin
Indian Towns and Natural Resources

○   "Breadbasket" Marsh

▢   Best Waterfront Corn-growing Soils

▣   Downstream Limits of Tuckahoe

Note: The prime corn-growing soils up the
Pamunkey and Mattaponi rivers, where they lie
within a floodplain, are moderately fertile. Arrow
arum and wild rice harvested from "breadbasket"
marshes upriver complemented the agricultural
yields of corn, beans, and squash.

5   2.5   0   5 miles

Modern Indians

The two York River drainage Indian communities of 1700 have since become three. The Pamunkey and Mattaponi reservations still exist, under a treaty signed in 1677, and the Pamunkeys operate a museum open to the public. The Mattaponis put on an annual powwow and have a privately run museum. A Chickahominy contingent returned to Charles City County 150 to 200 years ago (see chapter 6). Another group left the Mattaponi Reservation before that and became today's nonreservation Upper Mattaponis, who also put on an annual powwow and are recognized by the State of Virginia. The powwows are open to the public and announced in the media.

within an oxbow; come what may, the Pamunkeys have held onto the peninsula ever since. Why choose that place, out of all the other waterfront Pamunkey River land? The defensibility and isolation of the land within the oxbow very likely was one factor. But the natural resources there and nearby would have been additional reasons. The reservation itself is a combination of prime farmland and the swamp forest (supporter of deer and wild turkeys) that fills many of the meanders upstream. Much of the reservation's farmland is the very best: Pamunkey loam. The river water is fresh, which means that fish come there to spawn in the spring. But the clincher among natural resources may have been the "breadbaskets." Some of the largest expanses of tuckahoe in the York River drainage occur across the river to the west. And the very best stands of wild rice—today and probably back in 1701[22]—grow directly across from the reservation on Chamberlayne Point and in Holts, Big, and Old Town creeks. If drought came or the English turned hostile, that peninsula was definitely a place where people could survive. One can extrapolate from all this that the choice of which land to keep was made by both men (in charge of defense) and women (in charge of plant foods).

The Mattaponi Reservation has remained in Indian hands for overlapping reasons. The tract is small and mostly on the top of a bluff, so farming soil is not an issue. The adjacent river waters today are just barely fresh, so that fishing is good in the spring. It is impossible to know whether the ancestors of today's duck potatoes across the river were there four centuries ago; if salty water penetrated farther upstream, it is unlikely. But the Mattaponi Reservation has a topographical feature that made it extremely desirable, as bluff-top sites go: it has a natural ramp leading down to the river, called the "cliff landing" in the old land patents. There is also a nearby "breadbasket," a stand of wild rice on an island just above the reservation.

Native American Use of Fossils

The cliffs along the York River are rich in fossils. Along the Colonial Parkway west of Yorktown, people have long picked up shark teeth eroded from the nearby cliffs. One especially interesting fossil, however, comes from a late Pliocene source, the upper sediments of the Yorktown Formation (dated to approximately 3 million years ago). Those sediment beds contain small (half-inch or 1.3-centimeter) univalve mollusks usually called marginellas. Some, classified as *Prunum limatulum,* were the shells used to embroider the famous "Powhatan's Mantle" that is held in the Ashmolean Museum in Oxford, England. (A carefully made replica is on display at Jamestown Settlement.)

The mantle represents a tremendous amount of effort and also an enigma. The labor required to create it was partially in the shell gathering—in all, some seventeen thousand shells from sediments in which they are moderately common but not abundant. It would have taken a long time to collect enough marginellas to embroider something the size of a great chief's mantle, and each one had to be polished into a shine.[23] It then had to be separately prepared for sewing by having a spot on one "shoulder" grated off. The seamstress—this was all female work, in a culture where all women and girls already worked full-time—passed a needle into the shell's aperture (mouth) and then through the hole in the shoulder and drew the shell onto the deer-sinew thread. She then passed the needle partway through the elk hide of the mantle (no stitches at all show on the back), pulled the sinew thread taut, then threaded on another shell, and so on. It must have taken forever!

The enormous amount of female labor required, as well as the gleam of the white shiny shells on the finished product, would have made that mantle extremely valuable. But the enigma is whether it was made for Powhatan himself. There is no mention of such a garment in any Virginia record, only in a Maryland one. A Jesuit missionary there wrote of "a cloak, oftentimes ornamented with shells in circular rows" in 1639, the year after the mantle appeared in the records of the Tradescant "cabinet"[24] in England, so it would seem that the mantle was shipped from Maryland. Yet the shells themselves do not occur in Maryland, for the exposed cliff sediments there are too old. Marginellas do occur along the York and James rivers and

The Powhatan Mantle. Made of four elk skins stitched together, the garment measures 7 feet 8.5 inches (2.35 meters) at its longest and 5 feet 3 inches (1.6 meters) at its widest. (Ashmolean Museum, University of Oxford/The Bridgeman Art Library International)

points south, where sediments are younger. Logically, then, the mantle was made in Virginia, for either Powhatan (d. 1618) or for Opechancanough (d. 1646, after making a peace treaty in 1632), and once in English hands it somehow traveled to Maryland before being shipped overseas.[25]

Enter the English

John Smith was captured about midway between the James and Pamunkey rivers, out in the "wildernesse." From Opechancanough's hunting camp near the Chickahominy's headwaters, Smith was first taken on a junket around Pamunkey Neck in an effort to show him to Powhatan, then on the communal hunt with his people. When that failed, Smith was taken back to the camp, which was dismantled, and then the party headed down through the forest in what is now New Kent County, avoiding the many

John Smith's Chesapeake Voyages, 1607–1609

Indian towns along the Pamunkey. (Protocol dictated that Powhatan or his brothers should be the first to see the captive celebrity.) Then they crossed the Pamunkey near modern Romancoke and stayed at least one day there, at Menapucunt, which was governed by a younger brother, Kekataugh. After a journey to the Rappahannock River and back, Smith was taken to meet Powhatan at Werowocomoco, on modern Purtan Bay. There he was feasted, interrogated, rescued—maybe—by Pocahontas, and sent back to Jamestown with an alliance in his pocket.[26]

In February 1608 at Powhatan's invitation, Christopher Newport and John Smith made a formal diplomatic visit to the York River basin.[27] After a trading session of several days at Werowocomoco, they went to a reunion with Opechancanough at Pamunkey. They also visited a town on the Mattaponi River, where a mock battle was staged for their entertainment.[28] They stopped at Chiskiack on their return, but the people there were hostile, having been bypassed (and deprived of English trade goods) earlier in the expedition. A stop on the way upriver may not have helped, however: the Chiskiacks had been hostile to the English from as early as June 1607.[29]

Anglo-Powhatan relations deteriorated during the next year, with John Smith's voyages of exploration around the Chesapeake Bay being a major contributing factor. Matters did not improve when, in the autumn of 1608, Christopher Newport and John Smith went to Werowocomoco and tried to "crown" Powhatan, making him (in English minds) a subject of King James I.[30] They followed up that visit with an expedition into Monacan country against Powhatan's explicit wishes, after which, having laid in no provisions, the English faced starvation in the coming winter. In January 1609, Powhatan invited them to trade for the corn they needed, and both sides planned an ambush. The English prevailed and went on to extort corn from the native people along both the Pamunkey and Mattaponi rivers.[31] During that time, Powhatan moved his capital from Werowocomoco (which the returning English found all but deserted) to Orapax in the headwaters of the Chickahominy River, where English barges could not go.[32] And the alliance between Powhatan and John Smith was at an end.

In the next few years, the English concentrated their interests either along the James River, where they began expanding their settlements in 1611, or on the Potomac River, where they traded for corn with the Patawomecks. The settlements along the James were enough to cause the Powhatan leadership, ostensibly in Opitchapam/Itoyatin's hands after Powhatan's death in 1618 and actually in the hands of his heir Opechancanough, to attack with the interlopers in 1622, leading to a decade of warfare that eventually ended

English Expeditions on the York, 1607–9

(English dates and Powhatan seasons in parentheses)

Expedition 7 John Smith's captivity (ca. Dec. 9, 1607–Jan. 2, 1608; *Taquitock-Popanow*). As a captive, John Smith traveled from the headwaters of the Chickahominy through Pamunkey Neck up to the vicinity of Tappahannock, back down to Werowocomoco on the York, and then back to Jamestown.

Expedition 8 Diplomatic visit to Werowocomoco (ca. Feb. 1608; *Popanow*). The expedition made an outward-bound stop at Warraskoyack and stopped at Chiskiack coming back down the York; they reached as far as Menapacute on the Pamunkey River.

Expedition 10 First exploration of Chesapeake Bay (June 2–July 21, 1608; *Cohattayough*).

Expedition 11 Second exploration of Chesapeake Bay (July 24–September 2, 1608; *Cohattayough*) (delayed harvest, hence extended Earing of Corn).

Expedition 12 Smith carried message to Powhatan (autumn 1608; *Taquitock*). The expedition traveled to Werowocomoco and back to Jamestown.

Expedition 13 Smith and Newport "crowning" of Powhatan (autumn 1608; *Taquitock*). The party traveled to Werowocomoco and back.

Expedition 16 Trading for food at Werowocomoco (late autumn 1608; *Taquitock*). Party led by Matthew Scrivener; John Smith stayed in Jamestown.

Expedition 20 Taking corn by force from Powhatan and Opechancanough (Jan.–Feb. 1609; *Popanow*). The venture lasted about six weeks and included outward-bound stops at Warraskoyack, Kecoughtan, and Chiskiack. Corn was acquired at Werowocomoco and at towns up the Pamunkey and Mattaponi rivers. This trip marked the first push up Pamunkey above Menapacute and the first exploration of the Mattaponi via water.

Sources: Haile 1998; J. Smith 1986a [1608]; J. Smith 1986b [1612]; J. Smith 1986c [1624]; Wingfield 1969 [1608].

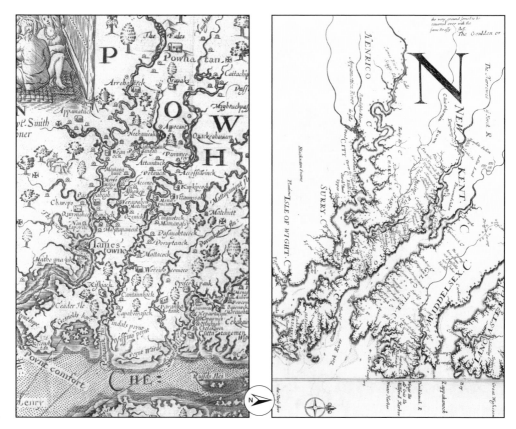

The York River and lower Pamunkey River as mapped by John Smith in 1608 (*left*) and by Augustine Herrmann in 1673 (*right*). Smith's map shows the high density of native sites in the heart of the Powhatan territory. Herrmann's map indicates native reservations on lands that were retained as English tobacco plantations spread upriver.

in a stalemate.[33] During that time, the English finally managed to establish a York River beachhead at the recently abandoned town of Chiskiack.[34] The town's inhabitants, later called "Cheesecake Indians" by the English, took themselves well out of the Englishmen's way (they hoped) and settled on the Piankatank River; the Piankatanks (formerly Kecoughtans) gradually lost their identity in the merger. The Chiskiacks would remain there until the terrible Seneca raids of 1683, when they apparently merged with another surviving Powhatan group.[35]

English tobacco farmers began patenting the banks of the York in the 1630s. For a time, they gave a wide berth to Pamunkey Neck (the "V" between the Pamunkey and Mattaponi rivers), where Opechancanough and his people were still both strong and defensive, but as more Englishmen claimed headrights (land in exchange for paying passage for more immigrants), the riverbanks closer to the Powhatan stronghold began to see pale "owners." In 1644–46, Opechancanough went to war again, despite being in advanced old age.[36] He lost this time. His successor signed a treaty,[37] but the English simultaneously passed a law, unknown to the Indian side, that reworded the treaty and allowed settlement north of the York.[38] Thereafter immigrants began pouring into the river valleys of coastal Virginia, taking up riverfront lands first and interiors of necks later on, until the coastal plain was all claimed and (in the 1680s) farmers began probing into the Piedmont. Pamunkey Neck was left as an Indian island and continued to be through the end of the century, not because it belonged to Indians but because the College of William and Mary claimed ten thousand acres (4,000 hectares) in it as an endowment and that tract had to be surveyed. The Treaty of Middle Plantation,[39] signed in 1677 and ratified with gifts to Indian leaders, allowed Indian communities only the land within a three-mile (4.8-kilometer) radius of their towns. And there were not many towns: the Youghtanunds had merged with the Pamunkeys, the Mattaponis were independent until the Seneca raids of 1683, and the Chickahominies, who had left their homeland in 1646 to get away from the English, took them in. Three communities then became two.[40] In 1701, the college survey was finally complete and the brand-new King William County was opened for settlement.

8

The Farmers and Fishermen
of the Lower Eastern Shore

JOHN SMITH MADE HIS FIRST STOP on the lower Eastern Shore after setting out on his initial exploration of the Chesapeake Bay.[1] He saw two "grim" men at Cape Charles, spearfishing with bone-headed javelins, and when he had reassured these men of his peaceful intentions, they directed him to the Accomac chief's town, where he received a friendly reception. The chief—possibly a predecessor of Esmy Shichans, the famous "Laughing King" of the 1620s—told him about the waterways and islands to the north, but not much about the people there. Although Smith claimed later to have visited "every inlet, and bay fit for harbours and habitations,"[2] all versions of his map show only a few towns, mainly Accomack and Accohannock. That may have been because most of the creeks of the Virginia Eastern Shore are small and obstructed enough[3] that they did not meet Smith's standard of "fit harbours" for navigation, so that their inhabitants were not very important. Yet we know that Smith was intent on seeking a Northwest Passage, and, knowing that the area was within striking range of Spanish ships entering the capes, he would have paid scant attention to the southern part of the Delmarva Peninsula. In fact, he missed a great deal there.

The Environment

The Virginia Eastern Shore differs in several ways from other regions within the Chesapeake drainage. The peninsula is flat or nearly so,[4] reflecting its origin as a southward-moving sand spit for the last 2 million years. It is also relatively narrow, so that no part of it is far from either the Atlantic Ocean or the Chesapeake Bay—an arrangement that tempers the heat of summer and the cold of winter. On its eastern, Atlantic side is seawater, while the water on its western side ranges from seawater near the capes to brackish farther north. Being surrounded by water has also isolated the peninsula—at least before the Chesapeake Bay Bridge-Tunnel was built—from many of the comings and goings of land animals, including people.

Especially at its Cape Charles end, the peninsula is narrow, so that animal resources, chiefly deer and other game, had limited forage opportunities and also could easily have been overhunted. The area's stream network was not extensive enough to sustain numerous beaver populations. Native Americans who lived on the seaside had access to shellfish and oceanic resources on the nine offshore barrier islands, such as Mockhorn and Parramore islands. Some of these islands are only now revealing archaeological evidence of pre-Contact human occupants and the living resources they harvested, such as sea turtles and sharks.[5]

The forest covering the shore formerly comprised hardwoods mixed with pines, except where the land was too low and the pines predominated. Near the tip of the shore are live oaks, a southern species living at its northern limit. Mockhorn Island is today the northernmost outpost of yaupon holly trees on the Atlantic coast. The wetland plants are all salt-tolerant species such as black needlerush and saltmarsh cordgrasses, the latter producing enough shoots and seeds even today to feed tremendous flocks of migratory waterfowl that pass through on the Eastern Flyway.

The shallows and tidal flats of the lower Eastern Shore are home to both hard clams and softshell clams, as well as to oysters that prefer a subtidal environment. Oyster reefs actually used to impede access to some creeks—notably Kings Creek, where the larger fishing boats could get in and out only at high tide.

The deepest channels of the bay are closer to the Eastern Shore than to the western one, and the water incoming with tidal flow is saltier along the Eastern Shore due not only to the Coriolis effect[6] but also to the small input of freshwater from the short bayside creeks. Many oceanic saltwater fishes—including species such as bluefish, sea trout, and mackerel—move along this route and up the bay in summer. Other, bottom-feeding species such as croaker, spot, black drum, and winter flounder move shoreward in warm weather, into shallows where fish weirs can catch them (see below).

The People

John Smith recorded only two Indian towns on the lower Eastern Shore, but there was actually a paramount chiefdom there, subject to the greater paramount chief Powhatan; county records from later times indicate considerably more towns. Smith discussed only the towns of Accomack (Accowmack) and Accohannock.

Accomac
This group consisted of one town, Accomack, whose inhabitants included 40 warriors. According to early colonial maps, the town Accomack was located in the vicinity of Old Plantation Creek, where several small Late Woodland sites have been found. The people, the Accomacs, subsequently wound up on the sea side of the Shore, where they became known as Gingaskins (1640s–1813).[7]

Occohannock
This group consisted of several towns whose inhabitants included 80 fighting men. E. Randolph Turner estimates 510 people for them and the Accomacs combined. That figure may be low; John Smith learned of an epidemic that had struck the Accomacs not long before he went there.[8] A later writer, John Pory (1621), estimated that "there may be on this shore two thousand people," and Pory mentioned visiting only the Accomacs and Occohannocks.

John Pory also discovered that the Accomac and Occohannock chiefs were brothers—Esmy Shichans and Kiptopeke, respectively—who ruled jointly.[9] The arrangement was broken by the late 1640s, for Northampton and Accomack County records show the Accomac/Gingaskins as separate, with several other groups living under one paramount chief, based variously at Accohannock, Onancock, or Nandua. Not all the groups noted below existed at any one time; the variety reflects voluntary changes of name (e.g., Gingaskin) and the tendency of county clerks to denominate Indians

Diet of Worms, Chesapeake Style

In the early 1600s, the bottom of the bay and its tributaries supported communities of worms, clams, and crustaceans collectively called the "benthos," which differed among sandy, muddy, or grassy bottoms. In precolonial times, these billions of organisms were fed by relatively diluted nutrients and detritus delivered by the bay's rivers and streams. Benthic organisms were literally the food base for the harvestable fish, crabs, and birds that so impressed later Chesapeake colonists. An example is the burrowing clamworm, which reaches several inches (perhaps 10 centimeters) in length and is a succulent meal for fish foraging on the bottom. Sturgeon, a dietary mainstay for the Jamestown colonists, feed directly on this resource. When those worms reproduce in spring, they transform into a swimming form called an epitoke that moves upward in the water and can become nutritious prey for fish that feed near the surface.

Cores taken from the bay bottom are time capsules revealing the bay's past. Scientists find the tiny jaws of these and other worms, indicating that they were abundant before the English came but were precipitously reduced (in some instances by 90 percent) in later centuries. Fish species known to feed on these worms are, like their prey, less abundant in the bay today.

In fresher waters, the larvae of midges overwinter and mature in bottom sediments in densities of thousands per square yard. The larvae emerge into successive broods of adults when the water warms, providing food for small fish as they surface, and more still are caught on the wing by swallows, martins, and other birds arriving after their migrations.

by where they were living (e.g., Currituicks,[10] who may have been part of the Nanduas). The settlements marked with an asterisk were listed by Robert Beverley as still surviving as subjects of an "empress" in 1705.[11]

On the bay side, south to north, the towns were: *Machipongo*, probably on Hungars Creek (an English name); *Nassawadox*, on the creek of that name; *Pungoteague*, on the creek of that name; *Nandua*, on the creek of that name; *Currituck/Craddock*, on the creek of that name; *Occohannock* (*Accohannock*), somewhere south of Occohannock Creek in 1608[12] (by the 1630s, the name applied specifically to the chiefdom on the creek that still bears the name); *Onancock*, on the creek of that name; and *Chesconessex*, on the creek of that name.

On the sea side, south to north (outside the purview of this volume), the

John Smith's Chesapeake Voyages, 1607–1609

One early writer describes a large bay "crab" species as having "a crustie taile" (Lankford 1967). This was not a true crab (decapod crustacean); it was the horseshoe crab, the females of which (in some areas) lay millions of eggs at the high tide mark along the bay's mostly small, sandy beaches. Female horseshoe crabs can grow to a length of two feet, including their spearlike tail, and they can be found, often as part of male-female pairs, on sandy Middle and Lower Chesapeake beaches near full-moon spring tides in May or June. Shorebirds, headed north along the Atlantic Flyway to their northern breeding grounds, gorge on this food-fuel in May or June. Smith records "dotterel" (i.e., plover) and "oxeye" among such birds. Native Americans only lightly harvested these birds, but their European successors would shoot and fish some species to near-extinction. Invertebrates are still abundant on the bay's bottom and shorelines, but near polluted urban and industrial areas such as Baltimore, Washington, D.C., and Norfolk, relatively few species survive. Also, in most of the bay's deep channel areas, plankton blooms—the result of terrestrial nutrient runoff—settle to the bottom and decompose, driving oxygen levels so low that every summer, over wide areas of the bay bottom in deep water, all bottom-dwelling species are killed. Both these conditions deny food and habitat to fish, crabs, and visiting birds.

Sources: Arnold 2003; Grace Brush personal communication to Kent Mountford; C. Timothy Morris, personal communication to Kent Mountford.

towns were: *Metomkin,* near the bay of that name; *Gargatha,* near the bay of that name; *Kegotank,* near the bay of that name; *Chincoteague/Assateague,* uncertain, but probably on those islands or Wallops Island, where farmland is better (by Beverley's time, these people had moved north to the Maryland coast).

John Smith naturally missed the Indian groups living on the Atlantic side of the peninsula. It is more difficult to explain his apparent missing of the bayside groups other than the Occohannocks, but one clue is the fact that the Accomacs he did visit spoke the Powhatan language, which Smith had begun to learn.[13] Smith may have limited his questions, asked only if there were deepwater creeks to the north that were suitable for ships (answer: no), and lost interest in the area. (For another possible reason, see the

Indians Towns: Sometimes Difficult to See from the Water

It is difficult to spot a town that is camouflaged, even if the inhabitants did not do the camouflaging deliberately.

Most Indian towns consisted of houses scattered among small fields, overgrown fields, and groves of older trees. Even after the harvest, much of the "town" would have vegetated areas interspersed among the houses. Then there were the houses themselves. Whether covered with bark or with mats, their outer shells were brown or dun-colored when new and grayish when weathered. They blended right in with deciduous trees and shrubs in winter and were shielded from view by foliage in summer.

The best way to find an Indian town was to watch for smoke rising above the trees on calm days and blowing into one's nostrils on windy ones—if the wind was right. The wind was not right, however, when John Smith passed by the lower Eastern Shore: it was onshore, perhaps from the southwest (see chapter 4), and it blew the telltale smoke from houses inland.

box on Indian towns.) To date archaeological survey of the creekside lands has been limited to shorelines and the surfaces of plowed fields.

Interplay between People and the Environment

Powhatan added the Virginia Eastern Shore—probably peacefully, just as the English later did—to his dominions as he spread his influence from his inherited territories near the fall line. Why bother with a peninsula lying across a major body of open water? The answer probably lies with the shells available there. Shell beads, and especially conch-shell pendants and column beads, were highly valued throughout the prehistoric Southeast, and Powhatan's heartland lacked the saltwater species that produced the shells.[14] (For a more detailed discussion of shell jewelry, see chapter 9.) He therefore had to procure such status symbols by trade, which meant paying out valuable copper and puccoon that he had had to import. So rather than buying the worked shells from the Accomacs and Occohannocks, or from the Kuskarawaoks/Nanticokes who specialized in making them, he managed to bring the former two groups under his influence, probably by

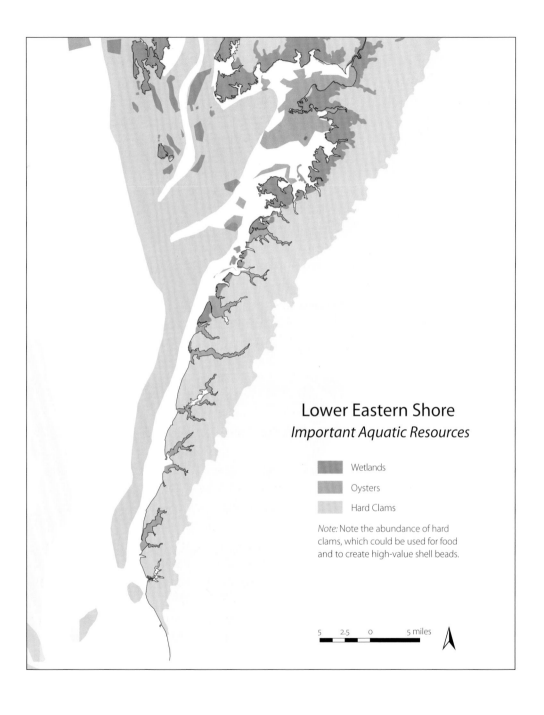

Lower Eastern Shore
Important Aquatic Resources

Wetlands

Oysters

Hard Clams

Note: Note the abundance of hard clams, which could be used for food and to create high-value shell beads.

5   2.5   0   5 miles

promising to revenge them (he could not defend them) from marauders like the Massawomecks, not to mention the Spanish.[15] After establishing this kind of connection, he could have received shell items annually as tribute; he is known to have sent canoes "over the Bay for tribute beads."[16]

The Virginia Eastern Shore is the easiest place in the Chesapeake to show a direct relation between the environment and the Native Americans' culture within it. John Pory observed of the Accomacs and Occohannocks: "Those are the best husbands of any savages we know: for they provide corn to serve them all the year, yet [enough and to] spare; and the other [mainland people] not for half the year, yet want [go without]. They are the most civill and tractable people we have met with."[17]

The intensive husbandry arose from necessity, for the lower Eastern Shore has no "breadbasket" marshes.[18] Instead it has a tremendous amount of good farmland—level, easily tilled Bojac soils that warm early in the spring[19]—much of which lies along the waterfront. The people's tractability arose partially from confidence in their isolation protecting them from enemies, a situation that for many years had made them less warlike than the Indians to the north, south, and west.[20] The men also had less practice in the methods of hunting deer and people because "by the narrownesse of the Land there is not many Deere, but most abundance of Fish and Fowle."[21] Instead of hunting down deer much of the year, the men would have tapped the abundant supplies of shellfish, which would have been easy to find if uncomfortable to harvest (by wading or diving) in the cooler months. Most of the large birds worth hunting on the lower Eastern Shore are migratory, with large numbers of waterfowl such as geese wintering there. So fowling would have been primarily a cold-weather occupation. Fishing was done mainly with weirs, so the time-consuming job there would have been the building and upkeep of those structures—work that would not have been a daily task. Altogether, the Accomac and Occohannock men probably had more time for involvement with farming, so that more hands produced the greater amounts of corn the people needed.

With prime farmland so abundant near the waterfront on the peninsula and without the "breadbaskets" found on the Western Shore, neither factor would have influenced the people in choosing the locations for their towns. Judging from the distribution of those towns, the deciding factor instead was the width of saltwater marsh dividing the land from the open water: Native Americans preferred that there be less of it to cross. Thus we see bayside towns below and seaside towns above a line running roughly from Chesconessex Creek, through the modern town of Accomac, to Metomkin

Accohannock

Accomack

Lower Eastern Shore
Indian Towns and Natural Resources

Best Waterfront Corn-growing Soils

Note: All the prime corn-growing soils here are
low in natural fertility, but they are remarkably
extensive. Although Smith noted only two
towns and chiefdoms in this area, later reports
indicated that there were many more.

5   2.5   0   5 miles

Oyster Shortage in the 1840s

The invention of technology for taking oysters from deeper water quickly had an effect on the oyster beds in the Chesapeake, and there were shortages by the 1830s (see chapter 6). Local watermen were not the only ones doing the harvesting; vessels from Maryland sailed down and took shellfish from creeks that were "public" waterways. By 1842, oysters were entirely gone from Old Plantation, Hungars, and Occohannock creeks and were almost gone from Nassawaddox Creek. Cherrystone still had plenty, but given the demands of the industry, they were in danger of being depleted soon. In that year, citizens of Northampton County asked the legislature in Richmond to pass a law prohibiting trading in oysters for the time being. Predictably, the matter remained controversial thereafter.

Sources: Commonwealth of Virginia, Legislative Petitions, Northampton Co., March 17, 1842; March 9, 1843.

Bay. North of Chesconessex, the marsh is wider and the land lower and less desirable for Indian farming; south of Metomkin, the marshes are wider and have fewer bays in which fish weirs would have been productive.

Weirs would have been the major source of animal protein in the people's diet, allowing trapped fish to be dipped out during the warm months. The weirs were a very old coastal Indian invention; part of one (the Boylston Street fish weir) was excavated in the 1920s after being found by workers digging a cellar in downtown Boston. It dated to before 2000 BC. The excavation uncovered part of the "hedging" or fence that led from shore into deeper water. The fence was made of sticks and reeds lashed together to create a barrier that only minnows could pass through. A similar weir was found in Delaware Bay in the 1890s.[22] Allowing for artistic license, that is what John White painted in 1585 and Theodor de Bry engraved in 1590. The actual fish trap, however, would be most workable if it were on the end of the fence, not built perpendicular to it partway along the length (and there would be no point, given the habits of fish, in building more hedging beyond the trap). The shape of the head, however, may not have mattered: it may have been the box form depicted in White's painting (and the modern version) or a heart-shaped chamber as shown in de Bry's engraving. It mattered more that there be at least one pair of heart-shaped areas (called

John Smith's Chesapeake Voyages, 1607–1609

"bays" in Hampton Roads and "hearts" on the lower Potomac) between the hedging and the head, as an outer trap for the fish.

English colonial records indicate that the native people began teaching weir building to the newcomers at Jamestown as early as 1608,[23] and in 1638 some Englishmen were still hiring Indians to build weirs for them.[24] The labor involved may not have been what daunted the English; rather their motivation in hiring out this task may have been that the "bays" have to be angled carefully—not too wide, not too narrow—to maximize the catch. Even today, methods of weir construction are taught by oral tradition.[25] The English seem not to have maintained an interest past the 1600s (even then, there are only a few records mentioning weirs), preferring to use floating gill nets or else haul seines pulled onto the beach. When, in 1858, someone tried building a weir based on the Indian model, presumably with only de Bry's illustration to go by; it was not particularly successful. After a second attempt in the early 1870s and a third one in Mobjack Bay in 1875, a workable version was devised and began spreading rapidly all over the Chesapeake and elsewhere.[26] The non-Indian trap, however, was made of poles with nets strung between them and came in various sizes: small fykes and very large "pound" nets (also known as "pond" nets, apparently because of fish being trapped in the enclosure). The latter are built in water twelve to thirty-four feet (3⅔ to 10⅓ meters) deep and employ poles over forty-five feet (13.7 meters) long using special tools[27]—well beyond the technological capability of the original Algonquian-speaking inventors.

Structure of a modern fish pound, similar to the devices that were used by Indians of the Chesapeake region in the 1600s. For the older version (presumably rendered accurately by John White), see the illustration on p. 26. (Helen C. Rountree)

Enter the English

The English first heard of the lower Eastern Shore in 1585, when John White painted a map that included a town "Mashawatec" (Nassawadox) up the bay from "Combec" (Accomack).[28] After John Smith's friendly contact with the Accomacs in 1608, the English attempted to establish a saltworks on a barrier island in 1611;

The Farmers and Fishermen of the Lower Eastern Shore

it was moved to Smith Island in 1619 and seems to have fizzled out in the early 1620s.[29] Archaeological remains of these efforts have not been found, which is not surprising, considering the dynamic eroding shoreline environment of the barrier islands. The failure of those saltworks meant that the English could not preserve the fish they caught among the riches of the Chesapeake, and that they had to go to New England and points north to obtain stores of salted fish.

The Jamestown colony also began buying corn regularly from the Accomacs, who were seemingly amenable to raising a surplus. The newcomers began acquiring land in 1620, sometimes by purchase and sometimes by gift from the "Laughing King."[30] In 1621, that chief broke his ties to the Powhatan leadership (Powhatan himself having died in 1618), when he informed the English that Opechancanough, brother to Powhatan's successor Opitchapam/Itoyatin, had tried to buy from him a noxious plant (probably spotted cowbane) with which to poison the English.[31] After a friendly visit from John Pory in the autumn of that year,[32] the Accomacs and Occohannocks sided with the English and refused to participate in the Great Assault of 1622. In the ensuing war, the Accomacs provided corn to the embattled colony, the grain sometimes being taken to Jamestown by interpreter Thomas Savage, who had settled there on land (Savage Neck) that Esmy Shichans had given him.[33] At times, Savage and the chief were so friendly that the English mistrusted him: in 1625, the colonial council at Jamestown issued a warning to him.[34]

In the 1640s, English farmers began taking up land at an increasing rate on the Virginia Eastern Shore, hoping to get rich raising tobacco, and it is fair to say that there was a "land boom" in the 1650s and early 1660s. Much of the land was legally purchased from Indian leaders such as Tapatiaton ("Debbedeavon"), Esmy Shichans's successor. As the land boom moved north, so did the holders of the Indian leadership: Wachiawamp (r. 1643–57) was originally from the Occohannocks, and his successor, Tapatiaton (local chief 1648–63, paramount chief 1663–72), was from the Nanduas but based farther north, as was his daughter and successor, Mary (r. 1663–at least 1703).[35] Any genealogical relationship among the first three men is impossible to trace. By about 1670, the Accomacs (now called Gingaskins) were left on a small reservation near Eastville, which they would hold on to until 1813. A county park at that site is named Indiantown Park today. The Occohannocks, comprising a half dozen or more named groups, were apparently all but landless and moving back and forth between their home

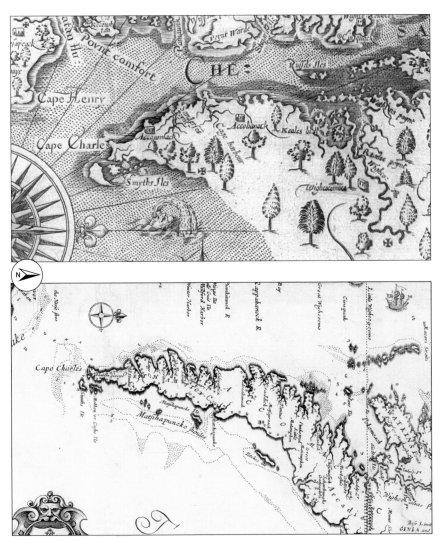

The lower Shore area as mapped by John Smith in 1608 (*top*) and by Augustine Herrmann in 1673 (*bottom*).

territories and the Indian communities in Maryland, where they eventually remained.

The English were fairly densely settled on the Virginia Eastern Shore by 1663, when Accomack County budded off from Northampton County. Like most Virginians and Marylanders of the time, they grew tobacco as a cash crop, preferring until after 1700 to concentrate on tobacco rather than diversify. In subsequent centuries, the inhabitants have made their

The Cape Charles Meteorite

Thirty-five million years ago, in the late Eocene period, a celestial object or bolide that could have been either a comet or a meteorite some two to three miles (3.2 to 4.8 kilometers) in diameter streaked out of the southwestern sky and plowed into the ocean-covered continental shelf. Sea level was much higher at the time, with the Atlantic lapping at the feet of the Blue Ridge Mountains, which were then clothed in tropical forest. The impact blasted out a crater over a mile (1.6 kilometers) deep and fifty miles (80 kilometers) in diameter. The center of impact is under a point near the modern town of Cape Charles, Virginia, and the crater lies under northern Virginia Beach and Norfolk, all of Hampton, Poquoson, Mathews County, eastern Newport News, York County, and Gloucester and Middlesex Counties, not to mention all of Northampton County and the southern part of Accomack County.

No one can fall into the crater, however, for not only did much of the debris kicked up by the crash fall back into the crater, but more than one thousand feet (about 400 meters) of sediments have accumulated in it since then. The hole is not discernable today to the naked eye. (It was discovered by geologists using drilling and remote sensing technology.) The object itself may have vaporized upon colliding with the Earth.

Source: Poag 1999.

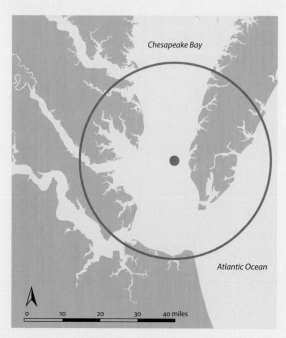

Area of the Eocene meteor crater at the southern end of Chesapeake Bay. (Helen C. Rountree)

living by farming and fishing, as their Indian predecessors did. The lower Eastern Shore's isolation and the peaceful relations with the native people have meant relative immunity from the destruction of war, so that the two counties have local records that are unbroken down to the present. The full complexity of English life in past centuries is there for historians to tap, and major studies of non-English people, Indians and free Africans, have already been published.[36]

Today the relative isolation of the Eastern Shore is ending, thanks to the building of the Chesapeake Bay Bridge-Tunnel in the 1950s and the steadily increasing traffic on it. It is ironic that two of the major features of that engineering marvel were caused by the need to deal with very ancient waterways. The southern tunnel burrows under the old Ice Age channel of the James River, which has followed that independent course out to sea since before the Pleistocene began. The northern tunnel goes under a modern dredged shipping channel. But the High-Rise Bridge, which looks peculiar as it juts into the bay rather than jumping off the south end of the Shore, is a necessity. It crosses the still-deep, rapid current of the last Ice Age's combined Susquehanna, Potomac, Rappahannock, and York rivers, just before it turns eastward around Cape Charles. That current is being slowly but steadily extended southward before turning out to sea by the continued growth of the Lower Eastern Shore.[37]

9

The Middle Eastern Shore:
Land of Marsh and Merchants

OF ALL THE PLACES VISITED by John Smith and crew in 1608, the Tangier Sound, Pocomoke marshes, and marshes of the Nanticoke to this day retain a wonderful sense of what the Chesapeake Bay looked like back then. The three thousand oyster-dredging boats of the 1880s are reduced to a dozen. The nineteenth-century-farmed hummocks in the marshes have reverted to forest. And the area today is viewed mostly as a preserve for plant species and wildlife. The Jamestown exploration party was looking for good harbors, abundant timber, cleared farm fields, and perhaps areas with low Algonquian populations as places for future English expansion, so for several decades this midbay area held little interest for the English. The low, flat, swampy, and marshy landscape, like the Norfolk fens back home, seemed good for cattle grazing and fishing, but for little else unless the land could be drained.

To the Nanticokes and related Algonquian-speaking chiefdoms of these drainages, the region was a rich one, able to sustain and defend a large population. Partly it was because they knew exactly how to use the natural resources available to them; partly it was because they produced trade goods valuable to other Indian people. For hundreds of years, the Algonquians of the middle Eastern Shore had gathered hard clams and whelks from beaches and bays to the east, converting those shells into beads and disks for trade. Their products were in demand from the Mississippi River to the Great Lakes and the St. Lawrence River. In 1608, the people of the Nanticoke paramount chiefdom were known as the "best merchants of all other [Indians]."[1]

The Environment

Since the end of the last Ice Age, a combined process of sea level rise and land subsidence has converted former uplands into a steadily enlarging mosaic of tidewater, marshes, islands, and flat surviving uplands. In 1608, the islands and hummocks fringing the Eastern Shore were much larger; for example, James Island, surveyed in 1650 at 1,330 acres (538.23 hectares), today consists of less than 100 acres (40.47 hectares) and is becoming increasingly fragmented.[2] Tangier, Bloodsworth, and nearby islands are the remnants of the land that used to divide the Nanticoke and Susquehanna rivers above their confluence. Tangier Sound is the almost completely drowned lower river valley of the Nanticoke.[3] As elsewhere in the Chesapeake, rising sea level pushed salty waters up the major rivers and backed up the flow of rainwater, creating extensive freshwater marshes and floodplains far into the uplands. Across the drainage divide, the same thing happened to the rivers that ran directly into the sea, although not always at the same rate. This dynamic dance between land and sea, combined with climate and the land-use practices of diverse cultures, has shaped the area and its people over time.[4]

The Rivers

The Pocomoke, Nanticoke, and Choptank are the largest tributaries of the Chesapeake on the Eastern Shore. The Pocomoke watershed, some 324,000 acres (131,118 hectares), is classified today as 80 percent upland forest and 20 percent wetlands; of those wetlands, 2,000 acres (almost 810 hectares) are brackish tidal marsh on Pocomoke Sound, and 55,000 acres (22,258 hectares) are freshwater tidal and nontidal swamp upriver. The majority of the upriver swamps are in forest, commonly bald cypress forest of which a part is known as the "Great Cypress" or "Burnt Swamp" (because of its decimation by fires in 1782 and 1931).[5]

The Nanticoke River has extensive marsh and hummocks to the west

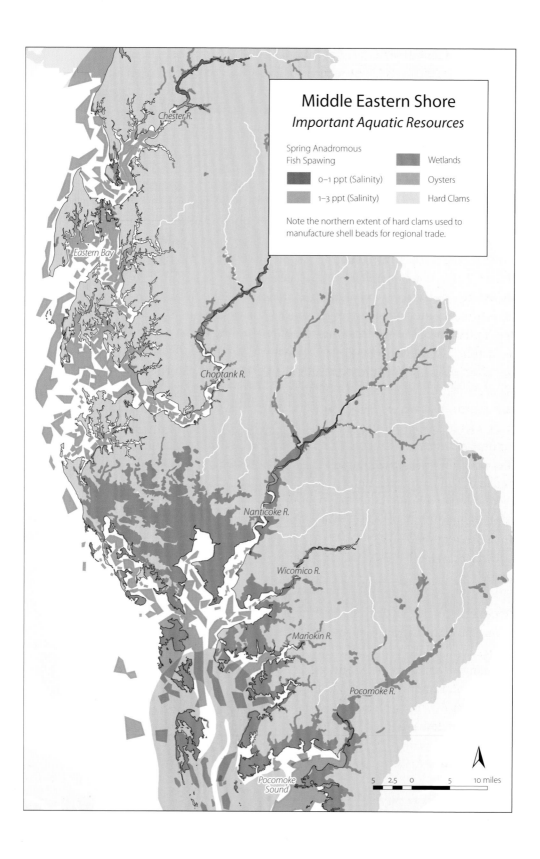

Middle Eastern Shore
Important Aquatic Resources

Spring Anadromous
Fish Spawing

0–1 ppt (Salinity)

1–3 ppt (Salinity)

Wetlands

Oysters

Hard Clams

Note the northern extent of hard clams used to
manufacture shell beads for regional trade.

Chester R.

Eastern Bay

Choptank R.

Nanticoke R.

Wicomico R.

Manokin R.

Pocomoke R.

Pocomoke
Sound

5   2.5   0   5   10 miles

of its mouth and uplands on the east side. This river, which has its headwaters in Delaware, drains 718,000 acres (290,564 hectares) of wetlands, over twice the size of the entire Pocomoke watershed. The ever-larger expanses of uplands, once forested and now mainly farmland, contain a mystery—small circular depressions of wetlands that have been variously called potholes, whale wallows, pingos, or Carolina bays (see chapter 1). Waterfront communities exist on their rims today, as Indian ones once did.[6]

The wide mouths of the Choptank and Little Choptank rivers were less obvious in 1608 than they are today because the present-day James Islands were then connected to the mainland as a long peninsula; Tilghman Island extended farther south, and Sharps Island (which no longer exists) filled much of the area in between. These features obscured John Smith's view, so that he did not include them in his landmark bay map. The two rivers' watersheds combined drain 580 square miles (1,502 square kilometers), with 240 of those (621.6 square kilometers) being wetlands until modern times, when all but 15 square miles (almost 39 square kilometers) have been drained and converted to farmland.

Wetlands

As one moves up the rivers of this region, the emergent plants poking up through the water change from black needlerush and salt-marsh cordgrass to species preferring freshwater. Today's downstream limits may be a little farther downriver than was the case in

1847

1942

1994

Erosion of James Island on Maryland's Eastern Shore. Surveys recorded the island's area at 1,330 acres in 1650, 1,134 acres in 1877, and a mere 85 acres in 1994. Since the mid-1990s the island has fragmented further. (Maryland Geological Survey)

1608. Tuckahoe and cow lily appear in the Pocomoke near Rehobeth, in the Wicomico near Princess Anne, in the Nanticoke near Vienna, and in

Island and Shoreline Erosion

Most bay islands resulted from the erosional "cutting off" of river-mouth peninsulas, or "interfluves," as sea level rise created a growing Chesapeake. These habitats were relatively isolated from predators and particularly suited for birds. On forested islands, rookeries could develop for treetop nesting species like herons and egrets, while open sandy and shelly beaches hosted dense colonies of skirling shorebird species like terns, skimmers, and oystercatchers.

Some colonists sought out and patented land on these islands for protection (for example, Claibourne's trading "fort" on Kent Island), for agriculture (such as James and Barren islands), or for actual villages with churches and schools (Smith, Tangier, and the vanished Sharps island). There livestock, especially the passive sheep,

could range freely without fences or threat from wolves, and the bay's fisheries were right at hand.

Sea level has inexorably advanced since well before the shorelines were first mapped in the early 1600s, bringing changes that at first were documented only anecdotally as people noted the disappearance of a point of land or freshwater pond, then as houses or a hunt club building fell into the bay. Some dwellings were taken by barge to the mainland and reerected on new foundations; others fell to rubble and were washed away.

Precise documentation of the loss of land only became possible with U.S. Coast Survey mapping of the bay's shorelines after the War of 1812, with the first accurate, triangulated maps being published in the 1845–52 period. We have only conjectural information about

the Choptank at the Maryland S.R. 331 bridge; softstem bulrush has much the same distribution but occurs farther down the Wicomico and also in Wetipquin and Quantico creeks, tributaries of the Nanticoke. Reedgrass (*Phragmites*), which tolerates some salt, appears in more rivers and lower down them. This plant occurs far more widely today than in the seventeenth century, when smaller populations of the native subspecies occupied this habitat. Cattails—in undisturbed places—are not common; they are found at only one site (in 1978) far up the Pocomoke, one on the lower Annemessex River, another in the headwaters of the Manokin River, in the Choptank from near the S.R. 331 bridge upward, at several places along the Nanticoke below its junction with Marshyhope Creek, and in the headwaters of the Wye River. Water hemp is more common, at least along the waterways from shoreline and island changes before those times, but in the record of 150–190 years of surveying alone the losses are dramatic. The vistas around these landmasses are radically changed from what they were then, and the changes since 1608 can only be guessed at.

The loss of protected offshore bird-nesting habitats is one reason why the numbers of some species such as terns, oystercatchers, and black skimmers are reduced today. A modern management strategy is to use vast quantities of mud and silt dredged from harbor channels, pumped and dewatered inside containment walls, to provide open and isolated offshore habitat over or adjacent to some "disappearing" islands. The jury is still out about whether these artificial structures (such as the ones at Hart and Miller islands in the upper bay, or Poplar and Coaches islands in the

mid-Chesapeake) will serve the birds well. They certainly do not have the natural appearance or rugged beauty of the original remnant islands.

Note: Mareen Waterman, principal organizer of James Island Gun Club, personal communication 2003 to Kent Mountford. Waterman, a Kent Island realtor, provided film footage of his house, well pump, and an acre-sized (.4-hectare) lake present during the 1950s–70s, all of which have vanished into the bay via erosion.

At this writing, shoreline erosion maps for Maryland are available online at http://www.mgs.md.gov/coastal/maps/schangepdf.html. The maps show erosion since 1845–52 and are complex enough that a high-speed Internet connection is advisable.

the Wicomico River northward, and it also appears in the fresher parts of the necks and islands projecting out into the bay. Wild millet is to be found in the Manokin's headwaters, in a few places in Blackwater National Wildlife Refuge, in the Choptank's headwaters above Tuckahoe Creek, and in a few places in the Wye River and one spot on Kent Island. It does not appear (as of 1978) along either the Pocomoke or the Nanticoke. Wild rice likewise is absent along the Pocomoke, but it occurs in the headwaters of the Manokin River, Wicomico River, and in several lower tributaries of the Nanticoke, plus more sites along the Nanticoke above Vienna; in the Choptank it appears at many places from Marsh Creek onward. Sweetflag, the roots of which were used as medicine by many Woodland Indian peoples, can be seen at one site near Rehobeth on the Pocomoke, one in Jones Creek (tributary of the Big Annemessex), at several places in Wicomico Creek and Wicomico River, at a cluster of sites above Vienna in the Nanticoke River and Marshyhope Creek, and at a very few places above Denton on the Choptank River and near Queen Anne on its tributary, Tuckahoe Creek.[7]

Oysters, Clams, and Snails

In the early 1800s, the Chesapeake Bay had 193 square miles (just under 500 square kilometers) of oyster beds on the harder bottoms of tidal waters between the depths of two to thirty feet (.61–9.1 meters). The Pocomoke Sound had a 40,000-acre (16,187.4-hectare) share of this total, exceeded only by the "Great Rocks" beds of Tangier Sound. These nurseries of life supported a rich diversity of organisms, including the shellfish that filtered the water and made it clearer. Once the waters of the sounds reached warm temperatures in early summer, the male and female oysters released their sperm and eggs in such numbers that the water over those huge beds turned white.[8] The lower Choptank and Little Choptank rivers also had extensive channel oyster beds, though they were in water deep enough to be inaccessible until long-shaft tongs and dredges were invented.

Hard clams reach their northern limit in the Chesapeake Bay in Pocomoke and Tangier sounds, specifically around the Wicomico River and Bloodsworth Island. The reason is salinity: hard clams grow only in waters that are mixed with up to two-thirds the salt of Atlantic Ocean waters. Across the Delmarva drainage divide, they occur in great abundance in the flats of Sinepuxent and Chincoteague bays. Hard clams near their upbay limit are therefore sensitive to changes in freshwater flows from the rivers; they do well during droughts and poorly during unusually rainy years.

Small snails called marsh periwinkles live on salt marsh plants of the intertidal zone. Ignored as food today, they were easily collected and processed as a food source by the Algonquian speakers.[9] But the marine snail most prized by the native people was the whelk, often and erroneously called "conch." Its large column could be drilled to make long beads and the broad "panels" of shell around the aperture could be fashioned into engraved pendants. The making and trading of these items will be discussed shortly. The whelks in the Chesapeake prefer even saltier water than hard clams do, so they are common only in the lowermost bay and along the Atlantic shore to the east. Nevertheless, the Nanticoke Indians, who must have acquired the shells by trade, became known as the premier whelk traders.

The lower Chesapeake Bay is home to two species, the channeled whelk and, less commonly, the knobbed whelk, which reach lengths of seven inches and nine inches (18 and 23 centimeters), respectively. The latter come in either "right-handed" or "left-handed" shells, referring to which side the aperture is on as one holds the shell with the aperture facing the viewer. (Another way to think of it is to hold up your right hand with the fingers curled. The heel of your hand is the aperture in a right-handed whelk, and your fingers represent the ever-smaller spirals of the shell.) Channeled whelks always have right-handed apertures. Knobbed whelks are also right-handed initially, but they do not always stay that way. The change from right to left is apparently triggered by warm temperatures during the mollusk's larval stages. Left-handed specimens—commonly called lightning whelks and formerly assigned to a separate species—are more common in southern and Gulf of Mexico waters but are often found on Virginia's lower Eastern Shore barrier islands.[10] Lightning whelks are found as far north as New Jersey, while the knobbed whelk species as a whole occurs all the way up to Massachusetts.[11]

Fishes
The fishes that live in the bay all year and anadromous species that visit the freshwater reaches of the rivers (see chapter 1) are all found in the waterways of the middle portion of the Eastern Shore, although in smaller numbers than in John Smith's time. The weir, a device discussed in chapter 8, was one of the most efficient methods the Algonquian speakers used to catch fish.

Forest
The canopy and understory species in this region have changed over time, as shown by the pollen in a sediment core collected in Red Fin Creek on the Nanticoke River.[12] Within the 1,500 years represented by the core, a pronounced warm, dry period occurred from seven hundred to nine hundred years ago (the Medieval Warm Period), followed by a cooler, wetter period. During the dry spell, the canopy trees were oaks, hickories, and pines, which then changed to river birch, sweet gum, and black gum when the climate became moist. The dry period also saw frequent fires and high erosion and sedimentation rates, especially on coastal-plain sandy soils like the ones on the Eastern Shore, which collectively explain the thick deposits with large amounts of charcoal revealed in the cores. The wetter period, often called the Little Ice Age, extended into the time of European colonization.

Divers and Dabblers: Bay Ducks

Some dabblers, known as puddle ducks, can dive, while the divers can also dabble. Dabblers are ducks that tip "bottoms up" in shallow water, stretch out their necks and graze on submerged vegetation and aquatic invertebrates. They can dive to feed or to evade danger, but they prefer dabbling. Most have a colorful iridescent or metallic wing patch (called a speculum) on the trailing edge of each wing. When alarmed, however, dabblers literally explode off the water.

Divers prefer to dive for their food in deeper water. Their legs are set farther to the rear of their bodies, and their feet are larger than those of dabblers—characteristics that make them ungainly when they leave the water. Because they do not walk readily on land, they are less likely than dabblers to graze on grass and grain ashore. They also cannot spring out of the water when alarmed, but instead must paddle or "run" across the surface for several yards before taking wing. Where dabblers ashore can take wing easily, startled divers ashore have a more difficult time and must run first. Those with legs set far to the rear, like common loons and long-tailed ducks (also called "old squaws") actually fall forward and must stand up, waddle over to the nearest water, and then paddle before they can fly away. Thus we rarely see diving ducks joining the hordes of dabblers (generally mallards) that frequent parks, golf courses, and other open areas, sometimes becoming permanent residents there.

Along the Pocomoke, the dominant wetland trees are bald cypresses, which—before the nineteenth-century logging that severely overcut them—reached a diameter of eight feet (nearly 2.5 meters) and had knees up to ten feet (3 meters) high.[13] The Pocomoke Great Cypress Swamp actually has species more typical of those found in the Great Dismal Swamp of southeastern Virginia and the Okeefenokee Swamp (Georgia-Florida).[14] Within this protected, relatively warm forest, mistletoe comes and goes from decade to decade, alternately driven south by unusually cold winters and reintroduced as migratory birds deposit its seeds. Spanish moss was recorded in the area in the mid-seventeenth century, when Colonel Henry Norwood called it the Indians' "linen of the country,"[15] but it is not found there now.

Thanks to the channelizing of the upper Pocomoke and the conversion of much of the surrounding country to farmland, it is not easy to find forest on the middle Eastern Shore that resembles the mature forest of previous centuries. However, there is one patch along the upper Pocomoke in an area of reddish clay soils that has the right combination: tulip poplar, several kinds of oak, hickory, sweetgum and black gum, dogwood, loblolly pine, ironwood, plus bald cypress and swamp azalea.[16] Along the Nanticoke and Choptank rivers there are patches of a rich forest dominated by oaks, hickories, and (formerly) chestnuts, which grow there because of dry soil conditions rare in the coastal plain in Delmarva and more typical of the well-drained soils of the Piedmont province where the abundant hickory, oak, and (formerly) chestnut trees provided for an abundant autumn harvest of nuts.[17] These small surviving patches suggest that the diversity of forest cover four centuries ago in the region was greater than we might suspect. One of the most accessible patches of mature forest is at the Adkins Arboretum, near Tuckahoe State Park.

Waterfowl and Other Animal Resources

The middle bay area's tremendous SAV beds and fresh and brackish estuarine marshes are second only to the Susquehanna Flats of the upper bay in supporting hundreds of thousands of migratory waterfowl. In the 1950s, wintering populations ranged from a low of 22,400 to a high of 234,500 with an average of 126,500, with mallards, black ducks, canvasbacks, American wigeons, and Canada geese being the most common species. These same marshes also support muskrats, otters, and minks.

Deer, bears, Eastern cougars, timber wolves, beavers, and twenty-eight other species of mammals are recorded for the Pocomoke drainage and elsewhere, although the larger predators are now gone. Wild turkeys were a major food resource that competed with the Algonquians and deer for acorns on the forest floor.[18]

The People

The Native American inhabitants of what are now Worcester, Somerset, Wicomico, Dorchester, Talbot, and Queen Anne's counties were scarcely recorded by Smith, so that their populations are impossible to estimate today. Later records have provided us with more names of groups, though we cannot be sure that all of them existed in 1608.[19] Even major groups such as the Kuskarawaoks changed their names voluntarily (to Nanticoke, the name of a minor town in 1608). John Smith's locations for towns along the Nanticoke River show that the people used a wide variety of natural resources; thus some of the "towns" may well have been only summer foraging base-camps—a situation that would have held true throughout the Chesapeake region. The Pocomokes spoke a dialect that Powhatan speakers could understand, but that was not true of their neighbors to the north.[20]

Given the fluid situation with settlements occupied seasonally and towns moved in the course of slash-and-burn farming, it is likely that Smith missed some settlements while others had not yet come into existence. In the following list, asterisks mark the towns that Smith did record in 1608.

Pocomoke River Valley

Here were four towns with an estimated 425 people including 100 fighting men. This was home to the "Wiccocomicos," whom John Smith described as short and crude people, for reasons known only to himself. In the late 1600s John Banister wrote that they were of the same stature as other native people.[21] The towns were: *Acquintica,* west of the mouth of the Pocomoke River, below Shelltown (mentioned as a separate group ruled by the Assateagues at Askiminikansen in 1679);[22] *Wighcocomoco,* east of the river, southwest of Cedar Hall; a town of unknown name (later known as Askiminikansen, the people as Pocomokes[23]) in the "V" between the Pocomoke River and Nassawango Creek; *Nassawango/Nassawaddox,* mentioned as a group under the Assateagues at Askiminikansen in 1679.[24]

The site likely to be Wighcocomoco is a large shell midden in which pottery was also found. That fact, plus the timing of Smith's visit, indicates that this settlement was a summer fishing camp for the chiefdom rather than a farming town. In the rest of the Pocomoke River valley, archaeological survey has been limited, though some pottery from the Patawomeck-Piscataway areas has been found in the upper drainage, indicating contact.[25]

Annemessex

Records about these two towns appear only in the 1660s–70s; by 1686, their people had merged with the Assateagues, who shared the Askiminikansen reservation with the Pocomokes.[26] The towns were: *Annemessex,* location uncertain (mentioned as a group under the Assateagues at Askiminikansen in 1679);[27] and *Marumsco,* mentioned as a group under the Assateagues at Askiminikansen in 1679.[28]

Archaeological survey has been limited in this area, but the Late Woodland sites that have been studied show more Potomac Creek pottery (the

Potomac River's mouth is opposite the Annemessex) than other pottery types.

Manokin
Manokin was a reservation at the junction of the Manokin River and Kings Creek; the name of the weroance was Katackeuweiticks.[29] These people appear in records of the 1660s–90s;[30] they eventually merged with the Pocomokes. The archaeological situation here is similar to that with Annemessex: survey has been limited, and Potomac Creek pottery predominates in the sites on the south shore nearer the Annemessexes. North shore sites show the same Townsend and Rappahannock wares as are usually found on the lower Potomac, the Pocomoke, and the Nanticoke rivers.

Wicomico and Monie Rivers
John Smith missed these drainages, but Native American towns (later reservations) persisted along these waterways through the late seventeenth century.[31] Historical and ceramic evidence shows them to have been affiliated with the Nanticokes. The Pine Bluff site near Shad Point on the upper Wicomico also yielded a smoking pipe like those found in Susquehannock and Massawomeck sites,[32] probably indicating trade relations.[33]

Nanticoke River (Kuskarawaok)
This group consisted of five towns with an estimated 850 people including 200 warriors. The name was Anglicized to Chicone and survives as the name of a creek near the old capital town. The people were known as Nanticokes after around 1640, and under that name their descendants still live in both Delaware and Ontario. This paramount chiefdom, which included the peoples of the Manokin, Monie, and Wicomico waterways, was one of the oldest ones in the Chesapeake region (see chapter 2), and its history has been extensively written about.[34] The towns were: *Nause,* near the river's mouth, opposite and a little above Ragged Point, within Fishing Bay Wildlife Management Area (probably a fishing camp);[35] *Soraphanigh,* mentioned only in Smith's text, not on his map (location uncertain); *Arsek,* mentioned only in Smith's text, not on his map (location uncertain); *Nantaquack,* near modern Lewis Wharf Road, opposite and above the mouth of Rewastico Creek; and *Kuskarawaok,* on Chicone Creek, north of modern Vienna[36] (this was the chief's town in 1608, and it gave its name to the river at that time). Nantaquack was later Anglicized to Nanticoke. This town—moved upriver to the area between Chicone Creek and the town of Vienna—later

Elbow pipe from a site on Poplar Island, south of Kent Island off the Eastern Shore. Such pipes were made by the native Algonquian speakers and became the model for English pipe styles. (Darrin L. Lowery)

became the chief's town and the tribe, and the river acquired the same name.[37]

Archaeological survey has been limited in the Nanticoke River valley, but the site of Chicone is known and has received limited excavation, which revealed Contact-period trade goods and also some pottery from the Patawomeck-Piscataway area.[38] The latter would tend to corroborate the Piscataway oral tradition of contact in the 1660s. The Nanticokes were one of the longest-surviving chiefdoms on the Eastern Shore.[39] Their pottery at the end of the Late Woodland period was that of their southern neighbors: shell-tempered Rappahannock Fabric Impressed, Townsend Corded Horizontal, and Yeocomico wares.

Choptank River Valley

John Smith did not explore this area, so its status in 1608 is unknown. Its inhabitants included the Transquaking, Ababco, and Hatsawap groups. Later known as Choptanks, they occupied the Locust Neck Reservation just upstream from modern Cambridge until 1792.[40] This was the only chiefdom in Maryland to have reservation lands deeded instead of being held by the government; the abandoned lands were sold in 1856.[41] At least some of these people also merged with Nanticokes by 1693.[42] Locations of their towns other than that reservation are uncertain, but the name of the Transquaking River southeast of Cambridge probably indicates that some of the people lived there rather than along the Choptank. Archaeological survey has shown the people's pottery to be similar to that of the Nanticokes.[43]

Interplay between People and the Environment

Like other Chesapeake Bay peoples, the native people of the middle Eastern Shore were savvy about locating their larger towns at waterfront locations on prime soils and near the most expansive freshwater marshes. The best corn-farming soils on the middle Eastern Shore most often occur on uplands inland from rivers and the bay; that is where immense farming operations go on today. But the soils are also to be found in numerous waterfront locations. They are low-fertility soils—Matapeake and Sassafras loams and fine sandy loams[44]—that warm early in the spring and are easy to cultivate. The Pocomoke, Nanticoke, and other rivers probably contain "breadbasket" marshes today and did so in 1608, but the National Wetlands Inventory is not fine-grained enough to locate them, as Virginia's tidal marsh inventories do.

The Pocomokes had a real treasure within their territory: huge stands of immense bald cypresses. Cypress is the most rot-resistant of trees, and it would have been correspondingly valuable as a source of logs for canoe building. The historical record is silent on the subject, but the Pocomokes may have traded in logs or ready-made canoes with their neighbors to the south, west, and north. They and their northern neighbors along the Eastern Shore would later engage in the fur trade with the Virginia and Maryland English, who were less interested in the thinner furs produced by animals in the warmer part of the Chesapeake to the south.

Shell for Jewelry

The natural resource for which the Nanticokes in particular were famous was marine shells. There were four types of shell items that Native Americans valued, according to John Banister and Robert Beverley.[45] The most common form of valuable made from shell was *roanoke,* which consisted of mussel shells broken into pieces, drilled through, and then ground around the edges to make thin, stringable disks. Banister wrote specifically that these shell objects came from the Eastern Shore. The other three forms came from thicker, harder shells—whelks and hard clams—that produced larger and more valuable pieces that were wonderfully shiny and showed pearlescent peach, yellow ,and deep-orange hues when they were fresh. (We get only faint impressions of their beauty when they are dug by archaeologists after spending a few centuries in the ground—also when fresh shells are exposed to sunlight for only a few years.) Few things in the Woodland Indian world were shiny, although freshwater pearls are naturally

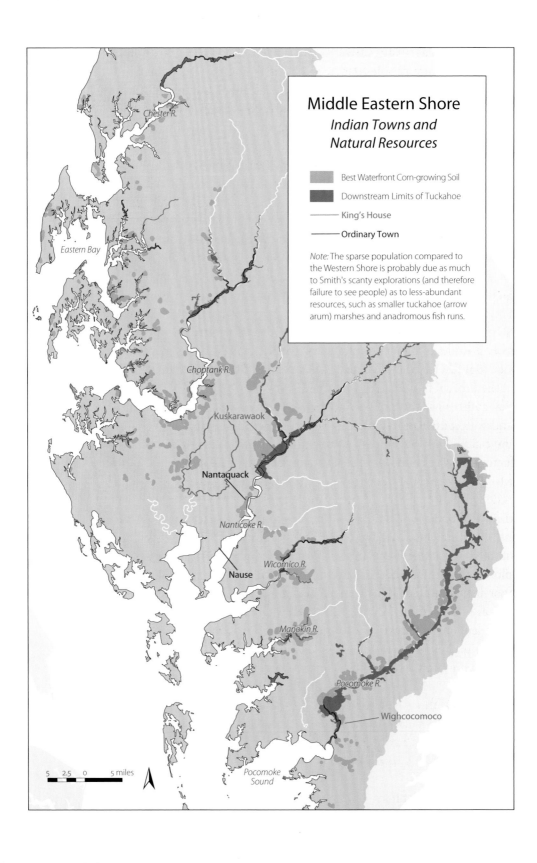

Middle Eastern Shore
Indian Towns and Natural Resources

Best Waterfront Corn-growing Soil

Downstream Limits of Tuckahoe

King's House

Ordinary Town

Note: The sparse population compared to the Western Shore is probably due as much to Smith's scanty explorations (and therefore failure to see people) as to less-abundant resources, such as smaller tuckahoe (arrow arum) marshes and anadromous fish runs.

Chester R.

Eastern Bay

Choptank R.

Kuskarawaok

Nantaquack

Nanticoke R.

Nause

Wicomico R.

Manokin R.

Pocomoke R.

Wighcocomoco

Pocomoke Sound

5   2.5   0   5 miles

opalescent, and shell and native copper can gleam when they are polished. The Eastern Shore peoples had access to thick marine shells that was unparalleled elsewhere in the Chesapeake. The Nanticokes in particular seem to have taken full advantage of this access, even though it meant traveling to the oceanfront or trading with people living near it. (The identity of those oceanfront dwellers is not known at present.)

Whelk shells were desirable mainly because of their size, which enabled chunks several inches (up to 10 centimeters) across to be cut out near the aperture, shaped into pendants (which Native Americans south of Virginia called *runtees*), polished, and engraved with designs such as the "weeping-eye" motif found in "maskettes" from various parts of the Eastern Woodlands. Five such maskettes were found at the Patawomeck site far up the Potomac River (see chapter 12); a slab ready for engraving was found downriver on Nomini Creek.[46] Whelks also have a fairly long columella in their centers, which can be broken out, drilled, and polished into beads up to two inches (5 centimeters) long (the native term for them is not known). Such beads are not mentioned in the seventeenth-century records, but they have been found archaeologically as far away as the Virginia mountains.[47]

The other two valuable shell commodities shared both their shape and their source. The interior of a hard-clam shell is mostly a lustrous, creamy mother-of-pearl color, but many specimens have a region of deep purple (the cause is unknown to science)[48]—in some cases where the strong adductor muscle is attached and in others around the shell's edge. Thus the two colors of Indian wampum (a New England Algonquian term), or half-inch (1¼ centimeters) beads laboriously made from these dense shells, are white *peak* and purple ("black") *wampumpeak*.[49] Because a hard-clam shell has only a small area of purple, wampumpeak was worth more than peak in Native American eyes.[50] Hence Powhatan's recorded preference for blue-colored glass beads in a trading session with John Smith early in 1608.[51] The labor-intensive value of clamshell beads was later destroyed by the proliferation of cheap European glass trade beads in Native American hands. But when John Smith was exploring the Chesapeake, he got the impression that white shell beads (which he called "roanoke") "occasion[ed] as much dissention among the [native people], as gold and silver amongst Christians."[52]

The Nanticokes (then called Kuskarawaoks) were rich not only in shells and shell jewelry but also in furs—"the best whereof is at Cuscaraweoke"[53]—that some of those furs may have been purchased at that early date from other native groups. Some of those groups may well have been distant peo-

Modern Indians

Today there are people holding an Indian identity living on the Maryland Eastern Shore. They include a strong, continuous Nanticoke community near Millsboro, Delaware (near the old Askakesky Reservation on Indian River), and other more recently organized groups bearing the historic chiefdom names of Pocomoke, Assateague, Nanticoke, and Occohannock. Several of these groups put on annual powwows that are open to the public.

Source: Weslager 1983; various personal communications to Helen Rountree.

ple to the northwest, well beyond the Chesapeake Bay's watershed.

Shell goods definitely went beyond the watershed by trade. Pieces of channeled whelk shells have been identified from a Neutral Iroquois site at the eastern end of Lake Erie. Pieces of whelk shells of uncertain species have been unearthed at sites associated with Huron, Petun, and other Neutral Iroquois people. Yet another Neutral site contained a piece that was clearly from a lightning whelk. These sites also yielded whelks from species that do not occur as far north as Chesapeake Bay, indicating trade routes not only to the Chesapeake (via the Susquehanna or Potomac rivers) but also to the Carolina Sounds (possibly via the Roanoke River) and the Gulf of Mexico (via the Ohio and Mississippi rivers).[54]

The Massawomecks have been proven to have traded marine shells, as middlemen, between the Chesapeake and the Great Lakes, for shell-disk beads have been found at their Susquehannock complex sites on the south and north branches of the upper Potomac River.[55] At Monongahela complex sites, whose distribution encompasses the far headwaters of the Potomac and across the eastern Continental Divide, and in the easternmost Madisonville phase of the Fort Ancient complex farther northwest, archaeologists have found abundant examples of clamshell and also engraved whelk-shell maskettes that clearly resemble—or indicate trade relations with—people far down the Mississippi River.[56] The distance from the Fort Ancient complex sites onward to Lake Erie is not great.

Enter the English

John Smith and his contemporaries paid little attention to the Eastern Shore as a whole, since their hopes were fixed upon a Northwest Passage (which proved to be mythical, unless one goes up to the Arctic Ocean in a modern ice-breaker) and mineral resources such as gold that normally occurred in much higher country. In the early 1630s, however, the area began to be visited by English fur traders based both on Kent Island to the northwest and on the lower Eastern Shore in Accomac territory.

From 1631 to 1661, the chiefdoms between the Choptank and Pocomoke rivers effectively maintained control of fur-trading

A copper square breast plate, jasper triangular point, brass points, clay pipe, and glass bead from Poplar Island, all dating to the early seventeenth century. (Darrin L. Lowery)

and other trading activities, partially by limiting their interactions with the English to mutually beneficial ones. The Nanticokes in the 1650s alternated between warfare and peace, which discouraged Maryland land grants and settlement. Also during the 1650s, the progressive northward granting of land to the expanding English populations of Virginia had reached the northern boundary of that colony. In 1651 and again in 1656, Lord Baltimore, alarmed by increasing efforts of the Virginia English to claim the area south of the Nanticoke, directed his authorities in the province to make every effort to organize settlements to establish claim by possession of this middle Eastern Shore region. In 1660, the Virginia General Assembly passed drastic anti-Quaker legislation that caused the Virginia Eastern Shore Quakers to request permission, granted by Maryland authorities in late 1661, to settle lands below the Choptank River. By May 1662, fifty property owners were living in two communities on the Annemessex and Manokin rivers and had agreed to pay the *tallak* of the Nanticokes six matchcoats for every plantation granted. From this initial foothold, the Virginia English began a campaign of hostility toward the Pocomokes to the south

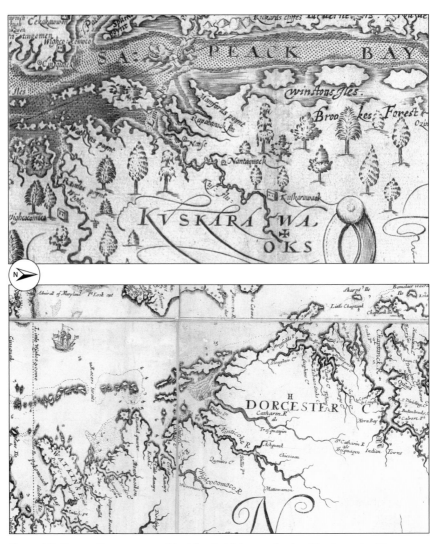

The middle Eastern Shore as mapped by John Smith in 1608 (*top*) and by Augustine Herrmann in 1673 (*bottom*). Smith's original map did not show all the Nanticoke towns he described. English settlement of the Nanticoke and Pocomoke areas began in earnest in the 1660s.

and the Assateagues to the east, an effort designed to drive them from their territories and thus expand areas for new land grants. Maryland's government did not support these actions and did not provide military assistance for them.[57]

It was not until 1668 that a permanent peace was established between the Maryland and Virginia English and the Nanticokes and other chiefdoms in the middle Eastern Shore. In 1669, the Nanticokes and others joined with

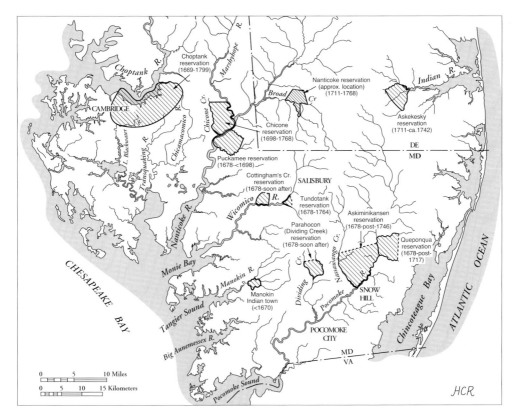

Indian reservations on the middle Eastern Shore, circa the late 1600s–mid-1700s. These places were chosen by the native people themselves; notice how they are all on the waterfront and (except for the Choptanks) located in the freshwater reaches of the rivers. (Helen C. Rountree)

the Marylanders to defeat the Wicomiss. The middle Shore Algonquians were granted reservations that would steadily be diminished by English squatters, who were sometimes removed by Maryland authorities and at other times granted the land they claimed simply because they settled it against the native peoples' wishes.

In 1678, however, with profits from furs declining, Maryland set aside lands for the Indian communities[58] and allowed English farmers to take up the rest. Settlement began along the rivers where it was convenient to ship out tobacco and unload imported European goods (local trades and crafts not becoming well-established until the eighteenth century). By 1700, only a handful of native communities remained on reservations, and those lands were being nibbled at by English neighbors.

The English required the remaining Nanticokes and Choptanks to fence

An End to Isolation on Kent Island: The Bay Bridge

Twenty-three years after John Smith sailed by, Kent Island was chosen by William Claiborne as a secure site for his settlement and trading fort. Claiborne figured prominently in opening up trade with the Susquehannocks and was in disagreement—and sometimes at war—with other English political interests on the Chesapeake. Kent Island, after wider settlement in Maryland, remained an isolated farming and waterman's community for about two hundred years, but the people maintained significant trade with Baltimore and Annapolis across the bay.

With the rise of steam power in the nineteenth century, ferries ran from Baltimore to Tolchester (near the Chester River) and to Love Point, and from Annapolis to Matapeake or Claiborne.

From 1907 onward, the Merchants and Manufacturers Association of Baltimore complained that their city was being bypassed: with improved rail and road connections on the Eastern Shore, goods were flowing north to Wilmington and Philadelphia rather than being hauled 130 miles (nearly 210 kilometers) around the head of the bay. They felt that a bridge would stem the flow, and by 1918 they envisioned a double-decked structure carrying both railroad and trolleys across the bay.

Bridge authorities floated several abortive proposals from 1926 onward, interrupted by the Great Depression. In 1938, the J. E. Greiner Company prepared a study for the State Roads Commission that proposed a bridge to (among other locations) Kent Island. Although bonds were issued, no construction began.

Summer resorts were also developing at Rehoboth and what became Ocean City on the Atlantic coast, and an increasingly automotive society became frustrated with long weekend ferry waits at the terminals. Ferries were only a stopgap, however, pending the inevitable future construction of a highway bridge.

In 1942, despite the fact that it was wartime, the Maryland legislature finally approved the building of a bridge, although construction was delayed until 1949, and the span did not open until 1952. Traffic doubled on the bridge within ten years, and by the early 1960s it had already approached capacity. A second span was built and opened in 1973. Now choked with traffic, a further expansion is being discussed at this writing.

Source: Kozel 2000–2003.

in their cornfields and not kill cattle and horses that ate their crops. For every Maryland government effort to settle conflicts, the Eastern Shore English developed ways to frustrate those measures—for example, by tearing down the Indian fences and driving their cattle into the cornfields. The Nanticokes wanted so badly to hold onto their traditional ways that many of them accepted the Iroquois invitation to move to New York and become a dependent nation in the 1740s. Families from other Eastern Shore tribes may have done the same. Other Nanticokes joined the few Choptanks who remained on their riverside plot, land that was lost to Indian ownership in 1799.[59]

The Maryland English were successful in retaining control of the southern boundary for the state, although watermen from both Maryland and Virginia would continue to fight wars over fishing rights into the twentieth century. Lord Baltimore also lost his battle to retain rights to game and fishes, opening the woods for hunting by all and the waters for fishing by all. In that sense, the Maryland and Virginia colonists were successful in adopting the Algonquian concept that game and bay resources belonged to the people, not the government. In fact, the government encouraged the populace in animal control by issuing bounties on predator species: bears, bobcats, wolves, and foxes, which attacked the pigs and cattle allowed to roam in the woods and marshes of the middle Eastern Shore.

10

The Head of the Bay:
The Iroquoian Speakers'
Northwest Passage

JOHN SMITH WAS ON ALMOST the right track when he fixed his interest on the Susquehanna River and the people who traveled along it. But the river was not a passage to the Pacific Ocean. Instead, it was a major corridor to the eastern continental divide. Portage trails were required to connect the native societies of the Chesapeake drainage with those of the St. Lawrence (including the Great Lakes) and the Mississippi (including the Ohio).[1] For the Algonquian speakers native to the head of the Chesapeake Bay, the Susquehanna meant access to fabulous trade goods but also danger if relations soured with the people to the north. The latter situation was predominant in 1608, with the result that Smith found relatively few Algonquian-speaking people using the natural riches of the area.

The Environment

The head of the bay is fed by a number of small rivers passing amidst high, rolling lands. Immediately to the northwest runs the fall line, just below present-day Conowingo, above which a series of falls impede larger water-craft and the land is higher yet.

Waterways and the Shellfish in Them

The Chesapeake's tributaries at its head are relatively small with the exception of the Susquehanna, which reaches 440 miles (708 kilometers) into the Piedmont and mountains to the west and north. However, navigation by craft other than lightweight canoes[2] stops about ten miles (16 kilometers) up the river, at the first rapids. The river carries an immense amount of rainwater out of its watershed—a billion gallons (3.8 billion liters) per day even during a drought year. In an extremely wet year, as 1972 was thanks to Tropical Storm Agnes, the river poured 650 billion gallons (2,469.5 billion liters) of freshwater into the bay each day, killing oysters as far south as the Chester River's mouth.[3]

Oysters today are found as far up the bay as halfway between the Chester and Sassafras rivers; in 1608, with more forests and less runoff to freshen the water, they extended to the mouth of the Sassafras, where they have been found archaeologically. The beds occur from a depth of thirty-five feet (10.5 meters) up to those exposed on reefs at low tide. Archaeologists find Late Woodland Period Indian sites with shell middens throughout the area, indicating heavy reliance on this resource by the native people.[4] The shellfish taken, however, would have been in shallower water, since they were gathered by wading or diving. Many of the middens represent seasonal foraging camps; that is probably what the town Ozinies on John Smith's map actually was. Limited amounts of blue crab remains among the shells indicate occupation during their greatest abundance in July and August. And that abundance is amazing, when the underwater grass beds favored by male crabs are plentiful.[5]

The upper Chesapeake above Pooles Island has reduced water transparency because that location is where ascending tidal brackish water meets descending fresh river water. There, chemical reactions cause organic and inorganic sediment particles to coalesce, "muddying" the waters in a zone called the turbidity maximum. Despite its turbidity, this zone is one of high biological activity and serves as a nursery for many estuarine species. Tidal freshwaters and turbidity maxima are also present in each of the bay's major rivers, notably the Potomac River near Alexandria, the James River near Richmond, the Pocomoke River, and the Chester, Choptank, and Wicomico rivers on the Eastern Shore. Farther down those rivers, the water is relatively clear again.

Submerged Aquatic Vegetation (SAV)

The Susquehanna Flats make up a broad, shallow sediment trap adjacent to that river's mouth, where the confined, rapidly flowing Susquehanna spreads out into the bay, slowing in velocity and depositing much of its sediment. The flats have a maximum depth of ten feet (3 meters) in most places. A half dozen species of freshwater rooted aquatic plants make up a thick bed of underwater grasses that extends from the northern tip of Spesutie Island to Furnace Bay, at the Chesapeake's head. Smaller beds occur in the lower and middle reaches of the North East, Elk, and Sassafras rivers, as well as in tributaries of the bay extending down to the Chester River. Extensive beds occur in Eastern Bay, east of Kent Island, as well.[6] Like oysters, SAV is a major contributor to water quality. While oysters filter water, underwater grasses capture sediment and diminish wave action. These functions greatly enhance water clarity and reduce erosion along the shoreline. Aquatic vegetation beds like the ones in the upper bay are also a major food source for overwintering waterfowl. The Susquehanna Flats suffered much-diminished SAV in the decades after Tropical Storm Agnes in 1972. Only in 2004 did these grasses regain their historic abundance on some areas of the flats.[7]

Wetlands

The waterways at the head of the Chesapeake have marshes that are somewhat more extensive than they were in John Smith's time, thanks to the erosion of adjacent lands due to clear-cut plow farming in the 1800s and 1900s. A letter written in 1634 reported that the Elk River had a yellow gravel bottom;[8] today eroded soils have changed that bottom and also extended marshlands a mile and a half (2.5 kilometers) farther downstream. Today's marshes tend to be limited in size by the relatively high lands around them; the waterways do not meander across wide floodplains, as the Chickahominy and Pamunkey rivers do.

Even with these limitations, in this region there are marshes useful to people because of the plants growing in them. Sweetflag, which the Five Nations and also perhaps the Susquehannocks and Algonquian speakers used for medicine, grows at the heads of most of the rivers, including the

John Smith's Chesapeake Voyages, 1607–1609

Chester at the Maryland S.R. 290 bridge, and at two sites in the middle reaches of the Sassafras. A wide variety of plants producing edible roots also occur in the area. Tuckahoe appears in the headwaters of the Wye and Corsica rivers and in the Chester from just below Chestertown upward; it begins growing in the tiny creeks close to the bay around the mouth of the Patapsco River and becomes more common to the north. Cow lily is found in the Chester River's headwaters above the U.S. 50/301 bridge and at that same highway's bridge over the Sassafras; it also grows in the headwaters of the Bohemia, Elk, Bush, Gunpowder, and Patapsco rivers and in Furnace Bay near the Susquehanna's mouth.[9]

Reedgrass (*Phragmites*) is common in disturbed, moist places all around the Chesapeake today, but in undisturbed conditions it is not very common. (The plant found in disturbed conditions is likely to be an invading Eurasian subspecies.) In the upper bay, it can be seen in many places around Kent Island and up the Chester River, as well as at the heads of creeks around Baltimore and (less commonly) up the tributaries of the bay from the Gunpowder/Sassafras area northward. Softstem bulrush also appears in the headwaters of creeks from the Annapolis area northward, being more common in the Elk River; along the Chester, it occurs at only two sites. Cattails are not frequently found in undisturbed areas, the main sites for them being the upper Chester River, upper Bush River, the upper Sassafras, Bohemia, and Elk rivers, and several sites around the mouth of the Susquehanna.

Numerous wetlands plants produce seeds that birds use as food. The ones that people can also gather and eat include water hemp, wild millet, and wild rice. Water hemp is found in many places in the tributary waterways from Kent Island on the east side of the bay upward and from the West River on the west side, although there are fewer sites to the north except for a dense cluster of places around the Bohemia River. Wild millet is rare in the upper bay, being limited to the northern tip of Kent Island, two sites in the Chester River's headwaters, one each in the headwaters of the Bush and Gunpowder rivers, and a few sites up the Sassafras River. Wild rice is more common, appearing at two sites in the Corsica River's headwaters, at the U.S. 50/301 bridge across the Chester River, at several places far up the South River, one spot far up the Patapsco, and in many small creeks from the Sassafras/Gunpowder area northward.

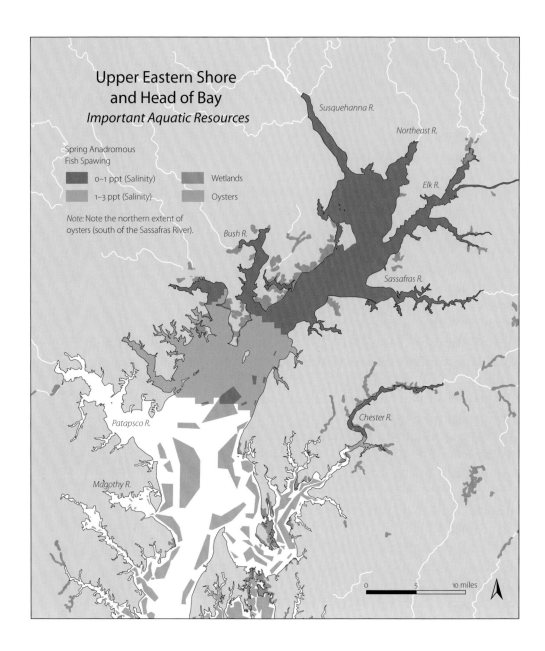

**Upper Eastern Shore
and Head of Bay**
Important Aquatic Resources

Spring Anadromous
Fish Spawning

0–1 ppt (Salinity)

1–3 ppt (Salinity)

Wetlands

Oysters

Note: Note the northern extent of
oysters (south of the Sassafras River).

Susquehanna R.

Northeast R.

Elk R.

Bush R.

Sassafras R.

Patapsco R.

Chester R.

Magothy R.

0   5   10 miles

Vegetation

The forest cover at the head of the bay resembles that of uplands to the
south, being an oak-hickory forest except where it has been cleared and
the land then colonized by pines. The area does, however, boast two tree
species that reach their northern limit on the Sassafras River—the willow
oak and the loblolly pine. Last but not least, there is one spot on the Chester

John Smith's Chesapeake Voyages, 1607–1609

River, at the Maryland S.R. 290 bridge, which boasts some of the north-ernmost bald cypress trees in eastern North America.[10] On the other hand, as one heads northward into the Susquehannocks' old territory, the cold-weather conifers increase. And in places in the Piedmont province, there are natural barrens free of trees as the result of annual forest fires or because of the hard serpentine rock that underlies them.

Sediment cores taken at Furnace Bay, near the Susquehanna's mouth, and on the Magothy River tell us about changes in the forest over time. The Furnace Bay core, which penetrated sediments dating to 1,500 years before John Smith's time, showed that the canopy trees had remained uniform: pine, hemlock, oak, and hickory. There were fluctuations, however, in the frequency of ash, walnut, alder, and birch, which prefer wetter habitats. Basswood appeared before European Contact but not afterward, for un-known reasons. Interestingly, the core gave no evidence of the dry period of 800–900 years ago that other cores have shown (see chapter 12). The core taken in the headwaters of the Magothy River[11] covered the last 4,000 years. At that time, black gum and sweetgum were the dominant species growing around the river, accompanied by river birch and cinnamon fern; then, about 2,500 years ago, the climate became drier, and chestnut, Ameri-can holly, and blueberries became dominant, as they are today. Within this drier period there have been two spells of exceptionally dry conditions: about 1,500 years ago and about 800–900 years ago.

In southeastern Pennsylvania and adjacent Maryland, running paral-lel to the fall line and northwest of it, is a band of stunted forest and grass meadowlands. The dry soil conditions of this area, particularly in the ser-pentine deposits of the region, result in open grasslands when the area is subjected to annual burning. In the late seventeenth century, the Mary-land and Pennsylvania English referred to these sapling, grass, and stunted blackjack oak forests as the York, Gunpowder (or Baltimore), and Patap-sco "barrens." To experience a small example of the Patapsco barrens, one need only visit the Soldiers' Delight barren in Baltimore County. Mary-land's rangers may have so named this barren while patrolling the colonial frontier as early as 1693 because of the ease of travel and the good sight distances across it.[12] Historical records indicate that these barrens were cre-ated by human activity, one example being the York Barrens that stretched along both sides of the Susquehanna River from Broad Creek upward for some twenty miles (32 kilometers), covering an estimated 130,000 acres (52,609 hectares). From Broad Creek, the barrens also stretched southwest-ward through the Gunpowder drainage, where they were nine miles (14.5

kilometers) wide, to reach the Piedmont province of the Patuxent River. Evidence that they extended to the Potomac drainage is inconclusive.[13]

The People

Two major Native language families—Algonquian and Iroquoian—were represented around the head of the bay in 1608, although speaking related languages did not make people into military allies here, any more than belonging to different language families automatically made people enemies. The Susquehannocks warred with their linguistic relatives the Massawomecks while keeping peace with the nonrelated Tockwoghs.

The Algonquian speakers, whose ancestors made Minguannan ceramics and may have migrated into the area with the Leni Lenape from the northwest,[14] lived to the east, not the west, of the bay. Away from the Chesapeake to the northeast were Atquanachukes on John Smith's map. Smith's text, however, hints that instead they lived to the northwest beyond the mountains, not on the ocean. Their identity and linguistic affiliation remains uncertain, but they may have been some St. Lawrence River Iroquoian speakers (tribe not recorded) who were pushed out by the Five Nations Iroquois before 1590.[15]

The two Iroquoian-speaking groups that were active at the head of Chesapeake Bay were the Susquehannocks, who lived up the Susquehanna River, and the Massawomecks, whose home country is still controversial and who came to the Chesapeake as raiders.

Much of the Algonquian speakers' territory—that is, Tockwogh, described below—has not been surveyed archaeologically at this writing; in the Kent Island–Queen Anne's County area there has been a thorough survey[16] but nothing more. The Susquehannocks are far better known archaeologically, and the Massawomecks are becoming so. Following are the known seventeenth-century settlements, with asterisks marking the ones John Smith saw in 1608.

*Tockwogh

This single, palisaded town had an estimated 425 people including 100 warriors. It was on the south bank of the Sassafras River, probably on Shrewsbury Neck, which has the best line of sight down the river.[17] What little information we have about the Tockwoghs comes from John Smith's brief visit with them. They were preyed upon by the Massawomecks, and that situation drove them and the Susquehannocks to palisade their towns and make an alliance with each other. A byproduct of the alliance was that French metal tools came into their hands.[18]

*Ozinies

This group inhabited at least one town, with an estimated total population of 255 including 60 fighting men. After 1630 they were known as Wicomiss. The town of theirs that John Smith visited was probably east of Swan Creek, north of Rock Hall.

Matapeake

This was a settlement on Kent Island near the isthmus to the mainland. John Smith missed this group, but they appear in fur traders' records in the 1630s. Their relation to the Wicomiss is uncertain.

Monoponson

These people had a settlement on the west side of Kent Island and north tip of the south bank of the mouth of the Chester River. Smith missed this group, too, but it appears in records of the 1630s, and in 1659 their chief Zakowan signed a treaty with the Maryland colony.[19] Their relation to the Wicomiss and the Matapeake is uncertain; the latter may have merged with them by 1659.

Susquehannock

This group consisted of six towns with an estimated total population of 1,700 including 600 fighting men.[20] These people were also known as White Minquas, Andastes, Andastehorrons, or Conestogas.

Archaeology has shown that these people were relative newcomers to the head of the Chesapeake, having moved from the Susquehanna's north branch southward to its lower shores around 1570–80. In that move they displaced earlier inhabitants whose ethnic and linguistic identity is unknown.[21] The motive for the relocation may have been economic: trade goods, including metal cutting tools, had become available from French fishermen visiting the Northeast. The Susquehannocks could buy such tools from their own linguistic relatives to the north if they could acquire marine shells (for jewelry) from Algonquian speakers in the Chesapeake. Archaeologists have found snow whelk shells—which come only from the mid-Atlantic coast—in Susquehannock and other Iroquoian sites all the way to Ontario.[22]

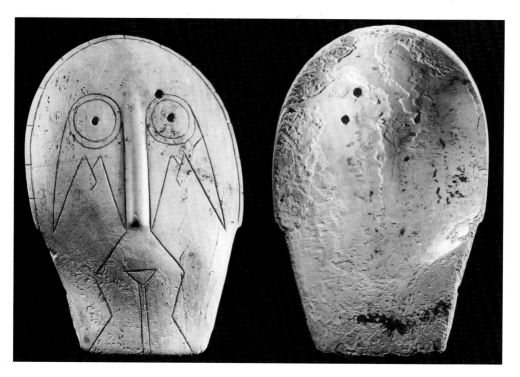

A Massawomeck conch shell "mask" gorget, front and back. The Massawomecks traded furs in exchange for conch and other marine shell beads that were important to the native trade network that extended from the Ohio River valley to the Atlantic coast. (West Virginia Geological and Economic Survey)

In 1608, the Susquehannock towns were: *Cepowig,* at the head of Winters Run, a tributary of the Bush River; *Sasquesahanough,* the capital and lowermost town, at Safe Harbor, Pennsylvania; *Attaock,* west of the Susquehanna River, up a tributary; *Quadroque,* east of the river; *Utchowig,* west of the river, up a tributary; and *Tesinigh,* the uppermost village, on the east side of the river.

Of these, only Sasquesahanough has been located, at the Washington Boro site near Millersville, Pennsylvania.[23] That town had a triple palisade and a large enough population—up to 1,700 people—that the other five towns on Smith's map may have been only foraging settlements, hence archaeologists' not recognizing them if found.

Incised Susquehannock pot from the Washington Boro site near Millersville, Pennsylvania. (Pennsylvania Historical and Museum Commission)

Massawomecks

This group consisted of at least four major towns (or tribes) according to the somewhat vague report of Henry Fleet, which also noted that each town was ruled by a "king." His brother Edward, who actually visited their mountain domain, reported that there were thirty towns altogether and some 30,000 people.[24] These people were called Black Minquas by the Dutch and Swedish and Pocoughtraonacks/Bocootawwonauks by the Powhatans. The four towns noted by Fleet were *Tohoga, Mosticum, Shannetowa,* and *Usserahak.*

The Massawomecks were enemies to all except the Nacotchtanks and possibly the Nanticokes.[25] They are recorded as meeting John Smith at the mouth of the Sassafras River in 1608, and in 1609–10 Henry Spelman saw them attack a Patawomeck town.[26] They arrived and departed in both cases in bark canoes, which were much lighter and faster than the dugouts paddled by their victims. Their home base lay up the Potomac River;[27] an effective way for them to reach the head of the Chesapeake and encounter John Smith would have been to ascend the Monocacy River, portage eastward, and come down the Patapsco. They lived near a large body of water and possessed metal hatchets purchased from the French to the north.[28]

The Jamestown English learned little about these people until the early 1630s, when fur traders became quite active in the Potomac area. Their "homeland" was still not located precisely, being simply "ten days" of travel up in the mountains, which would put them over the eastern continental divide.

The Head of the Bay

Their talent for making enemies ultimately undid the Massawomecks, for they were defeated by the Susquehannocks and the Senecas, and after 1638 the name "Massawomeck" disappeared from the English records.[29]

Scholars still argue about who the Massawomecks were and whether they were absorbed by the Five Nations Iroquois.[30] Archaeologists have found town sites dating to the late 1500s and early 1600s along the North Branch of the upper Potomac River and over the eastern continental divide along the tributaries of the Ohio River, but their ceramics do not belong to one single complex, as we would expect of close allies. Interestingly, however, one complex found along the Potomac in West Virginia shows clear connections with the Susquehannocks,[31] as if a subset of Massawomecks broke off—in animosity—from the main body of the tribe and headed west to control the Potomac River trade route to the Ohio River valley.

Interplay between People and the Environment

Oysters, crabs, and fish helped sustain the Algonquian speakers during the lean period from late spring to midsummer, and for longer periods as needed to make up for crops lost in dry years. Access to shellfish and abundant fin fisheries were advantages the Susquehannocks lacked, so smoking oysters not needed immediately for food provided the Algonquians with a possible delicacy to trade with their Piedmont neighbors for bear, elk, and deer meat and also furs. That said, the Susquehannocks were no slouches about harvesting fish, as excavations at their farthest downriver village of 1608 have demonstrated. The middens yielded bones from long-nosed gar, American shad, sucker, catfish, eel, walleye, and striped bass. From an affiliated historic-period Susquehannock site we may add sturgeon.[32] The presence of both freshwater and anadromous fishes indicates that the Susquehannocks fished locally, rather than going down into the bay. In the spring, they would have had no reason to leave home, for the Susquehanna River once boasted the largest annual shad run on the East Coast. The Algonquian speakers who remained their neighbors in 1608 were similarly blessed, and their towns, like the downriver Susquehannock one, were fishing "camps" as well as farming towns.[33]

Part of the Atlantic Flyway passes up the bay and along the Susquehanna River, where herbivorous ducks and geese take advantage of the grasses.[34] People in turn took advantage of the flocks. Archaeologists digging the Susquehannock village found the usual wild turkey bones that are found

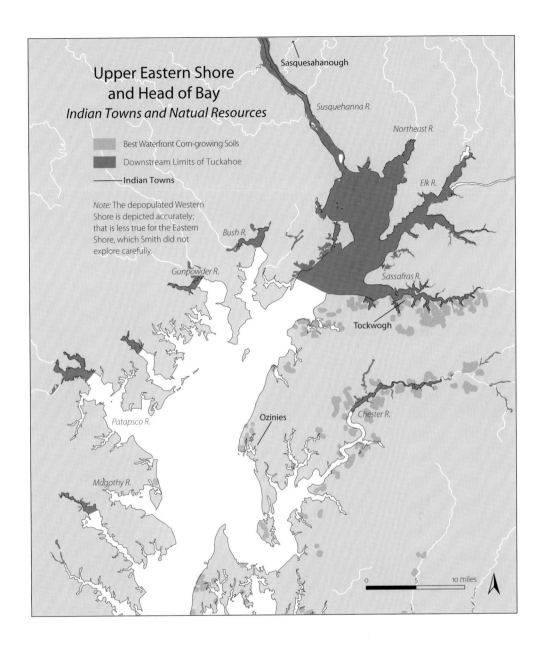

Upper Eastern Shore and Head of Bay
Indian Towns and Natural Resources

Best Waterfront Corn-growing Soils

Downstream Limits of Tuckahoe

Indian Towns

Note: The depopulated Western Shore is depicted accurately; that is less true for the Eastern Shore, which Smith did not explore carefully.

Sasquesahanough

Susquehanna R.

Northeast R.

Elk R.

Bush R.

Sassafras R.

Gunpowder R.

Tockwogh

Patapsco R.

Ozinies

Chester R.

Magothy R.

0   5   10 miles

in so many Late Woodland sites, but other avian species were represented as well: common loon, pied-billed grebe, whistling and trumpeter swans, Canada goose, blue/snow goose, black duck, mallard, redhead, scaup, common goldeneye, bufflehead, and merganser. The list indicates a seasonal focus on migrant birds that is not seen farther south in archaeological sites. In the Piedmont province, where tuckahoe (arrow arum) grows reluctantly in fast-moving waters, the abundance of bird life ("millionous multitudes" was George Alsop's phrase) was a welcome supplement to people's diet in later winter and the spring; the alternative was to disperse from the town and go hunting, which some people did.[35]

The Algonquian and Iroquoian speakers living near the head of the Chesapeake Bay probably used three kinds of settlements during the year, judging from the archaeological evidence (historical accounts are far too sketchy). First there were farming towns that were occupied mainly during the summer and autumn. The palisaded town of Tockwogh was one of these. Then there were fishing camps, if the main town was not well sited to encounter the spring fish runs; Ozinies may have been an example. Finally there were foraging camps in the interior, used during the intensive autumn hunts when venison and hides were stockpiled for the winter by the most able-bodied individuals. There is some evidence that the winter hunting villages of the Susquehannocks may have retained a smaller year-round population to continue to provide forest resources to the main village. The residents would also be able to alert the Susquehannocks of the arrival of Massawomeck enemies or allied trade partners.

The extensive seventeenth-century barrens already mentioned must reflect the use of fire to manage the forest and enhance habitat to greatly increase game resources throughout the Late Woodland period.[36] Similar barrens, underlain by drier limestone soils, existed in the Shenandoah River valley. Interestingly, these barrens may include some Massawomeck villages. If so, the barrens of the bay's upper eastern Piedmont and those of the Shenandoah Valley may have been an incentive for the Massawomecks' and Susquehannocks' move to their new territories (shown as their traditional territory on John Smith's map) during the first and third quarters, respectively, of the sixteenth century.

On the upper Eastern Shore there is ample good land that is flat or nearly so and warms up in the spring: Matapeake and Sassafras loams, silt loams, and sandy loams are excellent soils for native or modern agriculture.[37] Where such soils occurred next to major waterways, Indian towns (as opposed to foraging camps) could be built. Western Shore soils were also productive farther up the tidal rivers, although the rolling countryside made erosion more of a problem for early Indian agriculturalists and later European settlers. In John Smith's time, however, political and military forces had caused the native population to abandon most of the upper Chesapeake region.

Enter the English

From the mid-sixteenth to the early seventeenth centuries, the upper coastal plain, Piedmont, and ridge and valley provinces were dominated and controlled by the Susquehannocks and the Massawomecks, who, as we have seen, were each other's mortal enemies. They vied for access to and control of luxury trade goods: brass, copper, shell, furs, and other commodities from societies from the Atlantic Ocean west to the Ohio valley. The addition of European brass and iron goods after 1550 only intensified the competition, so in 1608 both the Susquehannocks and the Massawomecks sought the English as allies and trade partners. The Virginia English began taking an interest in the fur trade by 1620, but the First Anglo-Powhatan War delayed their doing much about it until 1631, when they established a trading post on Kent Island and created a partnership with the Susquehannocks. In the same year, a rival trading post was set up nearby by people who would become the Maryland English.[38] By that time, the Algonquian-speaking Tockwoghs had disappeared, probably moving in with linguistic relatives to the northeast, and the Ozinies, now called Wicomisses, were holding their own thanks to an alliance with the Patuxents and Nanticokes.[39] The groups that Smith missed, the Monoponsons and Matapeakes, appear to have joined them in making peace with the Susquehannocks, although by the treaty of 1652 the Maryland English claimed most of the region.[40]

Lord Baltimore, made Proprietor of the land north of Virginia, established his colony in 1634. By 1638, he had eliminated the Virginians' fur-trading post, but their former allies the Susquehannocks remained hostile to him and friendly to the Dutch to the north for another decade and a half, and the Wicomisses carried on the hostility until 1669.[41] The Virginia English remained hostile, too; alarms were periodically sounded in both colonies about planned attacks by the other colony and its Indian allies. In the 1640s, the Marylanders, both English and African, took up tobacco agriculture[42] and spread steadily northward along the Chesapeake and westward along the Potomac in the next several decades. After 1668, they also began settling on the Eastern Shore.[43]

The Susquehannocks were now a reduced population, harassed by the Five Nations. In 1675, the Maryland government talked them into moving to the Potomac River, where they built a square, European-modeled fort near the Piscataways' town. That is where they were attacked by a combined force of Virginia and Maryland English, with their Piscataway allies, in the opening salvo of Bacon's Rebellion, after which they went to war again. To

A Northeast Passage: The C & D Canal

In 1671, Bohemian immigrant Augustine Herrmann produced the first definitive
Chesapeake map that improved on John Smith's work. As payment for this
service, Lord Baltimore's Maryland government at St. Mary's City granted
Herrmann a large plantation on a tributary of the Elk that Hermann had named
the Bohemia River. With his extensive and excellent surveying abilities, in 1661 he
had written: "The Minquaskil [today's Appoquinimink Creek] and the aforesaid
Bohemia River run there within a league [3 miles or 4.8 kilometers] from each
other from where we shall in time have communication with each other by
water." Herrmann soon engineered a cart road enabling commerce between
the headwaters of these two streams, a route that interwove Maryland and
Delaware interests. But neither in Herrmann's lifetime nor in the following
160 years would the canal he dreamed of be built. In 1679, Benjamin Bullivant
wrote: "About 6 myles [nearly 10 kilometers] below New Castle is a creek by
w[hi]ch you may come to a neck of land about 12 myles [nearly 20 kilometers]
over . . . w[hi]ch are drawn goods to & from Maryland . . . by oxen." These were
but two of five possible canal routes surveyed in 1769 between the Chesapeake
and Delaware. It was not until 1824 that excavation began, with the "deep cut"
at today's Summit Bridge opened by moving 375,000 cubic yards [286,708 cubic
meters] of soil, a stupendous effort for the time.

  In 1829, just as railroads were putting competitive pressure on canals, the Elk
and Delaware rivers, 13.6 miles [21.9 kilometers] apart, were linked. Ships could
pass the canal by way of a series of four locks, later reduced to three. After
the 1830s, water was pumped by steam engines into the empty locks after a
ship had passed, an expensive process. Later, more modern power excavating
equipment was employed to extend the canal to sea level, eliminating the
need for locks; the canal reopened in 1928. Annual tonnage passing through
the canal increased from 700,000 to 1.2 million tons [636,364 to 1,090,908 metric
tonnes] in six years. The canal was deepened and widened in 1938, with a
second expansion started in 1954. By that time concern had begun to develop
about the effect of huge water exchanges between the two bays on fishes,
eggs, and larvae, concerns that persist today. With changes in ships and cargo
types, the number of vessel trips through the C & D Canal has declined. Despite
pressure from the Army Corps of Engineers and Maryland harbor officials for
yet another deepening in the mid-1990s, decreasing use by large oceangoing
vessels and natural resource concerns have maintained the status quo.

Sources: Mountford 2002a and 2002b.

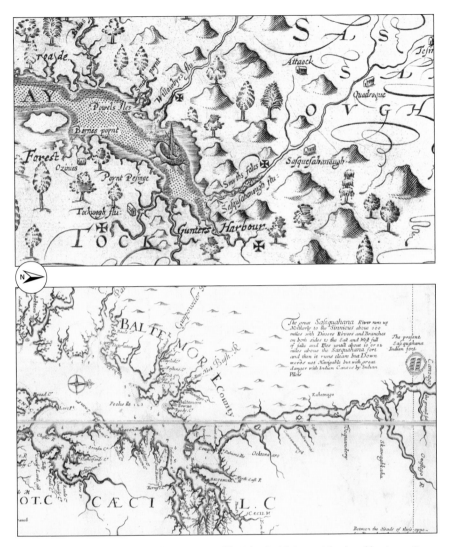

The upper shore and head of the bay as mapped by John Smith in 1608 (*top*) and by Augustine Herrmann in 1673 (*bottom*). Maryland bestowed on Herrmann a plantation on the Bohemia River on the Eastern Shore in payment for his survey and excellent map. The small boat on Smith's map is thought to represent his exploration barge.

gain allies and ensure their own survival, they made peace with the Five Nations; some went to live with their allies, while others returned to their old Susquehanna River territory.[44] Their town in Pennsylvania is known to archaeologists as the Conestoga Town site (1690–1763).

Tobacco farmers continued to pour into the lands near the upper Chesapeake Bay, and settlers from the new colony of Pennsylvania were moving in as well. The upper bay area was firmly established as part of Maryland by the 1690s, so it was Maryland that dealt with another group that moved in for a time: the Shawnees (1697–1707). The Leni Lenape were also using the region as a hunting territory, which occasionally caused difficulties. Eventually the native people of the region were pushed out of their lands by the influx of settlers. In the eighteenth century, they either moved westward, as the Lenape did, or they went north and joined the still-strong Five Nations. In English hands, and with the colony's governmental center in Annapolis, the area became a hub for trade and (later) industry.

11

*The Patuxent River Basin:
"Good Cheer" and "Infinite
Kinds of Fish"*

JOHN SMITH MET THE PEOPLE of the Patuxent River on his second voyage, probably with a sense of relief after finding no one on the Western Shore of the bay in the first voyage. The name "Patuxent" probably meant "at the place of the rolling water or little rapids."[1] Although he recorded little about the people who inhabited this region of the Chesapeake, he did note that they seemed more "civil" than the Indians he had previously met (which included the Accomac and Potomac River people he had seen on his first trip). He probably meant "polite" rather than "civilized," for the Accomacs were at least as dependent on agriculture and firmly settled in towns as the downstream Patuxents. As for the people's cordiality, Smith's possession of Massawomeck shields and other gear, which could be construed as war trophies, may have had an effect.

John Smith Exploring the Patuxent

As two of our authors (Mountford and Clark) have lived on the Patuxent over long periods, and one of them (Mountford) has sailed it avidly, we shall draw on their knowledge to reconstruct John Smith's exploration of the river more thoroughly than was possible in chapter 5. John Smith's visit would, at a minimum, have required protocol visits to each weroance village of the river's three chiefdoms in 1608, the "Acquintanacsuck, Pawtuxunt, and Mattapanient."[2] From them or a local guide the English may have taken on board, they would have learned the names of the river and the various villages they passed as they went.

Smith had bypassed the Patuxent on his first voyage, perhaps because he did not spot it to the south in the haze as he crossed the bay to Calvert Cliffs, but more likely because the wind and tide were against going in that direction. On his second expedition, perhaps with the previous day's northerly wind behind him, he rectified the omission, although still not without difficulty. He noted Mill and Cuckold creeks to port, but he was more concerned with the difficulties of traveling upstream than with exploring these minor tributaries.

Upstream from its mouth, the Patuxent makes a sharp bend around a point extending southwest into the river's deepest reach. Because the channel there is narrow, the currents during both flood and ebb tides accelerate to 1.2 or 1.3 miles (1.9 or 2.1 kilometers) per hour. The point would earn the name "Point Patience" because of the difficulty mariners had in rounding it during the age of sail. Being in a barge that at best was difficult to row, if Smith encountered an unfavorable ebb or flood tide there the only sensible thing for him to have done was to wait for the next flood tide. The tidal current also strengthens at Broome Island and Jack Bay, upriver, and when it is favorable, it is a significant assist all along the tidal part of the river. A stiff southerly wind can persist at least to Holland Cliff, twenty miles (32 kilometers) above the river's mouth, during an upstream passage, although its usefulness wanes farther up. Winds would be stronger in the afternoon, as the land warmed, so that morning travel might have to be human-powered with the assistance of a flood tide, if one occurred that early in the day.

Smith had been looking all along for harbors for oceangoing ships, so he took soundings here as well, even though the shape of the river did not augur well (in those days) for a naval base. He accurately reported that the depth of "the river," probably at that narrowing, was "16 or 18 fathom [96–108 feet or 29–33 meters] deep in some places."[3] From there, he proceeded up the east side of the Patuxent, where the flood tide would run stronger and the ebb slightly less strong. He may also have taken advantage of favorable winds.

Judging by the map he produced, Smith noted the entrance of Back Creek at today's Solomons but did not sail up it to see the split of St. John Creek. He sailed around today's Point Patience and failed to note the presence of several creeks in Calvert County. Neither Hellen Creek nor Hungerford Creek is readily visible from the river, and Mears Creek was visually blocked, up through the nineteenth century, by a vegetated bar that concealed its mouth. Smith headed for Parran Point, downstream from Mears Creek and Turner Cove, crossing over fairly deep underwater meadows that were reported, in the 1830s, to be clear enough that fish could be seen swimming through the grasses. The explorers, however, were interested in the Indian village, named Opanient, on the shore.[4] There they could go ashore and ask where the nearest chief's town was, what lay upriver, and so on. If they treated the villagers well, those people would send word ahead that the outlanders were friendly.

Continuing northward, Smith noted St. Leonard Creek, the river's largest tributary. That creek would be unattractive to sailors if they had the wind, for inside its mouth, under today's Rodney Point, the strongest up-Patuxent summer winds are blanketed to dead calm. In addition, in the late seventeenth century and possibly earlier, the creek's mouth was partially blocked by an island. Thus Smith noted but did not explore the creek. Instead he kept on going along the east side of the river, for the west side has high cliffs that would have shut off any useful wind. He passed what is now Jefferson Patterson Park and Museum and what was then the village of Quomocac. The shoreline there is only ten feet (3 meters) above the river, with a low, flat floodplain intersected by tidal marshes. The marshes have spits across their mouths due to sand drift along the shores, but the beaches shelve off fairly soon into water deep enough to accommodate the English barge. Smith may have stopped at the village, but he probably did not have to do so and kept on going, moving out into the broad river to avoid the shoals around Broome Island, which at the time, with lower sea level, may have extended even farther into the western channel.

Smith's goal lay upriver. The Patuxent chief's capital was on Battle Creek, and Smith definitely stopped there to parley, as protocol demanded. He would have stayed at least a few hours, given the nature of Native American hospitality, and there must have been an exchange of stories about the Massawomecks. Smith and the chief may also have discussed an alliance, exchanged goods to cement one, and arranged for a guide to accompany the party upriver.

Pressing onward the next day, Smith rounded Prison Point, at Battle Creek's mouth, and followed the covelike eastern riverbank past the village of Onatuck. The offshore shelf here is shallow, and as late as 1938 a lush underwater meadow of aquatic grasses grew on it. More small tributary streams have had their mouths closed up by sand drifting downstream along the shore. He passed Sheridan Point, where the channel narrows again and a flood tide would have been a significant help. The mariners were probably rowing again[5] as they passed the last Patuxent village, Wascocup, on Morsell Cove.

After passing this village, while noting the bends and direction of the river's course, Smith saw no human habitations from below the modern Maryland S.R. 231 bridge to what is now Lower Marlboro. Then villages appeared again, and the river began some serious meandering, with low-lying lands and extensive freshwater marshes alternating on each side. Much of the east bank of the river above Hall Creek, however, consists of cliffs up to sixty feet (18.3 meters) high. Smith does not seem to have gone up (or learned about) the river much farther, for his map does not show Jug Bay, which is a prominent feature on modern maps. Interestingly, he did not place a cross on his map anywhere on the Patuxent, as he did on other rivers to indicate how far he claimed to have explored. But he would have paid a courtesy (and information-seeking) call on the chief of Mattapanient.

Even if Smith made it as far as the modern Merkle Wildlife Sanctuary, that was a good forty-five miles (nearly 75 kilometers) of long, hot rowing for his men, even if the tides were somewhat stronger due to there being a full moon during their trek (August 15, on the old Julian calendar, August 25 on our modern, Gregorian one). All of those miles led northward, up toward the Piedmont province along a river they had already been told did not reach the mountains.

The trip back downriver, against the prevailing wind, would have been even more difficult, alleviated only by taking advantage of ebb tides. Having established good relations and been entertained by all three Patuxent chiefdoms, perhaps Smith concluded his alliance at Acquintanacsuck and promised to return the following year to revenge the Patuxent River chiefdoms on the Massawomecks. That meeting would have concluded when the ebb tide and favorable winds once again made feasible the voyage past Point Patience and the mouth of the Patuxent.

The Environment

The Patuxent is the Chesapeake's sixth-largest river. It extends for 110 miles (177 kilometers) from Drum Point to Parrs Ridge, which is the divide between the Patuxent and Monocacy river drainages; the river therefore lies wholly within the modern state of Maryland. For over two thousand years, the river served as a highway for the movement of people transporting goods from the Blue Ridge Mountains up the Monocacy River valley, across a portage to the upper Patuxent, and thence down to the Chesapeake Bay.[6] The valley itself provided its human inhabitants with hardwood forests containing nut-bearing trees, a lower river with oysters and softshell clams, an upper river with freshwater marshes containing edible plants, river shallows attractive to waterfowl, and a floodplain with good soils for farming.

Waters and the Plants beneath Them

In terms of salinity, the Patuxent passes from brackish water at its mouth—especially in drought years—to fresh by the time one reaches its meanders at Lower Marlboro. Four centuries ago, with more forest along its flanks, and the presumed drought in 1608, the river became fresh farther upstream. During John Smith's journey, the water was also probably much clearer than at present, as mentioned above, and grass beds flourished on the bottom in many places up and down the river.

Four centuries, including a century and a half of intensive clear-field agriculture, have muddied the Patuxent considerably. Upstream, the river's channel through these later-deposited soils has progressively eroded the outside edges of the meandering bends, redepositing sediments on the inside of downstream curves. Thus over the centuries the channel has been reworked more than once.[7] Thanks to all that sediment washing riverward, the Patuxent for much of its length is shallower today than it used to be, and significant parts of the river have actually been filled in.[8] This change was gradual: shallow waters along the shore became marshes and later some of these became low-lying land—a process that can be seen in the other tributaries of the Chesapeake as well. Marsh creatures have benefited, but for humans it was perceived as a waste of good farm soils that have eroded away. Elsewhere in the river, the channel in places became so shallow or narrow that commercial navigation ceased in the early 1900s. As late as the 1930s, aerial photographs showed extensive aquatic grass beds, but these have nearly disappeared since then.

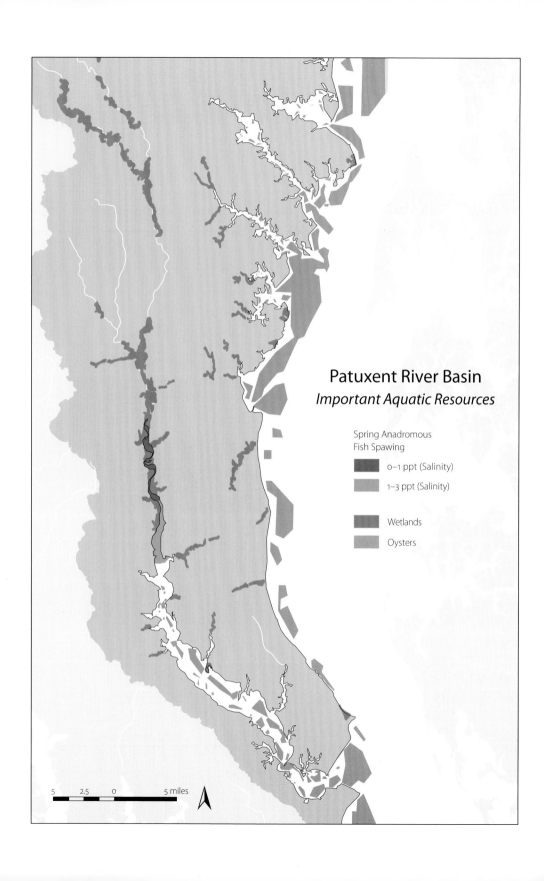

Patuxent River Basin
Important Aquatic Resources

Spring Anadromous
Fish Spawing

■ 0–1 ppt (Salinity)

▨ 1–3 ppt (Salinity)

■ Wetlands

▨ Oysters

5   2.5   0   5 miles

Fishes and Shellfish

It is likely that the Patuxent's transparency led John Smith to exclaim over the "infinite schools of diverse kinds of fish more than elsewhere."[9] In August 1608, these would have included different-aged schools of rockfish (striped bass), and equally possible would have been voracious bluefish slashing through circling schools of young menhaden—schools that could be acres (up to a hectare) in extent. Baitfish such as the Atlantic silverside and bay anchovy would also have been seen, as well as shoals of mummichogs (killifish) darting about in the shallows. All of these species were food for larger predator fish. The clear water would also have revealed spot and croaker some yards beneath the surface, while individual white perch would have been breaking the surface all over the tributary creeks as they fed near sunset. Cownose rays, in groups of five to a dozen, foraged on bottom-dwelling clams and worms, raising clouds of sediment in the shallows.

Extensive oyster beds once existed, rising above the bottom along the lower river, each bed given a name by nineteenth-century oystermen. The beds extended from the "Chinese mud" beds at the river's mouth all the way to the modern town of Benedict. Softshell clam beds, prior to the extensive harvest of the 1960s boom period, formerly occupied twelve thousand acres (4,856.2 hectares) of Patuxent River bottom.[10]

Wetlands

As with other waterways in the Chesapeake, the Patuxent River's marshes gradually change from salt water (2,600 acres or 1,052.2 hectares) to fresh (5,200 acres or 2,104.4 hectares) as the bay is left farther behind.[11] Thanks to the aforementioned sedimentation, these downstream marshes are more extensive today than they were four hundred years ago. Even so, the marsh plants most useful to humans are limited to specific areas. Tuckahoe (arrow arum) appears in the lower river only at Town Point and near Clark's Wharf but is common from the mouth of Swanson Creek upward. Cow lily appears from the mouth of Mattaponi Creek upward. Among the usable rushes and reeds, phragmites occurs at several sites along the river, softstem bulrush is currently found only at one site near the river's mouth and at three more in the far headwaters, and cattails grow in only six undisturbed places, three of them above the Anne Arundel County line. Water hemp is scattered along the whole river, but wild millet does not occur below Hunting Creek, nor wild rice below Ferry Point Landing. Sweetflag,

The Sneaker Index

Marylander C. Bernard "Bernie" Fowler was born and raised fishing and boating on the Patuxent at Broome Island. As a young man he ran a boat livery and in his spare time took a long-handled net and waded out chest-deep in the river. The water was so clear that he could see and catch soft crabs in the dense grass beds; he could also see his white sneakers on the bottom, even in five feet (1.5 meters) of water. By the 1960s, however, development and urbanization overtook the upper Patuxent, and agricultural fertilizer use mushroomed. As water quality in the river declined, Fowler was puzzled and disheartened when he could no longer see the bottom—or his sneaker-clad feet—and poorer fishing drove him out of the boat-rental business. Adding injury to insult, the Patuxent's grass beds all but disappeared after Tropical Storm Agnes ravaged the area in the late summer of 1972.

Playing afternoon community baseball with Dr. Don Heinle at the Chesapeake Biological Laboratory, Fowler learned about nutrient pollution and its insidious effects on the Patuxent. Heinle, a scientist working on the river and bay, told an emerging story about nitrogen pollution of waterways in an era when the phenomenon was largely unrecognized, politically unpopular, and dangerous for a government-funded biologist to discuss.

Campaigning on an environmental platform, Fowler ran for and was elected county commissioner, then becoming commission president. He galvanized the surrounding lower Patuxent counties around the need for proactive efforts to restore the health of the Patuxent and the bay, bringing suit against the upriver jurisdictions and the U.S. Environmental Protection Agency for failure to control nutrient pollution. The result was a landmark judgment that was one of the first efforts in establishing the Chesapeake Bay Program. Now retired, Fowler went on to serve multiple terms as senator in the Maryland legislature.

In the 1980s, a St. Mary's County schoolteacher who knew of Bernie Fowler's "sneaker test" for water clarity had her students wade in the river to test how deep they could go and still see their toes. Touched by this effort, poet Tom Wisner penned "Bernie's Measure" to add his voice to the rising chorus of citizens concerned about the Patuxent's health. The Patuxent Wade-In—with the condition of the Patuxent measured by what came to be called the Sneaker Index—soon became an annual community event, and each year since 1988, on the second Sunday in June, Fowler, his supporters, and a wide range of local, state, and federal elected officials have waded in to reaffirm their commitment to the Patuxent. The EPA now tracks and publicizes the Sneaker Index as one of its Chesapeake Bay environmental indicators.

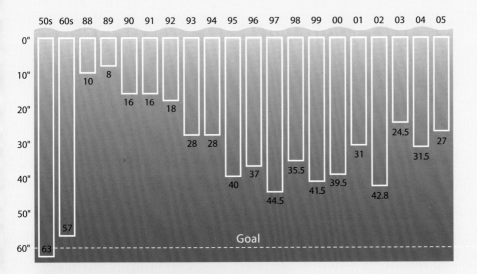

| 50s | 60s | 88 | 89 | 90 | 91 | 92 | 93 | 94 | 95 | 96 | 97 | 98 | 99 | 00 | 01 | 02 | 03 | 04 | 05 |

0"
10" 10   8
20"   16   16   18
30"   28   28   24.5   27
40"   40   37   35.5   31   31.5
50"   44.5   41.5   39.5   42.8
60" 63

57

Goal

How shallow does Patuxent River water have to be before you can see your feet clearly? Former Maryland senator Bernard Fowler has long monitored the river's health, seeking the clarity remembered from his youth. The graph (above) shows values for what has come to be called the Sneaker Index, from the 1950s to 2005. Contrasting symbols on shoes (left) are part of one wader's water-clarity testing equipment. (Graph: Nita Sylvester, United States Environmental Protection Agency, Chesapeake Bay Program. Photograph from the collections of The Mariners' Museum, Newport News, Va.)

which many Woodland Indians used for medicine, can be found only far up the river around the Maryland S.R. 4 bridge.[12]

Trees

While the standard oak-hickory forest still covers the lands around the Patuxent, two species reach their limit in the river's basin. One is the swamp white oak (also called basket oak), a southerly species that fades out along the southern Patuxent. The other is the bald cypress, with a large stand up Battle Creek,[13] another pocket on St. Thomas Creek, and yet another near the intersection of Route 231 and Sixes Road. Individual trees are found in other places in the Patuxent valley. Except for one site on the Chester River on the Eastern Shore, that is as far north as this famous tree-with-knees grows, and the Battle Creek stand has been purchased by the Nature Conservancy and ceded to Calvert County, which has turned it into a park with a nature center. The upper tidal half of the Patuxent's drainage is covered by the tulip poplar forest association and the lower half by the oak-hickory association, which before the blight of the 1930s included the valuable American chestnut.[14]

Biologists have taken sediment cores from Patuxent marshes to learn about the adjacent forests in ancient times. One of them[15] shows evidence of a warm, dry interval called the Medieval Warm Period, which lasted from around 1200 to 1400. The dominant trees at that time were oaks, hickories, and pines—like today's forest, only dryer with charcoal indicating frequent fires and high sedimentation rates indicating considerable erosion from the clearings. Intervening between 1400 and about 1800 was the "Little Ice Age" mentioned in chapter 1, during which the woods were wetter and supported more river birches, sweetgums, and black gums. An exception, however, was the late sixteenth to the early seventeenth century, which a core from Jug Bay shows to have been a period of drought (corroboration for the dendrochronology results from cypress trees to the south).[16]

The People

John Smith wrote that the towns in the Patuxent River valley had 200 fighting men, which would mean a population of about 850 people. Since Smith's penetration of the river was limited, those figures may be low. There were several chiefdoms along the river.[17]

Patuxent

This group consisted of five towns located on the east side of the lower part of the river; their foraging territory probably extended over the peninsula to Calvert Cliffs. The chief's name in 1608 was not recorded; in 1621, John Pory wrote that it was Namenicus and that he lived not at Pawtuxunt but at "Attoughcomoco" (perhaps Acquintanacsuck, Assomocomoco being rather far upstream).[18] The towns were: *Opanient,* on the north side of Turner Cove, upstream from the mouth of Hellen Creek; *Quomocac,* just downstream from the mouth of Island Creek, around the mouth of Swan Creek; *Pawtuxunt,* on the east side of Battle Creek, south of Long Cove; *Onuatuck,* between Prison Point and Kitts Point (a large, thick shell midden has been found there, possibly indicating the "town" was a summer fishing/shellfishing settlement); and *Wascocup,* between Sheridan Point and Sandy Point, around Morsell Cove.

Opanient has been identified as the Cumberland Palisaded Village, the only palisaded town along the river; a carbon date of 1575 AD has been recovered from it.[19] Quomocac has been located inside Jefferson Patterson Park and Museum, being one of several sites in the park. Thick shell middens, indicating long-term use as summer shellfishing base camps, probably mark the sites of Onuatuck and Wascocup, which may have been primarily spring/summer fishing camps. Ironically, the Pawtuxunt town area has not yet been extensively surveyed by archaeologists.

Acquintanacsuck

This group consisted of five towns located on the west side of the lower part of the river. Its relationship with the Patuxents is uncertain; when John Pory visited in 1621, its chief was dominant, but by 1634 there seems to have been a reversal. The towns were: *Acquintanacsuck,* east of Cole Creek, around Hollywood Shores; *Wasinacus,* between Cole Creek and Second Creek; *Acquaskack,* around Trent Hall; *Wasapokent,* either at Long Point/ Golden Beach or across Indian Creek from them; and *Macocanaco,* on the south side of Swanson Creek near Teague Point (this town may have been John Pory's "Assamocomoco" in 1621).

It is possible that the latter two towns comprised an autonomous, midriver chiefdom, which appears in John Pory's 1621 account as Assamocomoco, with its own chief named Cassatowap. This chiefdom and chief, together with a downriver town named Paccamaganant, appear only in Pory's report. Sites corresponding to the first two towns have been found during archaeological survey.

The Cumberland Palisaded Village

Opanient was the southernmost village of the Patuxent chiefdom on the eastern shore of the river. Named after the site's owner, the Cumberland Palisaded Village site was excavated as an emergency salvage recovery in 1983 and is in the area of Opanient as depicted on Smith's 1612 map. Detailed controlled surface collections, test squares, and plow-zone removal failed to reveal any historic period artifacts below the plow zone, although pre-Contact features were discovered below the zone. A C^{14} date of 1575 + 65 years (uncorrected), combined with 70 percent Yeocomico ware and 20 percent Rappahannock Fabric Impressed ware, suggests that the village dates from the late 1500s to the early 1600s. This time frame is reinforced by the recovery of Potomac-type triangular points made of quartz, chert, and jasper.

The fortified village was built on a point that provided sight distances three miles (4.8 kilometers) downriver and twelve miles (19.3 kilometers) upriver. Steep cliffs containing Miocene fossil deposits provided defenses on two sides of the village adjacent to the river and cove at an elevation of twenty feet (6 meters) above high tide. Three hundred years of farming at the site resulted in surface deflation that eroded any post molds from houses inside the palisade. The arching palisade is 171 by 171 feet (52 by 52 meters), an area of 23,681 square feet (2,200 square meters), but it, too, is partly eroded. The Patuxent people constructed the palisade by excavating a continuous trench, into which they dropped the palisade posts, which are estimated to have been twelve feet (over 3.5 meters) high. They used oyster shells and Miocene fossil concretions to wedge the posts in place. Between the posts they would have woven limbs of trees in a wicker-style pattern. They then excavated clay from a parallel trench and packed the wattle fence with clay daub. This wattle-and-daub technique was the same one that was used at the Massawomeck-related sites in the upper Potomac River and Ohio valley drainages. Two overlapping lines of posts were set at the major entrances as a trap, should attackers break through the first opening to the entrance. John Smith noted in 1608 that the Massawomecks were attacking the Patuxents; on retaliatory raids the Patuxents may have learned their enemies' method of fortification. Alternatively, they may have adopted it from the Potomac River Piscataways and Patawomecks, who were using this method by the fifteenth century. The Cumberland Palisaded Village is the only fortified village reported to date along the Patuxent River. Its location at the southern end of the Patuxent chiefdom indicates that during periods of conflict, villages on the edge of the territory required defenses.

Sources: Reeves 1996; Smolek 1986.

Upriver from the first two chief-doms there seems to have been a buffer zone between them and the Mattapanients, for reasons unknown. The zone extended between Swanson and Black Swamp creeks on the right side of the river (as one drifts downstream) and between Buzzard Island and Chew Creeks on the left side.

Mattapanient

This chiefdom consisted of seven towns. It was definitely autonomous, as evidenced not only by its separate appearance in the English records but also by the twelve-mile (19-kilometer) absence of settlements, resembling a "buffer zone," between its lowermost town and the uppermost one of Acquintanacsuck (or Assamocomoco).

East of the Patuxent, going upriver, the towns were: *Tauskus,* around Lower Marlboro; *Wepanawomen,* south of Hall Creek, opposite and a short distance upstream from White Landing; and *Quactataugh,* opposite and a little downstream from Nottingham.

West of the Patuxent, going upriver, the towns were: *Pocatamough,* south of the mouth of Black Swamp Creek, opposite Camp Mohawk; *Quotough,* at White Landing, upstream from Short Point; *Wosameus,* in the marsh, then a point of land, above White Landing; and *Mattapanient,* south of Spice Creek, opposite Jones Point (this was a commoners' village in 1608 but had become a chief's residence by 1621).

Numerous archaeological sites, apparently representing hamlets, have

A daub clay burrow trench and a wattle-and-post palisade line excavated at the Cumberland Palisaded Village site in Calvert County, Maryland. The poles of the palisade were erected first, then woven with twigs (wattle) and covered with mud-plaster (daub), which was fire-resistant. This site may be the one Smith called Opanient. (Jefferson Patterson Park and Museum)

Triangular projectile points from the Stearns site on the Patuxent River. Radiocarbon testing dates the site to around 1450; it is in the vicinity of the town John Smith called Quomocac. (Jefferson Patterson Park and Museum)

been found along this stretch of the river; some may be the villages of Smith's map. The site of Tauskus, however, seems to have been badly disturbed by the building of the modern settlement of Lower Marlboro. Interestingly enough, the pottery found thus far during survey of the sites indicates closer connections with the Piscataways/Moyaones than with neighbors down the river,[20] another indication of a buffer zone between upriver and downriver chiefdoms.

There were probably a few more towns upriver that Smith missed, especially around Jug Bay. The evidence is both archaeological and historical. A large Late Woodland site has been found just south of Jug Bay and north of the modern town of Nottingham. And Augustine Herrmann's map of 1673 shows a town far up the river called Wighkawamecg; it has not been precisely located archaeologically. That town was a reservation community (1652–92) located north of the mouth of Western Branch on the west side of the upper Patuxent, about two miles (3.2 kilometers) above Jug Bay. Its inhabitants were the Mattapanients and families from other districts who had gone to live with them under English protection.

Intertown and Intertribal Relations

The towns that John Smith saw along the Patuxent were not as scattered as the ones he was familiar with farther south; he wrote that the people there "inhabit together, and not so dispersed as the rest." The reason is not difficult to discern: the Massawomecks are known to have raided them.[21] And the Susquehannocks seem already to have been pushing their field of influence southward, which was another threat. By the 1630s, a state of war existed between them and the Wicomisses and Yoacomocos and possibly the Patuxents as well; the Patuxent and the Wicomisses are known to have been each other's allies in 1634.[22] The establishment of an English fur-trading outpost on Kent Island, exacerbating competition with the Susquehannocks in the upper bay region, would not have helped. That threat, if it existed as early as 1608, would have been a factor in the initial friendly reception accorded the English.

Most of the Powhatan chiefdoms between the York and the lower Potomac rivers produced the same type of shell-tempered pottery (Townsend, Rappahannock, Sullivan, and Yeocomico wares) as did those along the lower Patuxent.[23] The upper Patuxent sites have these wares plus increased percentages of Potomac Creek, Moyoane, and Camden wares with sand or quartz temper, indicating somewhat closer relations between the upriver people with (at least) the Moyaons across the peninsula of southern Maryland. Both ceramic groups, however, are associated

Late Woodland shell-tempered Yeocomico Ware vessel from the clay burrow trench of the Cumberland Palisaded Village site. This type of pottery was typical of sites along the lower Patuxent and Potomac rivers during the Contact period. (Jefferson Patterson Park and Museum)

with Algonquian-speaking chiefdoms. While archaeologists are reluctant to equate ceramic types with languages spoken in the early 1600s, correlations such as this build the case for associations when geographic maps, village names, and narratives such as Smith's allow such direct historical linking of chiefdoms and languages to associated material culture produced by native peoples circa 1550 to 1650.

There has been extensive archaeological survey within the Patuxent valley, and a fair amount of excavation.[24] As a result, the prehistory of this valley, and the changes of lifeways within it, are probably better understood than for any other part of the Chesapeake drainage. The Late Woodland period (AD 900–1692) sites suggest a steady increase of the valley's human population, focused on a combination of farming and foraging for wild plants and animals.[25] Corn carbon-dated to AD 900–1100 has been found at one site within the Acquintanacsuck chiefdom's area, and storage pits in the Patuxent area dating from AD 200 to 1450 point to a long-held practice

Archaeological Evidence of Patuxent Peoples' Diet

Since the 1930s, archaeological research in the lower Patuxent River valley has documented extensive oyster middens that extend from Patuxent Naval Air Station at the mouth of the river to Cocktown Creek in the north. At a site that may represent the village of Opanient, analysis of a small sample of oyster shells from the excavation indicates a preference for three- to four-year-old oysters; radial ridges and pinkish color indicate they were collected in a near-shore, shallow-water zone. The same excavation yielded box turtles and deer. On St. Leonard Creek, a small shell midden spanning the early Late Woodland period suggests progressively smaller oyster shell size over time, evidence for overharvesting of the adjacent shell beds. At an early Late Woodland storage pit north of St. Leonard Creek, oyster, blue crab, and white perch were found, along with corn and hickory, acorn, and black walnut shells.

As corn, bean, and squash agriculture increased during the Late Woodland period, the number of shell midden sites doubled, reflective of the overall increase in population during this period. Squash seeds were found in a shell pit at Myrtle Point on the lower west side of the river. Use of flotation at the Thomas Point site (ca. 900–1100) revealed corn, acorn, hickory, persimmon, cherry, elderberry, blueberry, grape, *Chenopodium,* knotweed, pokeweed, and bedstraw. Animal remains from the same site include deer, box turtles, and musk turtles, gray foxes, raccoons, rabbits, squirrels, turkeys, barred owls, fish crows, robins, toadfish, and white perch. Detailed analysis of the oysters at the Thomas Point site suggests a late summer to winter harvesting time.

There is still more to be learned, not only by further excavation but by detailed analysis of existing collections gathered by use of the flotation method.

Sources: Herbert 1993 and 1995; Herbert and Steponaitis 1998; Mountford and Mountford n.d.; Reeves et al. 1991; Scarry 1996; Smolek n.d.; Stearns 1951; Steponaitis 1985.

of producing a food surplus: extra seeds and nuts before maize agriculture was adopted, and extra corn thereafter.

Evidence from the Bay's Rim

Much of the country along the Western Shore was less than ideal for Late Woodland Period people, who were both farmers and watermen. Cliffs rim the bay for long stretches on the west—often, spectacular ones like Calvert

Cliffs—and elsewhere the lands near the shore are rolling uplands that are subject to erosion when cultivated. Along the South, Severn, and other rivers to the north are waterfront lands on which evidence has been found of Late Woodland occupation—but none of those sites dates to the Contact period. John Smith did not miss people there; rather, the people had moved away, perhaps to the upper tidal Patuxent River.

Interplay between People and the Environment

The Patuxent River flows through a floodplain whose lower reaches have been inundated by rising sea level. Along this floodplain are patches of the prime corn-growing soils that are typical of the uplands from the Northern Neck of Virginia northward: Matapeake and Sassafras loams, silt loams, and fine sandy loams.[26] Smith's map shows that there is a close correlation between the location of Indian towns in John Smith's time and where those productive soils are. Being watermen as well as farmers, the people naturally preferred to put their settlements on low ground, eschewing high cliffs that would have required up-and-down carrying. Consequently, there are shell middens on those low grounds as far upriver as the Maryland S.R. 231 bridge.

The upper Patuxent meanders for part of its length, and within the meanders are extensive marshes. The upstream marshes are far enough removed from brackish Chesapeake Bay waters that they contain the marsh plants—tuckahoe (arrow arum) and wild rice—so productive of food for Native Americans. Around Jug Bay there is a good "breadbasket"[27] that would have given the upriver women tubers to trade to the downriver people for oysters and other goods. If such trade did not go on, the downstream women would have had to raise more corn to see their families through the spring and early summer, as well as the winter. It is possible that they did just that, if John Smith's calling them "civil" meant he saw them doing intensive farming.

The towns the people built in Indian times are not only to be found on good soils and near productive marshes; they are also located at places where there is only minimal marsh to cross to reach the river. If canoes transported food and other items needed by people in the towns, it made sense to place the towns as close to the canoe landings as possible. Later, English settlements along the river would follow the same rule. In the case of Opanient, the town farthest downriver, there is an additional advantage:

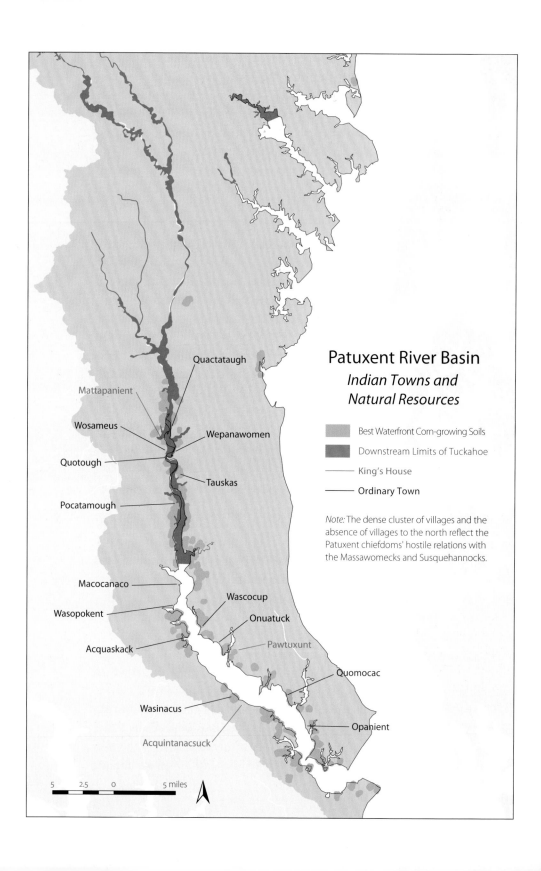

Quactataugh

Mattapanient

Wosameus

Wepanawomen

Quotough

Tauskas

Pocatamough

Patuxent River Basin
Indian Towns and Natural Resources

Best Waterfront Corn-growing Soils

Downstream Limits of Tuckahoe

King's House

Ordinary Town

Note: The dense cluster of villages and the absence of villages to the north reflect the Patuxent chiefdoms' hostile relations with the Massawomecks and Susquehannocks.

Macocanaco

Wascocup

Wasopokent

Onuatuck

Pawtuxunt

Acquaskack

Quomocac

Wasinacus

Opanient

Acquintanacsuck

5   2.5   0   5 miles

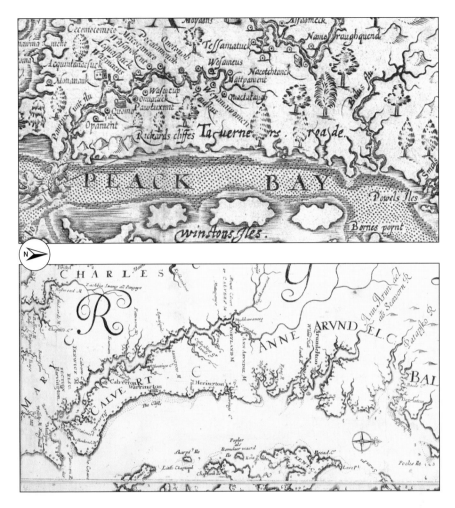

The Patuxent River area as mapped by John Smith in 1608 (*top*) and by Augustine Herrmann in 1673 (*bottom*). By 1673, the remaining Algonquians were settled on a 700-acre reservation along the upper Patuxent next to Mount Calvert.

a five-mile (8-kilometer) sight line to Point Patience. Approaching enemies would be seen as they rounded that point, and the petty chief of Opanient, which had a defensive palisade (apparently unusual on the Patuxent),[28] could send word to his overlord and have his people assume battle stations.

The premier Indian capital in 1608 was Pawtuxunt, which gave its name to the Patuxent River. Although surviving records provide no proof, the town's access to that large stand of cypress trees may have played a part in the town's prominence. Cypress is slower to rot than any other tree except red cedar, which does not grow to nearly the size. It is a first-class tree for making dugout canoes, and either logs or finished canoes could have been used as trade items. Perhaps the gift of a dugout canoe from the Patuxent weroance to John Pory in 1621 reinforces the suggestion that the cypress swamp in their territory enabled them to trade such a high-valued item for European goods.[29]

Enter the English

Smith was delighted by the cordial reception he received in 1608, but he recorded little about the Patuxent River area other than its people being "very tractable, and more civil than any," the meaning of which is uncertain. He promised the towns' leaders, as he had promised earlier at Patawomeck, that he would help them fend off the Massawomecks.[30] At least this time, with the Patuxents, he could make the promise having actually met some Massawomecks (see chapter 5).

Neither John Smith nor his compatriots at Jamestown had further contact with the Patuxents, as far as the surviving records show, until 1616, when a runaway Englishman took refuge with them; they refused to hand him over to John Pory in 1621. When the English interpreter Thomas Savage further demanded a child as a hostage and corn when the English asked for it, they became much less "tractable," for they already had serious differences of opinion with Savage. The rulers of Acquintanacsuck (Anglicized to Aquasack), who had specifically invited Pory to visit, were initially hospitable. But the atmosphere deteriorated rapidly, ending with a loud confrontation with the chiefs upriver when the English party went there.[31]

By 1624, the Patuxents were in the confidence of the Powhatan leadership and out of touch with the English, for in that year they were invited to send an observer to Pamunkey to watch a confrontation there between the English and Opechancanough's forces.[32] Nevertheless, they received fur trader William Claiborne in friendship in 1631, when he established his post on Kent Island.[33] Three years later, other Englishmen would begin a permanent settlement near them on St. Mary's River, a move that put the Patuxents in the middle of the competition between Virginia and Maryland Englishmen for furs and territory. The attempt at neutrality failed in 1639, when the Acquintanacsucks were involved in a killing.[34]

In 1638, with the Indians' permission, a Jesuit missionary came to work

Artist's rendering of a post-in-the-ground English dwelling at the King's Reach site on the Patuxent. Most English houses of the seventeenth-century Chesapeake consisted of this type of earth-fast building, since they were built on scattered plantations rather than in towns. Contrast with illustration on page 43. (Jefferson Patterson Park and Museum)

on the lower part of the river. However, the native people's relations with the English in general—and relations between the Maryland government and the Jesuits—soured in the early 1640s, especially when immigrant farmers began arriving and taking up land in competition with both Indians and Jesuits. Within another decade, most of the river would be in the hands of English tobacco farmers, who a century later would begin shifting to a greater diversity of crops. Tobacco culture, however, was labor-intensive, and English and later on Africans and West Indians were brought into the Maryland colony to perform that work, making for a diverse mix of non-Indians in the region. By the end of the seventeenth century, the river's native people would be living either with the Choptanks on the Eastern Shore or with several other groups at Choptico on the Wicomico River (the tributary to the Potomac River).[35] Their descendants are among the several modern groups living near U.S. 301, as described in chapter 12.

The Patuxent River Basin   259

The Patuxent River Indian Reservation

Following a period of strained relations, in January 1642 the Maryland English and the various chiefdoms along the Patuxent River agreed to a cessation of hostility and reestablishment of friendship. However, some anti-Indian English continued to steal corn and other goods, leading the government to enter into its first formal peace treaty in June 1644. Complaints by the native people did not diminish, for English hogs and cattle were destroying their corn crops and settlers were locating too close to them. In 1651, the Maryland government decided to define the lands reserved for the various chiefdoms on the lower Potomac and Patuxent Rivers. An 8,000- to 10,000-acre (3237.5- to 4046.9-hectare) Chopticon Resolving Preserve was established for those groups who wished to move there to "live together that they may neither injure the English nor the English them."

Chopticon was located along the Wicomico River on its eastern shore north of Choptico Bay. Another 1,000-acre (404.7-hectare) reserve, called "Calverton Manor," was established near the Patuxent River's junction with the Western Branch, in the freshwater marsh area of the river. Within these two reserves, chiefs were to receive up to two hundred acres (80.9 hectares) of land and warriors up to fifty acres (20.2 hectares) each. A year later, however, the Patuxents lost even more of their ancestral land when the Susquehannocks entered into a peace treaty with the English in which they ceded the lands from the Patuxent River to the head of the bay, which they claimed by right of conquest. The Patuxent and Mattapanient chiefdoms decided to settle on Calverton Manor, which was retained by the Maryland Proprietor and leased to them for their use. They apparently gave up seven hundred acres (283.3 hectares) of the land to Major John Billingsley, their agent, who died before the land could be patented. Billingsley's children then asked the colonial government to remove the natives. Instead, however, the government decided to allow the Indians a five-year resettlement period. By 1683, English settlements had spread up the river, there being sufficient settlers in that year to warrant an act that approved an English town at Mt. Calvert. By 1692, the Mattapanient and Patuxent groups decided to relocate to the larger Chopticon Resolving Preserve. "Two of the Indians appearing with those of Choptico acquaint his Excellency that they with some others that formerly belonged to Patuxent to the number of ten Men; were desirous to come and live with and amongst the Choptico Indians if they be permitted so to do: His Excellency gives Consent thereunto for which they are thankful." Those who made the move to Chopticon Resolving Preserve and who did not want to assimilate into English society may have relocated one last time, to the Choptank reserve of Locust Neck on the Eastern Shore (see chapter 9). The last reference to the Patuxent Indians under that name comes from Major Daniel Jenifer, Indian agent for Maryland, dated December 16, 1786: "there are not more than two or three persons, if so many, of the true race of the Locust Neck type [i.e., Choptank] now remaining, that the others settled on the Land are from Snow Hill [i.e., Pocomoke/Assateagues], Nanticoke and Patuxent."

Sources: Brown 1883–1972; document in Maryland State Archives.

12

The Potomac River: Conduit and Boundary

WHEN JOHN SMITH EXPLORED the Potomac on his first expedition in 1608, his reception varied from hostile downriver to friendly upriver near the fall line.[1] With the English colony still being in its treasure-hunting phase, he and his men spent a good deal of time in the Potomac valley hunting for mineral mines.

The Potomac River had long served as a major conduit of people and trade items between the Piedmont and mountains and the coastal plain. Reaching to the Shenandoah Valley and beyond, it connected with trading paths that extended all over eastern North America. Archaeology in the river valley therefore tells a complex story of migrations and other interactions, with the river as the center of it all.[2]

The Environment

The Potomac, like the Susquehanna and the James, has headwaters reaching far up into the Appalachians, so that its drainage basin is large (some 14,679 square miles or 38,018.4 square kilometers) and it contributes about

30 percent of the freshwater that enters the Chesapeake Bay. Some of the Potomac's tributary rivers, like the Occoquan and the Wicomico, drain large basins. Below the Little Falls on the fall line, the Potomac opens up into a vast subestuary running for over 110 miles (177 kilometers) to the bay. Including its three dozen tidal tributaries—rivers, creeks, and embayments—the river within the coastal plain has over a thousand miles (1,600 kilometers) of tidal shoreline, amounting to about one-seventh that of the entire Chesapeake Bay system.

Waters and the Shellfish in Them

The Potomac has the widest mouth of any Chesapeake tributary: eleven statute miles (17.7 kilometers) between Point Lookout and Smith Point. From Point Lookout to the nearest Virginia shore, upstream from Smith Point, is still six miles (almost 10 kilometers), so that the opposite shore is a mere smudge on the horizon even in clear weather. That long fetch means that winds can kick up a severe chop to hinder the progress of smaller craft, especially when wind turns against tide.

Though averaging less than twenty feet (6 meters) deep, the Potomac nonetheless has a generally consistently navigable channel all the way to the fall line. Depths of forty to sixty feet (12 to 18 meters) deep are not uncommon, and the Potomac has several "holes" in the range of one hundred feet (30.5 meters) deep, including one in the tidal river near Georgetown and a remarkable one in the bedrock of the nontidal river just downstream from the American Legion Memorial Bridge (I-495 Beltway). The Kettle Shoals, or Carters Lumps, off today's Colonial Beach are an obstruction for vessels drawing over ten feet (3.5 meters), and multiple right-angle turns in the river's course present sailing challenges like those in the James.

On each side, however, there are often broad, shallow shoulders where the depth is less than six feet (1.8 meters) and where clams live: brackish-water clams as far downstream as Nomini Bay, and plentiful soft clams below that. Today hard clams do not occur in the Potomac, although they may have been near the Potomac's mouth in John Smith's time when the water was saltier. There are also significant oyster beds or "rocks" at numerous deep places in the river.

Native American shell middens are understandably plentiful along the saltwater reaches of the Potomac; some date back several thousand years.[3] Euro-Americans later mined the middens at Maryland's Popes Creek as a source of lime. The size of these deposits indicates that the shellfish were harvested nearby, yet the middens are located farther upstream than shell-

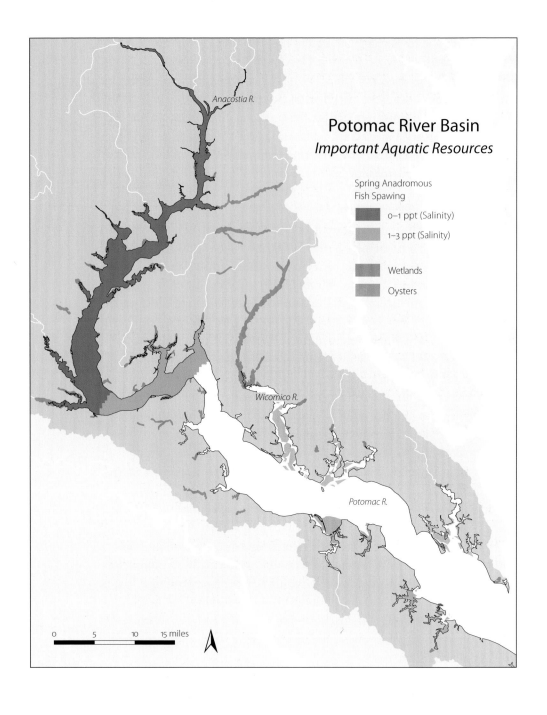

Potomac River Basin
Important Aquatic Resources

Spring Anadromous
Fish Spawing

▨ 0–1 ppt (Salinity)

▨ 1–3 ppt (Salinity)

▨ Wetlands

▨ Oysters

Anacostia R.

Wicomico R.

Potomac R.

0   5   10   15 miles

fish occur today. Today's upper limit on oysters is roughly Popes Creek, just above the U.S. 301 bridge, and die-offs occur there and downstream whenever tropical storms or unusually large spring freshets dilute the waters below survival salinity levels. For instance, after Tropical Storm Agnes swept through the region in 1972, most oysters were killed by freshwater for 25.1 miles (40.4 kilometers) below their current average limit, and for 42 miles (67.6 kilometers) below their pre-Contact limit.[4] The pre-European limit is marked by large shell deposits as far upstream as Douglas Point (19 miles [30.6 kilometers] above Popes Creek), which is also one of our best indications that the Potomac—and other tributaries of the Chesapeake—were generally saltier four centuries ago, when the much greater area of forested land resulted in less runoff. Large quantities of shell probably indicate that harvesting was done nearby.

The Potomac can carry massive floods downriver, delivering as much as 400,000 cubic feet (11,300 cubic meters) per second in peak flows. That is enough water to flood low-lying parts of the District of Columbia and Alexandria. In 1608, many parts of the modern District of Columbia were marshes, fed by numerous clear streams flowing over rocky substrates from the surrounding hills, which in turn were fed by the many artesian springs scattered throughout the wooded uplands.[5] One of the then-largest creeks, meandering Tiber Creek, is now completely filled in and entombed in storm water drains beneath the national monuments of downtown Washington.

On the other hand, the Potomac's flow has decreased to a record low of 609 cubic feet (17.245 cubic meters) per second during deep droughts. At such times, one can see the famous "drought rocks," a stone formation only above water only when the water level is extremely low; during such multiyear drought periods, the salt-loving shellfish like oysters slowly shift their distribution upriver. Four centuries ago, droughts were mitigated by the huge amount of groundwater sequestered in soils; even after trees and other plants of the forest withdrew the water they required, enough remained to feed a steady seepage from adjacent banks, which maintained stream flows at levels that may have been 20 to 30 percent higher than during modern droughts.

In dry summers, male blue crabs migrate as far upstream as the freshwater Potomac tributaries in Washington, D.C., being caught along Hains Point and in the mouth of Rock Creek. Crabs have always been abundant during warm months throughout the lower Potomac, and their remains are found at some Native American dwelling sites.

High water and low water: photographs showing a section of the Potomac River in flood in the winter of 1984, discharging water at the rate of 200,000 cubic feet per second (above), and after the drought summer of 1964, with the historic low flow of 600–700 cubic feet per second (below). (Photographs by Kent Mountford)

Fishes

The Great Falls of the Potomac prevent many anadromous fishes, such as sturgeon and striped bass, from moving farther upstream to breed—thus the bulk of these massive fish populations are concentrated in the main stem and freshwater tributaries below the falls. The visiting fish also include herring (that is, alewives and blueback herring), which spawn from Breton Bay on up. American shad and striped bass rarely enter the river's tributaries, preferring instead to travel up the main channel to fresh and nearly fresh (oligohaline) waters, with some shad passing up beyond the Little Falls (but not the Great Falls). Current populations of these fish are far below those of four centuries, ago, especially for the sturgeon, but American shad are showing strong signs of a comeback.[6] Archaeologist Wayne Clark has discovered a prehistoric petroglyph (rock carving) at the falls, which could represent a shad split open rather like a book. This would be typical of the Native American fashion of cooking them: split open and slowly roasting before an open fire for consumption or temporary preservation.[7]

Fisheries have been important to all people who have lived along the Potomac, including George Washington, who in 1772 took a half million herring from the river. The means of preserving them, however—salt from the Caribbean—had to be imported.[8]

Wetlands

The land bordering the Potomac River is nearly all high and gently rolling, so wetlands are limited except where tributary streams have carved floodplains into the lowlands. The Potomac is brackish for a long way up its course, which means that the freshwater emergent plants so useful to Native Americans were in short supply until the river turned northward. The limits of cow lily are Chicamuxen Creek on the left bank (as one heads downriver) and Potomac Creek on the right bank. The tributaries below those creeks tend to have tuckahoe (arrow arum) and cattails in their headwaters, which are fresher than the Potomac, but all creeks except Nomini lack sizable stream meanders, with emergent plants growing inside them. Cattails, *Phragmites,* and the various rushes are actually rather uncommon today in the coastal plain reaches of the Potomac River valley. Above Potomac Creek, on the other hand, the tributary streams on both sides of the river often have fairly wide mouths, even bays (such as Occoquan), and at the narrowing the creeks meander for a distance, producing sizable expanses of freshwater wetlands. These marshes, however, become increasingly constricted (compare Mattawoman and Piscataway Creeks) nearer the fall line.

There are sizable swamps in the headwaters of many tributary creeks. Prior to the seventeenth-century local extinction of beaver because of over-tapping by fur traders, these swamps would have contained a variety of beaver-changed areas: open ponds, abandoned ponds turned to wet meadows, and secondary swamp forest growth.

The Land and the Animals on It

The Potomac runs through uplands, if not hills and mountains, except for the low-lying tip of the Northern Neck. There are also low islands, such as

St. Clements, within its floodplain. The river has cut cliffs into the uplands in many places along its course. As with other tributaries of Chesapeake Bay, the oldest sediments, on the bottom, tend to be older the farther one goes upriver. Around Popes Creek (Maryland), just above the U.S. 301 bridge, they date to the early Eocene (ca. 55–45 million years old), with an overlay of early Miocene material (ca. 23–15 million years old) and then Pleistocene deposits on top. Upriver as far as Piscataway Creek, the cliffs on either side of Potomac Creek have in their bottom layer the Aquia Formation, which is late Paleocene (ca. 55 million years old). Earlier Cretaceous (over 100 million years old) Paleocene sediments can be found upriver from Piscataway Creek to the fall line.[9]

From the fall line upward, rocky outcrops occasionally yield things valuable to people. The Indians took an ore containing gold-colored iron pyrites and sparkling mica "tinctures" (called *matchqueon* by the Patawomecks; see chapter 4), separated out the glittery bits in a nearby stream, and then mixed them with grease to make sparkly body paint.[10] Real gold, however, was found only much later, and then in modest quantities, around the time of the Civil War, in the vicinity of the Great Falls, Rockville, Sandy Spring, and Bethesda; the last gold mine closed by 1950.[11] Outcrops of sandstone well up Aquia Creek proved hard enough to be used as building blocks. In the nineteenth and twentieth centuries, other outcrops of this "Aquia Freestone" was used in the facades of many public buildings in Washington, D.C.[12]

The animals and birds in the Potomac basin are the common species for this region with one exception: in the 1600s, bison were sighted beyond Great Falls.[13] They were very likely transients, for such large grass-eaters would have had to rely upon patches of woodland that had been cleared either by storms or by Native Americans conducting fire hunts. Above the fall line there were also natural, fire-maintained meadows that would have attracted those grazers. There were never many of them, however, and to date archeologists have found no bison bones.

Forests

The forest cover in the Potomac region is oak-hickory intermixed with pines and sweetgum up to the highest mountainsides, where conifers become dominant. Typical riverside forest, described in chapter 1, occurs only above the fall line, because below that most of the floodplain is bordered by estuarine waters. However, sediment cores show that these forests have changed greatly over longer stretches of time.

One of the longest continuous histories of postglacial vegetation in the coastal plain of the Chesapeake region was taken from Indian Creek, a tributary of the Anacostia River.[14] Around fourteen thousand years ago, the area was covered with a boreal forest of fir, spruce, and pine, but by thirteen thousand years ago alders, ashes, birches, hornbeams, and hazelnuts had appeared; there were few oaks and no hickories, sweetgums, or black gums. In the next five hundred years, fir and spruce declined and pine and ash increased, suggesting a warming trend, but then the trend reversed for the next thousand years. (This return of cooler conditions after an initial glacial retreat has been observed in many parts of the world.) Gradually spruce and fir would peter out for good around the Potomac's fall line.

For five thousand years, the landscape was dominated by hemlock, while black gum slowly increased. Pine gradually became co-dominant, with alder and birch coming in, but the paucity of herbaceous plants represented in the sediments indicates a closed-canopy, mixed coniferous-deciduous forest. Then large amounts of charcoal appear, representing a warmer and drier climate characterized by frequent fires—events that would have created openings in the forest for blueberry and arrowwood. Oaks and hickories also came in and increased, becoming dominant by 3,500 years before the arrival of Europeans; pines decreased accordingly. In the warmer climate, sweetgum appeared in the canopy and blueberries and their relatives became a major part of the understory. Cores show that since the arrival of English farmers, tree pollen in general has decreased and that of field plants—including Eurasian weeds like ragweed—has greatly increased.

Visitors can see a mature forest resembling that of 1608 in the Belt Woods in Prince George's County, Maryland. This woodland goes back at least two hundred years without significant disturbance. Interestingly, the trees do not have very large diameters. That is because they are not field-edge trees, which receive more sunlight and expand horizontally and look older. Instead the trees in Belt Woods put their energy into growing upward, and many have long lightning scars down their trunks because of their great height.

The People

The Potomac's role as a conduit is apparent in the Native American towns along its banks. As with the rivers to the south, most of these people lived in the inner coastal plain. But on the Potomac, that was a dangerous place to be in 1608, for Massawomeck raids from the west occurred frequently;

River as Boundary—But Not a Midriver One

Most state, county, or city boundaries in English-speaking America run down the centers of streams. That is the opposite of the way the Algonquian speakers thought: for those canoe-dependent people, streams were the centers of territories. Nonetheless, on maps we are accustomed to seeing lines down the centers of waterways—except between Virginia and Maryland. The Potomac River belongs to Maryland. Why? Because the capes at the entrance to Chesapeake Bay belong to Virginia, even though many ships passing through them have always been Maryland-bound. The deal was a compromise, worked out between Virginia and Maryland over the course of three centuries.

by the 1630s, the Susquehannocks would also be staging raids from the north, at the mouth of the river. The capitals of Moyaone/Piscataway and Patawomeck were both fortified, while the main Nacotchtank/Anacostian town was documented as a "fort" during the period 1620–53, even though those groups had managed to make peace and become middlemen in the trading between upland and tidewater peoples.[15]

Given the paucity of very early records about the Potomac River valley, we must rely heavily on archaeology to tell us about the native people. The English settled in the region late enough that many of the creek and river names used by the Indians were already familiar to them and were thus retained, albeit Anglicized and (usually) shortened. Unless otherwise noted, the towns listed below were recorded by John Smith in 1608.

Wiccocomico

This group consisted of two towns with an estimated 550 people including 130 warriors.[16] The name has been shortened to Wicomico, with the first syllable pronounced "wye." The towns were: *Wiccocomico,* at the head of Little Wicomico River; and *Cinquack,* on the north side of the mouth of the Great Wicomico River.[17] Neither village has yet been located archaeologically.

Yoacomoco

John Smith missed this town, so it is not possible to estimate its population. There was only one town in 1634, which Lord Baltimore bought from the Indians in that year and renamed St. Mary's City. The people moved first across St. Mary's River and then across the Potomac, settling by 1650 on the river (Yeocomico) that still bears their name.

The site of the town of Yoacomoco has been partially excavated along with many later English features in Historic St. Mary's City.[18] The town reflects a dispersed-settlement pattern, with houses scattered among gardens; pottery found there indicates contact with but not dominance by the Piscataways.[19]

Sekakawon

This group occupied a single town with an estimated 130 people including 30 fighting men. The spelling shown above is from John Smith's text. The name was Anglicized first to Chicacone and then shortened to Coan. The town was *Cekakawon* (spelling on Smith's map), around Boathouse Pond on the main branch of the Coan River. It has been confirmed archaeologically.[20]

The Coan River area has been extensively surveyed archaeologically, and some excavations have been done. The Sekakawons produced shell-tempered Townsend pottery, with a minority of Sullivan Cove and Potomac Creek wares suggesting relations with Native American groups to the north, east, and west. Later in the 1600s, they were relocated to the south, along with the Wiccocomicos, to a 4,400-acre (1,780.6 hectare) reservation in Lancaster County, Virginia.

Secomocomoco

This group consisted of two towns with an estimated 140 people including 30 warriors. The name (as spelled in Smith's text) was soon Anglicized to Choptico (now spelled Chaptico). The towns were: *Monanauk,* on the east side of St. Clements Bay near St. Clement Shores (this town, midway between Yoacomoco and Cecomocomoco, could have belonged to either chiefdom); and *Cecomocomoco* (spelling on Smith's map), considerably west of Monanauk, near Swan Point and west of Potomac View (the name was later Anglicized to Choptico).

Choptico was a later reservation (post-1650s), inhabited by the Secomocomocos and others and located at Indiantown Point on the northeast side of Chaptico Bay, off the Wicomico River.

Excavated potshards showing differences between Potomac Creek ware, which was common to the upper tidal Potomac and Rappahannock rivers during the Late Woodland period, and Camden ware (*left two rows*), which is named after a site on the Rappahannock River and was common during the historic period. (Virginia Department of Historic Resources)

In 1638, the Jesuits established a mission in the St. Clements Bay area and retained it until the 1940s, when the land was acquired for a military base. The capital town's area was extensively excavated in connection with the Swan Cove development, but only shell middens were found. The limited number of other sites surveyed within this chiefdom produced ceramics such as those from both the upriver Patawomecks and Piscataways and the downriver Yoacomocos and Patuxents, indicating that the Secomocomocos occupied a border area. Historical corroboration for this conclusion comes from the fact that in 1634 the local people (Monanauks) informed Lord Baltimore, who wanted to settle on St. Clements Island, that he should check with the Piscataway tayac first; thus the tayac's influence, but not his actual rule, extended that far down the Potomac.[21]

Onawmanient

This group consisted of two towns with an estimated 425 people including 100 fighting men. The name was soon Anglicized to Nomini, which may indicate where the accent fell on the longer original. The towns were: *Onawmanient,* on the west side of Nomini Creek across from McGuires Wharf; and *Uttamussamacoma,* east of Nomini Creek near Whiteoak Point.

A shell midden near the likely site of Uttamussamacoma has been excavated. It indicates that the people relied heavily on oysters and were in contact with the Patawomecks and/or the Piscataways upriver. Given the thickness of the oyster-shell midden, they may have dried oysters to trade with inland people, as some people on the James River did. The midden may represent a spring foraging camp. A 1978 survey indicated that the capital was located between Smarts Creek and Mathews Cove.[22]

Affiliation Uncertain

This group included two commoners' villages on Upper Machodoc Creek. They were: *Ozaiawomen,* east of the creek, on the west part of Pumpkin Neck; and a town of unknown name upstream, on the opposite side of the creek.

The two towns, which appear on Smith's map but in no other historical record, are not near any other cluster of towns forming a chiefdom.[23] In the mid-seventeenth century, the area was inhabited by Onawmanients who had been pushed upriver by English settlers.

Potapaco

This group consists of three towns with an estimated 140 people including 30 warriors. The name has been Anglicized to Port Tobacco, and under that name a portion of the people left Maryland in the 1650s and settled on the Rappahannock River on the bay that still bears their name. The towns were: *Potapaco,* above Fourth Point, well upstream; a town of unknown name on the east side of Port Tobacco River where it narrows at Warehouse Point;[24] and a town of unknown name on the west side of Port Tobacco River and north side of Goose Creek.

An archaeological site of the proper period has been found north of Goose Creek but not excavated. The Warehouse Point site, on the other hand, consisted of four ossuaries (the attached town has not been located), and its neighbor was an eroded ossuary at Fourth Point. All the ossuaries were excavated in the 1930s.[25] The late prehistoric ones at Warehouse Point produced clamshell beads, probably from the Eastern Shore (see chapter

Modern Indians

There are still Indian people in southern Maryland, living without a reservation in the vicinity of U.S. 301 between La Plata and Brandywine. They are formally organized into several groups, all bearing the Piscataway name. One group runs the American Indian Cultural Center in Waldorf and puts on an annual powwow that is open to the public; the others have people active in putting on other programs for the public. On the Northern Neck, there is an organized group bearing the name Patawomeck; they, too, put on a powwow. All these groups function within a short distance of the new National Museum of the American Indian (NMAI), and a Piscataway was involved in setting up exhibits for the NMAI opening.

Piscataway in seventeenth- and eighteenth-century regalia at the Prince George County Tricentennial observance held in Piscataway Park. (Rico M. Newman)

9), and copper that may have come east through Massawomeck hands; the fourth one at Warehouse Point and the eroded one at Fourth Point both yielded European glass trade beads and European copper. Sites within this chiefdom had predominantly Potomac Creek pottery, indicating that it fell under the Piscataway paramountcy, an interpretation reinforced by some Maryland colonial records.[26]

John Smith's Chesapeake Voyages, 1607–1609

Noushemouck/Nanjemoy

This group consisted of three towns with no warrior estimate by Smith. The people appear in later records as Nanjemoys centered around the creek of the same name. The towns were: a town of unknown name on the curve of the Potomac River at Wellington Beach, near Maryland Point; *Noushemouck,* on the east side of Nanjemoy Creek near Balls Point, between Kings and Burgess creeks; and *Mataughquamend,* on Little Creek, near Benny Gray Point.

Shell middens have been found around Maryland Point and in the Nanjemoy Creek area. In the early 1970s, however, three large ossuaries were excavated near Friendship Landing;[27] they must have served as the cemetery for as-yet unlocated villages elsewhere on the creek. Excavated terminal Late Woodland sites from here on up the Potomac contain mainly Potomac Creek pottery, indicating close ties among the district chiefs and, for those on the north bank, alliance with the Piscataways.

Patawomeck

This group included eleven towns with an estimated 850 people and 160 fighting men. In 1624, John Smith changed the warrior estimate to "more than 200." Almost immediately the English shortened the name to Potomac.

On the south bank of the Potomac River, the town was *Passapatanzy,* near the creek of that name, probably around Belvedere Beach. John Smith did not record this town, for reasons unknown. The town's viceroy, named Japazaws, betrayed Pocahontas into the hands of the English in 1613.

South of Potomac Creek the towns were: *Mattacunt,* opposite and a little upstream from Patawomeck; and a town of unknown name upstream from Mattacunt.

North of Potomac Creek the town was *Patawomeck,* on Marlboro Point; this town has been confirmed archaeologically.

South of Aquia Creek the towns were: *Quiyough,* where the creek narrows (the creek took its name from this town); and three towns of unknown name far upstream from Quiyough.

North of Aquia Creek the towns were: a town of unknown name opposite and a little upstream from Quiyough; and two towns of unknown name far upstream (the most distant one may have been a camp for people engaged in mining the glittering ore noted below).

Archaeologists have worked sporadically at Patawomeck (the Indian Point site) and its predecessor, an adjacent palisaded village (the Potomac

Creek site), for much of the last century.[28] Unfortunately, 98 percent of the village John Smith visited has now eroded into Potomac Creek, while its predecessor has been severely impacted by modern house-building. A third site, since destroyed by development, produced a high-status Contact period burial.[29] The name "Patawomeck" means something like "trading place," and the large number of villages in the chiefdom could have provided plenty of local goods for bargaining. At the time, oysters occurred not too far down the Potomac, and they could have been harvested and dried. The chiefdom's territory also contained a glittering ore that was in high demand for personal decoration.

Pamacocack

This group consisted of three towns with an estimated 250 people including 60 warriors. Their creek's name was Anglicized to resemble that of a Virginia tribe (name also Anglicized) but spelled *Pomonkey*. The people themselves appear in later Maryland records as two groups, Pomonkeys and Mattawomans. At this location, the Potomac River is narrow enough that the chiefdoms along it may have had towns on both sides. Evidence for this comes from John Smith's map, which shows a hiatus in towns from Aquia Creek to Occoquan Bay except for one intriguingly named town across from the Pamacocack capital.

East of the Potomac the towns were: *Nussamek,* the chief's town, on the north side of Mallows Bay near Sandy Point; and *Pamacocack,* on Stump Neck, north of Chicamuxen Creek.

West of the Potomac was a single town, *Pamacocack,* north of the mouth of Quantico Creek, with the same name as the town on Stump Neck.

There has been only limited archaeological survey in the area of this chiefdom. A location called the Posey Site, on Pamonkey Neck, has yielded Potomac Creek ceramics—an indication of the makers' close connections with the Piscataways.[30]

Tauxenent

This group consisted of two towns with an estimated 170 people including 40 fighting men. The name was later Anglicized to Doeg (Dogue). These people were Virginia Indians allied with Powhatan, who is known to have visited their town of "Mayumps" in his last years; until recently the town's name survived in an island that is now washed away. The towns were: *Tauxenent,* on Belmont Bay northeast of where it narrows into the Occoquan River; and *Namassingakent,* north of the mouth of Dogue Creek. The latter is far enough upriver that it might be taken as a Moyaone/Piscataway town, except for the name that still adheres to the creek.

Numerous archaeological sites have been found in the area, though none have been identified conclusively as towns of Smith's time. The pottery found thus far in the Tauxenents' area matches that of the Moyaone/Piscataways not far away.[31] Historical records, however, indicate that they were independent of Piscataway rule, being allies instead.

Moyaone

This group consisted of six towns with an estimated 425 people including 100 warriors. This paramount chiefdom seems to have been confined to the Maryland side of the river and had its center near Piscataway Creek. After the English allied themselves with the Patawomecks and began attacking them in the 1620s, they moved up Piscataway Creek itself, so that they were known as Piscataways by the time the English began settling in Maryland. By the 1630s, the Piscataway "emperor" was the paramount chief over the Mattawomans, Pomonkeys, Pamacocacks, Nanjemoys, Potapacos, and (as a "fringe") the Secomocomocos already noted. The towns were: *Cinquaeteck,* on the south side of the mouth of Pomonkey Creek; *Moyaons,* downriver from Mockley Point; a town of unknown name near Mockley Point (there are several archaeological sites in the area, although one of them, the Accokeek Creek site, is too early); *Tessamatuck,* on the south side of Piscataway Creek near Farmington (this town became the capital in the 1620s, apparently with a name change to "Piscataway"); and two towns of unknown name on the north side of Piscataway Creek upstream from Tessamatuck.

The premier archaeological site excavated so far in this area is the Accokeek Creek site, which predated John Smith's time (estimated 1300–1500).[32] The size of this palisaded town points to its having been a chief's town, perhaps the one preceding the chief's town that Smith did visit. A smaller, single-palisaded town southeast of the Accokeek Creek site may date somewhat later and be the site of the unnamed town near Mockley Point on Smith's map.[33] (Chapter 10 discusses the possibility that the Massawomecks, who were known to be active on the Potomac River below the falls, included a sector of the Susquehannocks.) Several Contact period sites have been excavated in the vicinity of Tessamatuck.[34] The style of the European goods discovered there fits with an occupation date of around 1630–80. Candidate sites for the other Moyaone-related towns have been found by archaeologists, but few of them have been published as yet.[35]

Nacotchtank

This group included five towns with an estimated 340 people including 80 fighting men. The name has been altered to Anacostia. These people were far enough up the Potomac, and friendly enough with the Massawomecks, that their linguistic affiliation has been questioned. The modern consensus is that they were Algonquian speakers, for Henry Fleet became fluent in their language but still needed an interpreter when dealing with Massawomecks.[36]

North of the Potomac the towns were: a town of unknown name upstream from the mouth of Broad Creek; *Nacotchtank,* downstream from the Anacostia River beneath what is now the runway area of Bolling Air Force Base; and a town of unknown name on the south side of the Anacostia River, a short distance upstream from the mouth.

South of the Potomac the towns were: *Assaomeck,* near Hunting Creek on the Fairfax County side; and *Namoraughquend,* in Alexandria near Ronald Reagan/Washington National Airport.

The latter two town names mean roughly "good fishing here."[37] The Nacotchtanks have not yet been located archaeologically, due to the rapid urbanization of the area.[38]

Interplay between People and the Environment

The banks of the lower Potomac, especially on the south side, often consist of bluffs fronted by beaches, the result of erosion due to cliff collapse and sediment transport by wind-driven waves across the broad fetch of the wide river. The larger creeks and tributary rivers tend to have bays at their mouths, while smaller creeks often have storm-created spits partially or entirely blocking their entrances. Those bays were fine locations for fish traps but not necessarily for waterfront living (except fishing camps). For their larger, more permanent towns, the people along the lower river chose to live up the Potomac's tributaries, partly for protection against wind and enemies and partly because wetlands could form only in those streams' headwaters. In the reach of the Potomac that heads northward, the riches of the freshwater marshes and the spawning areas of anadromous fishes supported a larger human population, as demonstrated both in John Smith's "warrior counts" and in the greater number of Indian settlements shown on his map.

Many of the wetlands above Potomac Creek are "breadbaskets" today,[39]

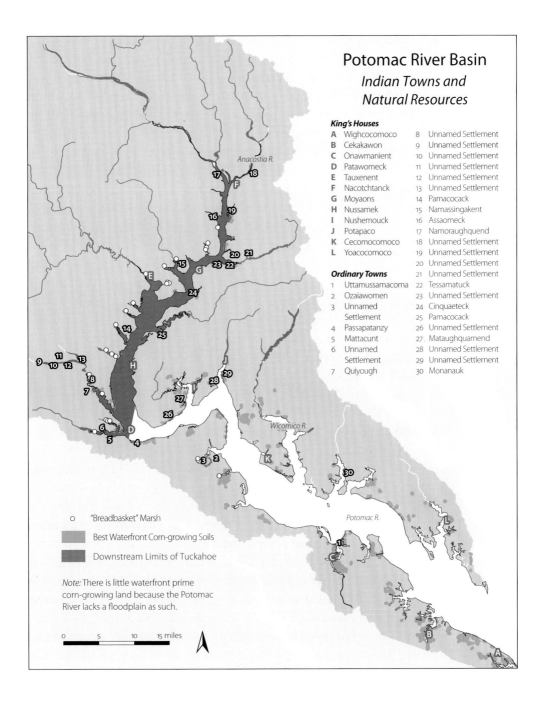

Potomac River Basin
Indian Towns and Natural Resources

King's Houses

A	Wighcocomoco	8	Unnamed Settlement
B	Cekakawon	9	Unnamed Settlement
C	Onawmanient	10	Unnamed Settlement
D	Patawomeck	11	Unnamed Settlement
E	Tauxenent	12	Unnamed Settlement
F	Nacotchtanck	13	Unnamed Settlement
G	Moyaons	14	Pamacocack
H	Nussamek	15	Namassingakent
I	Nushemouck	16	Assaomeck
J	Potapaco	17	Namoraughquend
K	Cecomocomoco	18	Unnamed Settlement
L	Yoacocomoco	19	Unnamed Settlement
		20	Unnamed Settlement

Ordinary Towns

1	Uttamussamacoma	21	Unnamed Settlement
2	Ozaiawomen	22	Tessamatuck
3	Unnamed Settlement	23	Unnamed Settlement
4	Passapatanzy	24	Cinquaeteck
5	Mattacunt	25	Pamacocack
6	Unnamed Settlement	26	Unnamed Settlement
7	Quiyough	27	Mataughquamend
		28	Unnamed Settlement
		29	Unnamed Settlement
		30	Monanauk

Anacostia R.

Wicomico R.

Potomac R.

○   "Breadbasket" Marsh

▨   Best Waterfront Corn-growing Soils

▨   Downstream Limits of Tuckahoe

Note: There is little waterfront prime corn-growing land because the Potomac River lacks a floodplain as such.

0   5   10   15 miles

but our data for the two sides of Potomac River are not comparable. In the 1970s, the Commonwealth of Virginia funded very detailed tidal marsh inventories, with areas of marshes calculated to hundredths of an acre and plant species estimates figured to single percentage points. No survey of comparable detail has been carried out in Maryland. As a result, at this writing we can only calculate which marshes are "breadbaskets" on the Virginia side of the Potomac.[40]

"Breadbaskets" were vital for Indians of the inner coastal plain along the Potomac because the rolling uplands near the river are not ideal for agriculture. Even nearly level places are few (such as Marlboro Point, where Patawomeck was located) and not large. Indian-style shifting agriculture required plenty of farmland, so that old fields had a substantial fallow period. The Patawomecks, at least, seem to have made up for their limited arable land by engaging in trade, for they had the glittering *matchqueon* that John Smith and his fellows dug so avidly in 1608.[41] With it and perhaps other items such as dried oysters from slightly downriver (back then) and marine shells traded from the east, they participated in a far-flung trade network. It had to be such a network that brought two known exotic objects to their town from far to the southwest: the design of the "weeping-eye" shell maskettes found by archaeologists (though the maskettes themselves may have been made locally; see chapter 12) and the "china boxe" made of palmetto leaves observed by an Englishman in 1621. The design is fairly common in the U.S. Southeast; the Patawomecks said the box also came from far to their southwest (perhaps from the Mobile Bay area).[42]

Even with the limited extent of near-level farmland along the Potomac's waterfront, there are patches of prime corn-growing soils.[43] Not surprisingly, those patches correlate well with the locations of Indian towns on Smith's map, and major settlements were located in the Mockley Point area: John Smith's Moyaons near Marshall Hall to the south, two slightly earlier palisaded towns immediately adjacent to the point, and the residence of the "Emperor of Piscataway" (1630s–80s) up Piscataway Creek near where it narrows. The two towns, one being the famous Accokeek Creek site,[44] were not only on prime farmland but also had a wonderful line of sight up the Potomac into what is now the heart of Washington, D.C.; they could see Massawomecks coming downriver to attack them. The later "emperor's" town was probably placed upcreek due to incursions by the English and their Patawomeck allies in the 1620s.

The Native Americans of the Potomac River were expert foragers, judging by animal remains found at some of their town sites. A Nomini Creek

A reconstructed Algonquian house. This circular building is representative of winter hunting quarters typical of the Chesapeake region. (Jefferson Patterson Park and Museum)

site (Onawmanients or their predecessors) yielded remains of white-tailed deer, raccoons, sturgeon, rockfish, white catfish, and huge quantities of oysters. A recent restudy of the Potomac Creek site (which shortly predated the Patawomeck town John Smith visited) found deer remains in the greatest abundance, followed by wild turkeys and box turtles, then by garfish, slider or cooter turtles, sturgeon, and several kinds of freshwater fish; also swans, Canada geese and crows; eastern cottontail rabbits, opossums, gray squirrels, cotton rats, beavers, black bears, bobcats, raccoons and musk-rats.[45]

The smaller animals would have been hunted by boys who were honing their skills for hunting larger game. The Virginia records contain a delightful story from 1621,[46] when "Powhatan" (either Powhatan before his 1618 death or his brother) visited the Patawomeck chief and was feasted grandly as befitted his status. One of the entertainments that followed was to have the young men of the tribe tell the visitor, one by one, what marvelous things they had accomplished in hunting and war. Before long, the accounts had become a competitive tall-story contest, with the visitor listening impassively while the chief gritted his teeth. Had the Great Man caught on that he was being lied to? Finally the last young man stepped forward, and knowing he could not top the others, he opted for deflating them. As for me, he said, this morning I went into a great marsh and valiantly killed six muskrats. Of course, our town's boys do that daily, but at least *I'm* telling the truth! Powhatan burst out laughing and then gave the young hunter a better present than anyone else, to reward his quick wit.

Archaeological excavations have also located numerous campsites used by foraging families during the semiannual periods of dispersal from the main towns. One such site, a few miles up Piscataway Creek, produced no evidence of cultigens but did yield a plant assemblage dominated by pokeweed, raspberries, blackberry/mulberry (summer occupation), and knotweed.[47]

Enter the English

John Smith was the first Englishman to visit the Potomac valley, in 1608 (see chapter 4). From the fall of 1609 onward, his countrymen began making fairly regular visits to the south bank of the Potomac, especially to the Patawomecks, for relations with the James River Indians had soured to the point that none of those Indians would sell the English food.[48] That put the Patawomecks in the middle between the English and the Powhatan leadership, a role that seems to have suited them just fine. For the better part of a year they harbored Henry Spelman—who had been persuaded to run away from his host Powhatan by the Patawomeck chief's brother Iopassus (Japazaws)—keeping him until Samuel Argall (on another trading junket) picked him up in 1610.[49] Three years later, Iopassus and Argall engineered the capture of Pocahontas, who was visiting among the Patawomecks. In 1622, when the Powhatans carried out a mass assault on the English, and the Wiccocomicos of the Northern Neck agreed to help while the Sekakawons declined, the Patawomecks did not show overt hostility, instead persuading the Anacostians upriver to do so.[50] They grudgingly helped the surviving colonists with corn thereafter, and when Henry Spelman was killed upriver they allayed the suspicions of the English by joining them in a retaliatory raid on the Piscataways and their neighbors.[51]

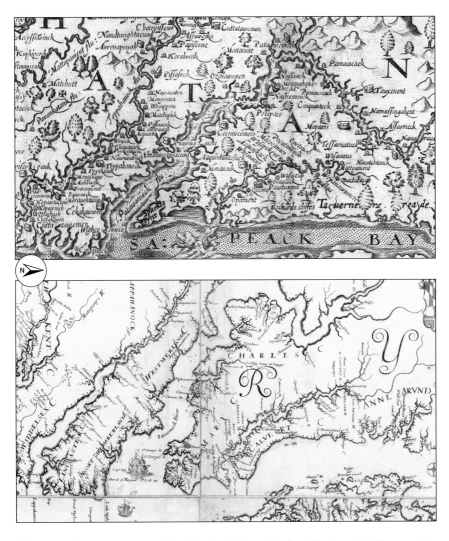

The Potomac River area as mapped by John Smith in 1608 (*top*) and by Augustine Herrmann in 1673 (*bottom*).

By the early 1630s, English fur traders like Henry Fleet were visiting the Potomac River peoples in search of beaver pelts,[52] and land-hungry tobacco farmers from the James River valley began eyeing all the rivers to the north. The first settlers began arriving after 1640, sparking another mass assault by the native people, the Northern Neck chiefdoms included. The English won the ensuing war and thereafter flooded into the area. By 1660, the native people had only a few reservations. Those lands in turn were lost, the

The Potomac River

Oyster Wars on the Potomac

The practice of dredging depleted the Potomac's oyster stock by 1820, but pressure to harvest the remaining mollusks continued due to the lucrative markets for them in Baltimore and Washington. Vessels from New England added to the competition, which abated only temporarily during the Civil War. By 1875, however, "oyster wars" were under way and continued sporadically well into the twentieth century. "War" was the operative word at times, for rivalry between local watermen and "intruders" from elsewhere in the Chesapeake sometimes escalated into shooting matches.

Source: Beitzell 2001 [1968].

Onawmanients (now called Machodocs) and Patawomecks both relocating to the Rappahannock River in the 1660s and the Sekakawons and Wiccocomicos losing the last claim to their land in 1718.[53]

The first permanent English settlement north of the Potomac was established in Yoacomoco territory in 1634 (St. Mary's City). The English were careful to purchase the land, after which the Yoacomocos moved across the Potomac River to join the Machodocs (modern Yeocomico River is named after them).[54] Jesuit missions were then established among the Piscataways and the Patuxents.[55] Thereafter there was a serious spreading-out of settlers on the lower Potomac. Beginning in 1651, Maryland encouraged settlement of the Piscataways' area, an effort that alienated the native people, especially the Piscataways, who wanted to retain the large land base needed to support their traditional mixed farming-and-foraging economy.[56] This intrusion of Europeans, coupled with Seneca and Susquehannock attacks in the late 1670s, induced a merging of the Algonquian-speaking chiefdoms into refugee communities. The Piscataways moved into Zekiah Swamp, after which some families departed for Iroquois country while others stayed behind.[57] The "Chopticos" (Secomocomocos, Patuxents and other small groups, later joined by Nanjemoys and others) had had a reservation near modern Chaptico since 1651; they remained on it until at least 1697[58] but were eventually pushed northwest onto less desirable land.

By 1670, English plantations dotted the shorelines on both sides of the Potomac from its mouth to the Mattawoman Creek–Occoquan Bay area. Upriver were still communities of Mattawomans, Pomonkeys, Tauxenents (now called Dogues), and Piscataways living on reservations. By the 1690s, English plantations had reached the fall line, and after that the activities of the Senecas from the Five Nations made a northward move palatable. Even so, some Indian families decided to remain in southern Maryland, where their descendants still live.[59]

The English who settled in Maryland were culturally somewhat different from those who established Jamestown: they were Catholics, not Protestants, and for several decades they were governed by a Proprietor (of the Calvert family) who held the (English) title to all the land in the colony in the name of King Charles I. There was considerable rivalry with the Virginia colony from the beginning, initially over the fur trade and later over issues such as fishing rights in the Potomac. In the nineteenth century there would be fiercely fought "oyster wars" between inhabitants of the two states.

13

The Rappahannock River Basin and the Piedmont Peoples

JOHN SMITH FIRST SAW the Rappahannock River in December 1607, when he was a captive. Opechancanough had taken him to see the Rappahannock chief's town, at a place near modern Tappahannock, so the people could look at him and tell whether he was the European ship's captain who a few years before had repaid their hospitality by killing their chief and kidnapping some of their relatives. Once exonerated—Smith was declared to be too short to be the culprit—he interviewed his hosts about who lived where on the river.[1] The next day he was hurried away and taken to meet the Rappahannocks' paramount chief, Powhatan. He did not return to this river before penning and sending home his wonderfully detailed "True Relation" in early June 1608.

Toward the end of August 1608, Smith came back and explored the area thoroughly, meeting and interviewing a Mannahoac man and settling a Rappahannock/Moraughtacund dispute over stolen women. He stopped in at Piankatank on the way home. His account of his Rappahannock River adventures is a rip-roaring yarn, but regrettably he did not write it down until 1624, so it may not be trustworthy in all details.

The Environment

The Rappahannock River has its source in the flanks of the Blue Ridge Mountains, in modern Fauquier County, Virginia. From its beginning at Chester Gap, it flows about 148 miles (238 kilometers) to the Chesapeake. It has two main heads in the Piedmont, the Rappahannock proper and the Rapidan; these two join ten miles (16 kilometers) above the modern city of Fredericksburg, where the river crosses the fall line. The river's watershed encompasses 2,715 square miles (7,032 square kilometers), and as with the Chesapeake's other riverine tributaries, most of the wetlands along it are found in and around its tributary creeks within the coastal plain.

Topography

The Rappahannock runs through uplands for nearly all of its length. Only at its very mouth are there low-lying lands grading into marshes, like the more extensive bayside areas to the south and, especially, on the Eastern Shore. Like its neighbors to the south, the James and the York, the river's shores alternate between wide floodplain terraces and the edges of the uplands, where wind and water have scoured cliffs. Those in the lower reaches of the river have Pleistocene deposits on top and below that are mid-Miocene layers (Calvert and St. Marys Formations, 14–9 million years old). Just above Port Royal the lowermost sediments are in the Nanjemoy Formation (early Eocene, ca. 30 million years old), and by the time one reaches five miles (8 kilometers) above the U.S. 301 bridge, they date to the Paleocene (65–55 million years old). The most spectacular cliffs along the Rappahannock, though, are Fones Cliffs, which rise more than 150 feet (45 meters) above the riverbank. Now home to numerous bald eagles, they represent about 8 million years of mid- and late Miocene (Calvert, St. Marys, and Eastover Formations, 6–14 million years ago).[2] Visitors to the area can see clearly the transition from floodplain to uplands in the Rappahannock's valley as they drive along U.S. 17 between Tappahannock and Port Royal. The cliffs can only be fully appreciated from the water, however.

The Piedmont province in Virginia and Maryland, with lands that range from gently rolling near the fall line to near-mountains at the foot of the Blue Ridge, varies from less than fifty miles (80 kilometers) in width along the Susquehanna to about one hundred miles (160 kilometers) in width along the James. It is drained by several major rivers—the Susquehanna, Potomac, and James—as well as by numerous lesser rivers such as the Rappahannock and the Patapsco, which originate within the Piedmont. Here

The Rappahannock River Basin and the Piedmont Peoples　　　　*287*

and there, floodplains occur along these waterways, but all are quite narrow. By comparison, in places the Rappahannock's floodplain above Tappahannock (locally called "the flats"), in the coastal plain, may be up to four miles (6.5 kilometers) wide.

Land Plants and Animals

Most of the Rappahannock's watershed lies within the coastal plain, with the remainder located in the Piedmont of northern Virginia. The uplands are covered in typical oak-hickory-pine forest, but there are also dry areas dominated by chestnut oak, blackjack oak, and post oak, as well as wet areas characterized by willow oak, red maple, black gum, and sweetgum. The trees that are more or less restricted to this section today include pale hickory, stiff dogwood, water ash, chickasaw plum, willow oak, and winged elm. A sampling of fifty-eight forest stands in the northern Virginia Piedmont showed three forest associations: white oak–tulip poplar, white oak–scarlet oak, and a Virginia pine group. That study concluded that white and red oaks were dominant before English colonization, but that a great deal of forest cutting for agriculture and the charcoal industry took place shortly after settlement. The study also showed that the Virginia pine stands are a result of farm abandonment, while many of the oaks prospered after logging.[3]

In 1612, William Strachey wrote: "It is supposed that the low land [coastal plain] hath more fish and fowl, and the high land more number of beasts."[4] That assessment of the coastal plain versus the Piedmont was accurate throughout Virginia and Maryland, where the coastal plain lands either graded into marshes and their associated bird life or narrowed into "necks" between waterways, inhabited by birds and fish alike.

The truly large expanses of forested territory lay in the Piedmont and were probably home to greater numbers of woodland animals. Toward the east side of the Blue Ridge, especially along the James, forest gave way to grasslands. Unlike the barrens in the upper bay (chapter 10), these ran parallel to the rivers and near the base of the mountains, and European explorers in the latter 1600s were impressed by the great numbers of deer, beavers, foxes, and wolves.[5]

Wetlands

Because both the Piankatank and Rappahannock flow almost entirely through uplands, both tend to have bluffs along their margins at their lower, easterly ends. (The exception is on the Northern Neck around Fleets Bay.) That topography greatly reduces the size of saltwater wetlands along the lower rivers and their tributaries. The larger tributaries, like Corroto-man River, have headwaters that become almost fresh, and there cattails and reeds grow. The Piankatank pushes far enough inland that its head-waters, before turning into Dragon Run, have a few freshwater meanders that harbor bald cypress trees and freshwater emergents such as tuckahoe (arrow arum). There is also a stand of bald cypress on the Rappahannock, near Cleve in King George County.

The Rappahannock has curves and meanders mainly in its middle reaches on the coastal plain; the lower meanders curl around marshes while the upper ones curl around low peninsulas of land. The tributary creeks, such as Cat Point Creek, also wind through sizable marshes. The farther upriver the creek, the more likely the headwaters and then the lower me-anders will be fresh enough to support broad-leaved emergents and wild rice. Traces of cow lily, which has edible roots, occur in the far headwaters of Piscataway Creek, but by Horsehead Point this species begins appear-ing along the river. Traces of tuckahoe (arrow arum) grow in the headwa-ters of Sturgeon Creek on the right bank (as one drifts downstream) of the river and Corrotoman River on the left, and the plant becomes dominant in the far headwaters of Totuskey Creek. It occurs on the Rappahannock riverfront from around the U.S. 360 bridge upward. The various bulrushes are uncommon in this river valley. The knotweeds are found mainly in the inner coastal plain and are rarely dominant in the marshes where they occur. Arrowheads are rare, even in the completely fresh marshes they re-quire, except for a few marshes above Portobago Bay, where they make up as much as 10 percent of the emergents. Cattails are found in nearly all marshes of the Piankatank and Rappahannock River valley, in the headwa-ters of downstream tributaries, and along the riverfront by the area of Ferry Creek in the Piankatank and Totuskey Creek in the Rappahannock. Water hemp follows a similar pattern, though is never dominant. As for wild rice, this plant grows upstream from Carvers Creek in the Piankatank, while its downstream limit in the Rappahannock valley is the headwaters of Little Totuskey Creek. Upstream, wild rice stands are occasionally large enough to earn the label "breadbasket" (see below). Finally, bald cypress occurs in Dragon Swamp (the headwaters of the Piankatank River) and in a small cy-press stand above My Lady's Swamp. The trees have also been found north of the Rappahannock in Lancaster, Richmond, and Westmoreland coun-ties, the individuals in the latter county being the northernmost ones in Virginia. Only the cypress trees in the Patuxent and Pocomoke river valleys in Maryland and Delaware grow farther north in the United States.[6]

The River and Its Fishes and Shellfish

Salinity of the Rappahannock ranges from a high of about 20 parts per thousand (ppt) at Windmill Point in the drier months to freshwater at Fredericksburg.[7] The dam at Fredericksburg was recently breached to allow anadromous fishes such as herring and shad to ascend the river above the city, and in 2004 a gravid (full of eggs) female shad was captured five miles (8 kilometers) above the dam.[8] Striped bass and their close relative the white perch range the entire river from Windmill Point at the river's mouth to Fredericksburg; striped bass spawn near Tappahannock close to where U.S. 360 crosses the river.[9] Shad, alewives, and blueback herring spawn in brackish and freshwater in the upper reaches of the Rappahannock; juvenile croakers sometimes range about twenty miles (32 kilometers) upstream and sea trout to about Urbanna, some ten miles (16 kilometers) upriver.[10] In years past, oysters were abundant as far upstream as the vicinity of Waterview on Parrots Creek, several miles above Urbanna, and there are small numbers of soft clams in the same area as well.[11]

The People

John Smith met representatives from two ethnic and linguistic groups when he explored the Rappahannock River Valley. The people living below the fall line spoke Algonquian dialects, identified themselves with similar people in the coastal plain of Virginia and Maryland, and considered themselves at least nominally to be part of the polity ruled by Powhatan. Less is known about the people living above the fall line of the Rappahannock and the James, not to mention the Potomac. John Smith or his compatriots had only one encounter each on the James and Rappahannock, none on the Potomac,[12] and each time the interaction was made difficult by a double language barrier: English to Powhatan and then Powhatan to the Piedmont inhabitants' dialect. Even with a competent interpreter present, understanding would not have come easily. To this day, scholars are not certain that the Monacans and/or the Mannahoacs spoke languages related to those of the Siouan speakers in the Carolina Piedmont, for no seventeenth-century Englishman wrote down a single word of their language(s) for us to examine.[13] One Englishman who heard some discourse wrote later that it sounded rather like Welsh[14]—so his companions asked him to be the interpreter for them (good luck!). Most of what we know about the

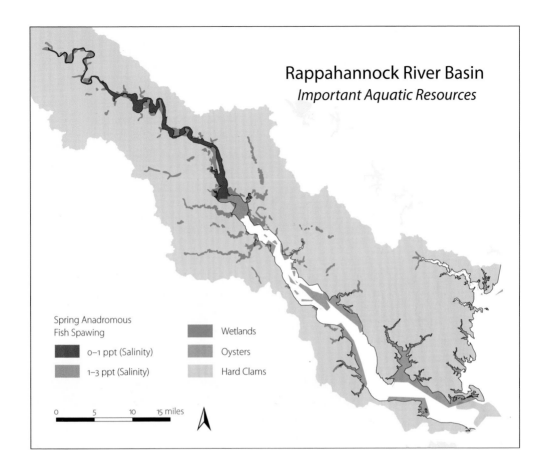

Rappahannock River Basin
Important Aquatic Resources

Spring Anadromous
Fish Spawing

0–1 ppt (Salinity)

1–3 ppt (Salinity)

Wetlands

Oysters

Hard Clams

0   5   10   15 miles

Piedmont peoples in 1607–9 has to do with their rivalry with Powhatan's paramount chiefdom and the names of their towns.

Following is the roster of chiefdoms and/or towns in the Rappahannock River Valley and the Piedmont portion of the James River Valley.

Piankatank
This group consisted of three towns with an estimated 170 people including 40 fighting men. The capital and both other towns were on the north side of the river: *Payankatank,* around modern Piankatank Shores; a town of unknown name west of My Lady's Swamp; and a town of unknown name halfway between the U.S. 17/33 bridge over Dragon Swamp and the Gloucester–King and Queen county lines.

Rays and Stingers

Smith's encounter at Stingray Point was almost certainly with a cownose ray, a species that visits the bay's tributary shallows, sometimes in large schools, to feed by dislodging clams and other organisms embedded in the soft bottom. The explorers described the creature as being "much the fashion of a thornback," but that rough-skinned fish, familiar to the English, is actually a skate that lays leathery egg cases and has no poisonous sting. On the other hand, the velvet-skinned rays that visit the bay have a "wing span" (actually, the span of their pectoral fins) of about thirty inches (76 centimeters), weigh twenty-five to thirty pounds (11.3 to 13.6 kilograms), and give birth to two or three live, dinner-plate-sized young before migrating to the Caribbean or the coast of Brazil each winter. Several ray species are found in Chesapeake Bay, but the cownose ray is the only one that commonly circles in tight schools while feeding in knee-deep water, as Smith found them doing.

Smith stabbed the rays with his "short sword," which means that his hands were close to these usually docile but now desperately thrashing animals. Using his free hand to brace against the fish to withdraw his sword for withdrawal, he put himself at risk of being jabbed by one or both of the sheathed spines (modified scales) that these fish have near the base of their tails. The spines are "bearded like a saw on both sides," extremely sharp, and contain a dangerous venom. Sequestered inside a mucus-filled sac around each spine, the venom contains a water-soluble protein that causes immediate, excruciating pain when it enters a victim's body, with subsequent rapid swelling and respiratory distress. Some sensitive victims require only a thumb-prick to suffer life-threatening anaphylactic shock.

People have been known to die after such an encounter with a cownose ray, and John Smith's expectation in that regard was hardly unrealistic. One of us (Mountford) witnessed a man in 2002 with a spine wound in his hand, writhing and screaming that he would cut off his hand to stop the pain. The acute symptoms usually subside within several hours, as Smith's did, but his suffering could have been alleviated by irrigating the wound with hot tap water or even hot seawater (about 120°F or as hot as can be tolerated), which denatures and flushes out the venom protein. Perhaps the "precious oil" that Smith's physician Dr. Russell used was heated before application. Russell was also wise to probe the wound, because retained spine fragments can cause a dangerous infection.

No archaeological sites have yet been found that are clearly identifiable as any of these villages.

Opiscopank (Opiscatumek)

We know little about the single Opiscopank town. By 1608, the members of this shadowy group had probably moved north of the river, where they appear under another name, possibly "Rappahannock." Smith's map shows a chief's town called "Opiscopank," but his writings say nothing about it or its inhabitants. Strachey mentions in passing that the native people of the region had "of old" called the river "Opiscatumeck" and more recently had been calling it "Rappahannock." Elsewhere he indicates that rivers took the name of the dominant people living on them (at least below the fall line).[15] The town was probably on the east side of Urbanna Creek, where Old and New Nimcock towns appear in mid-seventeenth-century records.[16] Archaeologists have identified a complex of Late Woodland sites precisely where Smith's map places Opiscopank, on the east side of Urbanna Creek.

Cuttatawomen I

This downriver group consisted of six towns with an estimated 135 people and 30 warriors. The group's name was subsequently Anglicized to "Corrotoman." The towns were located around Corrotoman River; heading up the Rappahannock's north shore they were: *Cuttatawomen,* northeast of Mosquito Point; *Chesakawon,* between Cherry Point and Mosquito Point; *Ottachugh,* east of the Virginia S.R. 3 bridge on Cherry Point; *Kapawnich,* west of the Virginia S.R. 3 bridge; *Nepawtacum,* on Orchard Point; and *Pawcocomocac,* on the northeast side of the Rappahannock, west of Bertrand.

Archaeological survey has turned up several promising Late Woodland sites around this area.

Moraughtacund

This group consisted of six towns with an estimated 340 people including 80 fighting men. The name was later Anglicized to "Morattico" and persists in a tributary of Lancaster Creek, which was called "Morattico Creek" in the mid-seventeenth century. The towns were: *Moraughtacund,* near Tarpley Point (Hales Point),[17] on the south side of Morattico Creek; *Oquomock,* on the west side of the mouth of Farnham Creek; *Powcomonet,* on the east side of Richardson Creek; *Auhomesk,* on the east side of Totuskey Creek; *Menaskunt,* on the west side of Totuskey Creek; and *Poyektank,* somewhere west of Wellfords Wharf.

The latter three towns could have belonged to either Moraughtacund or Rappahannock. Archaeologists have identified two large side-by-side Late Woodland sites on the west side of Farnham Creek. They very likely represent the location of Oquomock.[18]

Rappahannock

This group consisted of nine towns with an estimated 425 people including 100 warriors. Their chief had been killed by visiting (unidentified) Europeans around 1604, so the one John Smith met was relatively new. The Powhatans apparently pronounced their *r*s with a flap, so that English speakers were apt to hear it as either an *r* or (more usually) a *t*; hence the modern town's name of Tappahannock, on the Rappahannock River. Although all of the towns on Smith's map are on the north side of the river, Smith's writings make it plain that the tribe used both sides of the river. The towns were: *Toppahanock*, east of U.S. 360, probably northeast of Little Carter Creek;[19] *Nawnautough*, north of the mouth of Little Carter Creek; *Poykemkack*, north of the middle area of Little Carter Creek; *Tantucquask*, inside the bend of the headwaters of Little Carter Creek; *Winsack*, east of the mouth of Cat Point Creek; *Acquack*, west of the mouth of Cat Point Creek; *Cawwontoll*, upstream from the mouth of Wilna Creek; *Pissacoack*, around Smoots Landing; and *Matchopick*, around Lukes Island.

The latter two or three towns could have belonged to the Pissasecks. Several promising archaeological sites in the area have been found, but further testing is required to determine if they date to John Smith's time.

Pissaseck

This group consisted of five towns with an unknown number of inhabitants. John Smith seems to have combined this population with the Nandtaughtacunds. The Northern Neck is very narrow where they lived, with the headwaters of Popes and Mattox creeks almost reaching over to the Rappahannock. Later seventeenth-century records suggest that the Pissasecks claimed territory on the Potomac River.[20]

On the north bank of the Rappahannock, going upriver, the towns were: *Wecuppom*, on the cliffs below Brockenbrough Creek; *Mangoraca*, above Brockenbrough Creek, around Smith Mount Landing; *Nawacaten*, above the mouth of Peedee Creek; *Pissaseck*, at Leedstown (confirmed in the early 1900s with the finding of a large cache of glass trade beads; several adjacent archaeological sites could represent the town itself); and a town of unknown name between Pissaseck and Drakes Marsh.

Nandtaughtacund

This group consisted of ten towns with an estimated 640 people including 150 warriors (probably with Pissasecks added in). The name was later Anglicized to "Nanzatico," the name of a late seventeenth-century Indian reservation and the modern name of a bay and adjacent lands opposite Portobago Bay. In the 1650s, the tribe apparently was joined by Potopacos (from Maryland), another name that has stuck in Anglicized form.

North of the Rappahannock, going upriver, the towns were: *Kerahocak,* near the mouth of Jetts Creek; *Papiscone* (later called Gingoteague), on the upstream side of the mouth of Gingoteague Creek; *Assuweska,* east of the U.S. 301 bridge; *Monanask,* around Cleve; and *Waconiask,* west of Cleve, below the mouth of Jones Top Creek.

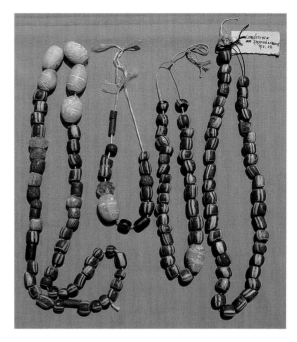

Glass trade beads from the Leedstown site. That site probably represents the Pissaseck chief's residence of 1608. (Ben C. Crary Collection/Helen C. Rountree)

South of the Rappahannock, going upriver, the towns were: *Anrenapeugh,* on the southwest side of Green Bay; *Nandtaughtacund,* on the southeast side of Portobago Bay; *Checopissowo,* around Hazelwood, opposite Goat Island; *Anaskenoans,* opposite Corbins Neck, above Skinkers Neck; and a town of unknown name somewhere around Dogue Run.

The latter two towns may have belonged to the upriver Cuttatawomens. Archaeological surveys have identified excellent candidates for the towns of Kerahocak and Papiscone. In addition, a mid-seventeenth-century town, probably the historical Portobacco, has been excavated at Camden, downstream from Port Royal.[21]

Cuttatawomen II

This upriver group consisted of at least five towns with an estimated 85 people including 20 fighting men. The Northern Neck narrows again in this group's territory, and they may have claimed two towns over in the headwaters of Upper Machodoc Creek.[22]

North of the Rappahannock, going upriver, the towns were: *Cuttata-women,* around Hop Yard Landing, on the "nose" of a convoluted meander known today as the Camel; *Sockobeck,* around the mouth of Lambs Creek; and *Massawoteck,* opposite the top of the bend around Moss Neck.

South of the Rappahannock, going upriver, the towns were: *Secobeck,* on the bluffs northeast of Garretts Store; and *Accoqueck,* north of Garretts Store below Springhill Bar.

Archaeological research has been limited in this area, but a Late Woodland site that may represent Sockobeck has been found at the mouth of Lambs Creek.[23]

Monacans

This group included five towns[24] (or chiefdoms in confederation),[25] population uncertain. The towns were: *Mowhemcho,* across from the modern settlement of Manakin, near Watkins Landing on the south bank of the James; *Massinacack,* downstream from the U.S. 522 bridge, near Michaux; *Rassawek,* at the junction of the James and Rivanna rivers, across from modern Columbia; *Monasukapanough,* north of the South Fork of the Rivanna River below the dam, north of metropolitan Charlottesville; and *Monahas-sanaugh,* on the north bank of the James River upstream from the Virginia S.R. 56 bridge at Wingina.

Archaeological research into these towns and their predecessors has been ongoing for several decades.[26]

Mannahoac

This group included five towns, or chiefdoms in confederation, population uncertain. The towns were: *Mahaskahod,* on the south bank of the Rappahannock just above Fredericksburg, west of the Interstate 95 bridge; *Hassinunga,*[27] at the confluence of the Rappahannock and Rapidan rivers; *Tauxsnitania,* at the next large westward bend upstream from the bridge at White Sulphur Springs, southwest of Warrenton; *Shackaconia,* a short distance downstream from Germanna Bridge, which carries Virginia S.R. 3 across not only the Rapidan River but also across the Orange-Culpeper county line; and *Stegarake,* at Dawsonville, on the Rapidan River west of the junction of Madison, Greene, and Orange counties.

To date, archaeological research in this area has been extremely limited.

The territory around the fall line of the Rappahannock was a buffer zone, inhabited by neither the Powhatans nor the Mannahoacs but hunted and

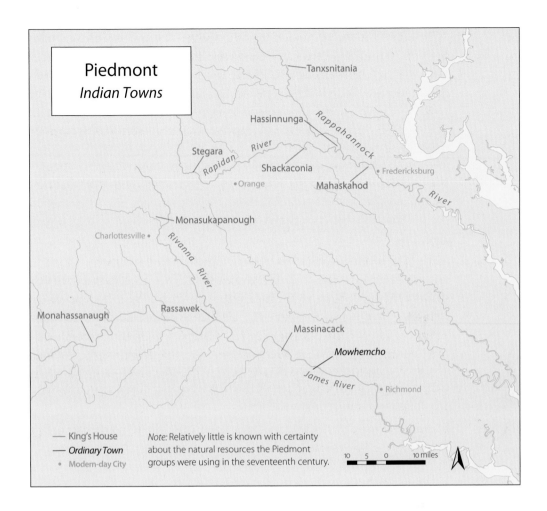

Piedmont
Indian Towns

Tanxsnitania

Hassinnunga

Rappahannock

Stegara

Rapidan River

Shackaconia

Orange

Mahaskahod

Fredericksburg

River

Monasukapanough

Charlottesville

Rivanna River

Monahassanaugh

Rassawek

Massinacack

Mowhemcho

James River

Richmond

—— King's House
—— *Ordinary Town*
• Modern-day City

Note: Relatively little is known with certainty about the natural resources the Piedmont groups were using in the seventeenth century.

10 5 0   10 miles

occasionally warred in by both. On the James, the Powhatans had been able to push the buffer zone upriver, so that most of it was above the fall line. Such pushing back and forth had probably gone on for a long time. Ceramics in the lower Piedmont region of the Rappahannock drainage match those of the nearest Algonquian-speaking chiefdoms—and also match those of the Patawomecks and Piscataways,[28] indicating influence, if not an actual migration, from the north.

Smith knew that the Algonquian speakers lived in district chiefdoms under Powhatan's sway. In watching the Mannahoacs and seeing war leaders (see chapter 5), he assumed that they, too, had chiefs (whom he called "kings"). The accuracy of that guess is uncertain, although archaeology in the Monacan area may support it.[29] It is of little help to consult the historical record about the Monacans, unfortunately. Smith did not go on that expedition beyond the falls of the James, and the report on it is disappointingly short. Captain Christopher Newport, who commanded it, turned Monacan wariness into sullenness by taking one of their leaders (a "petty weroance") hostage and "lead[ing] him bound" from place to place.[30] Altogether, so little was learned about the people of the Piedmont that all of the seventeenth-century English records contain only ten passages mentioning them,[31] and those concern mainly their location. Smith's assertion that they were mainly foragers is contradicted by Strachey's comment that they resembled the Powhatans, a statement corroborated by bioarchaeological studies showing that corn—the fruit of farming—provided up to half their diet.[32] They also had a hunting territory with more animals in it, and access to more large animals like elk, which prefer high country.

The Algonquian speakers' habitations along the Rappahannock were, as Smith showed them on his map, nearly all on the north side of the river in its lower reaches. That placement probably indicates that those people did not fully appreciate being subjects of Powhatan, a situation that must have come about not long before as the paramount chief expanded his domain. Once Powhatan established his capital at Werowocomoco on the York, he was within easy striking range of the south bank of the Rappahannock if his new subjects did not toe the line.[33]

Interplay between People and the Environment

Copper was highly valued by the native people of the Eastern Woodlands because of its reddish shininess when beaten and polished. "Native copper," or copper ore pure enough not to need smelting, occurred in the Virginia Piedmont, although much larger deposits were mined in ancient times in the Lake Superior area. The Powhatans obtained copper for jewelry by importing it, presumably bypassing the Monacans. It has been suggested that the Monacans and Mannahoacs dug their own copper within their own territory, which would have caused consternation among the Powhatans. However, no evidence of prehistoric mining operations has been found at the copper sites.[34]

There may have been other ecological differences between the Mannahoac and Powhatan areas that triggered competition for resources in the inner coastal plain. That possibility has yet to be studied, so the remainder of this section must be confined to the Powhatans' territory.

The English arrived late enough, and briefly enough, in the Rappahannock River valley that there is no record of the status of animals hunted by the Native Americans there. However, given the narrowness of the "necks" on each side of the Rappahannock, especially the Northern Neck, it is likely that deer were overhunted, just as they were on the Virginia Peninsula between the James and the York. If this was the case, then the quest for each winter's venison supplies would have forced the Algonquian speakers to sally westward into territory claimed by the Mannahoacs—lands that the latter were in fact hunting on when John Smith and his crew approached the fall line in 1608. Such "trespassing" would explain the hostility that is known to have existed between the two peoples.

Wetlands rich enough in edible plants edible to be "breadbaskets"[35] occur along the Rappahannock River and its tributaries, but only in certain places. The plants—tuckahoe (arrow arum) and cow lily for roots and wild rice for seeds—require shallow, slow-moving freshwater, and areas of such freshes are restricted to the meandering upper reaches of creeks from about Tappahannock up to Paynes Island, then to the lower part of creeks, and finally along the "horseshoe" of Horsehead Point on the riverfront itself. However, even the great horseshoes above Portobago Bay are mostly high ground, not marshes enclosed in river meanders. And where the river straightens out for its run up to Fredericksburg, marshes (rich or otherwise) all but disappear.

Hostility with the Mannahoacs plus the near-absence of freshwater marshes along the river for several miles below modern Fredericksburg probably account for the lack of Indian towns on John Smith's map in that stretch of river, even though the farming soils along it are good. Danger combined with a paucity of back-up marsh tubers during dry years would have been sufficient here, as it was in the head of the bay itself, to make the area not very desirable for settlement.

The Rappahannock's old floodplain, although now partially flooded, is readily visible along much of the valley in the coastal plain. Above Jones Point on the right bank (heading downriver) and Tarpley/Hales Point on the left bank, the prime farming soils are often moderately naturally fertile Pamunkey and Wickham ones. Like the State soils flanking them and the Suffolk and Kempsville loamy soils found downstream from the two points and along the Piankatank River, they are easy to till and warm up early in the spring due to a low wintertime water table.[36] Naturally fertile "warm" soils were a great blessing to people who wanted to stagger the planting of their fields in hopes of catching a 120-day period during Virginia's seven

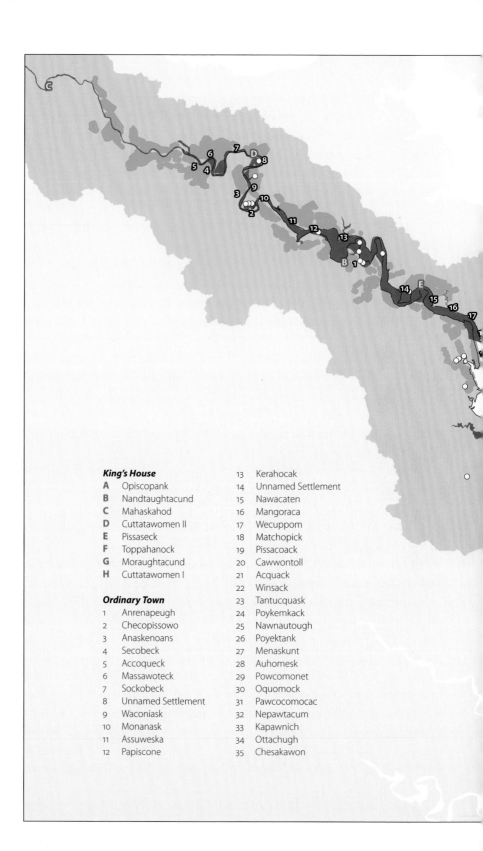

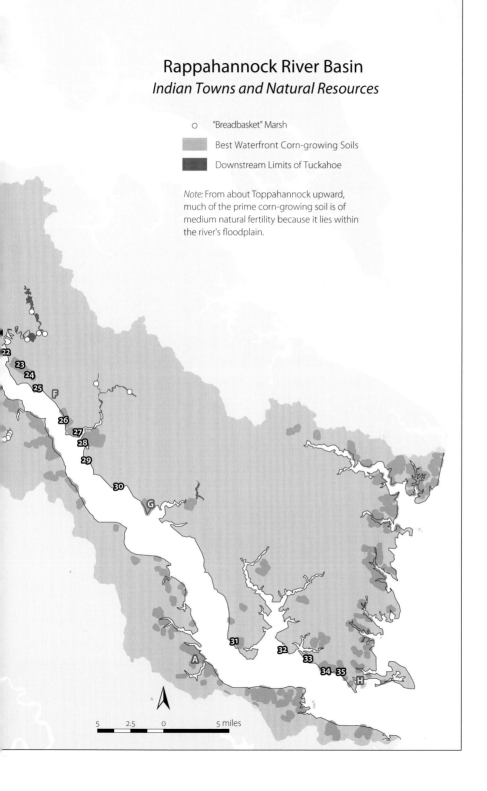

Rappahannock River Basin
Indian Towns and Natural Resources

○   "Breadbasket" Marsh

        Best Waterfront Corn-growing Soils

        Downstream Limits of Tuckahoe

Note: From about Toppahannock upward, much of the prime corn-growing soil is of medium natural fertility because it lies within the river's floodplain.

22

23
24
25
F

26
27
28

29

30
G

31
32
33
A
34 35
H

5   2.5   0   5 miles

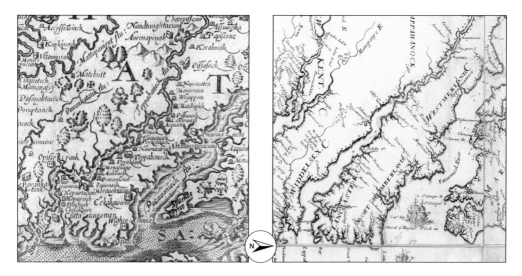

The Rappahannock River area as mapped by John Smith in 1608 (*left*) and by Augustine Herrmann in 1673 (*right*).

warm months in which plentiful rain fell. Thus it is not surprising that many of the Indian towns on John Smith's map, which would have been farming settlements, are found on such soils (see the map).

The part of the river richest in prime waterfront lands and access (up the creeks) to "breadbaskets" is the area between Tappahannock and the Richmond County–Westmoreland County line—precisely where the river's dominant tribe, the Rappahannocks, was living in 1608. Almost as rich was the stretch above it, inhabited by the Pissasecks and Nandtaughtacunds, with a combined "warrior count" one and a half times that of the Rappahannocks alone. When European settlers pushed up the river in the 1650s, the area the Indians chose to keep as their reservation was in Nandtaughtacund (by then called Nanzatico) territory.

Enter the English

After John Smith's expedition up the Rappahannock in the summer of 1608 (see chapter 5), the native people of that area saw little more of English people for a long, long time. There was an immediate repercussion from Powhatan, however, who punished his subjects' friendliness to the foreigners. (Smith claimed later that they had all promised to plant corn for the English.[37]) In the autumn of 1608, the paramount chief's forces wiped out

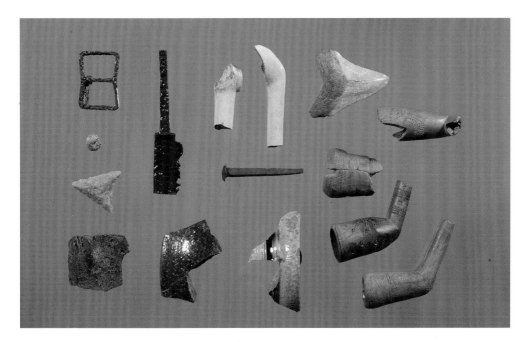

A combination of native and European artifacts found at the Camden site on the Rappahannock. During the second half of the seventeenth century, chiefdoms confined to reservations along the Rappahannock River manufactured native-style pipes to trade with the English, using shark teeth to make the designs. They also used a variety of European items received in exchange. (Virginia Department of Historic Resources/Camden National Register Archaeological District)

the Piankatanks, presumably as an object lesson for their Indian neighbors along the Rappahannock. Most of the Piankatank men were killed in an ambush, while the chief, the women, and the children were taken to Werowocomoco as prisoners and put to work (by custom, native warfare rarely provided for killing such useful people). The Piankatank towns were repopulated with loyalists and the Rappahannock River chiefdoms avoided trouble thereafter.[38]

As far as the surviving records show, it would be nearly three decades before the Rappahannock and Piankatank river basins again were visited by Englishmen, who were far more interested in trading for corn and furs on the Potomac River. What little contact the people did have with the foreigners was unpleasant. They sympathized enough with Opechancanough in the 1622–32 war that they were the target of English raids in the summer of 1623.[39] In 1641, they began unwillingly to see a trickle of English settlers into their area, a process that later was slowed by the 1644–46 war between the English and an ancient but still hostile Opechancanough.[40] The Rappahan-

The Rappahannock River Basin and the Piedmont Peoples   303

Modern Indians

In the regions covered by this chapter, two sets of modern people survive with an Indian identity, although without reservations. There are two formal organizations of Rappahannocks, both in Essex, Caroline, and King and Queen Counties; the one recognized by the Commonwealth of Virginia puts on an annual powwow. There are also state-recognized Monacans in Amherst County and Lynchburg; they too put on an annual powwow as well as a fall festival. All these events are open to the public and announced in the media.

nocks did not participate in that war or sympathize with anyone involved in it.[41] After the old paramount chief's death, the trickle of settlers became a flood, and by 1660 most of the native people's lands were in English hands.

The downriver Cuttatawomens (later called Corrotomans) went to live with the Wiccocomicos. The Rappahannocks were living up "on the ridge" between the Mattaponi and Rappahannock rivers, along with the Moraughtacunds. In the aftermath of a vicious attack by Seneca warriors in 1683, the "Rappahannocks" were all moved upriver to Portobacco. That refuge reservation was named for a sector of the Potopaco tribe that had moved down from Maryland in the 1650s. Its original inhabitants, the Nandtaughtacunds (now called Nanzaticos and probably including remnants of the Pissasecks and upriver Cuttatawomens) still lived across the river nearby, on Nanzatico Bay. The "Portobaccos" ultimately were joined by the Patawomecks and Machodocs from the Potomac River. These neighboring reservations endured until 1705, when the native occupants were forcibly evicted.[42]

Due to their avoidance of the English, the Monacans and Mannahoacs remained a dim presence in the historical record. By 1611, seeing the English beginning to take over the James River valley below the falls, they concluded that the interlopers were worse than the Powhatans and made an alliance with their fellow Indians.[43] After that the Virginia Piedmont natives all but disappear from the written record. They signed the Treaty of Middle Plantation in 1677, but the Monacan capital west of Richmond was abandoned by the time immigrant Huguenot refugees were settled there in the early 1700s. By then a tidal wave of English settlers was rolling into the Piedmont, and the native people were being pushed southwestward, into pockets in the foothills of the Blue Ridge Mountains.

Epilogue

Robert Carter

Four hundred years ago, the Chesapeake Bay and its tributaries offered a common area for Native Americans to travel along, draw sustenance from, and enjoy. Sparse in numbers and simpler in technology by today's standards, the native people accordingly treated the lands adjacent to the waterways relatively gently. The same cannot be said of the lasting impact of the Old World peoples who crossed the Atlantic and settled first in Virginia and later in Maryland. In the first century after settlement, they overran most of the native people with their greater numbers, while they imported others from Africa, first as indentured servants and later as slaves, to labor on the land under a hard yoke. In the last three centuries, the population of these immigrants' descendants, their numbers augmented by free or forced immigration from abroad and from elsewhere in the United States, has increased exponentially, so that today the bay is surrounded by more than 16 million human inhabitants.

The European settlers brought powerful technology to clear and plow the land, setting in motion, albeit unwittingly, a train of momentous changes in the bay environment. Subsequent generations introduced machines and chemicals of various kinds in creating a built environment increasingly out of harmony with the natural environment on which it depended—a process that has occurred in many parts of the world. But if John Smith returned to our region today, it is uncertain how many of the places he visited

Chesapeake Land Cover

- Wetlands
- Forest
- Croplands
- Development

0   7.5   15   30 miles

on his Chesapeake voyages he would recognize. The same would hold for his erstwhile ally and adversary Powhatan.

Some of the changes to the bay's environment have been distinctly harmful, and we hear about them regularly in the media. Other changes have been more subtle, often the natural consequence of moving human populations from one continent to another, such as the persistence of many so-called "weeds" in our yards that are in fact Eurasian wild field-plants.

Four hundred years ago neither the English nor the Algonquin-speaking peoples of the Chesapeake could see that the bay is a dynamic, changing ecological system. Our ability to look down on the Chesapeake from space—and to see it as an immense watershed—gives us the power to view the bay as a whole in a way that many (but not all) others before us could not. From this enlarged perspective, the evidence of science and history tells us that the bay as an ecosystem is profoundly out of balance.

Then and Now: How the Bay Is Different Today

In 1607, the forests of the bay and its tributaries conserved large amounts of nutrients and moisture, releasing great quantities of water into the atmosphere during the growing season—water that never made it into river flow. While these forests significantly moderated effects on water flow to the bay and reduced the severity of precolonial storm floods, their major effect was conserving water against drought.[1] In dry weather, what moisture did emerge from the forests was slow-processed through the groundwater aquifers and leaked into waterways as base flow through the soil. Floods in spring and during major storms were less dramatic because the forest's soil and duff layer—a great organic sponge—could hold so much more water. This terrestrial ecosystem was attuned to hold onto its biological and inorganic materials. The tributaries and the bay were thus more stingily fed, and because erosion was less, the water was much clearer than we see it today. In spring, the upstream portions of the bay's tributaries therefore received a significant boost when billions of migrating fish came upstream to spawn, leaving behind organics and nutrients incorporated into their bodies during years of living in the sea. The amount of water sequestered below the surface resulted in innumerable sweet-water springs and artesian wells burbling up clear, cool, groundwater-temperature water throughout the year.

Inorganic and organic nutrients that reached the bay provided sufficient

History of Forests and Land Use

The forests that we see today in the bay region are influenced not only by natural events but also by how they have been used by humans. Beginning in the seventeenth century, major trends were:

1600–1720 Subsistence farming, where small areas were cleared with an axe and hoe and farmed for a few years, whereupon they were left fallow; during this time less than 20 percent of the land was cleared at any one time. Ports were established at the heads of many tributaries.

1720–1840 Timbering for charcoal for the iron industry, as well as selective cutting for houses and boats. More land was cleared for agriculture, and plows came into general use—first wooden, then iron, and later steel. Crop rotation was introduced, and lime was applied to fields. As crops were grown farther inland, transport was overland rather than by water, which meant forests were also cleared for roads. The amount of land under cultivation ranged between 40 and 50 percent.

1840–1930 Sixty to 80 percent of the region was devoted to farming, and guano, bones, imported phosphates were used for fertilizer. After World War I, synthetic nitrogen fertilizers were introduced; soil erosion became widespread.

1930 onward Farms were abandoned in many areas; selective and clear-cutting was used to encourage growth either natural or by planting of loblolly pine for pulp. Many wetlands were drained for arable land.

Today An originally forested landscape, except for marshes and open plant communities (including grasslands, serpentine barrens, riversides, and others), has been converted to a landscape that is a mix of forest, agricultural fields, suburbia, and cities.

fertilizer for the submerged aquatic meadows that covered hundreds of thousands of acres in the shallower parts of the bay, its flats, and along its edges. The plants therein made fabulous food for visiting waterfowl and good hiding places for juvenile fish and crabs, and for small shellfish and snails that lived on the plants and among their rootlike rhizomes. Even the surfaces of the plants and the surface of the shallow bottoms were covered with a living turf of microorganisms that were themselves fodder for a host of critters. The bay efficiently utilized what the tributaries delivered, as well

John Smith's Chesapeake Voyages, 1607–1609

as what came in with the tides or swam in from the coastal ocean. Oysters were a special example of bay life, in their extraordinary abundance building over centuries massive reef structures with a living veneer that, like a home electrostatic filter, removed thousands of tons of particulate matter and left a still clearer bay.

Disruption of the Waterways

When the Europeans who settled around the bay pursued their course of cutting forests, plowing fields, fertilizing soils, channelizing some streams to get rid of water and damming others to hold or harness it, they started the flow of excess nutrient materials and sediment into the waterways that marks today's estuary. The initial disruption by sediment and chemicals in the runoff probably occurred during the first century after colonization, as agriculture became more invasive, but in the 1800s and 1900s it picked up tremendous speed. That flow has overfed the bay's ecosystem. Sediments shaded out the underwater grasses, nutrients stimulated increasing blooms of microscopic algae, and floods from the disrupted landscape dramatically increased the shocks to living communities. Early in the process, it is likely that natural resources became more abundant. However, the bubble began to collapse in the eighteenth and nineteenth centuries as too much organic matter accumulated—the inevitable result of so much microscopic plankton dying, sinking, and decomposing, consuming oxygen in large areas of the deep bay.

In the past three hundred years, the system has become overloaded—that is, overfertilized—resulting in an ecosystemwide shift away from a clear-water aquatic community, sustained chiefly by processes among bottom-dwelling species, to one overwhelmed by nutrient-fed plankton and bacterial processes in the water. Such systems are common now among the world's estuaries, which are less able than before to sustain fish and shellfish, while human harvest pressures on these food sources have intensified. The decline of estuaries, without doubt among the planet's most important nursery grounds, represents one of humanity's greatest challenges and most obvious management failures.

In the modern Chesapeake, with more things floating in the water and less light penetrating downward, the meadows of underwater grasses have been reduced to less than 10 percent of their former area and, since their low point in 1984, they have recovered only modestly and sporadically. Meanwhile, since 1900 several non-native plants, including hydrilla, Eurasian water milfoil, and water chestnut, have been introduced and become pests.

The Potomac, often dubbed "the Nation's River" since the War of Independence, became a poster child for egregious pollution. Abraham Lincoln was forced to leave Washington D.C., in summer because of the stench of raw sewage. Warm-weather epidemics made low parts of the city and neighboring environs unhealthy. In the tidal estuary, increasing sewage loads brought about massive blooms of blue-green algae, which coated the river like paint, a phenomenon totally unknown in precolonial times but that still troubles urban managers today despite billions of dollars spent for nutrient control and political protestations claiming the river's "restoration."

Upstream from Washington, agricultural erosion turned the river chocolate-brown with mud from valuable farmlands. The confluence of the Shenandoah, draining its fertile valley, and the mainstem Potomac at today's Harpers Ferry, became noted for the juncture of brown and clear streams. Historians once blamed the spread of tobacco agriculture from Jamestown for all the destructive soil erosion, but tobacco was planted and tended by hand, much like Indian corn. That method did not deeply disturb the soil. Furthermore, tobacco-farmed soils "played out" within a decade and were abandoned to return to forest for about two decades before they might be farmed again, or else left in ruins for "new" lands in the West. Records in the sediments[2] indicate instead that while massive storms struck the Potomac basin, and the Chesapeake at large, in precolonial times, huge flows carrying agricultural muds only began to accumulate in significant layers after about 1820, with the advent of massive deforestation and the use of deep, sod-breaking plows by an ever-expanding population of farmers. George Washington helped set the trend; in the period from 1793 to 1799, he used up to twenty plows at once at his Dogue Run farms alone.[3]

Fishes and Shellfish

Today there are fewer harvestable fish in the Chesapeake compared to the bay in 1607–9. It appears that the disappearance of submerged aquatic vegetation, plus runoff from a landscape being denuded of forest, eventually overwhelmed the resilience of this huge aquatic ecosystem. Its energy pathways shifted away from its precolonial state of clearer, relatively nutrient-poor runoff and a food supply dominated by organisms on and within the bottom sediments. The fish most abundant back then, as recorded by the English colonists, were those that fed on those bottom resources, and until the nineteenth century they were the ones most abundant in the refuse piles found at human settlements, suggesting that they were the fish most often caught.[4] The apparent dominance of bottom-feeding fish ceased as

John Smith's Chesapeake Voyages, 1607–1609

the bottom waters became increasingly anoxic from the decay of dead algae. Fish that fed in an increasingly turbid water column, and one that was richer in pollutant-fed plankton, became the most common species. The most abundant fish in the bay today is the bay anchovy, followed by menhaden and various small minnows, or shiners, which are efficient scavengers and grazers in the shallows. Their overall mass is small because of their size, but these and others are vital "forage species" for the larger predators.

Since colonial times, but mostly after the evolution of rail systems that could rapidly transport live fish, as many as ten other piscivorous (fish-eating) species have been introduced to Chesapeake watershed streams, including that popular sport fish, the largemouth bass. Thus it is possible that even if migratory populations of anadromous fishes were reestablished, they would fare more poorly than in past centuries because of the increase in predator species waiting for them.[5] One such major reintroduction program is under way in the Susquehanna above Conowingo Dam; the results, successful thus far, will be closely watched. Meanwhile, shad seem at this writing to be rebounding dramatically in the Potomac despite the predators.

Menhaden are caught today by pound nets (see chapter 6) throughout the bay and, in Virginia, with purse seines set from specialized boats that encircle the school. That kind of heavy fishing—the largest commercial fishery in the bay—is worrisome to fishery managers concerned about long-term sustainable yields. The dense schools still seen in the bay in summer may become depleted.[6] Ironically, despite their economic importance in the Chesapeake and other coastal areas, menhaden are unappreciated by the public, which consumes them not as food for the table but in other forms. The fish are rich in the omega-3 oils currently believed to help prevent heart disease; those oils are extracted and used in health-food supplements, cosmetics, and other products, while the flesh is cooked and dried into a protein-rich powder used as a chicken-feed additive.

Atlantic sturgeon, familiar to the Native Americans and to the English of the early Contact period, are now extremely rare due to habitat degradation and to overfishing in the nineteenth and twentieth centuries. The short-nosed sturgeon is listed as endangered throughout its range, which for both species is from the Canadian Maritimes to the St. Johns River in Florida.[7] Eels survive, but they are threatened by overharvesting in a fishery established in the 1970s; disease may also be a factor in their decline.

Blue crabs, a modern icon of the Chesapeake, were harvested but not intensely by both the Native Americans and the early colonists. This is a surprise because they are relatively easy to catch, especially the "doublers" or mating pairs that swim at the water's surface. Interest in a crab fishery seems to have increased in the first half of the nineteenth century, so their appeal as a food item may have risen as other species were fished down to commercially unproductive levels. Today blue crabs are heavily fished by both commercial and sport fishers.

Oysters have been depleted throughout the Chesapeake over the past four hundred years. Those in deep channels thrived until the last third of the nineteenth century, when they were sought with great intensity following the development of canning technology. They were dredged, shucked, canned, and shipped by rail to distant coastal cities and the interior of the United States. By the 1840s, in the lower bay, there was a serious shortage of oysters for watermen to harvest. It was only in the mid-nineteenth century that public-sponsored survey work revealed extraordinary "oyster rock" or reef systems in subestuaries like Tangier Sound and the Potomac, Rappahannock, and Choptank rivers.[8] New technology then triggered a serious, eventually devastating harvest of these deeper resources, simultaneously removing from the bay a living filter system that in past centuries helped maintain clear water conditions. In the main stem of the modern Chesapeake above the Rappahannock and in the York River, pollution-driven reductions in dissolved oxygen kill most oysters today at depths below about six meters (nearly twenty feet) and often in shallower water. Beginning in the 1950s, disease exacerbated the oyster decline; MSX (*Haplosporidium nelsoni*) and "dermo" (*Perkinsus marinus*), coupled with habitat degradation and continued harvesting, may have reduced oyster stocks by as much as 99 percent below their precolonial levels.

Some filtering function is still performed by the bay's vastly diminished oyster grounds, although there is very little hard-bottom habitat upon which oyster larvae can "strike" (settle permanently for growth). Oysters are still harvested by a few remnant sailing skipjacks that pull iron-framed dredges across oyster bars, but most harvesting is done by hand tongs or hydraulic "patent tongs." At first simply mechanical devices, modern versions are driven by hydraulic power. A few watermen harvest oysters by SCUBA diving. They take the premium oysters, visually selecting the largest and best, which would arguably have been the most successful and disease-resistant breeding stock, but at least divers are not damaging the remaining oyster bottom structure.

Today's harvests of soft clams also are much reduced, a decline that began in the last third of the twentieth century, when modern hydraulic conveyers were widely introduced and an apparently new disease called "DN" began affecting populations. Some consider it possible that soft clams may become extinct in the bay.[9]

Forests and Vegetation

We know of several differences in vegetation distributions that developed between 1600 and 2000. For example, the American chestnut made up about 25 percent of the forests in the drier habitats throughout the region before it became regionally extinct in the 1930s as a result of an introduced European fungal disease. Populations of the American elm have also been drastically reduced by an imported disease. The decline of agriculture and fire suppression during the twentieth century has probably led to decreases in pine species in existing woods and of grassy areas, both of which depend on periodic fires for regeneration. In the three centuries before that, deforestation by farmers resulted in higher freshwater runoff, so that more of the bay's upper tributaries, which are now mainly freshwater, were brackish at the time of settlement and supported brackish aquatic vegetation. We see evidence for these changes in pollen and seed profiles analyzed from sediment cores collected in the Chesapeake.[10] Prominent in cores from the last 350 years is ragweed, a native species, which invaded open plowed fields while trees became much less common.

The filling-in of tributary heads, coves, and bays and the narrowing of subestuaries have served to increase areas of swamp vegetation. The remains of loblolly pines some distance from modern pine forests, as well as half-dead trees out from the shoreline, indicate that marsh encroachment has been occurring at a rather rapid rate.[11] Soil erosion and siltation of the estuary have continued with ongoing deforestation and land cultivation.[12] Many of today's fresh tidal marshes are the outcome of delta progradation (outward growth) that resulted from soil erosion following European settlement.[13]

The vast freshwater swamps that once surrounded the Pocomoke and Nanticoke rivers are quite different today. Bald cypress is certainly not as extensive as it was at the time of John Smith's arrival, because the swamps have been drained to create arable land. Four hundred years ago, much of the middle Eastern Shore was wet woodland. To facilitate conventional tillage agriculture, complex systems of "tax ditches" were dug, initially by hand (usually slave) labor and later by machine. These systems, and sometimes systems of tile drains, conducted water off the landscape and (usually with a fair load of topsoil) into the adjacent streams. The ditching probably changed those ecosystems fundamentally, so that the native species may not be able to recolonize such areas even if the opportunity presented itself. In recent decades, significant private and government money has been invested in undoing this work, but restoration of some of the former wet habitat is far from complete.

Most of the (poorly preserved) pollen in sediment cores from Battle Creek, on the Patuxent, which go back two thousand years, came from bald cypress—a species that today has persisted in that location quite successfully.

Wetlands

Wetlands around the bay in general have decreased, and nationally about half have been lost since European Contact. The most notable loss has been around cities. Unlike the Native Americans of John Smith's time, incoming Europeans tended to regard marshes as a nuisance unless they wanted to graze livestock on them. Near settlements that were becoming towns and cities, people filled in the marshes to create more land. The Back Bay section of Boston, and the Marina District of San Francisco, both now urban land, are only the most famous American examples. There are hundreds of places around the Chesapeake where incoming people created more land, straightening out curvy shorelines, and their descendants forgot the land's origin. The frequent flooding of downtown Norfolk and parts of Washington, D.C., during rainstorms is actually the result of the filling-in of numerous small creeks to make low, flat land—which unfortunately does not drain. More intelligent "filling" in other cities involves laying underground pipes that collect water and connect with sewers, providing the drainage once supplied by the creeks.

The native subspecies of reedgrass (*Phragmites*) has been crowded out by an explosion of the Eurasian variety, familiar to lovers of thatched houses in England. Most of the "phrag" people see today is the invading subspecies.[14] Regrettably, the rather rare native version is often subject to extermination along with the invasive "pest" plant because few surveys recognize it.

When the Native American practice of driving game with fire ended, the vegetation changed on many of the barrens. A hopeful sign of restoration is the recently established policy of Maryland's Department of Natural Resources to reinstitute controlled burns in selected areas in order to preserve the unique flora that includes rare grasses, orchids, cardinal flower, and 90 percent of the world's population of sandplain gerardia.

Birds and Waterfowl

The past four centuries have seen alterations in numerous species, including two extinctions. Passenger pigeons, once numbering in the billions, were driven extinct by a combination of habitat loss and overhunting. Carolina parakeets, which wintered in Virginia and were called "grain robbers" by the Powhatans,[15] also succumbed to habitat loss. The heath hen was last recorded in 1860 in Prince Georges County, Maryland.[16]

For centuries the Delmarva Peninsula has been the migration corridor for millions of songbirds winging their way each autumn from summer breeding grounds to their winter homes in Central and South America. Without forest and shrub habitats to stop, rest, and refuel in, many do not have the energy reserves required to make the trip. Conservation groups and government agencies are working to protect critical feeding and resting habitat for these tiny travelers along the Delmarva, but it remains to be seen if the next generation will experience the mass migrations of songbirds that Native Americans and the first English colonists did.

Changes and intrusions among waterfowl have come more recently. The population of native black ducks has decreased, those shy birds being replaced, especially in urbanizing areas, by the gregarious mallards from the central North American Flyway.[17] Canada geese have become permanent residents in many fields, meadows, and city parks, and European "mute" swans have joined them; both species do further damage to marsh and SAV habitats. The snow goose has also become abundant enough to cause habitat problems. On a cheerier note, perhaps as a side-effect of global warming, the once threatened brown pelican, reported as a casual visitor in the tidewater areas of the bay's eastern and western shores in sightings from 1895 to 1958,[18] has extended its range northward from North Carolina in recent years at least halfway up the Chesapeake Bay and is now summering as far north as the mid–New Jersey coast.

Animals

The larger predators that existed in John Smith's time were systematically killed off by European-American farmers wanting to protect their livestock. The colonial legislatures of Virginia and Maryland repeatedly passed laws encouraging the killing of wolves, and sometimes of "wildcats" (cougars and their smaller relatives, bobcats) as well. Herbivorous animals like deer and wild turkeys and omnivores like raccoons and opossums were in competition with cattle, goats, and sheep that were favored by their human owners, and the owners shot and ate the wild animals, whose numbers correspondingly decreased. Deer were rare in the Chesapeake by the early twentieth century, except in places that were inaccessible to humans due to altitude or swampiness.[19] Raccoons and opossums flourished by becoming suburbanites and eating garbage; squirrels continued to thrive because some hardwood forests survived and also because the yard trees people planted were often nut-bearers.

Elk once were common in the uplands of the Chesapeake region, but the last known one in Virginia or Maryland was killed in the mountains of Clarke County, Virginia, in 1855.[20] The beaver population was decimated by the fur trade of the mid- and late seventeenth century in Virginia and Maryland, but beavers continued to be trapped for their pelts until they went extinct (locally) from the 1890s to the early 1900s.[21] River otters, once common in most waterways, were also hunted for their pelts, and by the twentieth century they were restricted to the less accessible river swamps,[22] although they have rebounded in areas where trapping has been curtailed. Martens and fishers in the Chesapeake region were trapped into extinction.[23] However, their relative the mink is more aquatic and adaptable and has sustained its numbers.[24]

British-style hunting in the Piedmont required a great deal of land clearing to allow hunters to "beat up" the game. Animals such as the red fox thrived in such cleared areas, but its brush-loving cousin the gray fox withdrew. The woodchuck and the skunk, previously adapted to a forested habitat, increased in numbers when fields and meadows (with their seeds and berries and their small rodent populations) became more plentiful.[25]

William Byrd of Westover unwittingly recorded the principal reason for the bison's disappearance from the Chesapeake region.[26] Colonel Byrd was commissioned in 1728 to survey the disputed border between North Carolina and Virginia. Traveling through the Piedmont, Byrd came upon a buffalo calf that impressed him mightily with its size and demeanor. Byrd's awe for the creature's beauty, mystery, and potential for domestication soon gave way to culinary curiosity as he and his party dispatched the young animal and transformed it into buffalo steaks. Hunted to extinction, the bison was last seen in Virginia in 1800.[27]

Deer and wild turkeys were nearly hunted out of existence not because they were dangerous, but because they were good to eat and inhabited the forests that the farmers were clearing. Then, in the late nineteenth century and throughout the twentieth, farms were steadily abandoned, some to become shrubby second-growth woodlands (the animals' preferred habitat) and others to become suburbs. In addition, for much of the twentieth century, hunting regulations limited the age and sex of deer that could be harvested. With these changes, plus stocking programs begun decades ago, populations of deer and wild turkeys have rebounded. Deer in particular have become suburbanites, troublesome grazers in gardens, and frequent highway casualties in ever-growing numbers.[28]

Bears have always survived in the Great Dismal Swamp in southeastern Virginia, as well as in the mountains. They are making a strong comeback throughout the region. In recent years, coyote sightings are on the rise in Virginia, Maryland, and Pennsylvania, and cougars are expanding their ranges. In the 1990s, a wolf was sighted in King William County, Virginia, as was a bobcat in Calvert County, Maryland.

Efforts to restock the region with beavers began in the 1930s, mainly in the James River basin.[29] Since the 1980s, beaver have appeared all over the Chesapeake watershed, in sufficient numbers to become regarded by homeowners and highway departments as a nuisance. River otters are also expanding their ranges. In the 1950s, an effort was launched to restock elk in the mountains, but since it remained legal to hunt them, the animals did not survive except across the Kentucky line, where elk hunting is illegal.

Human Population and Culture

Ask any environmental scientist to name the one dominant factor affecting the environment of the bay today, and the answer always comes down to the amazing post–World War II human population boom in the watershed. In 1950, the human population of the bay region numbered 8.1 million. By 2000, it reached 15.7 million, and the tally is projected to increase to 17.8 million in 2020. By contrast, in 1570 the human population of the bay watershed is known to have been seven Spaniards (at their Jesuit mission on the York River) and probably fewer than fifty thousand Algonquian-, Iroquoian-, and Siouan-speaking Native Americans. Between the arrival of 140 Jamestown men in 1607 and the establishment of Maryland's colony in 1634, one could add several thousand English speakers, some Dutchmen, and a handful of other Old World colonists and Africans. At the beginning of the seventeenth century, the English migrated to an Algonquian Chesapeake world that was involved in wars with the Iroquoian- and Siouan-speaking peoples to the west and north. The English were yet another group of outsiders with which the Algonquians had to contend and come to terms. But the worldview and ambitions of the English collided with the traditional ways of the Algonquians in a way that did not allow for cultural accommodation. The seventeenth-century record is replete with a mixture of trading, conflict, and mutual avoidance. By the end of the seventeenth century, the English had won the population contest. Members of the much-diminished Native American societies found themselves limited to established reservations or forced to migrate beyond the English frontier west and north of the fall line. There remain today only a few native speakers still fluent in one of the Algonquian languages of the Chesapeake region—the Oklahoma descendants of the Leni Lenape (Delaware). All the other Indian people in the region now speak English. This is important to note because how we see, describe, and understand our world is reflected in the language we speak. But although English has become the common language of the Chesapeake, embedded in it are the names of living creatures that the Algonquian speakers used: raccoon, opossum, and terrapin. Plants not found in Eurasia still bear their Algonquian-derived names: hickory, persimmon, and pecan. Soft-soled leather shoes are moccasins, and bread made from cornmeal is colloquially called "cornpone." And then there are the many waterways that still bear their old Indian names, the most famous being the Potomac River.

Archaeological Resources

Recent archaeological excavations at Werowocomoco and Jamestown Island in Virginia have vividly demonstrated how much archaeology can teach us about history and prehistory. Each discovery layer at Jamestown and Werowocomoco reveals hundreds of small insights into how both groups interacted with their natural world and glimpses into how they interacted with each other. For example, the remnants of food resources found at Jamestown include Bermudian cahows (a nesting seabird brought to Virginia as provisions by survivors of the 1610 shipwreck in Bermuda of the *Sea Venture*) and loggerhead sea turtles—federally designated as threatened today. The once-prolific cahow, believed extinct until the 1950s, was saved and its numbers are now slowly increasing in Bermuda. Their presence in the archaeological remains of the Virginia Company period reminds us of the rich resources the colonists encountered in New World ecosystems.

Regrettably, the sites available for such revealing studies are disappearing at an alarming rate. This is a natural consequence of successive generations wishing to live (and build) in choice locations along our waterways. Population growth is expected to require construction of 1.7 million new homes in the watershed by 2020, consuming an additional 600,000 acres of open land.[30] Unfortunately, archaeological sites are nonrenewable resources. Once destroyed through development, they are gone forever, along with all the knowledge they contained—information that could have helped expand our understanding of the Chesapeake Bay's remarkable natural and cultural history. As exciting as the early European accounts of exploration of the Chesapeake Bay are, they seldom scratch below the surface of the complexity of the world that Smith and his contemporaries encountered. The seventeenth-century records of the English settlers, while richer in detail, do not begin to yield what archaeology can tell us about housing, diet, and the degree of interaction between Chesapeake and world economies in the seventeenth century. Thus, archaeology has become one of the few remaining bridges to understanding more fully a world and its inhabitants of four hundred years ago.[31]

The Abiding Chesapeake Bay Connection

John Smith's Chesapeake voyages of 1607–9 give us a window on the Chesapeake at a point in time when the relationship of human beings to the bay and the impact of human activity on the bay environment were qualitatively and quantitatively different from today's. The growth in human population over four hundred years has fundamentally changed the landscape, the culture, the environment, and many ecological relationships within that environment. Understanding that earlier period in time reinforces the magnitude of change that has occurred and of our roles in this destructive process. It reminds us of the richness of the bay landscape, then as now, a complex ecological system. It shows us what is different and what abides.

The difficulty of understanding changes that have occurred in the bay's natural landscape is compounded by the short span of much of our "environmental memory." A long-term perspective is important because we need to know that the bay was once home to elk and bison. We may have seen evidence of this past in names like Buffalo Creek and Elk Ridge, but thought little of it. We need to remember the magnificence of the bay's original forests, old-growth forests now gone, probably forever, mostly destroyed by slash-and-burn agriculture, a technique that deeply disturbs us today when we see its effects in developing parts of the world. Here in the eastern United States, we need to know that trees fourteen feet (over 4.5 meters) in diameter once reached hundreds of feet into the sky. Jesuit Father Joseph-Pierre de Bonnecamps, writing in his 1749 diary, speaks of dining "in a hollow cottonwood tree which 29 men could be ranged side by side."[32] We have accounts of timbered logs from a single tree filling a whole train, trees so big around that once felled and sectioned they could only be "split" with gunpowder or dynamite to reduce them to manageable size.[33] Such trees are forever gone; no stands of such giants are preserved. A few trophy pictures are all that remain. We need to remember them.

We need to reflect deeply on John Smith's account of the bay in its abundance: "Beavers, Otters, Beares, Martins, and minks we found, and in diverse places that abundance of fish lying so thicke with their heads above the water, as for want of nets (our barge driving amongst them) we attempted to catch them with a frying pan, but we found it a bad instrument to catch fish with. Neither better fish more plenty or variety for small fish had any of us seene, in any place so swimming in the water, then in the bay of Chesapeack"[34] This comparison to "any place" is a remarkable statement, considering that it came from an explorer who had seen amazing abundance on his travels along pristine coastlines of Africa, the Caribbean, and other areas in North America. Such richness today seems beyond reality. We need to understand what the bay is capable of. We need to remember it.

With our present understanding of how ecosystems operate, scientists fear that we cannot return to the environmental conditions present four centuries ago. However, we must hold in our minds a clear picture of this pre-European ecosystem, how it changed, and what potential is there for restoration. This is extremely important when we set environmental goals for the future bay, for our children's children, for the bay four hundred years from now.

History, both written and recorded in sediments, has shown that the bay is always changing in response to fluctuations in climate and sea level. It was different during the Medieval Warm Period than at the time of John Smith. But the magnitude and speed of changes since the time of John Smith are vastly different. This disturbing, transformational process, which began in the eighteenth and nineteenth centuries, may not be possible to reverse. We anchor our hopes on a wisdom that urges us to cooperate across political, scientific, economic, social, racial, and cultural lines to bring it to a halt. Perhaps understanding the remarkable resources we have lost will stimulate strong action to stem—and reverse—the tide. History's witness is that the bay's resources are not limitless.

Not everything about the Chesapeake Bay has changed since 1609, however. Then as now, the vast water of this estuary, fed by its great rivers, serves as the lifeline of people and communities who depend upon it and as a principal thoroughfare for commercial and military traffic with the outside world.[35] For those who will wander far from the beaten path, there are hundreds, perhaps a thousand places where one can go and see vistas, and fragments of ecosystem, very much like the one that Smith and the Virginia adventurers of 1607 encountered. No doubt Great Falls and some of the Eastern Shore's wetlands would still be recognizable to Smith. One can stroll down a Chesapeake Bay beach and still encounter common beach and dune plant species such as switchgrass, American searocket, and American beach grass; and near eroding cliffs still find fossils that puzzled early colonists. Sandy habitats that shift with the wind and tides provide the last refuge on the East Coast of the United States for the federally threatened northeastern beach tiger beetle, which spends its entire two-year life cycle on the beach and low dunes around the bay. This species—once abundant from New England to the Chesapeake—can be found in large numbers on numerous bay beaches, but elsewhere it has been lost from all but one beach in Massachusetts.

The Indians of Virginia and Maryland feel a deep and abiding connection with their ancestral lands and waters on the bay's tributaries, even if their legal holdings of these traditional cultural properties have been vastly reduced. Many roads and towns reflect the footsteps of moccasin paths, following the lie of the land. Many of the bay's beautiful tributary names, such as the Susquehanna, Potomac, Rappahannock, Shenandoah, Conococheague, Monocacy, Antietam, Wicomico, Anacostia, and Tanyamentasacta recall the voices of the basin's first settlers—the First People of the Chesapeake—the ancestors of a People who raise their voices again, to ears which now may better hear.

Through historic preservation and historical interpretation, descendants of the African and English communities of the seventeenth-century Chesapeake also seek to renew their own cultural connection with the bay and its formative role in our national experience. Weaving the story of a unique estuary into a many-colored tapestry of peoples and cultures, these efforts, like the efforts to understand the Native American peoples of the Chesapeake four centuries ago, depend largely on primary historical and archaeological research without reference to the tangible remains of seventeenth-century buildings, of which only a handful remain standing.

We 16 million inhabitants of the Chesapeake Bay region today hold a dominant influence on the health of the system. We must know where we started, and how we got here, if we are to be effective stewards of the Chesapeake environment that is now our trust. Knowledge of the past, such as that of John Smith's voyages, enables us to set goals for the bay's restoration. Only a few people alive today remember the bounteous bay of clear waters and oyster reefs. History must supply what memory can no longer give us. Thus may our future depend on the past.

Notes

1. The Chesapeake Environment in the Early Seventeenth Century

1. A word on ambiguity, for those checking scholarly sources in geology or any other scientific field—not to mention the social sciences like anthropology and the humanities like history. What scholars observe, they interpret and categorize. The categories may be published, and taken by some readers as "the truth," but in reality these things are not written in stone. Different scholars can interpret the same things differently, and the same scholar can learn more and revise her or his interpretations later. (Genuine, active scholars do this all the time.) Therefore dates, the divisions of sediments into formations or living things into species or even the people into political groupings that you see in this volume are only the writers' (and no one else's) consensus—for now.

2. Poag 1997 and 1999. Poag's work shows that the impact, which created a massive, brine-filled crater that is now deeply buried, still has an effect upon us today. For one thing, the sharp angle of the mouths of the James and York rivers, after a long NW–SE run, is due to "differential subsidence of the Exmore breccia within the Chesapeake Bay impact crater" (1999: 111; see also map on that page). Second, deep drinking-water wells (400–1,200 feet [122–366 meters]) in Hampton and eastern Newport News find seawater, not freshwater, at these depths (1999: map on p. 116). There is a resulting cultural pressure: wanting to supply tap water for modern urban sprawl on the Virginia Peninsula and seeking to find other sources of water, the City of Newport News is pushing the currently proposed King William Reservoir, which in turn will impact the Mattaponi Indians' fisheries, which they have relied upon for many generations.

3. The ice front reached as far south as Scranton in Pennsylvania and New York City in New York; Long Island, Block Island, Martha's Vineyard, and Nantucket Island are remnants of the glacier's terminal moraine.

4. French et al., 2005.

5. For a reconstruction of those people's lifeways, see Dent 1995: 135–44; and McAvoy and McAvoy 1997.

6. J. Smith 1986b [1612]: 44; J. Smith 1986c [1624]: 101; Strachey 1953 [1612]: 38; Haile 1998: 599.

7. Fagan 2000.

8. Stahle et al. 1998. Things were no easier for the Powhatans: in 1608, the Quiyoughco-hannock chief sent presents to John Smith, then president of the English colony, asking him to "pray to his god for rain, for his god would not send him any" (W. White 1969 [1608?]: 150; Haile 1998: 141).

9. Lippson and Lippson 2006.

10. The water surface of the Chesapeake is about 1,342 square miles (3,475.8 square kilometers), and the watershed is about 64,000 square miles (165,759 square kilometers). This means that about 48 square miles (124.3 square kilometers) of watershed drains into each square mile (258 square hectares) of the bay (Cronin 1971). This ratio is exceeded among earth's water bodies only by the Gulf of Finland (William Matuszeski, personal communication to Kent Mountford).

11. James Smith, of the Interstate Commission on the Potomac River Basin, personal communication to Kent Mountford, 1984. In the 1960s drought, one of the deepest on record, Potomac River discharge reflected only the "base flow" of water stored in the soil, but reduced by the vast amounts being lost to the atmosphere through forest and understory plant evapotranspiration. The latter came to a halt when a sudden basinwide frost stopped photosynthesis virtually overnight across the entire basin, an area of about 14,670 square miles (37,995 square kilometers). Within a few days, and with no rainfall, Potomac River flows from upstream of Washington, D.C., increased by over 130 million gallons (492 million liters), representing the water previously taken up by vegetation.

12. Biggs (1981) demonstrates that boring sponges that attach to oysters reflect the salinity of their environment. At Hart Island, where oysters no longer grow in abundance, a core indicated that about 545± 90 years ago the salinity level was at least 10 parts per thousand (ppt) 25 percent or more of the time, and 15 ppt more than half the time. His core had only this single date determined, but high salinity still was indicated from greater depths. Today salinity at Hart Island only occasionally exceeds 10 ppt.

13. Calculated by ascertaining changes in level since 1900 (a rough average of 3.4 mm per year, J. Halka, personal communication to Kent Mountford) and extrapolating backward for four hundred years, which has some risk, but the overall stand of sea level is still markedly higher. Part of the observed "rise" is actually due to subsidence (settling) of the land. Grace Brush notes that there is no evidence from sediment cores that the diatom populations were affected by droughts, though there were changes in species of foraminifera that accompanied changes in salinity.

14. See, for instance, Wilke and Thompson 1977b.

15. Lippson and Lippson 2006.

16. Robert Beverley wrote in 1705 that there were "large Spots of Meadows and Savanna's wherein are hundreds of acres without any Tree at all; but yield Reeds and Grass of incredible Height" (1947 [1705]: 124).

17. Lippson and Lippson 2006; A. Lippson et al. 1981.

18. Garman and Macko 1998. Even today, after anadromous fish runs have been reduced by about 90 percent, resident predators have been found to derive 35.6 percent of their biomass from shad and herring in Ward Creek, a tributary of the James River.

19. Rohde et al. 1994.

20. J. Smith 1986b [1612]: 228; J. Smith 1986c [1624]: 168; Haile 1998: 262.

21. James Cummins, of the Interstate Commission on the Potomac River Basin, suggests these fish might also have been shad or herring.

22. Fay, Neves, and Pardue 1983a.

23. Danckaerts 1913 [1679–80].

24. Grosslein and Azarovitz 1982; Fay, Neves, and Pardue 1983a; Hildebrand and Schroeder 1928.

25. Thomas Horton, personal communication to Kent Mountford, 1998.

26. Lippson and Lippson 2006; Fay, Neves, and Pardue 1983a.

27. Kelso and Straub 2004.

28. Hildebrand and Schroeder 1928; Grosslein and Azarovitz 1982.

29. J. Smith 1986b [1612]: 228–29; J. Smith 1986c [1624]: 168–69; Haile 1998: 262–63.

30. J. Smith 1986b [1612]: 156; J. Smith 1986c [1624]: 111; Strachey 1953 [1612]: 28; Haile 1998: 684.

31. E.g., a Late Woodland component of the White Oak Point site (44WM119) on Nomini Creek (Stephen Potter, personal communication to the authors, 2004).

32. Donald Lear, personal communication to Kent Mountford, 1984.

33. Barrie and Barrie 1909 (records); Ulanowicz and Tuttle 1992 (frequency).

34. Lippson and Lippson 2006.

35. "Some boys were sent to dive for mussels" when an English party visited along the James River near the Appomattox's mouth (Archer 1969a [1607]: 92; Haile 1998: 113).

36. Rusnak 1967.

37. Kennedy, Newell, and Eble 1996.

38. Mountford 1986.

39. Another way to put it: "a coastal plain that tilts gently eastward into the Atlantic" (Rountree 1990: 4).

40. However, those alluvial deposits are highly susceptible to erosion, one of the reasons colonial farming practices caused such devastation to the landscape and filling of the waterways. That prompted Horace Greeley to suggest "go west" rather then trying to fix the problem.

41. On Tangier and Smith islands, bay author Tom Horton has seen the remains of walnut roots and stumps emerging; the wood is still solid enough to be carved by modern craftsmen (personal communication to Kent Mountford, 2004).

42. Mark Demitroff and Hugh French, personal communications to Kent Mountford, 2004. Wayne Newell, U.S. Geological Survey, personal communication to Kent Mountford about Delmarva Bays.

43. John Moss, quoted by Robert Walter of Franklin and Marshall College in a personal communication to Kent Mountford.

44. M. Williams 1990. After several millennia of agriculture and of cutting of firewood by an ever-larger population, very few forests were left in England except as hunting preserves for the wealthy. The poorer people's wood came from trees growing in hedgerows, where

coppicing was practiced: periodic cutting of branches, resulting in short, bushy-topped trees.

45. Metric conversion: oaks could be cut into square timbers 73.2 centimeters to a side and 18.3 meters long; biggest cypresses had trunks that ran straight for up to 24.4 meters.

46. J. Smith 1986b [1612]: 151, 162 (galloping); J. Smith 1986c [1624]: 109, 116 (galloping); Strachey 1953 [1612]: 128, 129; Haile 1998: 685, 686.

47. A. White 1910 [1634]: 40.

48. Daniel Boone (forester), introduction to Robbins and Blom 1996.

49. Rountree and Davidson 1997: 17–19.

50. Barber 2003.

51. Whitney 1996 [1994].

52. Harrison et al. 1965; Yuan and Brush 1992; Yuan 1995.

53. Maxwell and Davis 1972.

54. See, for instance, Brush 1986.

55. For a full list of such associations for Maryland, see Brush, Lenk, and Smith 1980. For Virginia, see Farrell and Ware 1991 (Piedmont only); and Fleming et al. 2004. Comparisons between the two states are difficult because Virginia has a geographical atlas of species but no manual giving frequencies, while Maryland has the latter but not the former.

56. The blight kills saplings after they reach a certain size. The species is not extinct, which is why there can be efforts to hybridize it with a blight-resistant European chestnut.

57. Percy 1969 [1608?]: 141; J. Smith 1986b [1612]: 151, 153; J. Smith 1986c [1624]: 108, 109; Strachey 1953 [1612]: 128–31; Haile 1998: 96, 685–87.

58. Strachey 1953 [1612]: 130; Haile 1998: 686.

59. Strachey 1953 [1612]: 127; Haile 1998: 683.

60. Ehrlich, Dobkin, and Wheye 1988: 273–77.

61. J. Smith 1986b [1612]: 154–56; J. Smith 1986c [1624]: 110–11; Strachey 1953 [1612]: 124–27; Haile 1998: 680–83. The Powhatan word for the bird—*maskawins,* or "grain robber"—represented the earlier farmers' view.

62. J. Smith 1986b [1612]: 155–56; J. Smith 1986c [1624]: 111; Strachey 1953 [1612]: 126; Haile 1998: 683; Alsop 1910 [1666].

63. Beaver tail, because it supposedly remained in the water, was classed with seafood as being permitted to Catholics on fast days (Kurlansky 2003: 110).

64. Argall 1904–6 [1613]: 642; Haile 1998: 754.

65. Fleet 1876 [1631–32]: 27; see also Anonymous 1910 [1635]: 80 for a Maryland sighting. As for Pennsylvania, in 1760 near Pomfret Castle, in a massive slaughter of wild game, hunters killed among other species 111 buffalo (Shoemaker 1917: 22).

66. Buffalo: Hulton and Quinn 1964. Puma: Hulton 1984: 182.

67. Steven Potter, personal communication to Kent Mountford, 2004.

68. Some historians feel that buffalo moved eastward after European settlement (e.g., Bakeless 1961: 268); it could, after all, only enter the area by following pasturage. To gain entry to West Virginia and Virginia, bison must necessarily have followed the narrow river floodplains where grass was available. However, through Late Woodland times, such passageways were blocked by Native American habitation in the form of large villages and, at the western end at least, any such animals "very easy to be killed" would have been quickly

harvested for food, hide, and tool material. Once the ecological niche was abandoned by the Native Americans in the sixteenth through eighteenth centuries, bison moved in but, due to limited grazing, probably never in large numbers (Guilday 1971; Belue 1996).

69. Charles Davis (naturalist), Maryland Department of Natural Resources, personal communication to Kent Mountford.

70. Middleton 1984: 190.

71. J. Smith 1986b [1612]: 155; J. Smith 1986c [1624]: 111; Strachey 1953 [1612]: 126; Haile 1998: 682.

72. Winne 1969 [1608]: 246; Haile 1998: 203–4. John Smith added (1986b [1612]: 155; 1986c [1624]: 111) that the dogs could howl but not bark, and Strachey (1953 [1612]: 125–26; Haile 1998: 682) noted further that they formed packs that hung around the charnel houses.

2. The World of Algonquian-Speaking Peoples

1. The lower, narrower parts of the necks in the region had become overhunted (J. Smith 1986b [1612]: 164 [having to go westward where there "is plenty of game"] and 165 [devouring "all they can catch"]). Strachey was more specific: "betwixt the Rivers the land is not so large below, that therein breed sufficient to giue them all content, considering especially how at all tymes and seasons they destroy them" and "Hares, Partridges, Turkeys, fatt or leane, young or old in eggs in breeding tyme, or however, they devowre, at no tyme sparing any that they can katch in their power" (1953 [1612]: 82, 83; Haile 1998: 639, 640). Even allowing for exaggeration, those hunters do not sound like members of Ducks Unlimited.

2. William Strachey, copying John Smith, wrote that there were "many severall nations of sondry Languages, which envyron Powhatans Territories, the Chawonocks [North Carolina Algonquians], the Mangougs [Iroquoian-speaking Nottoways and Meherrins], the [Siouan-speaking] Monacans, the [Siouan-speaking] Manahocks, the [Iroquoian-speaking] Sasquesahanougs, [and Algonquian-speakers] the Acquanachuks [Lenapes/Unamis] the Tockwoghes and the Kuskarawaoks [Nanticokes]. Of all these not any one vnderstandeth another but by Interpreters" (1953 [1612]: 49; Haile 1998: 608). Smith's list (1986b [1612]: 150) adds yet another: the Massawomecks, who may have been a branch of the Susquehannocks (see chap. 10).

3. Bartolomé Martínez, in Lewis and Loomie 1953: 161.

4. Most words collected in the Roanoke Sound area appear in Hariot 1972 (which is a facsimile reprint of the 1590 publication of his "Briefe and True Report" with de Bry's engravings; the original 1588 text of the "Report" is printed in Quinn 1955: 317–87, 403–62). However, artist John White recorded additional names of plants and animals in the captions of his paintings (Quinn 1955: 444ff.).

5. J. Smith 1986b [1612]: 136–39 (word list), 217 (serving as interpreter); Haile 1998: 208–9, 246.

6. Smith 1986b [1612]: 231; Haile 1998: 266.

7. That person was the half-European Wiccocomico guide, Mosco: J. Smith 1986c [1624]: 175; Haile 1998: 272. Since no words from the Piedmont people's language were recorded, scholars are uncertain what language family they belonged to; their neighbors in the Carolina Piedmont, however, were Siouan-speakers.

8. Rountree 1993: 50–51.

9. Barbour 1971: 287. In the 1580s records, the spelling is always a variant of "Chesapi-ock," with "-ock" or "-uck" being a Virginia Algonquian ending meaning "people."

10. Lewis and Loomie 1953. Blair A. Rudes (personal communication to the authors, 2004) suggests that this is a variant of *yeehawkawn,* the Powhatan word for "house." The Powhatan name for their country was Tsenacomoco (Strachey 1953 [1612]: 37; Haile 1998: 598), the ending "-comoco" meaning "place." The name probably translates to a full sentence: "it is a nearby dwelling-place" (James A. Geary, appendix B to Strachey 1953 [1612]: 211), or more colloquially, "our place." For other attempts at translation, see Barbour 1971; Rountree 1989: 9–12; and Tooker 1893, 1894a and 1894b, 1895, 1904a and 1904b, 1905, 1906.

11. A "blond" boy seen at an Appamattuck town in May 1607 (Percy 1969 [1608?]: 140; Haile 1998: 96) and the heavily bearded Wiccocomico man Mosco that John Smith met in the summer of 1608 (see chap. 4; J. Smith 1986c [1624]: 173; Haile 1998: 269). The former may have been a child of a "lost colonist," while Mosco was perhaps a by-blow of a Spanish expedition of 1588, rather than the "Frenchman's son" Smith took him to be.

12. Archer 1969a [1607]: 102–3; Haile 1998: 122–23; J. Smith 1986b [1612]: 160; J. Smith 1986c [1624]: 114–15; Strachey 1953 [1612]: 70–71; Haile 1998: 122–23 (Archer), 629–30 (Strachey); A. White 1910 [1634]: 42–43; Anonymous 1910 [1635]: 86.

13. Hairstyles: Archer 1969a [1607]: 94; Percy 1969 [1608?]: 142; Strachey 1953 [1612]: 57; Haile 1998: 114, 97–98, 615 [Strachey on Powhatan]; A. White 1910 [1634]: 43. Tattooing: Strachey 1953 [1612]: 73; Haile 1998: 631. Beards allowed to grow: A. White 1910 [1634]: 42–43; never going bald: Anonymous 1910 [1635]: 86. Tooth loss is corroborated by archaeologically excavated skeletons.

14. Archer 1969a [1607]: 103; Percy 1969 [1608?]: 136; J. Smith 1986b [1612]: 160–61; Strachey 1953 [1612]: 71 Haile 1998: 122, 92, 630; A. White 1910 [1634]: 43; Anonymous 1910 [1635]: 87.

15. J. Smith 1986b [1612]: 162; Strachey 1953 [1612]: 113; Haile 1998: 671.

16. Leanness: part of fitness, mentioned by J. Smith 1986b [1612]: 160; copied in Strachey 1953 [1612]: 74; Haile 1998: 632. Speed: Archer 1969a [1607]: 103; Haile 1998: 123; Kingsbury 1906–35: 4: 10.

17. A biological anthropologist who has examined many native women's skeletons from that time once remarked that the bones were "more robust" (denser, and with higher ridges for muscle attachment) than the bones of most modern males (Dr. Donna Boyd, personal communication to Helen Rountree, 1995).

18. J. Smith 1986a [1608]: 160; Anonymous 1910 [1635]: 83.

19. J. Smith 1986b [1612]: 150, 160; Strachey 1953 [1612]: 49; Haile 1998: 608.

20. Jennings 1978: 363.

21. Powhatan's bodyguards: J. Smith 1986b [1612]: 173; Strachey 1953 [1612]: 59; Haile 1998: 617. Face-off engraving: printed in J. Smith 1986c: 98. Variations: Smith 1986b [1612]: 149–50; Strachey 1953 [1612]: 49; Haile 1998: 608. Maryland and Virginia archaeological evidence compared with seventeenth-century London: Ubelaker 1993: 72 (this source gives references to specific studies).

22. J. Smith 1986b [1612]: 162–63; Strachey 1953 [1612]: 80; Haile 1998: 637. It is uncertain whether the Piedmont Siouan speakers relied as much on gardening as the Powhatans did;

if they did not, then foraging year-round (without a "fat" period at harvest time) may have caused somewhat less annual variation in body weight.

23. Dr. Mary C. Rountree (nutritionist at Riverside Regional Medical Center, Newport News, Virginia), personal communication to Helen Rountree.

24. J. Smith 1986b [1612]: 147, 153, 155–56, 162–64; Strachey 1953 [1612]: 79–80; Haile 1998: 636–37; with additions found only in Strachey 1953 [1612]: 121, 127; Haile 1998: 678, 684; Jesuit Letters 1910: 129.

25. The figure of 1,100-plus native species is the estimate Helen Rountree arrived at after several years of compiling data from books, botanical manuals, and atlases on edible plants. For a list of the most important plants, see appendix C in Rountree and Davidson 1997.

26. This word appears in Strachey's dictionary as "suttekapacatuwh," which may be closer to the Powhatan pronunciation (Strachey 1953 [1612]: 202). John Smith's version for this and the other seasons are arbitrarily used here due to their somewhat easier pronunciation by English speakers.

27. Based on timing of activities listed in J. Smith 1986b [1612]: 147, 153, 155–57, 158–59, 162–63; Strachey 1953 [1612]: 79, 80, 121, 124, 127; Haile 1998: 636, 637, 678, 680, 684.

28. Epidemic of 1617: Kingsbury 1906–35: 3: 92. Bloody flux: McIlwaine 1915: 1: 28; Haile 1998: 905. John Smith wrote of some kind of infectious disease attacking the Accomacs before 1608, but the initial deaths were of two children, and the disease spread only after the bodies were exhumed (J. Smith 1986b [1612]: 163; J. Smith 1986c [1624]: 163; Haile 1998: 255). Powhatan's statement about seeing "the death of all my people thrice" may have referred to major attacks on his hometown near the falls of the James (J. Smith 1986b [1612]: 247; J. Smith 1986c [1624]: 196; Haile 1998: 299; Rountree 2005: 42). Lack of archaeological evidence of other epidemics: Turner 1985: 212; Rountree and Turner 2002: 32. By 1698, Hugh Jones of Calvert County, Maryland, reported, "The small pox also has swept away a great many, so that they are dwindled almost to nothing" (Kammen 1963: 91).

29. Ubelaker 1993: 57, 67–69; Ubelaker and Curtin 2001: 131. While true for the Algonquian people, the Iroquoian-speaking people in the interior lived in larger villages. These included the Susquehannocks at the head of the bay and the Massawomecks in the upper drainages of the Potomac River (see chap. 8).

30. Fewer people: J. Smith 1986b [1612]: 160; Strachey 1953 [1612]: 116; Haile 1998: 673–74. Estimates: J. Smith 1986b [1612]: 160; Fleet 1876 [1631–32]: 25–26.

31. J. Smith 1986b [1612]: 146–50; Strachey 1953 [1612]: 45–46, 49, 64–69; Haile 1998: 605–6, 608, 621–28.

32. Rountree 1996.

33. Gallivan 2003: 28, 34, 70–73.

34. Serious doubt has been cast on New England Indians' use of fish for fertilizer, since it has been shown that Squanto spent time in England (where fertilizer was used) before returning to America and greeting the Pilgrims (Ceci 1975a and 1975b).

35. Exceptions to this model are the semipermanent, multiple palisaded villages of the Piscataway and Patawomeck chiefdoms on the freshwater tidal Potomac River. The Potomac Creek and the Accokeek Creek sites have multiple palisade lines and other evidence that suggests occupations lasting from 100 to 150 years (Blanton, Pullins, and Deitrick 1998: 91–97; Stephenson and Ferguson 1963: 38–39).

36. Indications of name changes with movements come from the later records in both Virginia and Maryland: e.g., Machodoc (formerly Onawmanient) in Virginia and Mattawoman (formerly Nussamek) in Maryland. Towns that were not permanent usually lacked cemeteries that saw long-term use. The dead, however, were always given a respectful ceremonial burial. Archaeologists have found evidence of several practices in the Chesapeake region, no one of them predominating in a given area. Many native people were buried immediately after death, either in a flexed position or laid out, among the houses of their kinsmen. Many bodies were kept aboveground, presumably in some kind of charnel house, until (ideally) only bones were left. Every few years the residents of some localities would hold a community interment, probably with elaborate ceremony: clean bones would be bundled, and still decomposing bodies would be wrapped, and everything would be placed in a large hole—located either inside or outside of the town—and covered over. These ossuaries, which contain from a few to hundreds of human remains, are biological anthropologists' best source of data on average height, longevity, health status, and other physical attributes of people from all over the Chesapeake region (For Maryland: Ubelaker 1974; Curry 1999. For Virginia: Potter 1993: 210–23; Stewart 1992; Turner 1992: 118–19). On the other hand, the bodies of chiefs, among the Powhatans at least, were not buried at all. Their mummified remains were wrapped and placed in temples, where they stayed until those sapling-and-mat buildings were abandoned and left to fall down. Burials other than ossuaries: J. Smith 1986a [1608]: 59; J. Smith 1986b [1612]: 169, 225; Percy 1921–22 [1612]: 263; Spelman 1910 [1613?]: cx; Strachey 1953 [1612]: 94–95; Haile 1998: 164, 255, 501, 491, 651–52. The Maryland accounts (Anonymous 1910 [1635]: 85, 90; J. Smith 1986c [1624]: 289) mention "burial" without details. That is what likely happened to the body of the great Powhatan himself; there was a "taking up of Powhatan's bones" (from the drying-out place, to move them into the temple) in 1621 (Kingsbury 1906–35: 4: 10. The bone bundle was presumably deposited in a temple, logically the holiest one at Uttamussak near modern West Point, Virginia).

37. Archer 1969a [1607]: 103; Haile 1998: 123.

38. Alfred Crosby, personal communication to Helen Rountree, 1991. The same cannot be said for the Iroquoian-speaking people, who achieved a considerable military advantage over their Algonquian rivals by consolidating their settlements into large fortified villages numbering from one thousand to seven thousand people (Kent 1984: 36–37; Pendergast 1991: 16).

39. In this volume, the spelling of settlements' names follows Edward Haile's two maps (1995, 1996), while the spelling of district/chiefdom names follows Rountree 1993.

40. Powhatans: J. Smith 1986 [1612]: 147, 173, Strachey 1953 [1612]: 44, Haile 1998: 603–4. Piscataways: Jesuit Letters 1910 [1639]: 125. Nanticokes: inferred from the Smith map, which lacks "kings houses" on rivers south of the Nanticoke, although later Maryland records show the Wicomico and Manokin rivers to have been inhabited (Rountree and Davidson 1997: 85). Assateagues: the Treaty of 1678 between Maryland and the paramount chief "emperor" of the Assateagues lists a number of weroances ("kings") representing the Pocomokes, Chincoteagues, Nassawangos (Nuswaddox), Annamessexes, Acquinticas and Marumscos (Browne et al. 1883–1972: 15: 213–15).

41. First suggested in Clark and Rountree 1993: 133–35.

42. Browne et al. 1883–1972: 3: 403.

43. J. Smith 1986b [1612]: 147.

44. Strachey 1953 [1612]: 56; Haile 1998: 614.

45. Jesuit Letters 1910 [1639]: 124.

46. Speck 1927: 49.

47. J. Smith 1986a [1608]: 59, 61; J. Smith 1986b [1612]: 174, 247; Strachey 1953 [1612]: 44, 77; Haile 1998: 164, 299, 604, 634; Anonymous 1910 [1635]: 84; Browne et al. 1882–1972: 3: 403.

48. Juan de la Carrera, in Lewis and Loomie 1953: 134; Archer 1969a [1607]: 104; J. Smith 1986a [1608]: 53; J. Smith 1986b [1612]: 174; Spelman 1910 [1613?]: cvii–cviii; Strachey 1953 [1612]: 61–62; Haile 1998: 123, 160, 488–89, 618–20; A. White 1910 [1634]: 44; Anonymous 1910 [1635]: 85; Jesuit Letters 1910 [1639]: 127.

49. Life and death: J. Smith 1986b [1612]: 174; Strachey 1953 [1612]: 59–60; Haile 1998: 617. Couldn't control: Strachey 1953 [1612]: 58; Haile 1998: 616.

50. Stolen wife: Strachey 1953 [1612]: 64–65; Haile 1998: 622. Bereaved father: J. Smith 1986a [1608]: 49; Haile 1998: 159.

51. Anonymous 1910 [1635]: 84, 86, 87.

52. Archer 1969a [1607]: 103 (living in "families of kindred and alliance"); Strachey 1953 [1612]: 113–14 (child-rearing done by parents), 116 (care of the elderly); Haile 1998: 123, 670–71, 673.

53. For the limited details available on deities, priests, temples, and rituals, see: J. Smith 1986b [1612]: 169–79; Spelman 1910 [1613?]: cv; Haile 1998: 486; Strachey 1953 [1612]: 62, 88–90, 94–96, 102–3; Haile 1998: 620, 645–47, 651–53, 659, 661; A. White 1910 [1634]: 44–45; Jesuit Letters 1910 [1639]: 130.

54. Strachey 1953 [1612]: 76–77, 88, 95; Haile 1998: 123, 670–71, 673.

55. Percy 1969 [1608?]: 141–42; J. Smith 1986b [1612]: 162; Strachey 1953 [1612]: 81; Haile 1998: 97, 638.

56. Bartolomé Martínez, in Lewis and Loomie 1953: 161 (every summer); Archer 1969a [1607]: 88 (every autumn); Strachey 1953 [1612]: 35; Haile 1998: 109, 596–97. Alliance against English: Strachey 1953 [1612]: 106 ("now the general cause hath united them"); Haile 1998: 663.

57. Professionalism: J. Smith 1986b [1612]: 164; Strachey 1953 [1612]: 83–84; Haile 1998: 640–41. Boys trained as hunters: Strachey 1953 [1612]: 113; Haile 1998: 671. Fate of captives: J. Smith 1986b [1612]: 166, 175; Strachey 1953 [1612]: 60, 109; Haile 1998: 617, 667. It is worth noting that Europeans likewise were not treating either captives or criminals gently in those times.

58. Hatchets: J. Smith 1986b [1612]: 232; canoes: J. Smith 1986b [1612]: 166; Strachey 1953 [1612]: 108; Haile 1998: 666; Fleet 1876 [1631–32]: 26.

59. J. Smith 1986b [1612]: 163; Strachey 1953 [1612]: 109, 115; Haile 1998: 633–34, 667.

60. Shovels: Spelman 1910 [1613?]: cxi; spades: Strachey 1953 [1612]: 75; Haile 1998: 492, 633–34.

61. Hariot 1972 [1590]: 67.

62. J. Smith 1986b [1612]: 150, 271; copied in Strachey 1953 [1612]: 49 (Tockwogh only); Haile 1998: 608.

63. Great Neck: Hodges 1998. Accokeek Creek: Stephenson and Ferguson 1963. Pata-womeke: Schmitt 1965; Blanton et al. 1999. Buck: McCary and Barka 1977: 83; Turner 1992: 108; Norman Barka, personal communication to Turner in 1974. Cumberland: C. Williams 1983: 15; Clark and Hughes 1983: 8.

64. Specifically, "native" copper, which in the Great Lakes region occurs in small quantities in nearly pure form, so that it can be cold-hammered into jewelry.

65. Marine shells: Beverley 1947 [1705]: 227. Nanticokes/Kuskarawaoks: J. Smith 1986c [1624]: 165. Puccoon: Harvill et al. 1992: 64; Radford, Ahles, and Bell 1968: 882. "Anoeg" middlemen: Strachey 1953 [1612]: 56–57; Haile 1998: 614. The Anoegs were probably the Enoes, whose linguistic identity is currently uncertain (Blair A. Rudes, personal communication to the authors).

66. English explorers encountered people in Arrohateck territory, paddling upstream with "baskets full of dried oysters" presumably used in trade (Archer 1969a [1607]: 83; Haile 1998: 103).

67. Kecoughtans having large fields: Strachey 1953 [1612]: 67; Haile 1998: 626. Accomacs raising corn to last year-round, and relying on fish and fowl: John Pory, in J. Smith 1986c [1624]: 290–91. Arrohatecks involved in trade of dried oysters: Archer 1969a [1607]: 83–84; Haile 1998: 103–4. Cakes of deer suet offered as sacrifice: J. Smith 1986a [1608]: 59; cakes of it traded to English: Strachey 1953 [1612]: 115; suet on bread: J. Smith 1986b [1612]: 153, Strachey 1953 [1612]: 120; Haile 1998: 673, 677.

68. Strachey 1953 [1612]: 115; Haile 1998: 673.

69. Henry Ford's cars were only part of the reason for a major change to land transportation; the rest was highway building and the paving of a great many county roads by FDR's Civilian Conservation Corps. Before that, the region's waterways bristled with wharves.

70. Maximum people: J. Smith 1986b [1612]: 163; Strachey 1953 [1612]: 82; Haile 1998: 639. Camping gear: J. Smith 1986a [1608]: 73; Haile 1998: 170. Canoe measured: Percy 1969 [1608?]: 134; Haile 1998: 90. Usual size and speed: Strachey 1953 [1612]: 82.

71. Hariot 1972 [1590]: 55; J. Smith 1986b [1612]: 163; copied in Strachey 1953 [1612]: 82; Spelman 1910 [1613?] cxiv; Haile 1998: 494, 638–39.

72. Illustrated in Beverley 1947 [1705]: 172. This practice may sound cruel to some readers, but to the babies it quickly comes to mean security. Modern on-the-go American parents have rediscovered the practice, though nowadays the babies are carried in front—since said parents are not weeding gardens or gathering firewood with baby aboard.

73. The description of Spanish moss by Norwood (1947 [1650]: 35–36) is unmistakable, and he was writing of the Kegotank area in northeastern Accomack County, Virginia (a fairly cool place for half the year). Today that warm-climate species fades out one hundred miles (160 kilometers) south (Virginia Beach city, Chesapeake city, Isle of Wight Co., Hampton city, Northampton Co.; Harvill et al. 1992: 7).

74. J. Smith 1986b [1612]: 163–64; Strachey 1953 [1612]: 75, 82; Haile 1998: 633, 639.

75. Little was recorded about the matter. Identification of plants comes from bioarchaeological sources and (for Indian hemp) the common name for it; Helen Rountree learned the optimum time of gathering the hard way (she encourages Indian hemp plants on the family farm by calculated mowing and harvests it for Jamestown Settlement's Indian Village).

76. Men probably helped during a time crunch. But John Smith was definite about all jobs other than hunting and war being primarily female ones (1986b [1612]: 162). Helen Rountree knows from participating in both house building and digging tuckahoe (arrow arum) roots that most tasks in the former are less strenuous than the latter.

77. Hancock and Rountree 2004.

78. William Sipple, personal communication to Helen Rountree, 2004. The species include: giant cane (*Arundinaria gigantea*; freshwater; common in the southeastern part of the Chesapeake region; tough enough to be made into a cutting tool [Kent Mountford ex-

periment, 2004]); reedgrass (*Phragmites australis;* fresh and oligohaline water; also usable for arrows [Kent Mountford experiment, 2004]); *Bulbostylis* (formerly *Scirpus*) *fluviatilis* (river bulrush; freshwater) and *B. robustus* (saltmarsh bulrush; brackish water); *Schoeno-plectus* (formerly *Scirpus*) *acutus* (hardstem bulrush; fresh or brackish water); *S. americanus* (common three-square; fresh to moderately brackish water); *S. pungens* (formerly *Scirpus olneyi;* Olney three-square; brackish water); *S. tabernaemontana* (formerly *Scirpus validus;* softstem or giant bulrush; uncommon in the region; fresh or brackish water); *Spartina alter-niflora* (saltmarsh or smooth cordgrass; prefers brackish water but will grow in freshwater) and *S. cynosuroides* (giant cordgrass (brackish and salt water); *Typha angustifolia* (narrow-leaved cattail; fresh or slightly brackish water) and *T. latifolia* (broad-leaved cattail; fresh or slightly brackish water).

79. J. Smith 1986b [1612]: 164; Spelman 1910 [1613?]: cvii; Strachey 1953 [1612]: 83; Haile 1998: 487–88, 639. Time to build: Strachey.

80. The soils were Pamunkey and Wickham loams and fine, sandy loams.

81. The best such soils are those classified variously as State, Matapeake, Sassafras, etc. (With the revision of 1950s and 1960s surveys, some of the names and mapped soil units are changing, but the areas with the best corn-growing soils remain the same.) The USDA Soil Surveys list some high-water-table "cold" soils such as Mattapex as prime corn-grow-ing soils today, but they probably were not so in the eyes of Native American women who wanted to get the year's first field planted in late March. Corn requires a certain amount of rainfall throughout its (minimum) 120-day growing season; in a dry late-summer, that first-planted field might be the only one to produce even seed corn for the next year.

82. The term is usually translated "wild rice," which grows in the Chesapeake region's freshwater marshes. But Frank Siebert's study of many Algonquian languages indicates that the word could be used more inclusively for the grains of other stiff-stalked grasses (Siebert 1975: 414–15). Grains from little barley have been found in numerous Middle and Late Woodland archaeological sites in the eastern United States, including an excavated Early Contact period Paspahegh village in James City Co., Virginia (Gardner 1994: 268). Gardner calls the plant a cultigen, but John Smith got the impression that it was wild (1986b [1612]: 153; 1986c [1624]: 109; copied in Strachey 1953 [1612]: ; Haile 1998: 678). It grows wild today in most parts of the Chesapeake region, especially the coastal plain.

83. For a detailed list by ecozone of edible and medicinal plants probably used by the Chesapeake region's native people, see Rountree and Davidson 1997: appendix C (focuses on the Eastern Shore but is usable for much of the mainland as well).

84. Beverley 1947 [1705]: 148; his wording is "the depth of eight or ten foot [2.5–3.5 me-ters]." Normal tidal amplitude in the lower bay varies between about 2½ and 4 feet (about 0.75–1.2 meters), depending on the phase of the moon; that means a maximum depth at mean low water of 6 feet (1.83 meters).

85. Diving for mussels: Archer 1969a [1607]: 92; Haile 1998: 113.

86. Two Late Woodland period Potomac Creek phase sites are situated above the bay beaches, with grand views of the bay, as noted by Wayne Clark for the northern section of Calvert Cliffs.

87. J. Smith 1986b [1612]: 162; copied in Strachey 1953 [1612]: 79; Haile 1998: 636.

88. Donna Boyd, personal communication to Helen Rountree, 1995.

89. Ubelaker 1993: 64–65. He was writing here of his own thorough study of two Nanje-

moy ossuaries: after a 30 percent infant mortality, people who lived to be fifteen years old could expect to live about another twenty years; only 2–3 percent of the population survived beyond age fifty. Note on so few living beyond fifty: before penicillin was discovered in the 1940s, the survival percentages for Virginians of all ethnicities were not a great deal higher (see the U.S. Census schedules); 150 years ago, before antiseptic childbirth practices were instituted, the percentage was about the same as for prehistoric Native Americans.

90. J. Smith 1986b [1612]: 169; closely paraphrased in Strachey 1953 [1612]: 88; Haile 1998:645. Henry Spelman wrote that rituals were performed not on a schedule but "upon necessity" (1910 [1613?]: cv; seconded by Strachey: 1953 [1612]: 96; Haile 1998: 486, 653).

91. Archer 1969a [1607]: 104; Percy 1969 [1608?]: 143, 145–46; Strachey 1953 [1612]: 97–98; Haile 1998: 123, 98–99, 141, 654–55; Anonymous 1910 [1635]: 88.

92. Strachey 1953 [1612]: 97; Haile 1998: 654.

93. J. Smith 1986b [1612]: 170; J. Smith 1986c [1624]:123; Strachey 1953 [1612]: 96; Haile 1998: 653; brackets ours.

3. Englishmen in the Chesapeake

1. Ferrar Papers, reel 2, item 364 (unpublished at this writing).

2. Quinn 1955.

3. Bridenbaugh 1967; Cressy 1997; Laslett 1984 [1965]; Morrill 1996; Palliser 1983; Sharpe 1987; Stone 1965 and 1977; Youings 1984.

4. Interestingly, John Smith wanted the first, advancement, but seems not to have been interested in the second. He is not known ever to have had even a girlfriend.

5. "Fostering out": Stone 1977: 106–7. Common in 1500: Sneyd 1847: 24–26. Indian response: Rountree 1990: 69, 70, 136–37, 168.

6. "Letters Patent and Instructions for Governments" in Barbour 1969: 24–44.

7. Strachey reported in 1610 that the newly rebuilt fort included houses covered with bark instead of clay daub, for better weatherproofing and summertime temperature control, a technique learned from the native people (1964 [1610]: 81–82; Haile 1998: 430). Evidence of such houses has been found archaeologically: Kelso and Straube 2004: 51.

8. An especially telling example of the latter occurred in September 1607, when the native people still hoped to make allies of the English. The Quiyoughcohannocks kept their promise of sharing their corn crop when it came in, but George Percy wrote: "It pleased God . . . to send those people which were our mortal enemies to relieve us with victuals" (1969 [1608?]: 145; Haile 1998: 100). John Smith was only a little less suspicious: "it pleased God (in our extremity) to move the Indians to bring us corn" (1986a [1608]: 35; Haile 1998: 148).

9. J. Smith 1986b [1612]: 213; J. Smith 1986c [1624]: 263; Haile 1998: 320.

10. Earle 1979.

11. Smith 1986b [1612]: 263; J. Smith 1986c [1624]: 212; Haile 1998: 319.

12. Not only that but a 1512 entry in the account books of George Percy's ancestors, the Earl and Countess of Northumberland, shows that at breakfast they shared a quart of ale and a quart of wine, while their children, aged eight and ten, shared a quart of ale (Meacham 2003: 119–20). Alcoholic beverages were often safer than the local water supply, and they had become ingrained in the lifeways of those who could afford them.

13. John Smith's 1608 letter (the "True Relation") shows it best; his later accounts say less about it.

14. J. Smith 1986a [1608]: 33; Haile 1998: 147.

15. J. Smith 1986b [1612]: 214–15; Smith 1986c [1624]: 153–54; Haile 1998: 242–43.

16. J. Smith 1986b [1612]: 233; J. Smith 1986c [1624]: 180; Haile 1998: 278.

17. Departure and assembling money for supplies: Strachey 1964 [1610]: 4, 100; Haile 1998: 384, 442. John Smith (1986b [1612]: 268; J. Smith 1986c [1624]: 218; Haile 1998: 327) places the departure in May 1609, but Strachey was actually aboard one of the departing ships. 1609 arrivals: Archer 1969b [1609]: 281; Haile 1998: 351. 1610 arrival and stopping the evacuation: J. Smith 1986b [1612]: 276–77; J. Smith 1986c [1624]: 234–35; Haile 1998: 341.

18. Boyd 1990: 16; "pathology" includes dental problems.

19. Owsley and Compton 1992: 35–37.

20. As evidence of both the death rate and the survivors' despair, archaeologists have found quantities of armor—helmets, chain mail, and breastplates—thrown onto trash heaps at Jamestown Fort, Martin's Hundred, Flowerdew Hundred, and Jordan's Journey.

21. Eric A. Speth, captain of the *Godspeed* and maritime program manager at Jamestown Settlement, personal communication to Helen Rountree, 2004.

22. The first detailed, truly architectural drawings we have of watercraft come from late seventeenth-century Holland: e.g., Ralamb 1943 [1691].

23. Thomas E. Davidson, personal communication to Helen Rountree, 2004. The "new" ships are to be in place by the 2007 Quadricentennial.

24. Imprecision: Eric A. Speth, personal communication to Helen Rountree, 2004. For modern thinking on the subject of building the large and small craft of that era, see Baker 1987 [1966] and 1983; Bruggerman 1999; Chapelle 1951: chap. 1; Lavery 1988 (section on fittings); and Phillips-Birt 1979 [1951] (section on colonial craft).

25. Haile 1998: 39.

26. The late seventeenth-century Dutch illustrations show a rounded bottom. Probable length and draft, and hull and sail uncertainties: Eric A. Speth, personal communication to Helen Rountree, 2004. Capt. Speth had sailed in the *Mayflower*'s shallop, with a sprit-rigged sail, and he found that boat "very able."

27. Barbour 1986: 1: 211n., citing an article on shallops by William A. Parker (*American Neptune* 17 [1957]: 105–13).

28. With the Second Supply, Capt. Christopher Newport brought "a 5 pieced barge" for the exploring expedition to the Monacan country (J. Smith 1986b [1612]: 234; J. Smith 1986c [1624]: 181; Haile 1998: 279).

29. Eric A. Speth, personal communication to Helen Rountree, 2004.

30. Perreault 2002.

31. These two verses come from the first—and later—of two creation stories in the biblical book of Genesis, probably recorded in the 500s BC under imperial Babylonian influence. The second and earlier story, which immediately follows the first, is probably much older; it lacks a seven-day motif and omits mention of dominion over plants and animals.

32. Printed in numerous places, such as Barbour 1969.

33. Linklater 2003: chaps. 1–3.

34. J. Smith 1986b [1612]: 228; J. Smith 1986b [1624]: 168; Haile 1998: 262.

35. The attack in April 1607, when the English landed and five Indian men assaulted them: when Christopher Newport had the ships guns "second" the Englishmen ashore, the warriors "little respected" the noise and kept on shooting until they ran out of arrows (J. Smith 1986a [1608]: 27; Haile 1998: 145). It is this reaction to English guns that led Rountree (1990: 21, 30) to suggest that those warriors had known and/or heard about the 1585–86 wintering among the Chesapeakes of an English party, whose members were undoubtedly armed.

36. Curious Pamunkeys asked John Smith to shoot his pistol while he was a captive, but by January 1609 the same people were attacking him and his men and only desisting when he held a similar pistol right to Opechancanough's head (J. Smith 1986a [1608]: 51; J. Smith; Haile 1998: 160.

37. There are several mentions of using the noise of firearms to bring the local people to heel as Smith explored around the Chesapeake Bay (e.g., at Kuskarawaok: J. Smith 1986c [1624]: 165; Haile 1998: 256)—but none of these is to be found in the 1612 version.

38. Strachey 1953 [1612]: 109 (distance); Percy 1969 [1608?]: 142 (shield); Haile 1998: 667, 95–96. Speed, specifically without encumbrance of armor: J. Smith 1986c [1624]: 310–11.

39. J. Smith 1986a [1608]: 51; Haile 1998: 160.

40. Calibers and shorter distances: Greg Schneck, armorer at Jamestown Settlement, personal communication to Helen Rountree, 2003. Longer distance for muskets, terminology, and setting-up and loading requirements: Featherstone 1998: 46–47, 59; Peterson 2000 [1956]: 21–22, 43. See also Brown 1980.

41. Morgan 1992: 119–21; Nash 1982: 50.

42. Morgan 1992: 115. Not all of them died there: many people gave up and returned to England.

43. Morgan 1992; Nash 1982; Scisco 1945. Later in the century, incidents of Indians killing English livestock became a frequent source of discord.

4. John Smith's First Voyage up the Chesapeake Bay

1. Scientific categorizing is interpretation of data in an effort to reach the "truth"; historical data are often even harder to categorize. But John Smith's accounts are vague enough, and in places jumbled enough, that this chapter literally represents the authors' thinking at the moment the publisher made them turn it loose.

2. Ultimately all were drawn by John Smith. Smith sent a sketch to England in late 1608, and because it fell into Spanish hands there, it has become known as the "Zuñiga map." Smith's polished version was first published in 1612 and thereafter went through a number of "states" in various publications. The differences between that and the Zuñiga map may or may not have been accurate corrections, since Smith was working from memory after leaving Virginia in late 1609. Therefore modern scholars try to juxtapose data from both maps.

3. Archaeological site data and synthesis also inform this discussion and will be covered in greater detail in the river basin chapters.

4. "Every inlet and bay fit for harbors and habitations," and "what other minerals [besides gold and silver], rivers, rocks, nations, woods, fishings, fruits, victual, and what other commodities the land afforded, and whether the bay were endless or how far it extended" (J.

Smith 1986b [1612]: 225, 227–28; J. Smith 1986c [1624]: 164, 168; Haile 1998: 255, 262; brackets ours).

5. Large enough not only for over a dozen Englishmen and their baggage but also for five Susquehannock leaders and two interpreters to ride with them during the second voyage (see chap. 5). The shallop built in Chestertown is 28 feet long, 7 feet wide, and 4 feet deep (8.5 by 2.1 by 1.2 meters) (John Swain, personal communication to Wayne Clark, 2005).

6. Eric Speth, personal communication to Helen Rountree, 2004.

7. Smith says nothing about what instrument he carried, and the Virginia Company recommended a compass, but he may also have used a pocket-sized quadrant to estimate latitude. Less likely was an astrolabe or cross staff, which was larger and required a carrying case. Smith's longitudes are off by 350 miles (563.2 kilometers) to eastward, his latitudes by only 12 miles (19.3 kilometers)—good work for the time.

8. J. Smith 1986b [1612]: 224; J. Smith 1986c [1624]: 163; Haile 1998: 254.

9. The source of our dates for lunar phases is NASA, which gives dates after 1582 in the modern Gregorian calendar: http://sunearth.gsfc.nasa.gov/eclipse/phase/phasecat.html.

10. The term is not related to the seasons. It means a semimonthly time in the lunar cycle with stronger currents, deeper water at high tide, and shallower water at low tide.

11. Based on 1946–70 averages for Norfolk, Virginia: Munday and Fredosh 1981: 81.

12. Maritime observations in this and the following chapter are by Kent Mountford, based on his decades of sailing experience in the bay and ocean. Additional information from William Gates, captain of the Maryland *Dove*, in 2004.

13. I.e., J. Smith 1986a [1608], his account of his experiences up to that point.

14. J. Smith 1986b [1612]: 224–25; Smith 1986c [1624]: 163–64; Haile 1998: 255.

15. They come in small numbers in March: Hildebrand and Schroeder 1928: 158. Large numbers of them were seen in a single year in the 1930s, however, as far north as Russell's Cliffs in Calvert County, Maryland. And a young cod was caught by a Potomac River net fisherman several years ago (Larry Chowning and A. C. Carpenter, personal communications to Kent Mountford, 2005).

16. Kingfish/whiting and sea trout are superficially similar; the former may spawn in the bay in June (Hildebrand and Schroeder 1928: 156, 290).

17. The precise location of the village is uncertain. Turner and Opperman (forthcoming) place it between Kings and Old Plantation creeks; Barbour (1964: 210) put it a few miles up Cherrystone Inlet. Wayne Clark (a coauthor of this volume) favors a point south of Elliots Creek.

18. Clark suggests an alternative here: that the Occohannocks' village was not on the creek to which they later gave their name, but was instead on the south of Nassawaddox Creek on Wellington Neck—though such a village may only represent that chief's summer fishing camp.

19. J. Smith 1986b [1612]: 225; J. Smith 1986c [1624]: 164; Haile 1998: 255.

20. That boat may have had two sails: a square or sprit-rigged mainsail and, in the bow, a triangular staysail or jib that was hoisted up the forestay. Smith's 1612 version indicates that there were two masts; his 1624 account simply says there was *a* mast.

21. One of the authors (Rountree) remembers seeing a hurricanelike gust in Norfolk in 1978; it was officially clocked at 98 mph.

22. I.e., not taken down.

23. J. Smith 1986b [1612]: 225; J. Smith 1986c [1624]: 164; Haile 1998: 255, 257.

24. J. Smith 1986b [1612]: 150; J. Smith 1986c [1624]: 107; Strachey 1953 [1612]: 49; Haile 1998: 608.

25. Fourteen miles (22.5 kilometers) round-trip overland, twenty-four (39.6) round-trip by water.

26. J. Smith 1986b [1612]: 225; J. Smith 1986c [1624]: 164; Haile 1998: 257.

27. J. Smith 1986b [1612]: 225–26; J. Smith 1986c [1624]: 164; Haile 1998: 257.

28. Ironically, a subsoil aquifer is present on the island, as on many islands and low-lying lands nearby; journalist Tom Horton reported to Kent Mountford that he saw a pipe driven deep into the aquifer on Bloodsworth in the 1990s, which made an artesian spring there. However, those aquifers easily become exhausted and invaded by salty water, as islanders and Eastern Shore residents have long known. When they become polluted by downward-leaching agricultural chemicals or residential septic wastes, the contamination not only affects shallow wells but also flows out to contaminate adjacent estuaries.

29. The Roman Catholic Church formally declared in December 2005 that this concept is inconsistent with Church doctrine. Protestants have long used the word only in a figurative sense.

30. J. Smith 1986b [1612]: 226; J. Smith 1986c [1624]: 164; Haile 1998: 257.

31. J. Smith 1986b [1612]: 226; J. Smith 1986c [1624]: 164–65; Haile 1998: 257–58.

32. J. Smith 1986b [1612]: 226; J. Smith 1986c [1624]: 165; Haile 1998: 258.

33. J. Smith 1986c [1624]: 168; Haile 1998: 261.

34. This conclusion was reached only after lengthy discussion and several field trips. A strong minority opinion favors an exploration of Marshyhope Creek, with Kuskarawaok being located east of modern Hurlock, several miles downstream from the end of exploration near modern Federalsburg.

35. J. Smith 1986b [1612]: 236; J. Smith 1986c [1624]: 183; Haile 1998: 282.

36. J. Smith 1986b [1612]: 226; J. Smith 1986c [1624]: 165; Haile 1998: 258.

37. Inference based upon Smith's mother coming from "the Rickards at great Heck in York-shire" (J. Smith 1986d [1630]: 153.

38. J. Smith 1986b [1612]: 226; J. Smith 1986c [1624]: 165–66; Haile 1998: 259.

39. Kent Mountford, a longtime sailor in these waters, notes that the main stem of the bay tends to channel the winds from the southerly quarters. A typical June day sees a light wind of 1–5 knots (up to 5.7 mph or 9.2 km/hr) blowing in the early morning, then consolidating direction and rising to a south to south-southeast breeze of 15–23 knots (17.3–26.5 mph or 27.8–42.6 km/hr) between 10 a.m. and 4 p.m., after which it drops to 6–11 knots (6.9–12.7 mph or 11.1–20.4 km/hr) as solar heating decreases. All that was helpful for people heading north; unless the crew rowed, however, a barge trying to go south would make no progress when opposed even by light southerly winds plus a flood tide.

40. J. Smith 1986b [1612]: 226–27; J. Smith 1986c [1624]: 165–66; Haile 1998: 259–60. Brackets in the quotation are ours.

41. Extensive silting in the last two centuries has ruined what used to be a port for ocean-going vessels. An estimated fifty feet (15.2 meters) of mud and silt was said to accumulate there every ten years in the 1920s, and at times it was flushed with hydraulic water cannon.

42. J. Smith 1986b [1612]: 226–27; J. Smith 1986c [1624]: 166; Haile 1998: 259–60; brackets ours.

43. J. Smith 1986b [1612]: 226–27; J. Smith 1986c [1624]: 165–66; Haile 1998: 259–60.

44. While June nor'easters are uncommon, similar storms are often seen in late spring today.

45. J. Smith 1986b [1612]: 227; J. Smith 1986c [1624]: 166–67; Haile 1998: 260.

46. J. Smith 1986b [1612]: 227; J. Smith 1986c [1624]: 166–67; Haile 1998: 260.

47. This group, ironically, is one of the best known in the Potomac River valley, thanks to the work of Stephen Potter (1982, 1993). For details on them and their neighbors, see chap. 12.

48. J. Smith 1986b [1612]: 227–28; J. Smith 1986c [1624]: 167–68, 173; Haile 1998: 260–62, 269. Smith was a soldier, not a sailor. Robert Juet's journal for Henry Hudson's voyage gives the sail changes and winds as well, making it occasionally possible to plot his courses from day to day.

49. J. Smith 1986b [1612]: 227; J. Smith 1986c [1624]: 167; Haile 1998: 260.

50. Native American beards were skimpy enough that complete plucking out was the fashion without being very time-consuming.

51. Nancy O. Lurie, personal communications to Helen Rountree, 1971 and 2006. A prime example of such teasing is Matoaka's nickname, "Pocahontas." Probably bestowed on her by her busy father, whose attention she was trying to get by playing court jester, it means "little wanton" (Strachey 1953 [1612]: 113; Haile 1998: 671); in modern terms, he was retorting, "you cruel, bawdy, undisciplined little girl!" (Rountree 2005: 38).

52. J. Smith 1986c [1624]: 173; Haile 1998: 269. Smith, unaware of the movements of the Spanish in the Chesapeake in 1588, supposed Mosco to be "some Frenchman's son."

53. J. Smith 1986b [1612]: 227; J. Smith 1986c [1624]: 167; Haile 1998: 260–61.

54. He is known to have gone to visit them in his last years (Kingsbury 1906–35: 3: 73–74), and he is also known to have been reluctant to leave his dominions.

55. J. Smith 1986b [1612]: 227–28; J. Smith 1986c [1624]: 167–68, 173; Haile 1998: 261–62, 269.

56. This region is in today's Eastern Piedmont province, in an area underlain by mica schist, gneiss, and granite. More important, the Aquia Creek drainage from the fall line to its head is along the northern exposure of a hornblende gabbro and gneiss formation. This is the closest formation of talc or soapstone deposits to the tidal Potomac. Minerals found here include talc, amphibole, chlorite schist, chloritic hornblende gneiss and some amphibolite, choritic diorite, and hornblende diorite, kyanite schist, and kyanite quartzite (Calver and Hobbs 1963). "Sparks" Valley could refer to the talc, antimony, or mica deposits found in these deposits. But the metal being mined would not be chrome as chrome is black in its natural state; also chrome was later mined elsewhere, at the Soldier's Delight serpentine barren on the Patapsco River, Maryland (Volks and Edwards 1974: 115). Edward Haile, after consulting with John Haynes, archaeologist at Quantico Marine Base, suggests that it could have been a graphitic slate, which is found on Beaverdam Creek at and just above its junction with Aquia Creek. For now, the metal Smith sought remains a mystery. Additional field research is needed in possible areas of the quarry, assuming the quarry location has survived modern suburban sprawl.

57. This name may have been a joke made by someone with a classical education. Democritus (ca. 470–360 BC) was known as the "laughing philosopher" because of his amusement with human foibles. The namer of the tree may have been thinking along the lines of "we're fools to look for mines around here!"

58. The James Fort excavations have revealed scores of fishhooks in varying sizes (Kelso

and Straub 2004). Profit, whatever his experience, would have had none of the Chesapeake habitat knowledge necessary to catch enough to feed fifteen men during the voyage.

59. Barbour 1971: 286, 293 in Potter 1993: 153.

60. J. Smith 1986b [1612]: 228; J. Smith 1986c [1624]: 168; Haile 1998: 262.

61. J. Smith 1986b [1612]: 228–29; J. Smith 1986c [1624]: 168; Haile 1998: 262–63.

62. A friend of Kent Mountford went through this experience not many years ago. With labored breathing he could have died before reaching a hospital.

63. J. Smith 1986b [1612]: 229; J. Smith 1986c [1624]: 169; Haile 1998: 263.

64. Slang expression used by modern Indian people in Virginia and elsewhere, meaning information spreading by whatever method.

65. J. Smith 1986b [1612]: 229; J. Smith 1986c [1624]: 169; Haile 1998: 263.

66. J. Smith 1986b [1612]: 229; J. Smith 1986c [1624]: 169; Haile 1998: 263. Harland (1984: 199–201) has reconstructed in detail how it can be done.

67. These had apparently been packed into the barge from the beginning, possibly to be able to disguise their barge as "friendly" in case Spanish military vessels caught them out in the bay.

5. John Smith's Second Voyage up the Chesapeake Bay

1. Even scientific data must be interpreted. John Smith's accounts of his voyages (which are all we have) are sufficiently obscure that this chapter does not represent the authors' "permanent" thinking, but rather their considered opinions as of this writing.

2. J. Smith 1986b [1612]: 229; J. Smith 1986c [1624]: 169; Haile 1998: 263–64. Smith may have left some of his crewmen behind in Jamestown simply because they were healthy, at a time when so many men in the fort were undernourished. A comparison of the lists of crew members in the boxes in this chapter and chapter 4 reveals that the skills of the crews on the two voyages were roughly the same, except that there was no blacksmith on the second voyage.

3. J. Smith 1986b [1612]: 230; J. Smith 1986c [1624]: 170; Haile 1998: 264.

4. Smith 1986b [1612]: 230; Smith 1986c [1624]: 170; Haile 1998: 265.

5. Winds in the region tend to "clock," or change direction around the compass points in succession. Thus the wind would probably become westerly and then southerly, as post-nor'easter warming occurred and the heated land drew a "sea breeze" up the bay.

6. J. Smith 1986b [1612]: 230; J. Smith 1986c [1624]: 170; Haile 1998: 265.

7. The flow of wind calms as the highest barometer readings are reached deep in the high pressure area. The wind not only dropped but may also have backed (i.e., shifted counterclockwise) to the southwest or south.

8. J. Smith 1986b [1612]: 230; J. Smith 1986c [1624]: 170; Haile 1998: 265.

9. Smith's map clearly shows Bodkin Neck and Bodkin Creek as well as the wide Old Road Bay.

10. There are several artesian springs along the west shore of Bodkin Creek (Kim Nielsen, director of U.S. Navy Museum, personal communication to Kent Mountford, 2005).

11. J. Smith 1986b [1612]: 230–31; J. Smith 1986c [1624]: 170–71; Haile 1998: 265–66.

12. Kent Mountford is uncertain how the shallows around the Susquehanna's mouth were configured in 1608.

13. The direction and the order of rivers visited are vague in Smith's account.

14. Smith makes that connection between bark canoes and the Massawomecks elsewhere: J. Smith 1986b [1612]: 166; J. Smith 1986c [1624]: 119; Strachey 1953 [1612]: 108; Haile 1998: 666. Seconded in Fleet 1876 [1631–32]: 26. The bark canoes are, in turn, evidence for a relatively calm day at the head of the bay.

15. J. Smith 1986c [1624]: 172; Haile 1998: 268. Smith added this in 1624, so his memory may not be accurate. If they ascended that river, it was to take cover, for the river would not have been a major route back to their homeland.

16. J. Smith 1986b [1612]: 231; J. Smith 1986c [1624]: 171; Haile 1998: 266.

17. The Tockwoghs were Algonquian speakers, as far as we know. But their distance from the James and York rivers would at the least have meant dialectal differences too great for mutual comprehension with the people on those rivers. It is also quite possible that the Tockwoghs spoke an Algonquian language closer to Leni Lenape of Delaware Bay, which differed significantly from the subfamily of Algonquian languages spoken along the Chesapeake Bay.

18. J. Smith 1986b [1612]: 231–32; J. Smith 1986c [1624]: 171–72; Haile 1998: 266–68.

19. In 1634, Cyprian Thorowgood met with the Susquehannocks at Palmer's Island and noted "this nation is vary valourous and stout people living in pallizaded townes about 40 miles [64 kilometers] from this land, they are commonly 2 daies in going home in their canowes but can come downe in halfe a day because of many falls which as [sic] in the river": Thorowgood (1634, in Dillow 1984: 202).

20. When Thorowgood (in Dillow 1984: 203) explored eight miles (12.9 kilometers) up the Big Elk Creek, he noted the high hills on both sides: plentiful deer, turkeys, and elk (thus the river's name); Indian beaver traps; and "one quarteringe house, where the Indians use to bee in time of hunting." The bottom of the creek itself was yellow gravel in those days. Modern NOAA charts show that estuary filled for at least a mile and a half (2.5 kilometers) downstream with eroded farmland soils, deposited over the last 370 years.

21. All activities at the Susquehannock village are educated guesswork; Smith says nothing about them.

22. Strachey (1953 [1612]: 48; Haile 1998: 607) added "swords" (war clubs) and "beads" of uncertain composition.

23. The Book of Common Prayer in the Anglican Communion's churches still has Morning Prayer and Evening Prayer services in it; the evening one, when entirely sung/chanted, is called Evensong.

24. The chants, still sung in some parishes in the Anglican Communion, would have been "lined out" in those days: the leader, a person able to read the Bible, sang a verse and the others repeated it, then the leader sang another verse, and so on.

25. Wampum belts were traditionally exchanged by the Five Nations to seal alliances; the designs in them (purple beads against a white background) served as mnemonic devices marking the occasions.

26. Such Virginia English help would not arrive until William Claiborne and one hundred colonists settled on Monoponson (Kent) Island in 1631 and opened a trade post on Palmer Island at the mouth of the Susquehanna River. The Massawomeck-Susquehannock war continued from 1608 to the defeat of the Massawomecks in the 1630s (see chap. 10).

27. None of the authors feels certain about when or how Smith learned about the Bush and Gunpowder rivers: by Indian descriptions or by visiting them himself, and if the latter, when he took the time to do it.

28. J. Smith 1986b [1612]: 232; J. Smith 1986c [1624]: 172; Haile 1998: 269.

29. They appear on the later maps by Alsop (1666) and Hermann (1673).

30. J. Smith 1986b [1612]: 232; J. Smith 1986c [1624]: 172; Haile 1998: 269.

31. Inference from comparing the plenitude of names along the other Western Shore rivers, where he is known to have had Indian companions (or captors) with him, and the paucity of Virginia Eastern Shore town names, where he is known to have had no such guide with him.

32. For a more detailed discussion of sailing conditions and the villages, people and archaeology, see chap. 11 on the Patuxent River.

33. J. Smith 1986b [1612]: 232; J. Smith 1986c [1624]: 172; Haile 1998: 269.

34. J. Smith 1986b (1612) in Haile 1998: 269. Smith spent three weeks exploring this long tidal river with its complex diversity of Algonquian chiefdoms, but he does not give daily accounts. The day-by-day interpretation presented next is based on Smith's narrative; Edward Haile's detailed knowledge of sailing, topography, and plotted village locations for the river (Haile 1996 map); and Randy Turner's and Wayne Clark's archaeological expertise and known Late Woodland site data.

35. J. Smith 1986c [1624]: 173–74; Haile 1998: 269–70.

36. J. Smith 1986c [1624]: 174; Haile 1998: 270–71.

37. J. Smith 1986b [1612]: 232; Smith 1986c [1624]: 174–75; Haile 1998: 271.

38. J. Smith 1986c [1624]: 175–77; Haile 1998: 271–74.

39. It would be a mile (1.6 kilometers) today, but sea level was three to four feet lower (.9–1.2 meters) back then.

40. J. Smith 1986c [1624]: 177; Haile 1998: 274.

41. J. Smith 1986c [1624]: 177–78; Haile 1998: 274–75.

42. John Smith never married, and he is not known to have had lovers of either sex. He seems to have been entirely a career-driven man.

43. J. Smith 1986b [1612]: 174; J. Smith 1986c [1624]: 126–27; Strachey 1953 [1612]: 62; Haile 1998: 620.

44. Strachey 1953 [1612]: 114; Haile 1998: 671.

45. J. Smith 1986c [1624]: 178; Haile 1998: 274–75.

46. J. Smith 1986b [1612]: 233; J. Smith 1986c [1624]: 178; Haile 1998: 275.

47. Stahle et al. 1998: fig. 3-B.

48. An alternate explanation for Smith's placing the "end of exploration" there is that he was taken across the run at that point as a captive back in December 1607.

49. Connection between promise and obliteration: Rountree 2005: 111, 119.

50. Smith 1986b [1612]: 232–33; Smith 1986c [1624]: 178; Haile 1998: 275.

51. Syzygy (in this context): times when the moon lines up with the sun (dark of the moon) or is opposite it (full moon). Perigee (in this context): reaching the point in its orbit when the moon is closest to Earth. For calculations of the phases of the moon, see www.nasa.gov, and access "lunar phases." For calculations of syzygy, see Wood 1976: 231 (table 16).

52. J. Smith 1986b [1612]: 233; J. Smith 1986c [1624]: 178–80; Haile 1998: 275–77.

53. J. Smith 1986a [1608]: 79–81; Haile 1998: 173–74.

54. Kelso and Straube 2004.

55. Smith, a well-read man in his later, inactive years, inserted numerous quotes from poets. In this one, according to Philip Barbour (in *The Complete Works of Captain John*

Smith (1580–1631), 180 n. 32, "Smith rewrote the first three lines of Fotherby's translation from Prosper's *De Providentia* (*Atheomastix*, 11–12), then quoted the rest almost verbatim."

56. J. Smith 1986b [1612]: 247; J. Smith 1986c [1624]: 196; Haile 1998: 299–300.

57. I.e., the First Anglo-Powhatan War, a term first used by Fausz (1985: 239) and followed by Rountree (1990: 55) and others since.

6. *The Powhatan River, Becoming "King James His River," and Hampton Roads*

1. The western rim referred to here extends from Fort Monroe to the mouth of Back River. The southern rim is now a resort area, part of the cities of Norfolk and Virginia Beach, although parts of it have been preserved as First Landing State Park and Fort Story, a U.S. Army base at Cape Henry.

2. Lauck W. Ward, personal communication to Helen Rountree, 2005.

3. Boon 2004.

4. James River Project Committee 1950: 491.

5. Stahle et al. 1998.

6. Saltiness, pollution: Earle 1979.

7. Barnard 1975; Doumlele 1976 and 1979b; Moore 1977a, 1980, and 1981, Moore and Dewing 1990, 1991a, and 1991b; Silberhorn and Priest 1987; Silberhorn and Dewing 1989a and 1989b; Silberhorn and Harris 1981.

8. Personal communication, William Jennings Hargis to Kent Mountford. Correspondence from the Civil War period indicated that Union sailors, stationed aboard "monitors"—gunboats patterned after the first ironclad *Monitor*—would row out to the oyster banks at low tide and simply walk about gathering shellfish.

9. Edmund Ruffin (1793–1865) wrote in the 1850s that "When our ancestors first reached this shore, nearly the whole country was in a state of nature. . . . The soil . . . was not exposed to be washed away by the rains into the rivers. The waters therefore were generally clear, instead of being generally muddy" (James River Project Committee 1950: 344).

10. For the nature of weirs, see chap. 8. Indians teaching: Perkins 1969 [1608]: 160; Haile 1998: 134.

11. Banister 1970: 354 (written before 1692; Indians could be Powhatans or Siouan speakers to the southwest. William Byrd [1966: 316] gives a vivid description of an Occaneechi man catching a sturgeon this way).

12. Archer 1969a [1607]: 97; J. Smith 1986a [1608]: 33; J. Smith 1986b [1612]: 210; J. Smith 1986c [1624]: 143; Haile 1998: 117, 148, 230.

13. J. Smith 1986b [1612]: 154; J. Smith 1986c [1624]: 110; Strachey 1953 [1624]: 124; Haile 1998: 680.

14. J. Smith n.d. [1612]; see also the maps in chaps. 6–7, 12, and 13.

15. James River Project Committee 1950: 274–75. The last Virginia bison were shot in the New River Valley in 1797. The authors of that "Mammals" chapter note: "It is not pleasant to see any animal exterminated from its native haunts, but . . . it would be virtually impossible for it [in the wild] to satisfy its range and food requirements in the Virginia of today." However, at this writing several commercial bison farms across the state (including one near the site of Werowocomoco!) are flourishing.

16. Harvill et al. 1992: 46 (yaupon), 86 (live oak), 6 (cypress), 7 (Spanish moss).

17. Rountree 2005: 32–33.

18. The locations given here come either from Turner and Opperman (forthcoming) or from published excavations of Powhatan sites that yielded English trade goods. Turner and Opperman also list surveyed archaeological sites that may be unconfirmed candidates for Smith map towns.

19. Hariot 1972 [1590]: 42–43.

20. Hodges 1998.

21. In a salvage dig in that developing residential area, several sets of human remains were found; after being analyzed, they were ceremonially reburied in First Landing State Park by members of the modern Nansemond tribe.

22. These and other sites that may represent Powhatan villages in the James and York river drainages are discussed in Opperman and Turner (forthcoming).

23. In the century or so before English arrival, the Chesapeakes, Nansemonds, Kecoughtans, and Paspaheghs all began to make Roanoke wares, like their neighbors to the south. Groups near the fall line used predominantly Gaston-Cashie ceramics, indicating links southwestward into North Carolina. Algonquian speakers in the York-Rappahannock area continued to use the formerly regionwide Townsend wares. For a map of those distributions, see Rountree and Turner 2002: 43.

24. Quinn 1955: 244–46.

25. Quinn 1985: 345ff.; Rountree 1998: 21–23.

26. Strachey 1953 [1612]; 104–5; J. Smith 1986c [1624]: 178; Haile 1998: 662, 275.

27. All the personal names of chiefs in this and the next chapter come from Strachey 1953 [1612]: 63–68 (Haile 1998: 621–27). Strachey gives no indication of how the names were pronounced.

28. Higgins, Downing, and Blanton 1995; Edwards et al. 1989.

29. J. Smith n.d. [1612]; Anonymous 1969 [1608], which was an early draft that fell into Spanish hands. The map that best indicates which of these two shows where things are is Haile 1995; the synthesis we use here is from Haile 1996.

30. Lucketti, Hodges, and Hodges 1994. Besides several dozen house outlines, the archaeologists found numerous burials; after analysis, the bones and associated grave goods were ceremonially reburied by members of the modern Virginia Indian tribes on nearby land donated by the developers.

31. Strachey 1953 [1612]: 69 (priests and elders); Hamor 1957 [1615]: 12; Haile 1998: 627, 810.

32. McCary and Barka 1977. The towns were Mamanahunt, Paspanegh, Moysonec, Righkahauk, Nechanicok, and Mansa, the latter apparently being palisaded. At this writing, there is a restudy of McCary and Barka's data in progress at the College of William and Mary.

33. J. Smith (1986c [1624]: 256) verbally places it across from Mamanahunt.

34. The only verbal clue: John Smith (1986a [1608]: 43) says it was forty miles (64 kilometers) from Jamestown, and measurement with a rolling planimeter on a modern map puts it above Providence Forge.

35. J. Smith 1986b [1612]: 147; Strachey 1953 [1612]: 57; Haile 1998: 615.

36. For stealing a wife of Opechancanough's: Strachey 1953 [1612]: 64; Haile 1998: 622.

37. However, ossuaries with remains of about 110 people (but no European trade goods) have been found at Claremont.

38. Deetz 1993. The town's name appears only on the "Zuñiga" map.

39. Mouer et al. 1992; McLearen and Mouer 1993 and 1994.

40. Gregory 1980.

41. J. Smith 1986b [1612]: 147; J. Smith 1986c [1624]: 104; Strachey 1953 [1612]: 44, 57; Haile 1998: 603–4, 615.

42. J. Smith 1986b [1612]: 147; J. Smith 1986c [1624]: 104; Strachey 1953 [1612]: 44, 57; Haile 1998: 603–4, 615.

43. J. Smith 1986b [1612]: 173; J. Smith 1986c [1624]: 126; Strachey 1953 [1612]: 56; Haile 1998: 614.

44. J. Smith 1986b [1612]: 271; J. Smith 1986c [1624]: 223. Gabriel Archer called the town "Powhatan's Tower" (Archer 1969a [1607]: 85; Haile 1998: 106).

45. Intertidal zone: Rountree's observations in the Hampton Roads area. Flourishing: Lippson and Lippson 2006: 242.

46. The only record of native shellfishing techniques: "Some boys were sent to dive for mussels" (Archer 1969a [1607]: 92; Haile 1998: 113).

47. Barber 1983; the sites in question date to before the Late Woodland Period began (Opperman 1992).

48. Barber, Madden, and Hardison 2004.

49. Klippel and Morey 1986.

50. Whyte 1988.

51. Weyanocks: Archer 1969a [1607]: 82; Haile 1998: 103. Unspecified Hampton Roads group, probably Nansemond: Ralph Lane in Quinn 1955 [1586]: 260–61.

52. Freshwater pearls are shiny; the region's oyster pearls, however, tend to be somewhat drab.

53. Archer 1969a [1607]: 93; Strachey 1953 [1612]: 132; Haile 1998: 114, 688. Native Americans cooked the shellfish first, which burned any pearls in them; the boring tools were coarse stone ones, not fine-bit steel drills like today's. Oyster pearls are hardly ever found today in the Chesapeake. Freshwater pearls are still occasionally extracted from upriver shellfish, though commercially farmed *Margaritifera margaritifera* produce the bulk of them for semiprecious jewelry today.

54. J. Smith 1986b [1612]: 168; Smith 1986c [1624]: 121; Strachey 1953 [1612]: 111; Haile 1998: 669. For a detailed discussion of the practice in the Southeast, see Hudson 1979. Helen Rountree, along with other participants in a seminar Hudson conducted in 1989, drank some of the brew; the participants agreed that it tasted like dirty sweat socks left in old hiking boots for several months.

55. Clay 1976; Jones et al. 1985; Hodges 1979; R. Hodges, Sabo, and Straw 1990; R. Hodges et al. 1985; Reber et al. 1981; Kitchel et al. 1986. Soil surveys have not yet been published for Surry Co. or Charles City Co., but they will eventually be available online. Meanwhile Helen Rountree was allowed to photocopy pages from the galley proofs for study (with thanks to local USDA staff, especially Kilby Majette).

56. Cleared: Kingsbury 1906–35: 3: 708; Strachey 1953 [1612]: 39; Haile 1998: 601. Best: Kingsbury 1906–35: 3: 557; in 1724, Hugh Jones would write (1956 [1724]: 55), "Wherever we meet with an old Indian field, or place where they have lived, we are sure of the best ground." For an expanded discussion of this practice and its impact on the native people of the Tidewater, see Potter and Waselkov 1994.

57. As defined in chapter 2, "breadbaskets" are marshes of at least ten acres (4 hectares) in which the plants consist of at least 30 percent wild rice and/or 50 percent tuckahoe (arrow arum) and/or 50 percent cow lily.

58. Barnard 1977; Doumlele 1976 and 1979b; Moore 1977a, 1980, and 1981; Moore and Dewing 1990, 1991a, and 1991b; Silberhorn and Dewing 1989a, 1989b, and 1991; Silberhorn and Harris 1981; Silberhorn and Priest 1987.

59. Turner 1993: 89.

60. J. Smith 1986b [1612]: 146; J. Smith 1986c [1624]: 103; Strachey 1953 [1612]: 68–69; Haile 1998: 627. Quote from Strachey.

61. Percy 1969a [1608?]: 133–34; J. Smith 1969a [1608]: 27; Haile 1998: 90, 145. The uncertainty comes from Strachey's vagueness about exactly when Powhatan annihilated the Chesapeakes, leaving that territory open for Nansemond use (Strachey 1953 [1612]: 104–5; Haile 1998: 662).

62. Percy 1969a [1608?]: 135–36; Haile 1998: 91–92.

63. Percy 1969a [1608?]: 136–37; Haile 1998: 92–93.

64. J. Smith 1986a [1608]: 51; Haile 1998: 160. The English, seeing a large concourse of people and assuming the chief examining them so carefully was the local chief, mistakenly called the Quiyoughcohannocks "Tappahannocks" (phonetically speaking, the Powhatans pronounced "R" as a flap, often heard by the English as a "T") for several years thereafter.

65. Archer 1969a [1607]: 82–94; Percy 1969a [1608?]: 139–41; J. Smith 1969a [1608]: 29–33; Haile 1998: 103–15, 96–97, 146–47.

66. For a detailed narrative of Anglo-Powhatan relations at that and other times, see Rountree 1990.

67. Well: J. Smith 1986b [1612]: 263; J. Smith 1986c [1624]: 212; Haile 1998: 319). Disease: Earle 1979; Rutman and Rutman 1976. The search for that early well continues at APVA Jamestown Rediscovery at this writing, for all the wells found in the remains of James Fort have proved later in date (Kelso and Straube 2004: 131–54).

68. For a comparison of effectiveness of Powhatan and English weapons, see Rountree 2005: 50–51.

69. J. Smith 1986a [1608]: 79, 81; Haile 1998: 173–74. A later version of Smith describes a very hostile first meeting on the way back from the second exploration of the Chesapeake Bay (J. Smith 1986c [1624]: 178–79; Haile 1998: 275–77).

70. Stahle et al. 1998, fig. 3-A; historical corroboration from colonists' writing that the Indians first had green corn ca. Sept. 10 (J. Smith 1986a [1608]: 35; Percy 1969 [1608?]: 145; Haile 1998: 148, 100), presumably for the fields planted in early April and expected to ripen by early August (J. Smith 1986b [1612]: 157; in optimal years, corn takes 120 days to ripen fully).

71. J. Smith 1986a [1608]: 35–39; Haile 1998: 149–51. Each subsequent version of Smith describes more violence: J. Smith 1986b [1612]: 211; J. Smith 1986c [1624]: 144–45; Haile 1998: 231–32.

72. J. Smith 1986a [1608]: 39–43; J. Smith 1986b [1612]: 211–12; J. Smith 1986c [1624]: 145–46; Haile 1998: 151–55, 233–24.

73. "Pounce" is the word, for the men Smith left behind at Apocant were attacked by the townspeople, and one Englishman was captured and tortured to death (J. Smith 1986b [1612]: 212; J. Smith 1986c [1624]: 146; Strachey 1953 [1612]: 60; Haile 1998: 334, 617). Smith

himself was captured when he went on into the Chickahominy's headwaters and ran into a communal hunt comprising Chickahominies, Paspaheghs, Youghtanunds, Pamunkeys, Mattaponis, and Chiskiacks (J. Smith 1986a [1608]: 91; Haile 1998: 179) and led by Opechancanough, who was based at Youghtanund. It is possible that after receiving information from Apocant, the hunters had angled their operations over to Chickahominy Swamp to intercept Smith.

74. Fausz 1977.

7. The "Pamunkey"

1. J. Smith 1986a [1608]: 47; Haile 1998: 157.

2. U.S. Geological Survey 2004.

3. Note the receding of an Indian name from a major waterway to one of its upstream tributaries. We shall see this again in chapter 13 in Morattico (formerly Moraughtacund) Creek.

4. Doumlele 1979b; Moore 1976 and 1980; Priest, Silberhorn, and Zacherle 1987; Silberhorn 1974 and 1981; Silberhorn and Zacherle 1987.

5. Harvill et al. 1992: 6. Specific locations and size of stands: James Vadas and Billy Mills, personal communications to Helen Rountree, 2004.

6. Dugout canoes, of course, in Indian times, and sailing ships and then steamboats in post-Contact times. Helen Rountree was told by one resident of Almondsville in 1973 that he had more knowledge of Baltimore, reached easily by the regular steam packet service plying the rivers, than of Richmond—until the 1930s when the Civilian Conservation Corps paved the dirt roads leading to his settlement. Shorter trips were made in a variety of canoes, bateaus, and other small craft.

7. Lauck W. Ward, personal communication to Helen Rountree, 2005.

8. Owners of Werowocomoco site, personal communications to Helen Rountree, 2003.

9. Lippson and Lippson 2006; Fay, Neves, and Pardue 1983b.

10. See map in Rountree 2005: 131. Centrality within a tribute-producing territory newly encompassing the Eastern Shore: various works by Rountree and Turner.

11. Archer 1969a [1607]: 84, 102; J. Smith 1986b [1612]: 173, 174–75; J. Smith 1986c [1624]: 126–27; Strachey 1953 [1612]: 63, 69; Haile 1998: 104, 122, 621, 627–28.

12. That assumption, which applies to much of the coastal plain, stems from the absence of mentions of palisades around them in the historical records and the lack of archaeological evidence for palisades in the area.

13. The locations given below come either from Turner and Opperman (forthcoming) or from published excavations of Powhatan sites that yielded English trade goods. Turner and Opperman's forthcoming work is our source of town assignments, and it also lists surveyed archaeological sites that may be unconfirmed candidates for Smith map towns.

14. In this chapter, as in the previous one, chiefs' names come from Strachey: 1953 [1612]: 69; Haile 1998: 627–28. Smith (1986b [1612]: 147; J. Smith 1986c [1624]: 104; copied by Strachey 1953 [1612]: 44; Haile 1998: 603–4) words his text so that Chiskiack appears to have been part of Powhatan's original inheritance, but Strachey gives a list of six territories that excludes Chiskiack (1953 [1612]: 57; Haile 1998: 615).

15. Lewis and Loomie 1953.

16. Cantaunkack: Opperman and Turner 1990. Werowocomoco: Turner 2003a. Location of Werowocomoco: Montague 1972; McCary 1981.

17. J. Smith 1986b [1612]: 147; J. Smith 1986c [1624]: 104; Strachey 1953 [1612]: 44, 57; Haile 1998: 603–4, 615.

18. R. Hodges et al. 1980; R. Hodges et al. 1985; Newhouse et al. 1980; Newhouse et al. 1985; and Clay et al. 1958. The soil surveys for King William Co. and King and Queen Co. have not yet been published, but they will eventually be available online. Meanwhile, Helen Rountree was allowed to photocopy pages from the galley proofs of them for study (with thanks to the local USDA staff).

19. Defined as marshes of at least ten acres (4 hectares) containing at least 30 percent wild rice and/or at least 50 percent tuckahoe (arrow arum) or cow lily.

20. James Perry, Virginia Institute of Marine Science (VIMS), personal communication to Helen Rountree, 2004.

21. This paragraph is based upon the VIMS Tidal Marsh Inventories (the operative word being "tidal"), which for the Pamunkey and Mattaponi rivers stop not at the fall line but at a point below Manquin Creek (the Pamunkey) and at Aylett on U.S. 360 (the Mattaponi). Sources for marsh locations: Doumlele 1979b; Moore 1976 and 1980; Priest, Silberhorn, and Zacherle 1987; Silberhorn 1974b; Silberhorn and Zacherle 1987.

22. James Perry, VIMS, personal communication to Helen Rountree, 2004.

23. The shells on the mantle shine, while the shells eroding from the cliff faces are a dull white (Rountree and Mountford's personal observation, 2005). Digging out less damaged shells with some nacre left on them is the likely explanation.

24. Private collections of diverse items of interest to the owners, called "cabinets," were the forerunners of modern museums.

25. Species identification: Gary Coovert, personal communication to Helen Rountree, 1991. Number: estimate by the replica's maker, Michael Taylor; personal communication to Helen Rountree, 1993. Common: Lauck Ward, personal communication to Kent Mountford, 2004. Sewing: Helen Rountree, personal close-up observation of the original, 1978 and 1992. Maryland record: Jesuit Letters 1910 [1639]: 125. Tradescant: Feest 1983. Distribution of shells: Lauck Ward, Gerald Johnson, and Jeffrey Halka, personal communications to Helen Rountree, 2004. The most logical candidate for the transport to Maryland would have been William Claiborne, one of the most active Indian traders of his day; he dealt with both the York River Indians (on behalf of Virginia) and the Maryland Native Americans in the 1630s (Jennifer Potter [author writing about the Tradescants] and Helen Rountree, discussions, 2005).

26. J. Smith 1986a [1608]: 57; Haile 1998: 162–63. Numerous historians have argued for and against the "rescue" actually happening. For a discussion in ethnological as well as historical terms, see Rountree 2005, chap. 6. Until a time machine is invented, however, no one will know what actually transpired.

27. J. Smith 1986a [1608]: 63–79; J. Smith 1986c [1624]: 155–57; Haile 1998: 166–73, 243–46.

28. J. Smith 1986b [1612]: 166–67; Strachey 1953 [1612]: 109–10; Haile 1998: 667–68.

29. Archer 1969a [1607]: 95, 98; J. Smith 1986a [1608]: 31, 33; Haile 1998: 115, 117, 147.

30. J. Smith 1986b [1612]: 234–37; J. Smith 1986c [1624]: 181–84; Haile 1998: 279–83.

31. J. Smith 1986b [1612]: 245–57; J. Smith 1986c [1624]: 194–205; Haile 1998: 297–310.

32. Avoiding English: Strachey 1953 [1612]: 57; Haile 1998: 615. Difficulty for English row-boats: J. Smith 1986a [1608]: 43, 45; Haile 1998: 155–56.

33. Termed the Second Anglo-Powhatan War by Fausz (1985: 246) and followed by scholars since then (e.g., see indexes in Rountree 1990 and Rountree and Turner 2002).

34. Sainsbury, Fortescue, and Headham 1860–1926: 5: 116 (1630 plan to seat the town, apparently carried out after peace was made in 1632).

35. Rountree 1990: chapters 4 and 5.

36. Termed the Third Anglo-Powhatan War since 1990 (indexes in Rountree 1990 and Rountree and Turner 2002).

37. Hening 1809–23: 1: 323–26.

38. Ibid.: 353.

39. Commissioners appointed . . . 1896 [1677].

40. Rountree 1990: chap. 5; for a revised history of the Mattaponi land, see Rountree and Turner 2002: 171–72.

8. The Farmers and Fishermen of the Lower Eastern Shore

1. J. Smith 1986b [1612]: 224–25; J. Smith 1986c [1624]: 163; Haile 1998: 254–55.

2. J. Smith 1986b [1612]: 225; J. Smith 1986c [1624]: 164; Haile 1998: 255.

3. Many of the bayside creeks have sandspits running across their mouths, requiring dredging nowadays.

4. The "spine" of Virginia's Eastern Shore rises to little more than fifty feet above sea level; see the map in Rountree and Davidson 1997: 2.

5. Lowery 2004, and personal discussions with Kent Mountford and Ralph Eshelman, 2004. For the latest archaeological surveys of Virginia Eastern Shore shorelines, see Lowery 2003.

6. I.e., the effect of the Earth's rotation upon water and air. In the lower Chesapeake and the lower portions of its larger tributaries, the heavier salty water tends to be pushed to the right (east) as it comes in on the flood tide, while the lighter, fresher water tends to move toward the Western Shore as it descends on the ebb.

7. The small sites produced burials whose skeletons were analyzed by the Virginia Department of Historic Resources and then ceremonially reburied in the late 1990s by Eastern Shore Indian descendants in Indiantown County Park, the site of the old Gingaskin Indian Reservation. Gingaskin history: Rountree: 1990: 179–86; Rountree and Davidson 1997: chap. 6.

8. J. Smith 1986b [1612]: 225; J. Smith 1986c [1624]: 163; Haile 1998: 255.

9. J. Smith 1986c [1624]: 289–91. The somewhat better known Debbedeavon (or more accurately, Tapatiaton) came still later; for a complete list with dates, see Rountree and Davidson 1997: 56, 58.

10. For those more familiar with North Carolina's Currituck Sound, the name "Currituck" is a common Algonquian place-name, and, like "Pamunkey," "Mattaponi," and "Piscataway," it is found in numerous places up and down the Atlantic coast. The Eastern Shore Currituck need not have had any connection, other than speaking related dialects, with the Outer Banks people.

11. Beverley 1947 [1705]: 232.

12. Smith's map is imprecise enough in showing creeks that the location could have been south of Nassawaddox Creek.

13. J. Smith 1986b [1612]: 150; J. Smith 1986c [1624]: 107; Strachey 1953 [1612]: 49; Haile 1998: 609.

14. Conch shells also wash up on the beaches in eastern Hampton, formerly the Kecoughtans' territory. But there is no historical reference to that group having worked the shells, possibly because that chiefdom consisted of loyal inlanders who had replaced the original Kecoughtans around 1596 (Strachey 1953 [1612]: 68; Haile 1998: 627).

15. People as far down the bay as Kecoughtan were known to fear the Massawomecks (J. Smith 1986b [1612]: 229; J. Smith 1986c [1624]: 169; Haile 1998: 263). The Spanish had made an indelible impression in 1572 when they revenged the Jesuit deaths on the Paspaheghs (word of their retribution would have spread), and they are known to have returned in 1588, kidnapping two children (who were never heard from again) in the Potomac River region (again, word would have spread).

16. J. Smith 1986a [1608]: 69; Haile 1998: 169.

17. J. Smith 1986c [1624]: 291; brackets ours.

18. Defined as marshes of at least ten acres (4 hectares) containing at least 30 percent wild rice and/or at least 50 percent tuckahoe (arrow arum) or cow lily. Sources: Moore 1977b; Silberhorn and Harris 1977.

19. Cobb and Smith 1989; Peacock and Edmonds 1994.

20. They lacked the mainland custom of making superwarriors through the horrific boys' initiation called the *huskinaw* (J. Smith 1986 [1624]: 291).

21. Ibid.: 290–91.

22. Darrin Lowery, personal communication to Wayne Clark, 2005, citing Cresson 1892. During a "low blow" (water wind-blown out of the bay, lowering water levels), wooden poles were seen, staggered to allow interweaving of branches in a wattle pattern. Prehistoric stone tools were found around this structure.

23. Teaching: Perkins 1969 [1608]: 160; J. Smith 1986a [1608]: 83; Haile 1998: 134, 175. Hiring: Norfolk Co., Minutes 1637–46: 6; published in *Virginia Magazine of History and Biography* 39 (1931): 9. Another reason the English did not bring the technology with them: such shallow-water weirs work only where the difference between high and low tides is not very great. The tidal amplitudes in England are too large: a weir built far enough offshore to contain water at low tide (to keep the fish alive) would require elaborate harvesting technology to raise the fish from deep water during the hours a boat could put out from shore and return home again—not to mention finding enough long poles in a country nearly denuded of forests.

24. Norfolk Co. (Va.), Minute Book 1637–46: 6.

25. Charles Elliott, personal communication to Helen Rountree, 1988; Mr. Elliott interviewed pound fishermen in Fox Hill, Hampton, Virginia.

26. Kennedy and Mountford 2001: 198.

27. Beitzell 2001 [1968]: 91.

28. Hulton 1984: 86. The latter name appears as "Comokee" on the map engraved by de Bry in 1590, and no other town appears on the Eastern Shore (Hariot 1972 [1590]: 42–43.

29. Kingsbury 1906–35: 3: 116, 279–80, 586, 476; 4: 176. Most saltworks are tropical, depending on extremely dry weather and abundant blazing sunlight to concentrate the brines until salt crystals form. In temperate climates like that of the Chesapeake, salt is a dicey economic venture, requiring moveable sheds to keep rain from diluting the brine, plus cheap local fuel sources to ensure evaporation. Salt making on the north Atlantic coast was not

practical until the mid- to late eighteenth century, when sheds and fuel transport were more available.

30. Giving: Northampton Co., Orders 9: 49; see also Thos. Savage reference, note 33 below. Purchase: Northampton Co.: Deeds: passim. Summary in Rountree 1990: chaps. 4 and 5, and Rountree and Davidson 1997: chap. 2; more details of English activities are in Perry 1990.

31. Kingsbury 1906–35: 4: 10; J. Smith 1986c [1624]: 298.

32. J. Smith 1986c [1624]: 288–91.

33. Sending Savage: McIlwaine 1979 [1924]: 11. Giving land to Savage: Nugent 1934: 35, 75, 524.

34. McIlwaine 1979 [1924]: 48.

35. Rountree and Davidson 1997: 56, 58.

36. Indians: Rountree and Davidson 1997: chaps. 2 and 5. Free Africans: Breen and Innes 1980. English expansion: Perry 1990.

37. Oertel and Foyle 1995. The Shore began as a sandspit about nearly 2 million years ago and built up to southward during the high sea levels of interglacials, gradually narrowing the distance between the Capes. This process is continuing as Fisherman Island, like the barrier islands north and east of it, grows through the deposition of sand by south-moving Atlantic currents along the coast. That means that the Susquehanna has had to push southward and then eastward around Cape Charles, especially during the low sea levels of glaciations, capturing the other rivers' channels one by one as it went. Oertel and Foyle expect the growing Eastern Shore eventually to push the Susquehanna into joining the James River (1995: 600, 602). The High-rise Bridge, by jumping the channel north of Cape Charles, makes the further southward growth of the shoals at the cape essentially irrelevant to the continued usefulness of the highway.

9. The Middle Eastern Shore

1. Merchants: J. Smith 1986c [1624]: 165; Haile 1998: 258. Oyster fleet in 1880s: Wennersten 2001: 122. Farming of hammocks: Lowery 2003: 61, 64. Time depth: Luckenbach, Clark, and Levy 1987: 18–25.

2. Cronin 2005: 74–76. On early maps, James Island appears joined to Taylors Island immediately to the south, but there was probably always a small creek or gut separating the two.

3. Judging by the current channels in the sound, fourteen thousand years ago the Nanticoke and Pocomoke flowed together before joining the Susquehanna.

4. For a contemporary analysis of the interplay between the geology, climate, and cultures of this area, see Lowery 2004b: 7–42; 2003: 15–93; Lowery 2001: 27–41.

5. A. Lippson 1973: 10–11; Sipple 1999: 205, 239–31. The smoke from the 1782 fire could be seen seventy miles (112.7 kilometers) to the north in Philadelphia.

6. Statistics and potholes: Sipple 1999: 278–79, 310–11. Pothole formation and settlement: Lowery 2003: 113–15; Lowery 2004b: 60, 112–13).

7. Sipple 1978: 157 (tuckahoe, or arrow arum); 90 (cow lily); 158 (reedgrass); 173 (softstem bulrush); 115 (cattails); 121 (water hemp); 135 (wild millet); 119 (wild rice); 29 (sweetflag).

8. Historical extent: Wennersten 2001: 126–27. Spawning: Lippson and Lippson 2006: 246–47.

9. Lippson and Lippson 2006: 48, 66 (distribution); Lowery 2003: 73 (eating). Whelks: Lippson and Lippson 2006: 53, 66. Live whelks can be captured using baited pots or traps, trawls, or steel-framed dredges similar to the oyster dredge.

10. Darrin Lowery, personal communication to Kent Mountford, 2004.

11. Abbott 1974: 222.

12. Brush 1986; Thornton 1991.

13. Sipple 1999: 205–6.

14. Ibid.: 240–42.

15. Norwood 1947 [1650].

16. Tom Horton, personal communication to Grace Brush, 2004. The oaks are black oak and southern and northern red oak; the hickories are pignut, shagbark, mockernut, and swamp hickory, and there are also beech trees. Other understory species reported there are dogwood, cherry, arrowwood, possum haw, persimmon, American holly, ironwood, spicebush, coastal pepperbush, rhododendron, deciduous clammy azalea, white ash, black walnut, black locust, and fringe tree. On the ground grow chain fern, sanicle, and bloodroot. Some of the trees were quite large; for instance, one black oak measured forty-four inches (1.1 meters) in diameter.

17. Sipple 1999: 282. In addition to the red oak, beech, tulip poplar, and flowering dog-wood trees were wild coffee in the understory and herbaceous species like bloodroot, pale Indian plantain, and May apple on the ground. According to the Nature Conservancy, in the patch on the Nanticoke near the town of Vienna "over thirty plant species known only from this Dorchester County location occur at this area." One can readily see why the Nanticokes selected this location for their Chicone reservation and stayed there well into the eighteenth century.

18. Waterfowl: A. Lippson 1973: 50–53; Sipple 1999: 154–59. Mammals: Sipple 1999: 206–9; Scott 1991: passim. Semmes (1929: 1–29) provides a good summary of the seventeenth-century situation.

19. For the appearance of these towns in later Maryland records, with maps of the reservations, see Rountree and Davidson 1997: chaps. 3 and 4.

20. J. Smith 1986b [1612]: 150; J. Smith 1986c [1624]: 107; Strachey 1953 [1612]: 49; Haile 1998: 608. The difference was probably not one of language, but of related dialects having diverged too much for mutual intelligibility.

21. J. Smith 1986b [1612]: 150; J. Smith 1986c [1624]: 107; Strachey 1953 [1612]: 49; Haile 1998: 608; Banister 1970: 372.

22. Browne et al. 1883–1972: 15: 213.

23. Ibid.; Rountree and Davidson 1997: 126.

24. Browne et al. 1883–1972: 15: 213.

25. Hughes 1980: 201–17.

26. Browne et al. 1883–1972: 5: 520.

27. Ibid.: 15: 213.

28. Ibid.

29. Ibid.: 14: 712.

30. Some were still living on their old land in Somerset Co. in 1700 (Browne et al. 1883–1972: 24: 103).

31. Rountree and Davidson 1997: 95–96, 105, 202.

32. Witt 1971: 4–9.

33. In addition, an ossuary discovered on the Wicomico River was documented and the skeletal remains reburied in 2004 in consultation with the (then) Maryland Commission on Indian Affairs.

34. Weslager 1983; Rountree and Davidson 1997.

35. Lowery 2004b: 61–65.

36. Our initial draft of this volume placed the *tallak*'s village on Marshyhope Creek, a large tributary once regarded as the Nanticoke's main stem (Herrmann map of 1673). However, after we toured the river and the creek in boats with a team of researchers in 2005 and considered the GIS analysis by Salisbury University colleagues, the majority opinion is now that Kuskarawaok was in the vicinity of Chicone Creek. Wayne Clark concurs but urges archaeological testing of an alternative area of Marshyhope Creek near Hurlock.

37. This Indian practice of the dominant town or tribe naming a river was followed on the Rappahannock River (see chap. 13) and probably elsewhere. Limited testing of the site has revealed evidence of a nucleated village with multiple post moulds but no definitive house pattern; there was also no clear evidence of a palisade. The ceramics were Townsend, appropriate to the Late Woodland period, and the presence of one glass bead brings the site into the Contact period.

38. Busby 1996 and 2000.

39. Weslager 1983: 180–200; Davidson 1993: 151–52; Rountree and Davidson 1997: 158–60.

40. Rountree and Davidson 1997: chap. 4.

41. State of Maryland, Acts of Assembly 1856: 193–94.

42. Weslager 1983; Rountree and Davidson 1997. Merging: Browne et al. 1883–1972: 8: 526.

43. More ossuary burials have been found in their territory than anywhere else on the Eastern Shore (Curry 1999: 52–57). No ossuaries at all have been found north of the Choptanks' area, at this writing. Schaffer 2005 provides a detailed analysis of traditional Nanticoke burial practices, which persisted into the eighteenth century.

44. Hutton et al. 1963; Hall 1970 and 1973; Ireland and Matthews 1974; Matthews and Hall 1966a and 1966b; Reybold 1971; Shields and Davis 2002 (revision of Matthews and Hall 1966b). The soil survey for Caroline County dates from about 1930 and is too general to be comparable with the ones used here. Hence no prime soils appear on our map in that county, although they undoubtedly exist.

45. Beverley 1947 [1705]: 227; see also Banister 1970: 373. John Smith and his contemporaries wrote only of "white beads" or "coral"; they had not yet been pushed by the native people into dealing in shell "money." The first historical mention of "roanoke" in Virginia was in 1615 by Hamor (Hamor 1957 [1615]: 41; Haile 1998: 834), who said it was very common among the Indians; it began to be used like money in transactions with the English after the 1620s. Native people persisted, however, in measuring it in "arms' length" even though peoples' arms varied considerably in length; they refused to adopt the English steelyard to standardize the measurement.

46. Potter 1993: 115–16; 214–19. Another slab and clamshell beads were found in ossuaries in the Nanjemoy–Port Tobacco areas: Curry 1999: 40–51.

47. Illustrated in Rountree and Turner 2002: 48.

48. Melbourne Carriker of University of Delaware (emeritus), personal communication to Kent Mountford, 2004.

49. "Wampum" is a New England Algonquian term, not a Chesapeake-region Algonquian one. There is no record—by name—of "wampumpeag" before 1634 in Maryland (Anonymous 1910 [1635]: 90) or of "peak" in Virginia before 1638 (Northampton Co., Orders, Wills, Deeds [transcribed version] 1: 95–96). Neither is there record of "belts" using black as well as white shells until Virginia began dealing with the Senecas in the 1680s; instead, there were bicolored coronets (Banister 1970: 373). Yet Powhatan ogled those blue glass beads, so he and his people must have seen some shell ones. For a history of New England Algonquian terms and bead making, see Malloy 1977: 14–35; and Ceci 1989: 67–73.

50. When the English began using it as money in transactions with Indian people, the black was given twice the value of the white.

51. J. Smith 1986a [1608]: 71; J. Smith 1986b [1612]: 217; J. Smith 1986c [1624]: 156; Haile 1998: 169, 246.

52. J. Smith 1986c [1624]: 168; Haile 1998: 261. Shell gorgets continued to be valuable, however: an engraved shell gorget was found in a Piscataway cemetery dating to the 1680s (Curry 1999: 28–40).

53. J. Smith 1986c [1624]: 168; Haile 1998: 261.

54. For whelk shell species found at Great Lakes sites, and theories about how they were traded there, see Pendergast 1991: 99–101; Sempowski 1989: 83–103; Stothers 2000: 53, 67–70.

55. North Branch sites: Wall 1999. South Branch sites: ibid.; Brashler 1987: 3, 16.

56. Monongahela sites: Boyce 1985: 43; W. Johnson 2001: 78–80; Pendergast 1991: 103. Fort Ancient sites: Brashler and Moxley 1990; Hanson 1975. For whelk-shell trade between Fort Ancient Complex people and Mississippian peoples, see Pollack, Henderson, and Begley 2002. For shell maskettes in general, see M. Smith and Smith 1989.

57. Virginia English: Perry 1990: 167. That plus Maryland activities: Semmes 1929: 379–427. Relations between Virginia and Maryland colonists: Torrence 1973: 9–54. Native Americans in late seventeenth century: Rountree and Davidson 1997: 93–121.

58. Rountree and Davidson 1997: chap. 4, with several maps.

59. Ibid.: chap. 5; summary map on 126.

10. The Head of the Bay

1. Wallace 1971; Rountree 1993: 34.

2. Cyprian Thorowgood noted in 1634 that Susquehannocks traveling between the river's mouth and their town forty miles (nearly 65 kilometers) upstream normally took a half day to descend the river but two days to ascend it (Gifford and Tinling 1958: 350; there is also a mention of an African interpreter living among them). The records are silent about whether their canoes were dugouts or made of birch bark (which is not plentiful in the Piedmont of Pennsylvania), but trade with towns upstream made the latter likely.

3. Horton 1987: 69–71.

4. Lowery 1992: 36–37; Lowery 1994: figs. 16–17, 32; Lowery 1995: 13–15; Custer 1988: 1–10; Wilke and Thompson 1977a and 1977b.

5. Wayne Clark (personal experience prior to the 1972 tropical storm) reports that it was possible to take two dozen softshell crabs and two bushels of hard crabs in a half a day of wading (at Eastern Bay SAV beds east of Kent Island), using a push net and a dip net.

6. A. Lippson 1973: 12–14; Orth et al. 1993: 46–53.

7. Michael Naylor, SAV coordinator, Maryland Department of Natural Resources, personal communication to Kent Mountford, 2004.

8. Cyprian Thorowgood: Gifford and Tinling 1958.

9. Sipple 1978: 29 (sweetflag); 157 (tuckahoe, or arrow arum); 90 (cow lily); 158 (reedgrass); 173 (softstem bulrush); 115 (cattails); 121 (water hemp); 135 (wild millet); 119 (wild rice).

10. Sipple 1978: 241. There are also some trees in Delaware: Grace Brush, personal communication to Helen Rountree, 2004.

11. Brush 1986. The river's high sedimentation rate provides a detailed sequence of variations.

12. Wayne Tyndall, regional ecologist, Maryland Department of Natural Resources, personal communication to Kent Mountford.

13. Marye 1955.

14. For discussions of the Minguannan Complex and migrations, see Custer 1987: 13–23; Custer 1996: 286–89; Custer and Griffith 1986: 10–17.

15. Engelbrecht 2003: 2; Snow 1994: 75.

16. Lowery 1992, 1994, and 1995.

17. MHT Site Archaeology files do not indicate a site location for the village. The site today should be a very low-density oyster shell, dark-stained soil midden around two acres in size. The villagers were only an hour's canoe trip to the oyster beds at the southern mouth of the Sassafras River (Wilke and Thompson 1977a: 79–80, 84). John Seidel and Darrin Lowery began trying to find this site in 2005.

18. Toghwogh palisade: J. Smith 1986b [1612]: 231; J. Smith 1986c [1624]: 171; Haile 1998: 266. Susquehannock palisade (Haile 1999: 6–7; Alsop 1910 [1666]: 370). Five Nations Iroquois palisades: Engelbrecht 2003: 98. For relation to Mahicans and River Indians, see Richter 1992: 28–29, 51–54; for Iroquoian trading partners to the north supplying Tockwoghs with French goods, see Snow 1994: 75–80.

19. Browne et al. 1883–1972: 3: 363–64.

20. A conservative estimate, since the Susquehannock village at the Stickler site occupied ten acres and was reported by the Jesuits of Canada to have 1,300 warriors, or an estimated population (using Kent's ratio of 3.3) of 4,239 people (Kent 1984: 37; Thwaites 1897–1901: 33: 129).

21. Their ceramics are in the Shenks Ferry Complex, which may have had affiliations with other complexes to the northwest. For Susquehannock origins, see Witthof and Kinsey 1969a.

22. Marine shell trade: Pendergast 1991; Engelbrecht 2003: 131–32; Kent 1984: 171–74; Richter 1992: 28–29, 51–54. Which Iroquoian speakers the Susquehannocks dealt with is uncertain; the best candidates are those St. Lawrence River people (suggested above as being the Atquanachukes) who were defeated by the Five Nations before 1590 (Snow 1994: 67, 75).

23. Excavations: Custer 1996: 310–12; Kent 1984: 333–38. Based on archaeological data from the site, the population estimate for this 1600–1625 period village ranges from 1,165 to 1,700 people, much larger than any contemporary Algonquian villages in the bay region (Schulenberg, Weets, and van Rossum 2003: 4, 10; Howard 2003: table 1).

24. Fleet 1876 [1631–32]: 25–26 (towns) and 27 (population). See also Pendergast 1991: 15–17.

25. Nanticokes: that group's chief "extolled" (praised) the Massawomecks during Smith's visit—not the usual report Smith heard of them. But the Nanticokes were major players in

the trade in marine shell and beads made from it, and unknown to the Jamestown English they could have conducted a trade with Massawomecks who came visiting.

26. J. Smith 1986b [1612]: 230; J. Smith 1986c [1624]: 170; Spelman 1910 [1613?]: cxiv; Haile 1998: 265, 494–95.

27. Strachey 1953 [1612]: 107; Haile 1998: 665.

28. J. Smith 1986b [1612]: 232; J. Smith 1986c [1624]: 172, 176; Haile 1998: 268, 272.

29. For historic references after their defeat by the Seneca and Susquehannocks, see W. Johnson 2001: 80–82. For continuation of the Tehaque nation of True Minquas in 1655, see A. Johnson 1911: 560 and note 20 in Becker 1987: 37–38. Analysis assumes that Tehaque of 1655 is the same name as Tohoga nation of 1632.

30. Hoffman (1964) suggested they were one and the same with the Erie confederated nations, but M. E. White disagreed (1978: 412). Pendergast (1991: 68) suggested that they were same as the (French name) Antohonorons, east of Niagara. Potter (1993: 176) says that name applied to all the Five Nations except the Mohawks, which accords with Fleet's comment that there were four tribes of them. Pendergast (1991: 72) points out that the lack of records about them after 1634 indicates being part of the Five Nations Iroquois; the individual names of the Five Nations began appearing instead. See Pendergast 1991 for the best summary of the primary records, even if we do not agree with some of his interpretations.

31. Brashler 1987. See also Wall 1999 and Wall and Lapham 2001.

32. Washington Boro site faunal analysis: Guilday, Parmalee, and Tanner 1962. Sturgeon remains at the Ibaugh site were mixed with two squirrels recovered from a pottery vessel from a burial. The burial also contained a brass kettle with preserved corn remains and part of a wooden ladle (Witthof and Kinsey 1969b: 113). The Ibaugh site is one of several cemeteries dating from 1600 to 1625 associated with (but located outside of) the Susquehannocks' Washington Boro site (Kent 1984: 335). Placing burials outside the village is a practice different from the Massawomecks of the upper Potomac, who buried their deceased within the inner edge of the palisade (Brashler 1987: 5, 11–13).

33. Lowery 1994: 21–22; 1995: 13–21, fig. 17: Custer and Griffith 1986: 33–49; Custer 1996: 287–89.

34. A. Lippson 1973: 50–53.

35. Susquehannocks' use of swan feathers as decoration: Alsop 1910 [1666]: 367; abundance of birds, ibid.: 347.

36. For a detailed discussion of the methods and value of fire forest management in the early historic Southeast, see Hammett 1992. For trails along the barrens and the nature and extent of the barrens historically, see Marye 1920 and 1955; for archaeological evidence of locations adjacent to the barrens for winter quarters for hunters, see Clark 1976: 113–141, 218–19; Custer 1986. As a rule, modern historians and archaeologists have not incorporated the impact of these barrens on Algonquian, Iroquoian, and European settlement patterns of the upper bay region.

37. Kirby and Matthews 1973; Matthews 1971; H. Smith and Matthews 1975; E. White 1982. The soil survey for Cecil County dates from about 1930 and is too general to be comparable with the ones used here. Hence no prime soils appear on our map in that county, although they undoubtedly exist.

38. Jennings 1984: 68 n. 33; see also Fausz 1983.

39. Patuxents: Anonymous 1910 [1635]: 89; Nanticokes: Browne et al. 1883–1972: 3: 191–92 (1647).

40. Browne et al. 1883–1972: 3: 277–78. "English" lands by that treaty were to be the Eastern Shore up to the northeast branch of the Elk River and the Western Shore south of Palmers (now Garrett) Island; the area north of those limits remained in Susquehannock hands.

41. Fausz 1983, 1984.

42. Main 1982. A small proportion of the Africans in Maryland were always free, and they took up tobacco farming just as the English did; see Berlin 1974.

43. Rountree and Davidson 1997: chap. 3.

44. Jennings 1984: 102–44; Ferguson and Ferguson 1960: 31–41.

11. The Patuxent River Basin

1. Blair A. Rudes, personal communication to Wayne Clark, 2004.

2. J. Smith 1986b [1612]: 148; J. Smith 1986c [1624]: 105; Strachey 1953 [1612]: 47; Haile 1998: 606.

3. J. Smith 1986b [1612]: 148; J. Smith 1986c [1624]: 105; Strachey 1953 [1612]: 47; Haile 1998: 606; brackets ours.

4. Clark 1996; Steponaitis 1980, 1985.

5. Rowing or sailing at three knots (3.5 mph or 5.6 km/hr), a modest pace especially if a twelve-knot wind (13.8 mph or 22.2 km/hr) was behind them, and with the tide pushing them another 1.3 miles per hour (2.1 km/hr), and using the four hours of favorable tide available to them every twelve hours, they may have made as many as twenty-five statute miles (40.2 kilometers) per half day (flood going up, ebb going down).

6. An indirect route to the upper Chesapeake, but useful if one wanted, for whatever reason, to avoid the lower Potomac River people.

7. Don Shomette, personal communication to Kent Mountford.

8. Sedimentation due to plow agriculture: Wennersten 2001: 66–67. Four to five feet (up to 1.5 meters) of sediment covered the remains of *Scorpion,* a scuttled War of 1812 block sloop, when archaeologists explored the wreck some 160 years later (Ralph Eshelman of Eshelman Associates, personal communication to Kent Mountford).

9. J. Smith 1986b [1612]: 148; J. Smith 1986c [1624]: 105; Strachey 1953 [1612]: 47; Haile 1998: 607.

10. P. Johnson 1988: 16–17.

11. Sipple 1999: 93–95.

12. Sipple 1978: 157 (tuckahoe, or arrow arum); 90 (cow lily); 158 (*Phragmites*); 173 (softstem bulrush); 115 (cattail); 121 (water hemp); 135 (wild millet); 119 (wild rice); 29 (sweetflag).

13. Sipple 1978: 241. Kent Mountford adds from personal observation that this stand was logged in the early 1900s but has come back well, "although virtually no new [shoots are] succeeding." Some well-grown young cypress trees are being planted in the area and are doing well. Very young cypress seems to prefer wet-dry cycles.

14. Brush, Lenk, and Smith 1980. Behind the modern Fox Run Shopping Center north of Prince Frederick, six-foot (almost 2-meter) diameter chestnut stumps still remain from the 1930 harvesting of those trees (Wayne Clark, personal observations, 1998). Several stricken

chestnut saplings survive on the 2,000-acre American Chestnut Land Trust lands along Parkers Creek to the south of Prince Frederick. These survivors are but shadows of a magnificent species.

15. Khan 1993.

16. Stahle et al. 1998.

17. Clark 1996.

18. J. Smith 1986c [1624]: 289.

19. R. C. Williams 1983.

20. Wayne Clark's interpretation (for this volume) of Reeves 1992 and Steponaitis 1980: 31–34.

21. J. Smith 1986b [1612]: 166; J. Smith 1986c [1624]: 119; Strachey 1953 [1612]: 107; Haile 1998: 665.

22. A. White 1910 [1634]: 42; Anonymous 1910 [1635]: 74, 88–89.

23. Potter 1993: 77–100; Rountree and Turner 2002: 36–45: Steponaitis 1980: 31–35; 1985: 162–65.

24. Clark 1996; Steponaitis 1980, 1985.

25. For discussion of the latter, see Steponaitis 1985: 72–90.

26. Gibson 1978; Hall and Matthews 1974; Kirby and Matthews 1973; Kirby, Matthews, and Bailey 1967; Matthews 1971.

27. William Sipple, personal communication to Helen Rountree, 2004. Kent Mountford notes, however, that two centuries of Euro-American agriculture, with resulting silting of riverfront, may mean that there were considerably smaller expanses of tuckahoe (arrow arum) then than there are now.

28. This is how things appear, until more test excavations are done.

29. J. Smith 1986c [1624]: 289.

30. J. Smith 1986b [1612]: 232; J. Smith 1986c [1624]: 172; Haile 1998: 269.

31. J. Smith 1986c [1624]: 288–91.

32. Kingsbury 1906–35: 4: 507–8.

33. See Fausz 1983.

34. Browne et al. 1883–1972: 3: 85ff.

35. Eastern Shore: Browne et al. 1883–1972: 15: 413–17 ("Mattaponis" who may have been upstream Patuxent people). Western Shore: ibid.: 1: 329–30; 2: 354, 359–61; 3: 293–94; 10: 45. The Western Shore group retained a Patuxent identity as late as 1692 (ibid.: 13: 274). For the subsequent history of the Choptanks, see Rountree and Davidson 1997; the Chopticos were probably among the ancestors of today's Conoy/Piscataways (chap. 10 of this volume).

12. The Potomac River

1. Smith was exploring without Powhatan's permission, so the downriver hostility may indicate where Powhatan's influence was strong. Another explanation could be that the downriver tribes remembered an unpleasant contact with the Spanish in 1588 (Lewis and Loomie 1953: 56). Spanish visitors to the Western Shore "near the Potomac" had kidnapped a young man, presumably to convert him and make him a missionary to his people; the youth died before that could happen.

2. Trade routes: Rountree 1993: 32. Archaeology: Potter 1993. Contact period history: Potter 1993; Rountree 1990.

3. Waselkov 1982.

4. Scaled from shellfish distribution map in A. Lippson et al. 1981.

5. Hawkins 1991.

6. Jim Cummins of the Interstate Commission on the Potomac River Basin (personal communication to Helen Rountree, 2006) notes that the number of adult American shad collected during spring brood-stock collections has nearly doubled since 1995, the start of a restoration project led by the ICPRB. Young shad have also become substantially more numerous, reaching eight times prerestoration record highs recorded in Maryland surveys, which started in 1958. American shad numbers in the Potomac River should significantly increase each year for the foreseeable future.

7. Shad identification: Kent Mountford, 2004.

8. Fusonie and Fusonie 1998: 46–48. Salt making was not a success in Virginia, where the solar-evaporation method was tried on the lower Eastern Shore. Later, however, in New Jersey, the abundant pine forests were harvested for cordwood to boil seawater into a briny slurry to speed up the process; the makers also invented moveable sheds to cover the evaporation pans during wet weather.

9. Lauck W. Ward and Jeffrey P. Halka, personal communications to Helen Rountree, 2005.

10. Debate continues on what the silver-appearing ore might be; see chap. 4, note 56.

11. Sween and Offut 1999: 104. The gold, first mined commercially in 1868, was sold to the U.S. Mint.

12. Arthur Pierce Middleton, personal communication to Kent Mountford. Middleton's father, of the same name, owned these quarries in the early twentieth century. The industry is now defunct.

13. Argall 1904–6 [1613]:642; Haile 1998: 754.

14. Yuan and Brush 1992. A longer one (40,000 years) is currently being analyzed in Virginia (Gerald Johnson, personal communication to Helen Rountree, 2007).

15. Marye 1938: 134–37.

16. The estimates are from Turner 1982 for southside Potomac; we have applied his ratio of 4.25 people per warrior to the north side of the river, though the archaeological and historical evidence is uneven enough to warrant a great deal of caution before accepting these figures (Potter 1993: 22–23).

17. This is the third town in this volume with the name. In addition to this town, there was Cinquactock on the James, and Cinquoteck on the York; a Cinquaeteck also existed farther up the Potomac. These names were probably all the same, and their meaning (which is uncertain) may have had something to do with the fact that the first three were on points protruding into the junctions of major waterways (the fourth was not). Alert readers may also have noticed multiple Pamunkeys, Mattaponis, Wicomicos, and Piscataways; there are even more such oft-used names and more examples of them up and down the Atlantic coast (e.g., the Piscataqua River between Maine and New Hampshire). Like the English, the Algonquian speakers repeatedly used certain place names.

18. Miller 1983, 1986a.

19. Majority ware: Rappahannock Complex; Minority ware: Potomac Creek.

20. Potter 1993: 92–93. Smith spelled the name with an initial "S" in the text of his "Map of Virginia."

21. A. White 1910 [1634]: 40–41; Merrell 1979: 555.

22. Oysters: Waselkov 1982: 83, 200–208, 235–37; Potter 1993: 115. Minority percentage of Potomac Creek pottery: Potter 1993: 125. Drying oysters for transport: Archer 1969a [1607]: 83; Haile 1998: 103.

23. Waselkov (1982: 19) suggested that they were an outlier of the Cuttatawomen chiefdom (on the Rappahannock River), but that does not seem probable to us at this writing.

24. Several small ossuaries were excavated there in the early 1900s.

25. Curry 1999: 46–51.

26. Clark and Rountree 1993: 114–15, 122 n. 50; Browne et al. 1853–1972: 2: 25–26; 5: 34–36.

27. Ubelaker 1974. This analysis is one of the most informative studies of a pre-Contact Algonquian-speaking population's size, stature, health, and life expectancy to come from the Chesapeake region.

28. Schmitt 1965; Stewart 1992; Potter 1993: 210–20; Blanton et al. 1998.

29. Discussed in detail in Potter 1993: 213ff.

30. Comparison of Posey site on Potomac River and Camden Site on Rappahannock River (both mid- to late seventeenth century): Galke 2004. Mattawoman history: Clark and Rountree 1993: 112–14; Ferguson and Ferguson 1960: 38–43.

31. Potter 1993: 146, 150, 204–5.

32. Stephenson and Ferguson 1963.

33. Ibid.: 32, 42. Several ossuaries connected with these towns have been excavated; no European goods were found, indicating a pre-Contact date, but Susquehannock-influenced pottery was present (Curry 1999: 23).

34. Stephenson and Ferguson 1963: 15–40; ossuary burials were among the findings.

35. Most have been written up in recent Cultural Resource Management reports, which are not published. An exception from before CRM days is Ferguson and Stewart 1940, describing the excavation of a Contact period Piscataway ossuary.

36. Fleet 1876 [1631–32]: 25.

37. Ives Goddard, personal communication to Stephen Potter.

38. The ossuaries possibly associated with their capital were uncovered during the building of runways for Bolling Air Force Base, but no European trade goods were found (Curry 1999: 9–15).

39. Defined as marshes of at least ten acres (4 hectares) containing at least 30 percent wild rice and/or at least 50 percent tuckahoe (arrow arum) or cow lily.

40. Mercer 1978; Moore 1975a, 1975b, and 1975c; Silberhorn 1975.

41. J. Smith 1986b [1612]: 227; J. Smith 1986c [1624]: 166–67; Haile 1998: 260–61.

42. Maskettes: illustrated in Rountree 1989: 75; Rountree and Turner 2002: 50; and elsewhere. Box: Purchas 1904–6 [1625]: 19: 151.

43. Elder 1989; Elder, Henry, and Pendleton 1963; Gibson 1978; Hall and Matthews 1974; Isgrig and Strobel 1974; Kirby, Matthews, and Bailey 1967; Nicholson 1981.

44. Stephenson and Ferguson 1963.

45. Nomini Creek (at White Oak Point): Waselkov 1982. Patawomeck: Duncan 1999: C3–24.

46. Kingsbury 1906–35: 3: 438.

47. Barse 1992: sec. 4, 15–35.

48. The first known food-buying expedition was by Francis West soon after John Smith left (Percy 1921–22 [1612]: 266; Haile 1998: 504–5).

49. Spelman 1910 [1613?]: ciii-civ; Haile 1998: 485–86.

50. J. Smith 1986c [1624]: 304ff.

51. Kingsbury 1906–35: 4: 58 and passim (killing); 4: 450 (revenge); J. Smith 1986c [1624]: 320–21.

52. Fleet 1876 [1631–32].

53. Rountree 1990: chaps. 4 and 5.

54. Anonymous 1910 [1635]: 73–74; Browne et al. 1883–1972: 3: 281. In 1652, the Yoacomocos and Machodocs were both crossing the river to go hunting, which bothered the Maryland English.

55. A. White 1910 [1634]; Jesuit Letters 1910 [various years].

56. Merrell 1979. Archaeological corroboration: the Posey site on Mattawoman Creek (Harmon 1999). The finds at the site show relatively few English goods, compared to an overwhelming majority of Potomac Creek potsherds and other traditional material goods; most of the faunal remains were from wild animals with a few pig bones thrown in.

57. Cissna 1986.

58. Browne et al. 1883–1972: 1: 329–30; 2: 25–27; 5: 34–35; 8: 53–54 and passim; 13: 258–65 and passim; 15: 78, 286, and passim; 17: 5–7 and passim; 19: 383–86 and passim; 20: 412; 24: 102–4; 25: 76; 27: 29 and passim; 38: 104–5. The last mention of the group by name in the colonial records was in 1710, but as their land ownership was challenged in 1696–97, they may not have been living on a reservation by then.

59. See Savoy and Harley 1999, for a present-day Maryland Piscataway Indian perspective written for a K-6 audience.

13. The Rappahannock River Basin and the Piedmont Peoples

1. J. Smith 1986a [1608]: 51, 53; Haile 1998: 160.

2. Lauck W. Ward, personal communications to Helen Rountree, 2004 and 2005.

3. Orwig and Abrams 1994.

4. Strachey 1953 [1612]: 34; Haile 1998: 596.

5. The major early explorer account of the Piedmont is that of John Lederer (1958 [1672]), who traveled up the James and then headed southwest. For modern map analysis of his and others' itineraries, see Briceland 1987.

6. Cypress north of Rappahannock: Harvill et al. 1992: 6. All other data: Doumlele 1979a; Harris and Mizell 1979; Mercer 1978; Moore 1975a, 1975b, and 1976; Priest 1981; Priest and Dewing 1990; Silberhorn 1973 and 1974a. Northernmost limit: Grace Brush, personal communication to Helen Rountree, 2005.

7. *Tidewater Virginia Atlas,* Virginia Marine Resources Commission, 1977.

8. Jack Travelstead, Virginia Marine Resources Commission fisheries manager; personal communication to Robert Lippson.

9. Ibid. Freshwater begins at Hicks Landing, twenty nautical miles (23 statute miles or 37 kilometers) below Fredericksburg.

10. *Tidewater Virginia Atlas,* Virginia Marine Resources Commission, 1977.

11. Ibid.

12. No one pushed beyond the falls of the Potomac until Samuel Argall's journey in 1613 (Argall 1904–6 [1613]: 642; Haile 1998: 754). Who the Piedmont people were, or whether there were any in that period, is still under discussion by archaeologists.

13. Blair Rudes, personal communication to Helen Rountree, 2005. The Monacan and Mannahoac linguistic assignment has therefore rested almost entirely upon their geographical location in the Piedmont, adjacent to better-attested "Siouan" languages in the Piedmont of North and South Carolina (apparently the reasoning in Mooney 1970 [1894]), as well as the documented language difference from the Algonquian speakers of the Virginia coastal plain.

14. Winne 1969 [1608]: 246; Haile 1998: 203. Welsh is one of the Celtic languages within the Indo-European language family and is unrelated to any American Indian language. Winne's account is evidence that no bilingual Powhatan- and Monacan-speaking person was taken along, due either to bad luck or bad planning. The youth Namontack, by then bilingual in English and Powhatan, was present (Strachey 1953 [1612]: 131; Haile 1998: 687), and his knowledge of Monacan, if any, must have been minimal.

15. Strachey 1953 [1612]: 45, 41; Haile 1998: 605, 603.

16. Nugent 1934: 181. Not living in a state-level society, with surveyed boundaries and censuses of the citizens, the Virginia Algonquians seem to have been more casual than we are about the names of towns and polities—assuming that the early seventeenth-century English understood them correctly through the language barrier.

17. Tarpley Point on maps; Hales Point in local usage.

18. Potter 1993: 178.

19. No large Late Woodland site has yet been found at that location, but the old plantation of Sabine Hall is there, and English settlers were known to take up Indian towns whenever possible (see chap. 6).

20. When he visited the Rappahannocks during his captivity, John Smith heard of a place called Appamattuck somewhere upriver (1986a [1608]: 53; Haile 1998: 160); the way he lists it in that river's chiefdoms indicates that he meant Pissaseck (a name missing from the list). There was also a "Nanzatico" man named Mattox Will among the last Nanzaticos (descendants of the Nandtaughtacunds and Pissasecks) to occupy their reservation (McIlwaine et al. 1918: 410).

21. Nanzatico: Turner 2003b. Papiscone: Woodlawn Community Associates 1990. Camden: MacCord 1969; M. E. Hodges 1987.

22. Clark and Rountree 1993: 114.

23. MacCord 1965, 1997.

24. Placement of Monacan and Mannahoac towns by Jeffrey Hantman (personal communication to Helen Rountree, 1992, and published in her map for Hantman 1993 [97]).

25. Hantman 1990.

26. Gallivan 2003: 33–37.

27. This is the spelling in Smith's text. The name is spelled "Hassniunga" on Smith's map, apparently in error.

28. I.e., Potomac Creek wares: Bushnell 1935; Clark 1980: fig. 1. An alternative explanation, offered by Clark, is that the Mannahoac segment nearest the fall line consisted of Algonquian speakers—a multilingual situation apparently echoed by the Massawomecks (see chap. 10). Although Albemarle ceramics have traditionally been considered the Mannahoac pottery, a more complex picture of wares and people is emerging (Hantman and Klein 1992: 145–48).

29. Hantman 1990; Gallivan 2003.

30. J. Smith 1986b [1612]: 238; J. Smith 1986c [1624]: 184; Haile 1998: 283–84.

31. May 1607 interview with enemy Powhatans: Archer 1969a [1607]: 87; Haile 1998: 108. December 1607 information from enemy Rappahannocks: J. Smith 1986a [1608]: 53; Haile 1998: 160. Summer 1608 encounter with Mannahoacs (written sixteen years later): J. Smith 1986 [1624]: 175–76; Haile 1998: 272. Smith's report of autumn 1608 encounter with Monacans: J. Smith 1986b [1612]: 238; J. Smith 1986c [1624]: 184; Haile 1998: 183–84. Strachey's account of autumn 1608 encounter with Monacans: Strachey 1953 [1612]: 131; Haile 1998: 687. Winne's eyewitness report of autumn 1608 encounter with Monacans: Winne 1969 [1608]: 245; Haile 1998: 203. Smith's overview of Piedmont peoples (paraphrased by Strachey): J. Smith 1986b [1612]: 165; J. Smith 1986c [1624]: 119; Strachey 1953 [1612]: 49; Haile 1998: 608. Strachey's account of Monacans as enemies of Powhatan: Strachey 1953 [1612]: 105–6, 107; Haile 1998: 663–64, 665. Strachey's comment on Monacans being "more daring" in attacking the English: Strachey 1953 [1612]: 34–35; Haile 1998: 596–97. Locations of Piedmont towns, all but Mowhemcho being shown as "kings houses" or capitals of chiefdoms: Smith map.

32. Trimble 1996.

33. This anomaly and reasoning were first presented in Mook 1944: 200.

34. Monacans and (mainly) Mannahoacs: Hantman 1990: 106, 108 (map). No mining: Palmer Sweet, of Virginia Geological Survey, personal communication to Lisa Heuvel, 2004; Helen Rountree's thanks to Heuvel for forwarding the information.

35. Defined as marshes of at least ten acres (4 hectares) containing at least 30 percent wild rice and/or at least 50 percent tuckahoe (arrow arum) or cow lily.

36. Clay et al. 1958; Elder 1985; Elder, Henry, and Pendleton 1963; Hoppe 1989; Isgrig and Strobel 1974; Newhouse et al. 1980; Newhouse et al. 1985; Nicholson 1981. A soil survey has not yet been published for Caroline County, but it will eventually be available online. Meanwhile Helen Rountree was allowed to see pages from the galley proofs for study (with thanks to local USDA staff).

37. J. Smith 1986c [1624]: 178; Haile 1998: 275.

38. Eliminating: Strachey 1953 [1612]: 44; Haile 1998: 604. Loyalists: the original Kecoughtans, who had been captives of Powhatan since around 1596 (Strachey 1953 [1612]: 68; Haile 1998: 627).

39. Kingsbury 1906–35: 4: 9–12.

40. Termed the Second and Third Anglo-Powhatan Wars by scholars today.

41. McIlwaine 1979 [1924]: 501, 563.

42. Rountree 1990: chaps. 4 and 5.

43. Strachey 1953 [1612]: 106; Haile 1998: 663–64.

Epilogue

1. Biggs 1981. Biggs estimated, for example, that the densely vegetated "all forest" Susquehanna basin had 10–15 percent higher flows in drought and 25–30 percent less intense floods than during the late twentieth century.

2. E.g., Brush 1989.

3. Fusonie and Fusonie 1998.

4. Miller 1986b.

5. Garman and Macko 1998.

6. Lippson and Lippson 2006.

7. Ibid.; Hildebrand and Schroeder 1928.

8. Rusnak 1967.

9. Mitchell Tarnowski, Maryland Department of Natural Resources, quoted in the *Capital* (Annapolis, Md., September 22, 2004).

10. Brush and Hilgartner 2000; Arnold 2003.

11. Shreve et al. 1969 [1910].

12. Gottschalk 1945; Froomer 1980; Brush 1984.

13. Hilgartner and Brush 2006; Pasternack and Brush 1998.

14. Saltonstall 2002; Robert Meadows, Delaware Department of Natural Resources, personal communication to Kent Mountford, 2005.

15. Wintering: Strachey 1953 [1612]: 127; Haile 1998: 683. Name: Siebert 1975: 364.

16. Daniel Boone, personal communication to Kent Mountford, 2005.

17. Mallards began spreading out as Euroamericans built canals and farm ponds across the landscape.

18. See Stewart and Robbins 1958.

19. James River Project Committee 1950: 270–71.

20. Scott 1991: 68–69.

21. James River Project Committee 1950: 260–61.

22. Ibid.: 252.

23. Ibid.

24. Ibid.: 250, 252.

25. Ibid.: 259 (woodchuck); 250 (skunk); Scott 1991: 92 (woodchuck).

26. Byrd 1966: 300–302.

27. James River Project Committee 1950: 274.

28. Ibid.: 271, 273; and Scott 1991: 70 (deer).

29. James River Project Committee 1950: 261.

30. Herbst 2002: 48.

31. Another bridge is historical: going through colonial and later documents (e.g., Virginia's Legislative Petitions) and sifting out references to natural phenomena and nonhuman species.

32. Bonnecamps 1920 [1749].

33. Clarkson 1964: 7.

34. J. Smith 1986c [1624]: 168; Haile 1998: 262.

35. See Abbot 1975: 19.

Bibliography

Abbot, William W. 1975. *The Colonial Origins of the United States: 1607–1763.* New York: Wiley.

Abbott, R. Tucker. 1974. *American Seashells.* 2nd ed. New York: Van Nostrand.

Alsop, George. 1910 [1666]. A Character of the Province of Maryland. In *Narratives of Early Maryland, 1633–1684,* edited by Clayton Colman Hall, 335–87. New York: Scribner's.

Ames, Susie May. 1940. *Studies of the Virginia Eastern Shore in the Seventeenth Century.* Richmond: Dietz Press.

Anonymous. 1910 [1635]. A Relation of Maryland, 1635. In *Narratives of Early Maryland, 1633–1684,* edited by Clayton Colman Hall, 70–112. New York: Scribner's. Reprint, New York: Scribner's, 1967; and Maryland Hall of Records' 350th Anniversary Document Series, 1984.

———. 1969 [1608]. "Map of Virginia" (Zuñiga map). In *The Jamestown Voyages under the First Charter,* edited by Philip L. Barbour, ser. 2, 137: facing page 239. Cambridge: Hakluyt Society.

Archer, Gabriel. 1969a [1607]. "Relatyon of the Discovery of Our River, Description of the River and Country, Description of the People" (authorship uncertain). In *The Jamestown Voyages under the First Charter,* edited by Philip L. Barbour, ser. 2, 136: 80–104. Cambridge: Hakluyt Society. Also printed, verbatim but with modernized spelling, in *Jamestown Narratives: Eyewitness Accounts of the Virginia Colony: The First Decade: 1607–1617,* edited by Edward W. Haile, 101–24. Champlain, Va.: RoundHouse, 1998.

———. 1969b [1609]. Letter from Jamestown, August 31, 1609. In *The Jamestown Voyages under the First Charter,* edited by Philip L. Barbour, ser. 2, 136: 279–82. Cambridge: Hakluyt Society.

Argall, Samuel. 1904–6 [1613]. "A Letter of Sir Samuel Argall Touching His Voyage to Virginia, and Actions There: Written to Master Nicholas Hawes." In *Hakluytus Posthumus or Purchas His Pilgrimes,* edited by Samuel Purchas, 19: 90–95. Glasgow: James MacLehose and Sons. Also printed, verbatim but with modernized spelling, in *Jamestown Narratives: Eyewitness Accounts of the Virginia Colony: the First Decade: 1607–1617,* edited by Edward W. Haile, 752–56. Champlain, Va.: RoundHouse, 1998.

Arnold, Angela. 2003. "An Interglacial (Sangamon) and Late Holocene Record of Chesapeake Bay." Ph.D. diss., Johns Hopkins University. Ann Arbor: University Microfilms.

Baker, William A. 1983. *The Mayflower and Other Colonial Vessels.* Annapolis: Naval Institute Press.

———. 1987 (1966). *Sloops and Shallops.* Columbia: University of South Carolina Press.

Bakeless, John. 1961. *The Eyes of Discovery. The Eyes of Discovery.* New York: Dover.

Banister, John. 1970. *John Banister and His Natural History of Virginia, 1678–1692.* Edited by Joseph Ewan and Nesta Ewan. Urbana: University of Illinois Press.

Barber, Michael B. 1983. *The Vertebrate Faunal Analysis of the Middle Woodland Mockley Ceramic Users: Maycocks Point Shell Midden (44PG51), Prince George County, Virginia.* Richmond: Virginia Department of Historic Resources.

———. 2003. "Archaeology in a Post–September 11th World: Excavations of 44PU72, Radford Army Ammunitions Plant, Pulaski County, Virginia." Paper presented at the annual meeting of the Eastern States Archaeological Federation, Mt. Laurel, N.J.

Barber, Michael B., M. J. Madden, and J. C. Hardison. 2004. *The Excavations of Feature 04-1 at the Hatch Site (44PG51), Prince George County, Virginia.* Richmond: Virginia Department of Historic Resources.

Barbour, Philip L. 1964. *The Three Worlds of Captain John Smith.* Boston: Houghton Mifflin.

———, ed. 1969. *The Jamestown Voyages under the First Charter.* Ser. 1, vols. 136, 137. Cambridge: Hakluyt Society.

———. 1971. "The Earliest Reconnaissance of the Chesapeake Bay Area: Captain John Smith's Map and Indian Vocabulary, Part I." *Virginia Magazine of History and Biography* 79: 280–302.

Barnard, Thomas A., Jr. 1975. *City of Hampton Tidal Marsh Inventory.* VIMS Special Report in *Applied Marine Science and Ocean Engineering,* no. 60.

Barrie, Robert, and John Barrie. 1909. *Cruises, Mainly in the Bay of the Chesapeake.* Philadelphia: Franklin Press.

Barse, William P. 1992. "Phase I and II Terrestrial Archeological Survey, Maryland Route 210 Wetland Mitigation at the Parker Berry Farm, Prince George's County, Maryland." Maryland State Highway Administration Report no. 285. Baltimore.

Becker, Marshall. 1987. "An Analysis of the Human Skeletal Remains from 46HM73: A Susquehannock Population of the Mid-Sixteenth Century." *West Virginia Archaeologist* 39, no. 2: 37–56.

Beitzell, Edwin W. 2001 [1968]. *Life on the Potomac River.* Bowie, Md.: Heritage Books.

Belue, Ted F. 1996. *The Long Hunt: Death of the Buffalo East of the Mississippi.* Mechanicsburg, Pa.: Stackpole Books.

Berlin, Ira. 1974. *Slaves without Masters: The Free Negro in the Antebellum South.* New York: Pantheon Books.

Beverley, Robert. 1947 [1705]. *The History and Present State of Virginia.* Edited by Louis B. Wright. Chapel Hill: University of North Carolina Press.

Biggs, Robert B. 1981. "Freshwater Inflow to Estuaries, Short and Long Term Perspectives." In *Proceedings of the National Symposium on Freshwater Inflow to Estuaries,* edited by R. D. Cross and D. L. Williams, Coastal Ecosystems Project, OBS, vol. 2. Washington, D.C.: U.S. Fish and Wildlife Service.

Bland, Edward, Abraham Wood, Sackford Brewster, and Elias Pennant. 1911 [1651]. "The Discovery of New Brittaine, Began August 27, Anno Dom. 1650 . . ." In *Narratives of Early Carolina, 1650–1708,* edited by Alexander S. Salley, 5–19. New York: Scribner's.

Blanton, Dennis B., Stevan C. Pullins, and Veronica Deitrick. 1998. *The Potomac Creek Site (44ST2) Revisited.* Research Report Series, no. 10. Richmond: Virginia Department of Historic Resources.

Bonnecamps, Father Joseph Pierre de. 1920 [1749]. "Account of the Voyage on the Beautiful River Made in 1749, under the Direction of Monsieur de Celeron." *Ohio Archaeological and Historical Quarterly* 39: 397–423.

Boon, John. 2004. *Secrets of the Tide.* Portland, Ore.: International Specialized Book Services.

Bourne, Michael Owen. 1998. "Prehistoric Kent County." In *Historic Houses of Kent County: An Architectural History: 1642–1860,* edited by Eugene Hall Johnstone, 1–15. Chestertown: Historical Society of Kent County.

Boyce, Hettie L. 1985. "The Novak Site: A Late Woodland Upland Monongahela Site." *Pennsylvania Archaeologist* 55, no. 3: 21–40.

Boyd, Donna C. 1990. "Osteological Analysis of Prehistoric Ossuary at Jordan's Point (44PG333/1)." Appendix (with separate pagination) to McLearen and Mouer 1994 (q.v.).

Brashler, Janet G. 1987. "A Middle 16th Century Susquehannock Village in Hampshire County, West Virginia." *West Virginia Archeologist* 39, no. 2: 1–30.

Brashler, Janet G., and Ronald W. Moxley. 1990. "Late Prehistoric Engraved Shell Gorgets of West Virginia." *West Virginia Archaeologist* 41, no. 1: 1–10.

Breen, T. H., and Stephen Innes. 1980. *"Myne Owne Ground": Race and Freedom on Virginia's Eastern Shore, 1640–1676.* New York: Oxford University Press.

Brewington, Marion Vernon. 1963. *Chesapeake Bay Log Canoes and Bugeyes.* Cambridge, Md.: Cornell Maritime Press.

Briceland, Alan Vance. 1987. *Westward from Virginia: The Exploration of the Virginia-Carolina Frontier.* Charlottesville: University Press of Virginia.

Bridenbaugh, Carl. 1967. *Vexed and Troubled Englishmen, 1590–1642.* New York: Oxford University Press.

Brittingham, Joseph B., and Alvin W. Brittingham Sr. 1947. *The First Trading Post at Kicotan (Kecoughtan), Hampton, Virginia.* Newport News: Franklin Printing.

Brown, M. L. 1980. *Firearms in Colonial America: The Impact on History and Technology, 1492–1775.* Washington, D.C.: Smithsonian Institution Press.

Browne, William Hand et al., eds. 1883–1972. *The Archives of Maryland.* Baltimore: Maryland Historical Society.

Bruggerman, Seth. 1999. "Notes on Early Seventeenth-Century Boatbuilding with Preliminary Suggestions Concerning the Construction of an Interpretive Shallop for Use at Colonial Jamestown." Jamestown Fellow Research Paper, Jamestown Settlement, Williamsburg, Va.

Brush, Grace S. 1984. "Patterns of Recent Sediment Accumulation in Chesapeake Bay (Virginia-Maryland USA) Tributaries." In "Geochronology of Recent Deposits," edited by J. A. Robbins. *Chemical Geology* 44: 227–42.

———. 1986. "Geology and Paleoecology of Chesapeake Bay: A Long-term Monitoring Tool for Management." *Journal of the Washington Academy of Sciences* 76: 146–60.

———. 1989. "Rates and Patterns of Estuarine Sediment Accumulation." *Limnology and Oceanography* 34: 1235–46.

Brush, Grace S., and W. B. Hilgartner. 2000. "Paleoecology of Submerged Macrophytes in the Upper Chesapeake Bay." *Ecological Monographs* 70: 645–67.

Brush, Grace S., Cecilia Lenk, and Joanne Smith. 1976. "Vegetation Map of Maryland." Manuscript on file, Johns Hopkins University, Dept. of Geography and Environmental Engineering.

———. 1980. "The Natural Forests of Maryland: An Explanation of the Vegetation Map of Maryland [with 1:250,000 map]." *Ecological Monographs* 50, no. 1: 77–92.

Burns, Jaspar. 1991. *Fossil Collecting in the Mid-Atlantic States.* Baltimore: Johns Hopkins University Press.

Bushnell, David I., Jr. 1935. *The Manahoac Tribes in Virginia, 1608.* Smithsonian Miscellaneous Collections 94, no. 8. Washington, D.C.

Busby, Virginia. 1996. "Interim Report on Archaeological Research at Nicholas Farms." Manuscript on file, Maryland Historical Trust, Crownsville, Md.

———. 2000. "Report of Archaeological Investigations at Site 18DO11 (the Chicone Site #1), Dorchester County, Maryland, 1994–1995 Season." Manuscript on file, Maryland Historical Trust, Crownsville, Md.

Byrd, William. 1966. *The Prose Works of William Byrd of Westover.* Edited by Louis B. Wright. Cambridge: Harvard University Press.

Calver, James, and C. R. B. Hobbs Jr., eds. 1963. *Geographic Map of Virginia.* Charlottesville, Va.: Division of Mineral Resources, Department of Conservation and Economic Development.

Canner, Thomas. 1904–6 [1603]. "A Relation of the Voyage Made to Virginia in the Elizabeth of London . . . in the Yeere 1603." In *Hakluytus Posthumus or Purchas His Pilgrimes,* edited by Samuel Purchas, 18: 329–35. Glasgow: James MacLehose and Sons. Reprint, in *New American World: A Documentary History of North America to 1612,* edited by David B. Quinn, 163–66. New York: Arno Press.

Ceci, Lynn. 1975a. "Fish Fertilizer: A Native North American Practice?" *Science* 188: 26–30.

———. 1975b. [Reply to letters on Ceci 1975a] *Science* 189: 946–49.

———. 1989. "Tracing Wampum's Origins: Shell Bead Evidence from Archaeological Sites in Western and Coastal New York." In *Proceedings of the 1986 Shell Bead Conference,* edited by Charles F. Hayes III and Lynn Ceci, no. 20: 63–80. Rochester, N.Y.: Rochester Museum and Science Center Research Records.

Chapelle, Howard I. 1951. *American Small Sailing Craft.* New York: Norton.

Cissna, Paul B. 1986. "The Piscataway Indians of Southern Maryland: An Ethnohistory from Pre-European Contact to the Present." Ph.D. diss., American University. Ann Arbor: University Microfilms.

Clark, Wayne E. 1976. "The Application of Regional Research Designs to Contract Archaeology: The Northwest Transportation Corridor Archaeological Survey Project." Master's thesis, American University, Washington.

————. 1980. "The Origins of the Piscataway and Related Cultures." *Maryland Historical Magazine* 75, no. 1: 8–22.

————. 1996. "The Patuxent Indians at the Dawn of History." *Calvert Historian* 22, no. 2: 6–20.

Clark, Wayne E., and Richard Hughes. 1983. "Proposal for Intensive Archaeological Investigations of the Cumberland Palisaded Village Site, Calvert County, Maryland." Manuscript on file, Jefferson Patterson Park and Museum, St. Leonard, Md.

Clark, Wayne E., and Helen C. Rountree. 1993. "The Powhatans and the Maryland Mainland." In *Powhatan Foreign Relations, 1500–1722,* edited by Helen C. Rountree, 112–35. Charlottesville: University Press of Virginia.

Clarkson, Roy B. 1964. *Tumult on the Mountain: Lumbering in West Virginia, 1770–1920.* Parsons, W. Va.: McClain Printing.

Clay, John W. 1975. *Soil Survey of Henrico County, Virginia.* U.S. Department of Agriculture. Washington, D.C.: U.S. Government Printing Office.

Clay, John W., H. H. Perry, E. A. Perry, J. R. Moore, F. F. Nickels, and G. C. Wilson. 1958. *Soil Survey of Mathews County, Virginia.* U.S. Department of Agriculture. Washington, D.C.: U.S. Government Printing Office.

Cobb, Philip R., and David W. Smith. 1989. *Soil Survey of Northampton County, Virginia.* U.S. Department of Agriculture. Washington, D.C.: U.S. Government Printing Office.

Commissioners Appointed under the Great Seale of England for the Virginia Affairs. 1896 [1677]. "Articles of Peace between the Most Mighty Prince . . . Charles the II . . . And the Severall Indian Kings and Queens &c . . . the 29th Day of May: 1677." *Virginia Magazine of History and Biography* 14: 289–96.

Cresson, Hilborne T. 1892. *Report upon Pile-Structures in Naaman's Creek near Claymont, Delaware.* Cambridge, Mass.: Peabody Museum of Archaeology and Ethnology, vol. 1, no. 4.

Cressy, David. 1997. *Birth, Marriage and Death; Ritual, Religion and the Life-Cycle in Tudor and Stuart England.* Oxford: Oxford University Press.

Cronin, William B. 1973. *1971–72 Chesapeake Bay Statistics.* Special Report 20, Chesapeake Bay Institute, Johns Hopkins University.

————. 2005. *The Disappearing Islands of the Chesapeake.* Baltimore: Johns Hopkins University Press.

Curry, Dennis C. 1999. *Feast of the Dead: Aboriginal Ossuaries in Maryland.* Crownsville, Md.: Maryland Historical Trust.

Custer, Jay F. 1986. "Late Woodland Cultures of the Lower and Middle Susquehanna Valley." In *Late Woodland Cultures of the Middle Atlantic States,* edited by Custer, 116–42. Newark: University of Delaware Press.

————. 1987. "Late Woodland Ceramics and Social Boundaries in Southeastern Pennsylvania and Northern Delaware." *Archaeology of Eastern North America* 15: 13–28.

————. 1988. *Prehistoric Cultures of the Delmarva Peninsula: An Archaeological Study.* Newark: University of Delaware Press.

————. 1996. *Prehistoric Cultures of Eastern Pennsylvania.* Harrisburg: Pennsylvania Historical and Museum Commission.

Custer, Jay F., and Daniel R. Griffith. 1986. "Late Woodland Cultures of the Middle and Lower Delmarva Peninsula." In *Late Woodland Cultures of the Middle Atlantic Region,* edited by Custer. Newark: University of Delaware Press.

Danckaerts, Jasper. 1913 [1679–80]. *Journal of Jaspar Danckaerts, 1679–1680.* Edited by Bartlett Burleigh James and J. Franklin Jameson. New York: Scribner's.

Davidson, Thomas E. 1993. "The Powhatans and the Eastern Shore." In *Powhatan Foreign Relations, 1500–1722,* edited by Helen C. Rountree, 136–53. Charlottesville: University Press of Virginia.

Deetz, James. 1993. *Flowerdew Hundred: The Archaeology of a Virginia Plantation, 1619–1864.* Charlottesville: University Press of Virginia.

Denny, Emily Roe. 1959. *Indians of Kent Island.* Centerville: Kent Island Historical Tour Commission.

Dent, Richard J. 1995. *Chesapeake Prehistory: Old Traditions, New Directions.* New York: Plenum Press.

Dillow, Joseph A. 1984. "A Relation of a Voyage Made by Mr. Cyprian Thorowgood (from the Patuxent) to the Head of the Baye: April 24-May 5, 1634." *Chronicles of St. Mary's* 32, no. 11: 201–6.

Doumlele, Damon G. 1976. *City of Virginia Beach Tidal Marsh Inventory.* VIMS Special Report in *Applied Marine Science and Ocean Engineering,* no. 118.

———. 1979a. *Essex County Tidal Marsh Inventory.* VIMS Special Report in *Applied Marine Science and Ocean Engineering,* no. 207.

———. 1979b. *New Kent County Tidal Marsh Inventory.* VIMS Special Report in *Applied Marine Science and Ocean Engineering,* no. 208.

Duncan, Gwenyth. 1999. "Faunal Analysis of the Potomac Creek Site (44ST2)." Appendix C (with separate pagination) to Blanton 1999 (q.v.).

Earle, Carville V. 1979. "Environment, Disease, and Mortality in Early Virginia." In *The Chesapeake in the Seventeenth Century: Essays on Anglo-American Society,* edited by Thad W. Tate and David L. Ammerman, 96–125. Chapel Hill: University of North Carolina Press.

Edwards, Andrew C., William E. Pittman, Gregory J. Brown, Mary Ellen N. Hodges, Marley R. Brown III, and Eric E. Voight. 1989. *Hampton University Archaeological Project: A Report on the Findings.* Richmond: Virginia Department of Historic Resources.

Ehrlich, Paul, David Dobkin, and Darryl Wheye. 1988. *The Birder's Handbook.* New York: Simon and Schuster.

Elder, John H., Jr. 1985. *Soil Survey of Spotsylvania County, Virginia.* U.S. Department of Agriculture. Washington, D.C.: U.S. Government Printing Office.

———. 1989. *Soil Survey of Prince William County, Virginia.* U.S. Department of Agriculture. Washington, D.C.: U.S. Government Printing Office.

Elder, John H., Jr., Elvin F. Henry, and Robert F. Pendleton. 1963. *Soil Survey of Northumberland and Lancaster Counties, Virginia.* U.S. Department of Agriculture. Washington, D.C.: U.S. Government Printing Office.

Eliot, Jonathon. 1830. *Historical Sketches of the Ten Miles Square Forming the District of Columbia.* Washington: J. Eliot Jr.

Engelbrecht, William. 2003. *Iroquoia: The Development of a Native World.* Syracuse: Syracuse University Press.

Fagan, Brian. 2000. *The Little Ice Age.* New York: Basic Books.

Farrell, J. D., and Stewart Ware. 1991. "Edaphic Factors and Forest Vegetation in the Piedmont of Virginia." *Bulletin of the Torrey Botanical Club* 118: 161–69.

Fausz, J. Frederick. 1977. "The Powhatan Uprising of 1622: A Historical Study of Ethnocentrism and Cultural Conflict." Ph.D. diss., College of William and Mary. Ann Arbor: University Microfilms.

———. 1983. "Profits, Pelts, and Power: English Culture in the Early Chesapeake: 1620–1652." *Maryland Historian* 14, no. 2: 13–31.

———. 1984. "Present at the 'Creation': The Chesapeake World That Greeted the Maryland Colonists." *Maryland Historical Magazine* 79, no. 1: 7–20.

———. 1985. "Patterns of Anglo-Indian Aggression and Accommodation along the Mid-Atlantic Coast, 1584–1634." In *Cultures in Contact: The European Impact on Native Institutions in Eastern North America, A.D. 1000–1800,* edited by William W. Fitzhugh, 225–68. Washington, D.C.: Smithsonian Institution Press.

Fay, C. W., R. J. Neves, and G. B. Pardue. 1983a. *Species Profiles: Life Histories and Environmental Requirements of Coastal Fishes and Invertebrates (Mid-Atlantic)—Striped Bass.* Division of Biological Services: FWS/OBS-82/11.8. Washington, D.C.: U.S. Fish and Wildlife Service.

———. 1983b. *Species Profiles: Life Histories and Environmental Requirements of Coastal Fishes and Invertebrates (Mid-Atlantic)—Alewife/Blueback Herring.* Division of Biological Services: FWS/OBS-82/11.9. Washington, D.C.: U.S. Fish and Wildlife Service.

Featherstone, Donald. 1998. *Armies and Warfare in the Pike and Shot Era, 1422–1700.* London: Constable.

Feest, Christian F. 1983. "Powhatan's Mantle." In *Tradescant's Rarities,* edited by Arthur MacGregor, 130–35. Oxford: Clarendon Press.

Ferguson, Alice L. L., and Henry G. Ferguson. 1960. *The Piscataway Indians of Southern Maryland.* Accokeek: Ferguson Foundation.

Ferguson, Alice L. L., and T. Dale Stewart. 1960. *The Piscataway Indians of Maryland.* Accokeek, Md.: Ferguson Foundation.

The Ferrar Papers. 1992 [1590–1790]. Originals housed in Magdalene College, Cambridge University. First published in six microfilm reels in 1960; more complete collection published in fourteen microfilm reels in 1992.

Fleet, Henry. 1876 [1631–32]. "A Brief Journal of a Voyage Made in the Bark *Virginia*, to Virginia and Other Parts of the Continent of America." In *The Founders of Maryland,* edited by Edward D. Neill, 19–37. Albany, N.Y.: Joel Munsell.

Fleming, Gary P., Phillip P. Coulling, Karen D. Patterson, and K. M. McCoy. 2004. *The Natural Communities of Virginia: Classification of Ecological Community Groups. 2nd approximation.* Virginia Department of Conservation and Recreation. Richmond: Division of Natural Heritage. Also available at: http://www.dcr.virginia.gov/dnh/ncintro.htm.

French, Hugh M., Mark Demitroff, D. Forman, and W. Newell. 2005. "Late Pleistocene Permafrost Events in Southern New Jersey, Eastern U.S.A." *Permafrost and Periglacial Processes* 16: 173–86.

Froomer, N. L. 1980. "Morphologic Changes in Some Chesapeake Bay Tidal Marshes Resulting from Accelerated Soil Erosion." *Zeitschrift für Geomorphologie* (N. F. Supplement) 34: 242–54.

Fusonie, Alan, and Donna Fusonie. 1998. *George Washington, Pioneer Farmer.* Mt. Vernon, Va.: Mt. Vernon Ladies Association.

Galke, Laura J. 2004. "Perspectives on the Use of European Material Culture at Two Mid- to

Late Seventeenth-Century Native American Sites in the Chesapeake." *North American Archaeologist* 25: 91–113.

Gallivan, Martin D. 2003. *James River Chiefdoms: The Rise of Social Inequality in the Chesapeake.* Lincoln: University of Nebraska Press.

Gardner, Paul S. 1994. "Carbonized Plant Remains." In *Paspahegh Archaeology: Data Recovery Investigations of Site 44JC308 at the Governor's Land at Two Rivers, James City County, Virginia,* edited by Nicholas M. Lucketti, Mary Ellen N. Hodges, and Charles T. Hodges, 267–78. Richmond: Virginia Department of Historic Resources.

Garman, Gregory C., and Stephen Macko. 1998. "Contribution of Marine-derived Organic Matter to an Atlantic Coast, Freshwater, Tidal Stream by Anadromous Clupeid Fish." *North American Benthological Society* 17, no. 3: 277–83.

Gibson, Joseph W. 1978. *Soil Survey of St. Mary's County, Maryland.* U.S. Department of Agriculture. Washington, D.C.: U.S. Government Printing Office.

Gifford, George E., Jr., and Marion Tinling. 1958. "A Relation of the Voyage to the Head of the Bay." *Historian:* 20, no. 3: 347–51 (Cyprian Thorowgood account).

Gottschalk, L. C. 1945. "Effects of Soil Erosion on Navigation in Upper Chesapeake Bay." *Geographical Revue* 35: 219–37.

Gregory, Leverett B. 1980. "The Hatch Site: A Preliminary Report (Prince George County, Virginia)." *Quarterly Bulletin of the Archeological Society of Virginia* 34: 239–48.

Grosslein, Marvin D., and Thomas R. Azarovitz. 1982. *Fish Distribution, MESA New York Bight Atlas.* Monograph no. 15. New York: New York Sea Grant Institute.

Guilday, John E. 1971. "Biological and Archaeological Analysis of Bones from a 17th Century Indian Village (46 PU 31), Putnam County, West Virginia." *Report on Archeological Investigations,* no. 4. Morgantown: West Virginia Geological and Economic Survey.

Guilday, John E., P. W. Parmalee, and D. P. Tanner. 1962. "Aboriginal Butchering Techniques at the Eschelman Site (36LA12), Lancaster County, Pennsylvania." *Pennsylvania Archaeologist* 32, no. 2: 59–83.

Haile, Edward W. 1995. *Virginia Discovered and Described by Captayn John Smith.* Champlain, Va.: Globe Sales Publications.

———. 1996. *England in America: The Chesapeake Bay from Jamestown to St. Mary's City, 1607–1634.* Champlain, Va.: Globe Sales Publications; distributed by Dietz Press, Richmond, Va.

———, ed. 1998. *Jamestown Narratives: Eyewitness Accounts of the Virginia Colony: The First Decade: 1607–1617.* Champlain, Va.: RoundHouse.

Hall, Richard L. 1970. *Soil Survey of Wicomico County, Maryland.* U.S. Department of Agriculture. Washington, D.C.: U.S. Government Printing Office.

———. 1973. *Soil Survey of Worcester County, Maryland.* U.S Department of Agriculture. Washington, D.C.: U.S. Government Printing Office.

Hall, Richard L., and Earle D. Matthews. 1974. *Soil Survey of Charles County, Maryland.* U.S. Department of Agriculture. Washington, D.C.: U.S. Government Printing Office.

Hammett, Julie E. 1992. "Ethnohistory of Aboriginal Landscapes and Land Use in the Southeastern United States. *Southern Indian Studies* 41: 1–50.

Hamor, Ralph. 1957 [1615]. *A True Discourse of the Present State of Virginia.* Richmond: Virginia State Library. Also printed, verbatim but with modernized spelling, in *Jamestown*

Narratives: Eyewitness Accounts of the Virginia Colony: The First Decade: 1607–1617, edited by Edward W. Haile, 795–856. Champlain, Va.: RoundHouse, 1998.

Hancock, William H., and Helen C. Rountree. 2004. "Building a Powhatan House: A Guide to Yeehawkawn Construction for Museums." Manuscript on file, Jamestown Settlement.

Hanson, Lee H., Jr. 1975. "The Buffalo Site: A Late 17th Century Indian village site (46Pu 31) in Putnam County, West Virginia." *Report on Archaeological Investigations,* no. 5. Morgantown: West Virginia Geological and Economic Survey.

Hantman, Jeffrey L. 1990. "Between Powhatan and Quirank: Reconstructing Monacan Culture and History in the Context of Jamestown. *American Anthropologist* 92: 676–90.

———. 1993. "Powhatan's Relations with the Piedmont Monacan." In *Powhatan Foreign Relations, 1500–1722,* edited by Helen C. Rountree, 94–111. Charlottesville: University Press of Virginia.

Hantman, Jeffrey L., and Michael J. Klein. 1992. "Middle and Late Woodland Archaeology in Piedmont Virginia." In *Middle and Late Woodland Research in Virginia: A Synthesis,* edited by Theodore Reinhart and Mary Ellen N. Hodges, 137–64. Archeological Society of Virginia Special Publication no. 29. Richmond.

Hariot, Thomas. 1972 [1590]. *A Briefe and True Report of the New Found Land of Virginia.* New York: Dover.

Harland, John. 1984. *Seamanship in the Age of Sail.* Annapolis, Md.: Naval Institute Press.

Harmon, James M. 1999. "Archaeological Investigations at the Posey Site (18CH81 and 18CH82), Indian Head Division, Naval Surface Warfare Center, Charles County, Maryland." Report on file, Maryland Archaeological Conservation Laboratory, St. Leonard, Md.

Harris, Arthur F., Jr., and Joseph C. Mizell. 1979. *Spotsylvania and Caroline County Tidal Marsh Inventory.* VIMS Special Report in *Applied Marine Science and Ocean Engineering,* no. 167.

Harrison, W. R., J. Malloy, G. A. Rusnack, and J. Terasmae. 1965. "Possible Late Pleistocene Uplift at the Chesapeake Bay Entrance." *Journal of Geology* 73: 201–29.

Harvill, Alton McCaleb, Jr., Ted R. Bradley, Charles E. Stevens, Thomas F. Wieboldt, Donna M. E. Ware, Douglas W. Ogle, Gwynn W. Ramsey, and Gary P. Fleming. 1992. *Atlas of the Virginia Flora.* 3rd ed. Burkeville: Virginia Botanical Associates.

Hawkins, Don Alexander. 1991. "The Landscape of the Federal City." *Washington History* 3, no. 1: 10–24. Washington, D.C.: Washington Historical Society.

Hening, William Waller, comp. 1809–23. *The Statutes at Large, Being a Collection of All the Laws of Virginia from the First Session of the Legislature.* 13 vols. New York: R. and W. and G. Bartow.

Herbert, Joseph M. 1992. "Descriptions of the Shallop in Western Europe and the New World, 1587–1671." *American Neptune* 50: 167–79.

———. 1993. "Prehistoric Settlement at the Myrtle Point Site and the Structure of Low Density Lithic Assemblages along the Lower Patuxent River, Maryland." *Occasional Papers,* no. 4. Jefferson Patterson Park and Museum, St. Leonard, Md.

———. 1995. "Thomas Point: Emerging Late Woodland Traditions in Southern Maryland." *Occasional Papers,* no. 5. Jefferson Patterson Park and Museum, St. Leonard, Md.

Herbert, Joseph M., and Laurie Cameron Steponaitis. 1998. "Estimating the Season of Harvest of Eastern Oysters (*Crassostrea virginica*) with Shells from the Chesapeake Bay." *Southeastern Archaeology* 17, no. 1: 53–71.

Herbst, Robert. 2002. *The State of the Chesapeake Bay: A Report to the Citizens of the Bay Region*. Chesapeake Bay Program. Annapolis, Md.: U.S. Environmental Protection Agency.

Higgins, Thomas F., III, Charles M. Downing, and Dennis B. Blanton. 1995. *Archaeological Survey at Veterans Administration Medical Center, City of Hampton, Virginia*. Report from William and Mary Center for Archaeological Research submitted to Sasaki Associates. Richmond: Virginia Department of Historic Resources.

Hildebrand, S. F., and W. C. Schroeder. 1928. *Fishes of Chesapeake Bay*. Bulletin no. 1024. Washington, D.C.: U.S. Bureau of Fisheries.

Hilgartner, W. B., and Grace S. Brush. 2006. "Human Impact and Late Holocene Habit Dynamics in a Chesapeake Bay Freshwater Tidal Wetland Delta." *Holocene* 16: 479–94.

Hobbs, Carl H., III. 2004. "Geologic History of Chesapeake Bay." *Quaternary Science Reviews* 23: 641–61.

Hodges, Mary Ellen N. 1987. "Camden: Another Look Seventeen Years after Registration." *Notes on Virginia* 27: 21–24.

———. 1998. *Native American Settlement at Great Neck: Report on VDHR Archaeological Investigations of Woodland Components at Site 44VB7, Virginia Beach, Virginia, 1981–1987*. Research Report Series, no. 9. Richmond: Virginia Department of Historic Resources.

Hodges, Mary Ellen N., and Charles T. Hodges. 1994. *Paspahegh Archaeology: Data Recovery Investigations of Site 44JC308 at the Governor's Land at Two Rivers, James City County, Virginia*. Richmond: Virginia Department of Historic Resources.

Hodges, Robert L. 1978. *Soil Survey of Chesterfield County, Virginia*. U.S. Department of Agriculture. Washington, D.C.: U.S. Government Printing Office.

Hodges, Robert L., Glenn Richardson, J. Paul Sutton, James E. Belshaw, Thomas W. Simpson, W. Scott Barnes, and James E. Keys, Jr. 1980. *Soil Survey of Hanover County, Virginia*. U.S. Department of Agriculture. Washington, D.C.: U.S. Government Printing Office.

Hodges, Robert L., P. Ben Sabo, David McCloy, and C. Kent Staples. 1985. *Soil Survey of James City and York Counties and the City of Williamsburg, Virginia*. U.S. Department of Agriculture. Washington, D.C.: U.S. Government Printing Office.

Hodges, Robert L., P. Ben Sabo, and Ronald J. Straw. 1988. *Soil Survey of New Kent County, Virginia*. U.S. Department of Agriculture. Washington, D.C.: U.S. Government Printing Office.

Hoppe, Diane A. S. 1989. *Soil Survey of Essex County, Virginia*. U.S. Department of Agriculture. Washington, D.C.: U.S. Government Printing Office.

Hoffman, Bernard G. 1977. "Observations on Certain Ancient Tribes of the Northern Appalachian Province." Anthropological Paper 70, *Bulletin of Bureau of American Ethnology* 191: 191–245.

Horton, Tom. 1987. *Bay Country*. Baltimore: Johns Hopkins University Press.

Howard, J. Smoker. 2003. "Chronological Placement of the Hershey Site and Implications on a Dynamic Socio-Cultural Landscape." *Pennsylvania Archaeologist* 73, no. 2: 15–30.

Hudson, Charles M. 1979. *Black Drink*. Athens: University of Georgia Press.

Hughes, Richard. 1980. *A Preliminary Cultural and Environmental Overview of the Prehis-*

tory of Maryland's Lower Eastern Shore Based upon a Survey of Selected Artifact Collections. Manuscript series, no. 26. Annapolis: Maryland Historical Trust.

Hulton, Paul. 1984. *America 1585: The Complete Drawings of John White.* Chapel Hill: University of North Carolina Press.

Hulton, Paul, and David B. Quinn. 1964. *The American Drawings of John White, 1577–1590.* 2 vols. Chapel Hill: University of North Carolina Press.

Hume, Ivor Noel. 1994. *The Virginia Adventure: Roanoke to James Towne: An Archaeological and Historical Odyssey.* New York: Knopf.

Hurley, Linda M. 1991. *A Field Guide to the Submerged Aquatic Vegetation of Chesapeake Bay.* Chesapeake Bay Estuary Program. Annapolis, Md.: U.S Fish and Wildlife Service.

Hutton, Frank Z., Sr., A. P. Faust, R. Feuer, H. R. Frantz, F. J. Gladwin, A. H. Kodess, and J. E. McCuen. 1963. *Soil Survey of Dorchester County, Maryland.* U.S. Department of Agriculture. Washington, D.C.: U.S. Government Printing Office.

Hutton, Frank Z., Sr., A. P. Faust, F. J. Gladwin, A. H. Kodess, J. E. McCuen, and William U. Reybold III. 1964. *Soil Survey of Caroline County, Maryland.* U.S. Department of Agriculture. Washington, D.C.: U.S. Government Printing Office.

Ireland, William, Jr., and Earle D. Matthews. 1974. *Soil Survey of Sussex County, Delaware.* U.S. Department of Agriculture. Washington, D.C.: U.S. Government Printing Office.

Isgrig, Dan, and Adolph Strobel Jr. 1974. *Soil Survey of Stafford and King George Counties, Virginia.* U.S. Department of Agriculture. Washington, D.C.: U.S. Government Printing Office.

James River Project Committee of the Virginia Academy of Science. 1950. *The James River Basin, Past Present and Future.* Richmond: Virginia Academy of Science.

Jennings, Francis. 1978. "Susquehannock." In *Handbook of North American Indians,* vol. 15, *Northeast,* edited by Bruce G. Trigger, 362–67. Washington, D.C.: Smithsonian Institution Press.

———. 1984. *The Ambiguous Iroquois Empire.* New York: Norton.

Jesuit Letters. 1910 (various years, 1634 onward). Extracts from *Annual Letters of the English Province.* In *Narratives of Early Maryland, 1633–1684,* edited by Clayton Colman Hall, 118–44. New York: Scribner's.

Johnson, Amandus. 1911. *The Swedish Settlements on the Delaware.* New York: D. Appleton.

Johnson, George. 1989 (1881). *History of Cecil County, Maryland.* Baltimore: Genealogical Publishing.

Johnson, Paula. 1988. *Working the Water: The Commercial Fisheries of Maryland's Patuxent River.* Solomons, Md.: Calvert Marine Museum.

Johnson, William C. 2001. "Protohistoric Monongahela and the Case for an Iroquois Connection." In *Societies in Eclipse: Archaeology of the Eastern Woodlands Indians, A.D. 1400–1700,* edited by David S. Brose, C. Wesley Cowan, and Robert C. Mainfort Jr., 67–82. Washington, D.C.: Smithsonian Institution Press.

Jones, David L., Ian A. Rodihan, Louis E. Cullipher, John W. Clay, and Michael J. Marks. 1985. *Soil Survey of Prince George County, Virginia.* U.S. Department of Agriculture. Washington, D.C.: U.S. Government Printing Office.

Jones, Hugh. 1956 (1724). *The Present State of Virginia.* Edited by Richard L. Morton. Chapel Hill: University of North Carolina Press.

Kammen, Michael G., ed. 1963. "Maryland in 1699: A Letter from the Reverend Hugh Jones."

Chronicles of St. Mary's 11, no. 11: 89–93. Reprinted from the *Journal of Southern History* 29, no. 3 (August 1963): 362–72. (Rev. Jones was one of four Hugh Joneses in the Chesapeake region at the time.)

Kelso, William M., with Blythe Straube. 2004. *Jamestown Rediscovery 1994–2004.* Richmond: Association for the Preservation of Virginia Antiquities.

Kennedy, Victor S., and Kent Mountford. 2001. "Human Influences on Aquatic Resources in the Chesapeake Bay Watershed." In *Discovering the Chesapeake: The History of an Ecosystem,* edited by Philip D. Curtin, Grace S. Brush, and George W. Fisher, 191–219. Baltimore: Johns Hopkins University Press.

Kennedy, Victor S., Roger I. E. Newell, and Albert F. Eble. 1996. *The Eastern Oyster: Crassostrea virginica.* College Park: Maryland Sea Grant College.

Kent, Barry C. 1984. *Susquehanna's Indians.* Anthropological Series no. 6. Harrisburg: Pennsylvania Historical and Museums Commission.

Khan, Humaira. 1993. "A Paleoecological Study of a Freshwater Tidal Marsh." Ph.D. diss., Johns Hopkins University. Ann Arbor: University Microfilms.

Kingsbury, Susan Myra, comp. 1906–35. *Records of the Virginia Company of London.* 4 vols. Washington, D.C.: Library of Congress.

Kirby, Robert M., and Earle D. Matthews. 1973. *Soil Survey of Anne Arundel County, Maryland.* U.S. Department of Agriculture. Washington, D.C.: U.S. Government Printing Office.

Kirby, Robert M., Earle D. Matthews, and Moulton A. Bailey. 1967. *Soil Survey of Prince George's County, Maryland.* U.S. Department of Agriculture. Washington, D.C.: U.S. Government Printing Office.

Kitchel, William F., H. Thomas Saxton III, Ruch A. Strauss, Steve K. Thomas, and Carl D. Peacock Jr. 1986. *Soil Survey of Isle of Wight County, Virginia.* U.S. Department of Agriculture. Washington, D.C.: U.S. Government Printing Office.

Klippel, Walter E., and D. F. Morey. 1986. "Contextual and Nutritional Analysis of Freshwater Gastropods from Middle Archaic Deposits at the Hayes Site, Middle Tennessee." *American Antiquity* 51: 799–813.

Kozel, Scott M. 2000–2003. Roads to the Future. Chesapeake Bay Bridge History. http://www.roadstothefuture.com/chesa_bay_bridge_history.html.

Kurlansky, Peter. 2003. *Salt: A World History.* New York: Penguin Books.

Lankford, John. 1967. *Captain John Smith's America.* New York: Harper Torchbooks.

Laslett, Peter. 1984 [1965]. *The World We Have Lost: England before the Industrial Age.* New York: Scribner's.

Lavery, Brian. 1988. *The Colonial Merchantman: Susan Constant, 1605.* Annapolis: Naval Institute Press.

Lederer, John. 1958 [1672]. *The Discoveries of John Lederer.* Edited by William P. Cumming. Charlottesville: University Press of Virginia.

Lemay, J. A. Leo. 1991. *The American Dream of Captain John Smith.* Charlottesville: University Press of Virginia.

Lewis, Clifford M., and Albert J. Loomie. 1953. *The Spanish Jesuit Mission in Virginia, 1570–1572.* Chapel Hill: University of North Carolina Press.

Linklater, Andro. 2003. *Measuring America: How an Untamed Wilderness Shaped the United States and Fulfilled the Promise of Democracy.* New York: Plume.

Lippson, Alice J. 1973. *The Chesapeake Bay in Maryland: An Atlas of Natural Resources.* Baltimore: Johns Hopkins University Press.

Lippson, Alice J., and Robert L. Lippson. 2006. *Life in Chesapeake Bay.* 3rd ed. Baltimore: Johns Hopkins University Press.

Lippson, Alice J., Michael S. Haire, A. Frederick Holland, Jorgen Jensen, R. Lynn Moran-Johnson, Tibor T. Polgar, and William A. Richkus, eds. 1981. *Environmental Atlas of the Potomac Estuary.* Baltimore: Johns Hopkins University Press.

Lippson, Robert L., and Alice J. Lippson. Forthcoming. *The Inner Coast.* Chapel Hill: University of North Carolina Press.

Lowery, Darrin L. 1992. "Archaeological Survey of Kent Island, Queen Anne's County, Maryland." Unpublished report, Maryland Historical Trust, Crownsville, Md.

———. 1994. "Archaeological Survey of Queen Anne's County, Maryland." Unpublished report, Maryland Historical Trust, Crownsville, Md.

———. 1995. "Archaeological Survey of Interior Queen Anne's County, Maryland." Unpublished report, Maryland Historical Trust, Crownsville, Md.

———. 2001. *Archaeological Survey of the Chesapeake Bay Shoreline Associated with Accomack County and Northampton County, Virginia.* Survey and Planning Report Series, no. 6. Richmond: Virginia Department of Historical Resources.

———. 2003. *Archaeological Survey of the Atlantic Coast Shorelines Associated with Accomack County and Northampton County, Virginia.* Survey and Planning Report Series, no. 7. Richmond: Virginia Department of Historic Resources.

———. 2004a. *A Landscape Sculpted by Wind and Water: Additional Archaeological and Geomorphological Investigations on Mockhorn Island in Northampton County, Virginia.* Easton, Md.: privately published.

———. 2004b. "Archaeological Survey of the Fishing Bay and the Fairmount Wildlife Management Areas within Dorchester and Somerset County, Maryland." Unpublished report, Maryland Historical Trust, Crownsville, Md.

Luckenbach, Alvin H., Wayne E. Clark, and Richard Levy. 1987. "Rethinking Cultural Stability in the Eastern North American Prehistory: Linguistic Evidence from Eastern Algonquian." *Journal of Middle Atlantic Archaeology* 3: 1–33.

Lucketti, Nicholas M., Marry Ellen N. Hodges, and Charles T. Hodges, eds. 1994. *Paspahegh Archaeology: Data Recovery Investigations of Site 44JC308 at the Governor's Land at Two Rivers, James City County, Virginia.* Richmond: Virginia Department of Historic Resources.

MacCord, Howard A., Sr. 1965. "The DeShazo Site, King George County, Virginia." *Quarterly Bulletin of the Archeological Society of Virginia* 19, no. 4: 98–104.

———. 1969. "Camden: A Postcontact Indian Site in Caroline County." *Quarterly Bulletin of the Archeological Society of Virginia* 24, no. 1: 1–55.

———. 1997. "The DeShazo Site, King George County, Virginia, the 1973 Excavations." *Quarterly Bulletin of the Archeological Society of Virginia* 52, no. 1: 1–22, 28–31.

Main, Gloria. 1982. *Tobacco Colony: Life in Early Maryland, 1650–1720.* Princeton: Princeton University Press.

Malloy, Anne. 1977. *Wampum.* New York: Hastings House.

Marye, William D. 1920. "The Old Indian Road." *Maryland Historical Magazine* 15: 107–24, 208–29, 345–95.

———. 1938. "The Anacostian Indian Fort." *Maryland Historical Magazine* 33, no. 2: 134–48.

———. 1955. "The Great Maryland Barrens." *Maryland Historical Magazine* 50: 11–23, 120–42.

Matthews, Earle D. 1971. *Soil Survey of Calvert County, Maryland.* U.S. Department of Agriculture. Washington, D.C.: U.S. Government Printing Office.

Matthews, Earle D., and Richard L. Hall. 1966a. *Soil Survey of Somerset County, Maryland.* U.S. Department of Agriculture. Washington, D.C.: U.S. Government Printing Office.

———. 1966b. *Soil Survey of Queen Anne's County, Maryland.* U.S. Department of Agriculture. Washington, D.C.: U.S. Government Printing Office.

Maxwell, J. A., and M. B. Davis. 1972. "Pollen Evidence of Pleistocene and Holocene Vegetation on the Allegheny Plateau, Maryland." *Quaternary Research* 2: 506–30.

McAvoy, Richard M., and Lynne D. McAvoy. 1997. *Archaeological Investigations of Site 44SX202, Cactus Hill, Sussex County, Virginia.* Research Report Series, no. 8. Richmond: Virginia Department of Historic Resources.

McCary, Ben Clyde. 1981. "The Location of Werowocomoco." *Quarterly Bulletin of the Archeological Society of Virginia* 36: 77–93.

McCary, Ben Clyde, and Norman Barka. 1977. "The John Smith and Zuniga Maps in the Light of Recent Archeological Research along the Chickahominy River." *Archaeology of Eastern North America* 5: 73–86.

McClure, N. E., ed. 1939. *Letters of John Chamerlain.* Memoir 12, pts. 1 and 2. Philadelphia: American Philosophical Society.

McIlwaine, Henry Reade, comp. 1979 [1918]. *Legislative Journals of the Council of Colonial Virginia.* 2nd ed. 3 vols. Richmond: Virginia State Library.

———. 1979 [1924]. *Minutes of the Council and General Court of Virginia, 1622–1632, 1679–1676.* 2nd ed. Richmond: Virginia State Library.

McLearen, Douglas C., and L. Daniel Mouer. 1993. *Jordan's Journey II: A Preliminary Report on the 1992 Excavations at Archaeological Sites 44PG302, 44PG303, and 44PG 315.* Richmond: Virginia Department of Historic Resources.

———. 1994. *Jordan's Journey III: A Preliminary Report on the 1992–1993 Excavations at Archaeological Site 44PG307.* Richmond: Virginia Department of Historic Resources.

Meacham, Sarah. 2003. "'They Will Be Adjudged by Their Drink, What Kind of Housewives They Are': Gender, Technology and Household Cidering in England and the Chesapeake, 1690–1760." *Virginia Magazine of History and Biography* 111: 117–50.

Mercer, James L. 1978. *Westmoreland County Tidal Marsh Inventory.* VIMS Special Report in *Applied Marine Science and Ocean Engineering,* no. 59.

Merrell, James H. 1979. "Cultural Continuity among the Piscataway Indians of Colonial Maryland." *William and Mary Quarterly,* 3rd ser., 36: 548–70.

Middleton, Arthur Price. 1984. *Tobacco Coast.* Baltimore: Johns Hopkins University Press.

Miller, Henry. 1983. *A Search for the "Citty of St. Marys": Report on the 1981 Excavations in St. Mary's City, Maryland.* St. Mary's City, Md.: St. Mary's City Archaeological Series, no. 1.

———. 1986a. *Discovering Maryland's First City: A Summary Report on the 1981–1984 Archaeological Excavations in St. Mary's City, Maryland.* St Mary's City, Md.: St. Mary's City Archaeological Series, no. 2.

———. 1986b. "Transforming a "Splendid and Delightsome Land": Colonist[s?] and Ecological Change in the Chesapeake, 1607–1820." *Journal of the Washington Academy of Science* 76, no. 5: 173–87.

Montague, Ludwell Lee. 1972. "Powhatan's Chimney, Gloucester County." *Discovery* 4, no. 3: 1, 6–10.

Mook, Maurice A. 1944. "The Aboriginal Population of Tidewater Virginia." *American Anthropologist* 46: 193–208.

Mooney, James. 1970 [1894]. *Siouan Tribes of the East*. New York: John Reprint Co. Originally published as Smithsonian Institution Bureau of American Ethnology Bulletin no. 22.

Moore, Kenneth A. 1975a. *Stafford County Tidal Marsh Inventory*. VIMS Special Report in *Applied Marine Science and Ocean Engineering*, no. 62.

———. 1975b. *King George County Tidal Marsh Inventory*. VIMS Special Report in *Applied Marine Science and Ocean Engineering*, no. 63.

———. 1975c. *Prince William County Tidal Marsh Inventory*. VIMS Special Report in *Applied Marine Science and Ocean Engineering*, no. 78.

———. 1976. *Gloucester County Tidal Marsh Inventory*. VIMS Special Report in *Applied Marine Science and Ocean Engineering*, no. 64.

———. 1977a. *City of Newport News and Fort Eustis Tidal Marsh Inventory*. VIMS Special Report in *Applied Marine Science and Ocean Engineering*, no. 137.

———. 1977b. *Northampton County Tidal Marsh Inventory*. VIMS Special Report in *Applied Marine Science and Ocean Engineering*, no. 139.

———. 1980. *James City County Tidal Marsh Inventory*. VIMS Special Report in *Applied Marine Science and Ocean Engineering*, no. 188.

———. 1981. *Surry County Tidal Marsh Inventory*. VIMS Special Report in *Applied Marine Science and Ocean Engineering*, no. 187.

Moore, Kenneth A., and Sharon Dewing. 1990. *Charles City County Tidal Marsh Inventory*. VIMS Special Report in *Applied Marine Science and Ocean Engineering*, no. 308.

———. 1991a. *Henrico County, Chesterfield County, Colonial Heights, Petersburg, and the City of Richmond Tidal Marsh Inventory*. VIMS Special Report in *Applied Marine Science and Ocean Engineering*, no. 309.

———. 1991b. *City of Suffolk Tidal Marsh Inventory*. VIMS Special Report in *Applied Marine Science and Ocean Engineering*, no. 311.

Morgan, Ted. 1992. *Wilderness at Dawn: The Settling of the North American Continent*. New York: Simon and Schuster.

Morrill, John, ed. 1996. *The Oxford Illustrated History of Tudor and Stuart Britain*. Oxford: Oxford University Press.

Mouer, L. Daniel, Douglas C. McLearen, R. Taft Kiser, Christopher P. Egghart, Beverly J. Binns, and Dane T. Magoon. 1992. *Jordan's Journey: A Preliminary Report on Archaeology at Site 44PG302, Prince George County, Virginia, 1990–1991*. U.S. Department of Agriculture. Washington, D.C.: Virginia Department of Historic Resources.

Mountford, Kent. 1986. "Ecological Change through History." In "Chesapeake Bay: A Study of Ecological Change through History," edited by J. Thomas and R. Monahan, special issue, *Journal of the Washington Academy of Science* 76: 141–45.

———. 2002a. "C&D Canal: Charting the Course That Began with Mapmaker's Dream." Past Is Prologue. *Bay Journal*, Jan.–Feb., 8–10. Alliance for the Chesapeake Bay, Baltimore.

———. 2002b. "Chesapeake & Delaware Canal Dilemma: Is Bigger Always Better?" *Past Is Prologue. Bay Journal,* March, 8–9. Alliance for the Chesapeake Bay, Baltimore.

Munday, John C., and Michael S. Fredosh. 1981. "Chesapeake Bay Plume Dynamics from LANDSAT." In *Proceedings of the Chesapeake Bay Plume Study "Superflux" Symposium,* edited by J. W. Campbell and J. P. Thomas, 79–92. NASA Conference Publication no. 2188.

Nash, Gary. 1982. *Red, White, and Black: The Peoples of Early America.* 2nd ed. Englewood Cliffs, N.J: Prentice-Hall.

Newhouse, Michael E., Phillip R. Cobb, W. Scott Barnes, and David V. McCloy. 1980. *Soil Survey of Gloucester County, Virginia.* U.S. Department of Agriculture. Washington, D.C.: U.S. Government Printing Office.

Newhouse, Michael E., Phillip R. Cobb, Larry F. Baldwin, and David V. McCloy. 1985. *Soil Survey of Middlesex County, Virginia.* U.S. Department of Agriculture. Washington, D.C.: U.S Government Printing Office.

Nicholson, John C. 1981. *Soil Survey of Westmoreland County, Virginia.* U.S. Department of Agriculture. Washington, D.C.: U.S. Government Printing Office.

Norwood, Col. Henry. 1947 [1650]. "A Voyage to Virginia by Col. Norwood." In *Tracts and Other Papers,* edited by Peter Force, vol. 3, no. 10. New York: Peter Smith.

Nugent, Nell Marion, comp. 1934. *Cavaliers and Pioneers: Abstracts of Virginia Land Patents and Grants, 1623–1800,* vol. 1. Richmond: Dietz Press.

Oertel, G. F., and A. M. Foyle. 1995. "Drainage Displacement by Sea-Level Fluctuation at the Outer Margin of the Chesapeake Seaway." *Journal of Coastal Research* 11: 583–604.

Opperman, Antony F. 1992. "Middle Woodland Subsistence at Maycock's Point (44PG40), Prince George County, Virginia." Master's thesis, University of Tennessee-Knoxville.

Opperman, Antony F., and E. Randolph Turner III. 1990. "Archaeology at Shelly, Gloucester County." *Notes on Virginia* 34: 24–27.

Orth, Robert J. 2005. *Chesapeake Bay Program Annual SAV Aerial Survey.* Gloucester Point: Virginia Institute of Marine Science. Available as e-publication at http://www.vims.edu/ bio/sav/sav04.

Orth, Robert J., Judith F. Nowak, Gary F. Anderson, and Jennifer R. Whiting. 1993. *Distribution of Submerged Aquatic Vegetation in the Chesapeake Bay and Tributaries and Chincoteague Bay—1993.* Chesapeake Bay Program. Annapolis, Md.: U.S. Environmental Protection Agency.

Orwig, D. A., and M. D. Abrams. 1994. "Land-use History (1790–1992), Composition, and Dynamics of Oak-Pine Forests within the Piedmont and Coastal Plain of Northern Virginia." *Canadian Journal of Forestry Research* 24: 1216–25.

Owsley, Douglas W., and Bertita E. Compton. 1992. *Osteological Investigation of Human Remains from "Jordan's Journey" (site 44PG302), a 17th Century Fortified Settlement in Prince George's County, Virginia.* Appendix (with separate pagination) to Mouer et al. 1992.

Palliser, D. M. 1983. *The Age of Elizabeth: England under the Later Tudors, 1547–1603.* London: Longman.

Pasternack, G. B., and Grace S. Brush. 1998. "Sedimentation Cycles in a River-Mouth Tidal Fresh Water Marsh." *Estuaries* 21: 407–15.

Peacock, Carl D., Jr., and William J. Edmonds. 1993. *Soil Survey of Accomack County, Virginia.* U.S. Department of Agriculture. Washington, D.C.: U.S. Government Printing Office.

Pendergast, James. 1991. "The Massawomeck: Raiders and Traders into the Chesapeake Bay in the Seventeenth Century." *Transactions of the American Philosophical Society* 81, no. 2.

Percy, George. 1921–22 [1625?]. "A Trewe Relacyon." *Tyler's Quarterly* 3: 259–82. Also printed, verbatim but with modernized spelling, in *Jamestown Narratives: Eyewitness Accounts of the Virginia Colony: The First Decade: 1607–1617,* edited by Edward W. Haile, 499–519. Champlain, Va.: RoundHouse, 1998.

———. 1969 [1608?]. "Observations Gathered out of a Discourse of the Plantation of the Southern Colonie in Virginia by the English 1606." In *The Jamestown Voyages under the First Charter,* edited by Philip L. Barbour, ser. 2, 136: 129–46. Cambridge: Hakluyt Society. Also printed, verbatim but with modernized spelling, in *Jamestown Narratives: Eyewitness Accounts of the Virginia Colony: The First Decade: 1607–1617,* edited by Edward W. Haile, 85–100. Champlain, Va.: RoundHouse, 1998.

Perkins, Francis. 1969 [1608]. Letter of March 18, 1608. In *The Jamestown Voyages under the First Charter,* edited by Philip L. Barbour, ser. 2, 136: 158–62. Cambridge: Hakluyt Society. Also printed, verbatim but with modernized spelling, in *Jamestown Narratives: Eyewitness Accounts of the Virginia Colony: The First Decade: 1607–1617,* edited by Edward W. Haile, 131–36. Champlain, Va.: RoundHouse, 1998.

Perreault, Melanie. 2002. "Waterways in the Atlantic World: Contact and Cultural Negotiation across a Liquid Landscape." In *New Perspectives in Transatlantic Studies,* edited by Heidi Slettedahl McPherson and Will Kaufman, 1–15. Lanham, Md.: University Press of America.

Perry, James. 1990. *The Formation of a Society on Virginia's Eastern Shore, 1615–1655.* Chapel Hill: University of North Carolina Press.

Peterson, Harold L. 2000 [1956]. *Arms and Armor in Colonial America, 1526–1783.* New York: Dover.

Phillips-Birt, Douglas H. C. 1979 [1951]. *Building of Boats.* London: Stanford Maritime.

Poag, C. Wylie. 1997. "The Chesapeake Bay Bolide Impact: A Convulsive Event in Atlantic Coastal Plain Evolution." *Sedimentary Geology* 108: 45–70.

———. 1999. *Chesapeake Invader: Discovering America's Giant Meteorite Crater.* Princeton, N.J.: Princeton University Press.

Pollack, David A., Gwynn Henderson, and Christopher T. Begley. 2002. "Fort Ancient/Mississippian Interaction of the Northeastern Periphery." *Southeastern Archaeology* 21, no. 2: 206–20.

Potter, Stephen R. 1982. "An Analysis of Chicacoan Settlement Patterns." Ph.D. diss., University of North Carolina. Ann Arbor: University Microfilms.

———. 1989. "Early English Effects on Virginia Algonquian Exchange and Tribute in the Tidewater Potomac." In *Powhatan's Mantle: Indians in the Colonial Southeast,* edited by Peter Wood, Gregory Waselkov, and Thomas Hatley, 151–72. Lincoln: University of Nebraska Press.

———. 1993. *Commoners, Tribute, and Chiefs: The Development of Algonquian Culture in the Potomac Valley.* Charlottesville: University Press of Virginia.

Potter, Stephen R., and Gregory A. Waselkov. 1994. "Whereby We Shall Enjoy Their Cultivated Places." In *Historical Archaeology of the Chesapeake,* edited by Paul A. Shakel and Barbara J. Little, 22–33. Washington, D.C.: Smithsonian Institution Press.

Priest, Walter I., III. 1981. *Middlesex County Tidal Marsh Inventory.* VIMS Special Report in *Applied Marine Science and Ocean Engineering,* no. 218.

Priest, Walter I., III, and Sharon Dewing. 1990. *Richmond County Tidal Marsh Inventory.* VIMS Special Report in *Applied Marine Science and Ocean Engineering,* no. 306.

Priest, Walter I., III, Gene M. Silberhorn, and Andrew W. Zacherle. 1987. *King and Queen County Tidal Marsh Inventory.* VIMS Special Report in *Applied Marine Science and Ocean Engineering,* no. 291.

Purchas, Samuel, comp., ed. 1617. *Purchas His Pilgrimes.* 3rd ed. London.

———. 1904–6 [1625]. *Hakluytus Posthumus or Purchas His Pilgrimes.* 20 vols. Glasgow: James MacLehose and Sons.

Quinn, David B. 1955. *The Roanoke Voyages, 1584–1590.* Ser. 2, vol. 104. Cambridge: Hakluyt Society.

———. 1977. *North America from Earliest Discovery to First Settlements: The Norse Voyages to 1612.* New York: Harper and Row.

———. 1985. *Set Fair for Roanoke: Voyages and Colonies, 1584–1606.* Chapel Hill: University of North Carolina Press.

Radford, Albert E., Harry E. Ahles, and C. Ritchie Bell. 1968. *Manual of the Vascular Flora of the Carolinas.* Chapel Hill: University of North Carolina Press.

Ralamb, Ake Classon. 1943 [1691]. *Skeps Byggerij eller Adelig Öfnings Tionde Tom.* Facsimile reprint. Stockholm: Museet. Available at the Mariners' Museum library, Newport News, Va.

Reber, Earl J., Moreton A. Bailey, Paul J. Swecker, and Jerry S. Quesenberry. 1981. *Soil Survey of City of Suffolk, Virginia.* U.S. Department of Agriculture. Washington, D.C.: U.S. Government Printing Office.

Reeves, Stuart A. 1992. "The Items of Living: The Material Relationships between Prehistoric Societies of the Western Chesapeake Bay, Maryland." Grant application to Maryland Historical Trust, on file at Jefferson Patterson Park and Museum, St. Leonard, Md.

———. 1996. "The Cumberland Palisaded Village (18CV171)." Grant proposal to Maryland Historical Trust, on file at Jefferson Patterson Park and Museum, St. Leonard, Md.

Reeves, Stuart A., Jean B. Russo, Dennis J. Pogue, Joseph M. Herbert, Camille Wells. 1991. "Myrtle Point: The Changing Land and People of a Lower Patuxent River Community." *Jefferson Patterson Park and Museum, Occasional Papers,* no. 3. St. Leonard, Md.

Reybold, William U., III. 1970. *Soil Survey of Talbot County, Maryland.* U.S. Department of Agriculture. Washington, D.C.: U.S. Government Printing Office.

Richter, Daniel K. 1992. *Ordeal of the Longhouse: The Peoples of the Iroquois League in the Era of European Colonization.* Chapel Hill: University of North Carolina Press.

Robinette, Carl E., and Diana A. S. Hoppe. 1982. *Soil Survey of Richmond County, Virginia.* U.S. Department of Agriculture. Washington, D.C.: U.S. Government Printing Office.

Robbins, Chandler S., and Erik Blom. 1996. *Atlas of the Breeding Birds of Maryland and the District of Columbia.* Pittsburgh: University of Pittsburgh Press.

Rogers, S. G., and M. J. van den Avyle. 1983. *Species Profiles: Life Histories and Environmental Requirements of Coastal Fishes, Invertebrates (South Atlantic)—Atlantic Menhaden.* Division of Biological Services. Washington, D.C.: U.S. Fish and Wildlife Service.

Rohde, Fred C., Rudolph G. Arndt, David G. Lindquist, and James F. Parnell. 1994. *Freshwater Fishes of the Carolinas, Virginia, Maryland, and Delaware.* Chapel Hill: University of North Carolina Press.

Rountree, Helen C. 1989. *The Powhatan Indians of Virginia: Their Traditional Culture.* Norman: University of Oklahoma Press.

————. 1990. *Pocahontas's People: The Powhatan Indians of Virginia through Four Centuries.* Norman: University of Oklahoma Press.

————. 1993. "The Powhatans and Other Woodland Indians as Travelers." In *Powhatan Foreign Relations, 1500–1722,* edited by Helen C. Rountree, 21–52. Charlottesville: University Press of Virginia.

————. 1996. "A Guide to the Late Woodland Indians' Use of Ecological Zones in the Chesapeake Region." *Chesopiean* 34, no. 2–3.

————. 2005. *Pocahontas, Powhatan, Opechancanough: Three Indian Lives Changed by Jamestown.* Charlottesville: University of Virginia Press.

Rountree, Helen C., and Thomas E. Davidson. 1997. *Eastern Shore Indians of Virginia and Maryland.* Charlottesville: University Press of Virginia.

Rountree, Helen C., and E. Randolph Turner, III. 1998. "The Evolution of the Powhatan Paramount Chiefdom in Virginia." In *Chiefdoms and Chieftaincy: An Integration of Archaeological, Ethnohistorical and Ethnographic Approaches,* edited by Elsa M. Redmond, 265–96. Gainesville: University Press of Florida.

————. 2002. *Before and after Jamestown: Virginia's Powhatans and Their Predecessors.* Gainesville: University Press of Florida.

Rusnak, Gene A. 1967. "Rates of Sediment Accumulation in Modern Estuaries." In *Estuaries,* edited by George H. Lauff, American Association for the Advancement of Science publication no. 83, 180–84. Washington, D.C.

Rutman, Darret B., and Anita H. Rutman. 1976. "Of Agues and Fevers: Malaria in the Early Chesapeake." *William and Mary Quarterly,* 3rd ser., 33: 31–60.

————. 1979. "Now-Wives and Sons-in-Law": Parental Death in a Seventeenth Century Virginia County." In *The Chesapeake in the Seventeenth Century: Essays on Anglo-American Society,* edited by Thad W. Tate and David L. Ammerman, 153–82. Chapel Hill: University of North Carolina Press.

Sainsbury, W. Noel, J. W. Fortescue, and Cecil Headham, comps. 1860–1926. *Calendar of State Papers, Colonial Series.* 60 vols. London: Longman, Green, and Roberts.

Saltonstall, Kristin. 2002. "Cryptic Invasion by a Non-native Genotype of the Common Reed, *Phragmites australis,* into North America." *Proceedings of the National Academy of Sciences* 99, no. 4: 3445–49.

Savoy, Mervyn A., and Yvonne Harley. 1991. *A Piscataway Story: The Legend of Kittamaquund.* Waldorf, Md.: Piscataway-Conoy Confederacy and Subtribes, Inc.

Scarry, C. Margaret. 1996. Appendix E: The Archaeology of Thomas Point. In *Thomas Point: Emerging Late Woodland Traditions in Southern Maryland,* edited by Joseph Herbert. *Jefferson Patterson Park and Museum Occasional Papers,* no. 5. St. Leonard, Md.

Schmitt, Karl, Jr. 1965. "Patawomeke: An Historical Algonkian Site." *Quarterly Bulletin of the Archeological Society of Virginia* 20: 1–36.

Schulenberg, Janet, Jaimin Weets, and Peter van Rossum. 2003. "The Hershey Site: An Update." *Pennsylvania Archaeologist* 73, no. 2: 2–15.

Scisco, Louis. 1945. "Discovery of the Chesapeake Bay." *Maryland Historical Magazine* 40: 277–86.

————. 1946. "Voyages of Vicenti Gonzalez in 1588." *Maryland Historical Magazine* 42: 95–100.

Scott, Jane. 1991. *Between Ocean and Bay: A Natural History of Delmarva.* Centreville, Md.: Tidewater.

Semmes, Raphael. 1929. "Aboriginal Maryland, 1608–1689." *Maryland Historical Magazine* 24: 157–72, 195–209.

Sempowski, Martha L. 1989. "Fluctuations through Time in the Use of Marine Shell in Seneca Iroquois Sites." In *Proceedings of the 1986 Shell Beach Conference: Selected Papers,* edited by Charles F. Hayes III and Lynn Ceci, no. 20, 81–96. Rochester, N.Y.: Rochester Museum and Science Center Research Records.

Shaffer, Gary D. 2005. "Nanticoke Indian Burial Practices: Challenges for Archaeological Interpretation." *Archaeology of Eastern North America* 33: 141–62.

Sharpe, J. A. 1987. *Early Modern England: A Social History, 1550–1760.* London: Arnold.

Shields, Diane, and Susan L. Davis. 2002. *Soil Survey of Queen Anne's County, Maryland.* U.S. Department of Agriculture. Washington, D.C.: U.S. Government Printing Office.

Shoemaker, Col. Henry. 1917. *Extinct Pennsylvania Animals: Part VI: The Slaughter.* Landisville, Pa.: Arment Biological Press.

Shreve, Forrest, M. A. Chrysler, Frederick H. Blodgett and F. W. Wesley. 1969 [1910]. *The Plant Life of Maryland.* New York and Codicote, Hertfordshire, U.K.: Verlag von J. Cramer. Originally published by Johns Hopkins University Press.

Siebert, Frank T., Jr. 1975. "Resurrecting Virginia Algonquian from the Dead: The Reconstituted and Historical Phonology of Powhatan." In *Studies in Southeastern Indian Languages,* edited by James M. Crawford, 285–453. Athens: University of Georgia Press.

Silberhorn, Gene M. 1973. *Lancaster County Tidal Marsh Inventory.* VIMS Special Report in *Applied Marine Science and Ocean Engineering,* no. 45.

———. 1974. *York County and Town of Poquoson Tidal Marsh Inventory.* VIMS Special Report in *Applied Marine Science and Ocean Engineering,* no. 53.

———. 1975. *Northumberland County Tidal Marsh Inventory.* VIMS Special Report in *Applied Marine Science and Ocean Engineering,* no. 58.

———. 1981. *Mathews County Tidal Marsh Inventory.* VIMS Special Report in *Applied Marine Science and Ocean Engineering,* no. 47.

Silberhorn, Gene M., and Sharon Dewing. 1989a. *Prince George County Tidal Marsh Inventory.* VIMS Special Report in *Applied Marine Science and Ocean Engineering,* no. 293.

———. 1989b. *City of Portsmouth Tidal Marsh Inventory.* VIMS Special Report in *Applied Marine Science and Ocean Engineering,* no. 299.

———. 1991. *City of Chesapeake Tidal Marsh Inventory.* VIMS Special Report in *Applied Marine Science and Ocean Engineering,* no. 312.

Silberhorn, Gene M., and A. F. Harris. 1977. *Accomack County Tidal Marsh Inventory.* VIMS Special Report in *Applied Marine Science and Ocean Engineering,* no. 138.

———. 1981. *Isle of Wight County Tidal Marsh Inventory.* VIMS Special Report in *Applied Marine Science and Ocean Engineering,* no. 213.

Silberhorn, Gene M., and Walter I. Priest III. 1987. *City of Norfolk Tidal Marsh Inventory.* VIMS Special Report in *Applied Marine Science and Ocean Engineering,* no. 281.

Silberhorn, Gene M., and Andrew W. Zacherle. 1987. *King William County and Town of West Point Tidal Marsh Inventory.* VIMS Special Report in *Applied Marine Science and Ocean Engineering,* no. 289.

Sipple, William. 1978. *An Atlas of Vascular Plant Species Distribution Maps for Tidewater Maryland.* Annapolis: Maryland Department of Natural Resources.

———. 1999. *Days Afield: Exploring Wetlands in the Chesapeake Bay Region*. Baltimore: Gateway Press.

Smith, Horace, and Earle D. Mathews. 1975. *Soil Survey of Harford County Area, Maryland*. U.S. Department of Agriculture. Washington, D.C.: U.S. Government Printing Office.

Smith, John. 1986a [1608]. "A True Relation." In *The Complete Works of Captain John Smith (1580–1631)*, edited by Philip L. Barbour, 3 vols., 1: 3–118. Chapel Hill: University of North Carolina Press. Also printed, verbatim but with modernized spelling, in *Jamestown Narratives: Eyewitness Accounts of the Virginia Colony: The First Decade: 1607–1617*, edited by Edward W. Haile, 143–82. Champlain, Va.: RoundHouse, 1998.

———. 1986b [1612]. "A Map of Virginia." (Historical section compiled from various texts by William Simmond). In *The Complete Works of Captain John Smith (1580–1631)*, edited by Philip L. Barbour, 3 vols., 1: 119–90. Chapel Hill: University of North Carolina Press. Also printed in part, verbatim but with modernized spelling, in *Jamestown Narratives: Eyewitness Accounts of the Virginia Colony: The First Decade: 1607–1617*, edited by Edward W. Haile, 205ff., 569ff. Champlain, Va., RoundHouse, 1998.

———. 1986c [1624]. *Generall Historie of Virginia, New-England, and the Summer Isles*. 1624. In *The Complete Works of Captain John Smith (1580–1631)*, edited by Philip Barbour, 3 vols., 2: 25–488. Chapel Hill: University of North Carolina Press. Also printed, verbatim but with modernized spelling, in *Jamestown Narratives: Eyewitness Accounts of the Virginia Colony: The First Decade: 1607–1617*, edited by Edward W. Haile, 215–347, 857–64 (partial version, cut off in 1617). Champlain, Va.: RoundHouse, 1998.

———. 1986d [1630]. "The True Travels, Adventures, and Observations of Captaine John Smith. In *The Complete Works of Captain John Smith (1580–1631)*, edited by Philip Barbour, 3 vols., 3: 153–302. Chapel Hill: University of North Carolina Press.

———. n.d. [1612]. "Virginia Discouered and Described by Captayn John Smith, 1606." [Map, various editions]. Richmond: Virginia State Library.

Smith, Marvin T., and Julie Barnes Smith. 1989. "Engraved Shell Masks in North America." *Southeastern Archaeology* 8, no. 1: 9–18.

Smolek, Michael A. 1986. "The Cumberland Palisaded Village Site: A (Very) Preliminary Report." Manuscript on file, Jefferson Patterson Park and Museum, St. Leonard, Md.

Sneyd, Charlotte Augusta, trans. 1847. *A Relation, or Rather a True Account, of the Island of England, with Sundry Particulars of the Customs of these People, and of the Royal Revenues under King Henry the Seventh, about the Year 1500*. London: Printed for the Camden Society by John Bowyer Nichols and Son.

Snow, Dean R. 1994. *Iroquois*. Oxford: Blackwell.

Sorg, David. 2003. "Linguistic Affiliations of the Massawomeck Confederacy." *Pennsylvania Archaeologist* 73, no. 1: 1–7.

Speck, Frank G. 1927. "The Nanticoke and Conoy Indians, with a Review of Linguistic Material from Manuscript and Living Sources: An Historical Study." *Papers of the Historical Society of Delaware*, n.s., vol. 1.

Spelman, Henry. 1910 [1613?]. "Relation of Virginea." In *The Travels and Works of Captain John Smith*, edited by Edward Arber and A. G. Bradley, ci–cxiv. New York: Burt Franklin. Also published, verbatim but with modernized spelling, in *Jamestown Narratives: Eye-*

witness Accounts of the Virginia Colony: The First Decade: 1607–1617, edited by Edward W. Haile, 481–95. Champlain, Va.: RoundHouse, 1998.

Stahle, David W., Malcom K. Cleaveland, Dennis B. Blanton, Matthew D. Therrell, and David A. Gay. 1998. "The Lost Colony and Jamestown Droughts." *Science* 280: 564–67.

Stearns, Richard E. 1951. "The Indian Survey of the Patuxent River, Maryland." *Maryland Naturalist* 21: 2–20.

Stephenson, Robert L., and Alice L. L. Ferguson. 1963. *The Accokeek Site: A Middle Atlantic Seaboard Culture Sequence.* University of Michigan Museum of Anthropology, Anthropological Papers 20. Ann Arbor.

Stephonaitis, Laurie Cameron. 1980. *A Survey of Artifact Collections from the Patuxent River Drainage, Maryland.* Maryland Historical Trust Monograph Series no. 1. Crownsville.

———. 1985. "Prehistoric Settlement Patterns in the Lower Patuxent Drainage, Maryland." Ph.D. diss., State University of New York, Binghamton. Ann Arbor: University Microfilms.

Stewart, Robert E., and Chandler S. Robbins. 1958. *Birds of Maryland and the District of Columbia.* North American Fauna, no. 62, U.S. Dept. of the Interior, U.S. Fish and Wildlife Service.

Stewart, T. Dale. 1992. "Archaeological Exploration of Patawomeke: The Indian Town Site (44ST2) Ancestral to the One (44ST1) Visited in 1608 by Captain John Smith." *Smithsonian Contributions to Anthropology,* no. 16

Stone, Lawrence. 1965. *The Crisis of the Aristocracy, 1558–1641.* Oxford and New York: Oxford University Press.

———. 1977. *The Family, Sex and Marriage in England, 1500–1800.* New York: Harper and Row.

Stothers, David M. 2000. "The Protohistoric Time Period in the Southwest Lake Erie Region: European-derived Trade Material, Population Movement, and Cultural Realignment. In *Cultures before Contact: The Late Prehistory of Ohio and Surrounding Regions,* 52–94. Columbus: Ohio Archaeological Council.

Strachey, William. 1953 [1612]. *The Historie of Travell into Virginia Britania.* Edited by Louis B. Wright and Virginia Freund. Ser. 2, vol. 103. Cambridge: Hakluyt Society. First book also published, verbatim but with modernized spelling, in *Jamestown Narratives: Eyewitness Accounts of the Virginia Colony: The First Decade: 1607–1617,* edited by Edward W. Haile, 569–89. Champlain, Va.: RoundHouse, 1998.

———. 1964 [1610]. "A True Reportory of the Wreck and Redemption of Sir Thomas Gates . . ." In *A Voyage to Virginia in 1609, Two Narratives,* edited by Louis B. Wright. Charlottesville: University Press of Virginia. Also printed, verbatim but with modernized spelling, in *Jamestown Narratives: Eyewitness Accounts of the Virginia Colony: The First Decade: 1607–1617,* edited by Edward W. Haile, 381–443. Champlain, Va.: RoundHouse, 1998.

Sween, Jane C., and William Offutt. 1999. *Montgomery County: Centuries of Change.* Sun Valley, Calif.: American Historical Press.

Thornton, Peter. 1991. "A Paleoecological Study of Salt Marsh Sediments from the NOAA Estuarine Research Reserve Site at Monie Bay, Maryland: The Application of Principal Components Analysis to Fossil Seed Data." Master's thesis, Johns Hopkins University.

Thwaites, Reuben Gold, comp. 1897–1901. *The Jesuit Relations and Allied Documents.* 72 vols. Cleveland: Burrows Brothers.

Tiner, Ralph W., Jr. 1981. *Coastal Wetland Plants of the Northeastern United States.* Amherst: University of Massachusetts Press.

Tooker, William Wallace. 1893. "The Kuskarawaokes of Captain John Smith." *American Anthropologist,* o.s., 6: 409–11.

———. 1894a. "The Algonquian Terms Patawomeke and Massawomeke." *American Anthropologist,* o.s., 7: 171–85.

———. 1894b. "On the Meaning of the Name Anacostia." *American Anthropologist,* o.s., 7: 389–93.

———. 1895. "The Name Chickahominy, Its Origin and Etymology." *American Anthropologist,* n.s., 8: 257–63.

———. 1904a. "Derivation of the Name Powhatan." *American Anthropologist,* n.s., 6: 464–68.

———. 1904b. "Some Powhatan Names." *American Anthropologist,* n.s., 6: 670–94.

———. 1905. "Some More about Virginia Names." *American Anthropologist,* n.s., 7: 524–28.

———. 1906. "The Powhatan Name for Virginia." *American Anthropologist,* n.s., 8: 23–27.

Torrence, Clayton. 1973. *Old Somerset on the Eastern Shore of Maryland: A Study in Foundation and Founders.* Baltimore: Regional Publishing.

Trimble, Carmen. 1996. "Paleodiet in Virginia and North Carolina as Determined by Stable Isotope Analysis of Skeletal Remains." Master's thesis, Department of Anthropology, University of Virginia.

Turgeon, Donna D., Arthur E. Govan, Eugene V. Coan, William K. Emerson, William G. Lyons, William L. Pratt, Clyde F. E. Roper, Amelie Scheltema, Fred G. Thompson, and James D. Williams. 1988. *Common and Scientific Names of Aquatic Invertebrates from the United States and Canada: Mollusks.* American Fisheries Society Special Publication 16. Washington, D.C.

Turner, E. Randolph, III. 1982. "A Re-examination of Powhatan Territorial Boundaries and Population, ca. A.D. 1607." *Quarterly Bulletin of the Archaeological Society of Virginia* 37: 45–64.

———. 1985. "Socio-Political Organization within the Powhatan Chiefdom and the Effects of European Contact, A.D. 1607–1646." In *Cultures in Contact: The European Impact on Native Cultural Institutions in Eastern North America, A.D. 1000–1800,* edited by William W. Fitzhugh, 193–224. Washington, D.C.: Smithsonian Institution Press.

———. 1992. "The Virginia Coastal Plain during the Late Woodland Period." In *Middle and Late Woodland Research in Virginia: A Synthesis,* edited by Theodore R. Reinhart and Mary Ellen N. Hodges, 97–136. Archaeological Society of Virginia, Special Publication no. 29.

———. 1993. "Native American Protohistoric Interactions in the Powhatan Core Area." In *Powhatan Foreign Relations, 1500–1722,* edited by Helen C. Rountree, 76–93. Charlottesville: University Press of Virginia.

———. 2003a. "Werowocomoco, Ye Seate of Powhatan." *Notes on Virginia* 47: 40–45.

———. 2003b. "Nanzattico Archaeological Site." National Register of Historic Places Registration Form, on file at Virginia Department of Historic Resources, Richmond.

Turner, E. Randolph, III, and Anthony F. Opperman. Forthcoming. "Searching for Virginia Company Period Sites: An Assessment of Surviving Archaeological Manifestations of Powhatan-English Interactions, A.D. 1607–1624."

Ubelaker, Douglas H. 1974. *Reconstruction of Demographic Profiles from Ossuary Skeletal*

Samples: A Case Study from the Tidewater Potomac. Smithsonian Miscellaneous Collections No. 18.

———. 1993. "Human Biology of Virginia Indians." In *Powhatan Foreign Relations, 1500–1722,* edited by Helen C. Rountree, 53–75. Charlottesville: University Press of Virginia.

Ubelaker, Douglas H., and Philip D. Curtin. 2001. "Human Biology of Populations in the Chesapeake Watershed." In *Discovering the Chesapeake: The History of an Ecosystem,* edited by Philip D. Curtin, Grace S. Brush, and George W. Fisher, 127–48. Baltimore: Johns Hopkins University Press.

Ulanowicz, Robert, and John Tuttle. 1992. "The Trophic Consequences of Oyster Stock Rehabilitation in Chesapeake Bay." *Estuaries* 15: 298–306.

United States Geological Survey. 2004. *York River Basin.* Reston, Va.

Virginia Marine Resources Commission, Richmond, Va. 1977. *Tidewater Virginia Atlas.* 1st ed.

Volks, Harold E., and Jonathan Edwards Jr. 1974. *Geology and Geography of Maryland.* Maryland Geological Survey, Bulletin 19. Baltimore.

Wall, Robert D. 1999. "Late Woodland Ceramics and Native Populations of the Upper Potomac Valley." *Journal of Middle Atlantic Archaeology* 17:15–38.

Wall, Robert D., and Heather Lapham. 2001. "Material Culture of the Contact Period in the Upper Potomac Valley: Chronological and Cultural Implications." *Archaeology of Eastern North America* 31: 151–78.

Wallace, Paul A. W. 1971. *Indian Paths of Pennsylvania.* Harrisburg: Pennsylvania Historical and Museum Commission.

Waselkov, Gregory. 1982. "Shellfish Gathering and Shell Midden Archaeology." Ph.D. diss., Department of Anthropology, University of North Carolina. Ann Arbor: University Microfilms.

Wennersten, John R. 2001. *The Chesapeake: an Environmental Biography.* Baltimore: Maryland Historical Society.

Weslager, C. A. 1983. *The Nanticoke Indians—Past and Present.* Newark: University of Delaware Press.

White, Fr. Andrew. 1910 [1634]. "A Briefe Relation of the Voyage vnto Maryland, by Father Andrew White, 1634." In *Narratives of Early Maryland, 1633–1684,* edited by Clayton Colman Hall, 25–45. New York: Scribner's.

White, Edgar A., Jr. 1982. *Soil Survey of Kent County, Maryland.* U.S. Department of Agriculture. Washington, D.C.: U.S. Government Printing Office.

White, Marian E. 1978. "Erie." In *Handbook of North American Indians,* vol. 15, *Northeast,* edited by Bruce G. Trigger, 412–17. Washington: Smithsonian Institution Press.

White, William. 1969 [1608?]. Fragment (published before 1614). Printed, with authorship assigned to George Percy, in *The Jamestown Voyages under the First Charter,* edited by Philip L. Barbour, ser. 2, 136: 146–147. Cambridge: Hakluyt Society. Reprinted, with modernized spelling, in *Jamestown Narratives: Eyewitness Accounts of the Virginia Colony: The First Decade: 1607–1617,* edited by Edward W. Haile, 141. Champlain, Va.: Round-House.

Whitney, Gordon G. 1996 [1994]. *From Coastal Wilderness to Fruited Plain: A History of Environmental Change in Temperate North America from 1500 to the Present.* Cambridge: Cambridge University Press.

Whyte, Thomas. 1988. *Zooarchaeology of the Addington Site, a Middle and Late Woodland*

Fishery. Vol. 4 of *Archaeological Mitigation of Two Components (44VB9 and 44VB92) of the Great Neck Site Complex, Virginia Beach.* Harrisonburg, Va.: Archaeological Research Center, James Madison University.

Wilke, Steve, and Gail Thompson. 1977a. "Archeological Survey of Western Kent County, Maryland." Unpublished report, Maryland Historical Trust, Crownsville, Md.

———. 1977b. "Prehistoric Resources of Portions of Coastal Kent County, Maryland." Unpublished report, Maryland Historical Trust, Crownsville, Md.

Williams, Michael. 1990. *Americans and Their Forests: A Historical Geography.* Cambridge: Cambridge University Press.

Williams, R. Christopher. 1983. "A Preliminary Site Report for the Cumberland Palisaded Village Site, Calvert County, Maryland." Report on file, Jefferson Patterson Park and Museum, St. Leonard, Md.

Wingfield, Edward Maria. 1969 [1608]. "Discourse." In *The Jamestown Voyages under the First Charter,* edited by Philip L. Barbour, ser. 2, 136: 213–34. Cambridge: Hakluyt Society. Also printed, verbatim but with modernized spelling, in *Jamestown Narratives: Eyewitness Accounts of the Virginia Colony: The First Decade: 1607–1617,* edited by Edward W. Haile, 183–201. Champlain, Va.: RoundHouse.

Winne, Peter. 1969 [1608]. Letter [November 16, 1608] to Sir John Egerton. In *The Jamestown Voyages under the First Charter,* edited by Philip L. Barbour, ser. 1, 136: 245–246. Cambridge: Hakluyt Society. Also printed, verbatim but with modernized spelling, in *Jamestown Narratives: Eyewitness Accounts of the Virginia Colony: The First Decade: 1607–1617,* edited by Edward W. Haile, 203–4. Champlain, Va.: RoundHouse.

Witt, Bill. 1971. *Preliminary Archaeological Investigations at Site 18SO20, Somerset County, Maryland.* Report on file, Maryland Historical Trust, Crownsville, Md.

Witthof, John, and W. Fred Kinsey III. 1969a. "Ancestry of the Susquehannocks." In *Susquehannock Miscellany,* edited by John Witthof and W. Fred Kinsey III, 19–60. Harrisburg: Pennsylvania Historical and Museum Commission.

———. 1969b. A Susquehannock Cemetery: The Ibaugh Site. In *Susquehannock Miscellany,* edited by John Witthof and W. Fred Kinsey III, 99–135. Harrisburg: Pennsylvania Historical and Museum Commission.

Wood, Fergus J. 1976. *The Strategic Role of Perigean Spring Tides in Natural History and North American Coastal Flooding.* Washington, D.C.: National Oceanographic and Atmospheric Administration.

Woodlawn Community Associates. 1900. Woodlawn Historic and Archaeological District. National Register of Historic Places Registration Form, on file at Virginia Department of Historic Resources, Richmond.

Wroth, Lawrence C. 1970. *The Voyages of Giovanni da Verrazzano, 1524–1528.* New Haven: Yale University Press.

Youings, Joyce. 1984. *Sixteenth-Century England.* Pelican Social History of Britain Series. London: Penguin.

Yuan, Shaomin. 1995. "Postglacial History of Vegetation and River Channel Geomorphology in a Coastal Plain Floodplain." Ph.D. diss., Johns Hopkins University. Ann Arbor: University Microfilms.

Yuan, Shaomin, and Grace S. Brush. 1992. "Postglacial Vegetation History of the Coastal Plain of Maryland." *Bulletin of the Ecological Society of America* 73: 396.

Index

birds *(continued)*
    passenger (*Ectopistes migratorius*), 315; plovers
    (*Charadrius* and *Pluvialis* spp.), 189; quail/bob-
    white (*Colinus virginianus*), 22; robin, American
    (*Turdus migratorius*), 255; skimmer, black (*Ryn-
    chops niger*), 204, 205; swallows, 188; swans (*see
    subentries below*); terns (*Sterna* spp.), 204, 205;
    turkey, wild (*Mealeagris gallopavo*), 21, 22, 23, 47,
    49, 51, 151, 178, 232, 254, 210, 281, 315, 316–17
—ducks: black (*Anas rubripes*) 210, 233, 315; buffle-
    head (*Bucephala albeola*), 233; canvasback
    (*Aythya valisinera*), 210; goldeneye (*Bucephala
    clangula*), 233; grebe, pied-billed (*Podilymbus
    podiceps*), 233; green-winged teal (*Anas crecca*),
    22; mallard (*Anas platyrynchos*), 48, 209, 210,
    233, 315; merganser (*Megsu* sp.), 233; old squaw/
    long-tailed (*Clangula hyemalis*), 22; pintail (*Anas
    acuta*), 22; redhead/scaup (*Aytha* sp.; archae-
    ologist was uncertain which), 233; ring-necked
    (*Aythya collaris*), 22; scaup (*Aythya affinis*), 22;
    wigeon, American (*Anas americana*), 210; wood
    (*Aix sponsa*), 22
—swans, 281; mute (*Cygnus olor*), 315; trumpeter (*Olor
    buccinator*), 233; whistling (*Olor columbianus*), 233
Blue Ridge Mountains, 137, 198, 287, 288, 304
"breadbasket marshes," 51, 154–55, 175, 178–79, 192,
    213, 255, 278, 280, 289, 299, 302; defined, 51
bridges, modern: American Legion Memorial, 263;
    Bottoms, 148, 171; Chatham, 127; Chesapeake
    Bay Bridge, 220; Chesapeake Bay Bridge-Tun-
    nel, 186, 199; County Road 614, 173; Germanna,
    296; Interstate 95 (over Rappahannock R.), 296;
    Interstate 495, 263; Maryland Route 290, 225,
    227; Maryland Route 331, 204; Summit, 236;
    U.S. 17/33, 291; U.S. 50/301, 225; U.S. 301 (over
    Potomac R.), 265, 268; U.S. 301 (over Rappahan-
    nock R.), 289, 295; U.S. 360 (over Pamunkey R.),
    173; U.S. 360 (over Rappahannock R.), 289, 290;
    U.S. 522 (over James R.), 296; Virginia Route 3
    (over Rappahannock R.), 293; Virginia Route 3
    (over Rapidan R.), 296; Virginia Route 56 (over
    James R.), 296
buffer zones (between tribes), 91, 99, 143, 155, 251,
    252, 296–97, 299

canoes: birch bark, 41, 112, 223, 231, 341n14; log dug-
    out, 28, 32, 41, 44–45, 63, 76, 82, 85, 88, 94, 98, 99,
    100, 113, 116, 117, 124; modern log, 174; size and
    limitations of dugouts, 44, 116
capes: Charles, 81, 143, 185, 186; —, meteorite, 1, 198;
    Henry, 81, 158, 160; Virginia Capes (i.e., both), 76,
    136, 144, 185, 186, 270, 351n37
ceramics, 144, 155, 210, 211, 212, 232, 252, 272, 277,
    297; Albemarle, 362n28; Camden, 253; Fort An-
    cient Complex, 216; Gaston-Cashie, 344n23;

Madisonville Phase, 216; Minguannan, 228;
    Monongahela Complex, 216; Moyaone, 253;
    Potomac Creek, 210–11, 253, 271, 274, 275, 276,
    362n28; Rappahannock Complex, 211, 250,
    253, 359n19; Roanoke, 212, 344n23; Shenks
    Ferry Complex, 355n21; Sullivan Cove, 253, 271;
    Townsend, 211, 212, 253, 271, 344n23, 353n37; Yeo-
    comico, 212, 250, 253, *253*
changes since 1607–9: in bird populations, 21, 22,
    205, 315; erosion of soil, 4–5, 22, 243, 255, 307,
    308, 310, 313; in fish/shellfish populations, 9, 14,
    246, 309–13, 320; in forests, 17, 20, 200, 308, 313,
    319–20; in human populations, 32, 317, 321; in
    islands and points, 203, *203*, 204–5, 251; in mam-
    mal populations, 23–24, 315–17; rain runoff, 4–5,
    265, 307–10; in river bottoms, 243, 341n20; in
    salinity, 5, 138, 175, 178, 280; in sea level, 1, 2, 5, 14,
    15, 203, 204–5; in soils, 310; in swamps, 313–14; in
    underwater vegetation, 7, 243, 309, 315; in water
    clarity, 5, 246; in waterways in urban areas, 265;
    in weather, 17, 310; in wetlands, 200, 203, 314
Chesapeake Bay, 1–24; bird life, 22; climate of, 2–3,
    15; depth of, 5–6; fish and shellfish in, 7–12, 14–15,
    13; forests around, 16–21; land animals around,
    22–24; origin of, 1; salinity of, 5, 6; size of, 3–4;
    sources of water, 4; tides in, 6, 79, 81, 83, 88, 89,
    90, 91, 93, 98, 100, 101, 103, 104, 106, 108, 110, 111,
    114, 117, 118, 120, 121, 122, 125, 126, 131, 240, 242;
    turbidity in, 138, 223–24
Chesapeake Bay Program, 246
cliffs: Calvert, 49, 89, *90*, 105, 240, 249; Fones, 287;
    Holland, 240; Randle, 89; Rickards (*see* Calvert
    above)
climate: Little Ice Age, 3, 207, 248; Medieval Warm
    Period, 3, 207, 248, 320; modern, 2–3; post–Ice
    Age changes, 207, 227. *See also* Ice Ages, effects of
Conowingo Dam, 134
creeks: Adams, 171; Ape Hole, 85; Appoquinimink,
    236; Aquia, 97, 100, 105, 268, 275, 276, 339n56;
    Back, 241; Battle, 19, 121, 314; Beaverdam, 339n56;
    Big, 178; Big Elk, 116; Black, 172; Black Swamp,
    251; Bodkin, 111; Broad (trib. Anacostia R.),
    278; Broad (trib. Nanticoke R.), 88; Broad (trib.
    Pamunkey R.), 175; Broad (trib. Susquehanna
    R.), 227; Brockenbrough, 294; Buffalo, 319; Bur-
    gess, 275; Carter (trib. York R.), 171; Carvers,
    289; Cat Point, 124, 125, 289, 294; Cedar Hall,
    85; Chesconessex, 83, 188, 193, 194; Chew, 251;
    Chicamuxen, 276; Chicone, 211; Chuckatuck,
    140; Clayborne, 175; Cocktown, 254; Cohoke
    Mill, 172; Cole, 249; Craddock, 188; Crouch,
    155; Cuckhold, 240; Deep, 140; Diascund, 148;
    Dividing, 101; Dogue, 96, 276; East, 85; Elliots,
    81; Falling, 150; Farnham, 293, 294; Ferry, 289;
    Fishing, 89; Fox, 171; Garnetts, 175; Gingoteague,